The Technological Unconscious in German Modernist Literature

Studies in German Literature, Linguistics, and Culture

The Technological Unconscious in German Modernist Literature

Nature in Rilke, Benn, Brecht, and Döblin

Larson Powell

CAMDEN HOUSE
Rochester, New York

Copyright © 2008 Larson Powell

All Rights Reserved. Except as permitted under current legislation,
no part of this work may be photocopied, stored in a retrieval system,
published, performed in public, adapted, broadcast, transmitted,
recorded, or reproduced in any form or by any means,
without the prior permission of the copyright owner.

First published 2008
by Camden House

Camden House is an imprint of Boydell & Brewer Inc.
668 Mt. Hope Avenue, Rochester, NY 14620, USA
www.camden-house.com
and of Boydell & Brewer Limited
PO Box 9, Woodbridge, Suffolk IP12 3DF, UK
www.boydellandbrewer.com

ISBN-13: 978–1–57113–382–3
ISBN-10: 1–57113–382–8

Library of Congress Cataloging-in-Publication Data

Powell, Larson, 1960–
 The technological unconscious in German modernist literature : nature in Rilke, Benn, Brecht, and Döblin / Larson Powell.
  p. cm. — (Studies in German literature, linguistics, and culture)
 Includes bibliographical references and index.
 ISBN-13: 978–1–57113–382–3 (hardcover : alk. paper)
 ISBN-10: 1–57113–382–8 (hardcover : alk. paper)
  1. German poetry—20th century—History and criticism. 2. German literature—20th century—Themes, motives. 3. Nature in literature. 4. Modernism (Aesthetics) I. Title. II. Series.

PT553.P65 2008
831'.910936—dc22

2008004955

A catalogue record for this title is available from the British Library.

This publication is printed on acid-free paper.
Printed in the United States of America.

Contents

Acknowledgments	vii
Introduction	1
1: The Limits of Technocracy	20
2: Rilke's Unnatural Things: From the End of Landscape to the *Dinggedicht*	66
3: Nature on Stage: Gottfried Benn — Beyond the Aesthetics of Shock?	97
4: The Limits of Violence: Döblin's Colonial Nature	134
5: Nature as Paradox: Brecht's Exile Lyric	178
Appendix: Niklas Luhmann	227
Bibliography	231
Index	251

Acknowledgments

THIS BOOK WAS ORIGINALLY CONCEIVED while I was in the Department of Germanic Languages and Literatures at Columbia University, working with Andreas Huyssen and Harro Müller; it bears, however, little resemblance to the original project (which was in large part devoted to Oskar Loerke). Portions of the manuscript were read and commented on by Tom Brockelman, Carl Caldwell, Ted George, Aaron Lercher, Ralph Schoolcraft, Bob Shandley and Lora Wildenthal. My thanks to Jim Walker for his editorial patience and collaborative ear. Bob Shandley was unfailingly good-humored in supporting his junior colleague. Rick Rentschler, Barton Byg, Sara Lennox, and Martin Puchner have offered advice and encouragement at points along the way. Last but not least, thanks to Brenda Bethman for listening to many *Fragen eines lesenden* (and *schreibenden*) *Arbeiters*.

L. P.
January 2008

Introduction

OUR CURRENT HORIZON of ecological disaster has made catastrophe theory into something far more immediate than a mathematical problem. After decades of cyberfashion and grandiose claims for virtual reality and post-history, Nature has returned to History in a form as apocalyptic as was the Cold War threat of nuclear destruction. Even in commercial cinema, the sublime fantasy of disaster films now includes the destructive effects of global warming (in Roland Emmerich's 2004 *The Day After Tomorrow*). Theories of a supposed "clash of civilizations" must then coexist with theories of the perishability of all human civilization as such. So Jared Diamond, the same biogeographer and psychologist who, less than a decade ago, wrote a bestselling environmentalist narrative of Why The West Won, has recently published a more sobering consideration of *Collapse: How Societies Choose to Fail or Succeed*.[1] Implicit in Diamond's account of the failure of Easter Island civilization is the possibility that the skyscrapers of the American metropolis may suffer the same fate as Easter Island's famous stone statues. Bertolt Brecht already described this prospect from the vantage point of 1920s Germany: "Von diesen Städten wird bleiben, der durch sie hindurchging, der Wind!" (Of these cities will remain what passed through them, the wind!)[2]

The horizon of apocalypse has been central to modernism for over a century, at least since Rimbaud's "ça ne peut être que la fin du monde, en avant" (from *Les Illuminations*). It has, however, become harder to respond with Brecht's concluding stanza, in which the poet hopes he will not let his cigar go out "in the earthquakes that will come," given that such natural disasters are no longer metaphorical or imaginary. Books like Diamond's accordingly want to help us understand the historical lesson of failed civilizations in hopes that we may not repeat their fate. Others, such as Richard Posner's *Catastrophe: Risk and Response*,[3] look for prognostications and offer calculations of how current civilization might avert the risk of ecological catastrophe. Common to both is a sober ethical and reflective note, indicative that a certain type of technophile party — an intellectual techno-rave, perhaps — is definitively over. If postmodernism was defined by the loss of any "critical distance" in a saturated, suffocating space where everything was "always already" culture or information,[4] then the prospect of global natural catastrophe opens up that distance again in very jarring fashion. It is almost as if humanity had been given back its old Marxian "species being" (*Gattungswesen*) in negative form.

The following book has more in common with Diamond's historical perspective than Posner's prognostic one. That environmental questions can and should be viewed ethically has been reiterated from perspectives as different as those of Hans Jonas and Jürgen Habermas.[5] The ethical perspective, however, presumes a freedom of choice or will that has been more self-evident in social theories of action than in the context of literary criticism. As the following chapters will show, nature and our relation to it are often too complex to be reduced to a simple question of responsible choice, or to Posner's calculations of economic viability. The problem goes much deeper, to the very roots of technological modernity itself. This last notion united philosophers otherwise as sharply opposed in politics and method as Martin Heidegger (in *The Question Concerning Technology*, 1949) and Theodor Adorno and Max Horkheimer (in *Dialectics of Enlightenment*, 1947). These two approaches to the problem were formulated in the immediate wake of one of the most destructive wars in human history, and under the threat of the arms race. If, however, in Hegel's familiar image, philosophy's owl of Minerva only flies at dusk (that is, in the retrospective wake of cultural production), then one should expect to find intimations of this question concerning technology in art and literature even earlier on.

This is indeed the case, as the following five chapters will show. The choice of modern German literature to illustrate the problem of technological civilization has much to recommend it. It has often been recognized that the Weimar Republic was a paradigmatic test case for European modernization. What was lost in the traumatic process of that modernization was not only a traditional and often socially conservative agrarian order, one which was transformed into urban modernity with greater rapidity than in the case of England or the United States, but also an entire high culture and its alternately pastoral or utopian thematics of nature. That the idea of nature need not be *only* a reactionary ideology masking traditional social hierarchies is evident in the role played by natural-law traditions in revolutionary political movements from the Middle Ages to Marx.[6] That political ambivalence of nature, at once deeply nostalgic and atavistic, saturated with the peculiar German theological inheritance and charged with hope for a reconciliation of the human and the natural, was unquestionably one of the central themes of German philosophy right up to the 1960s and 1970s. Only with the linguistic or communicative turn taken by Habermas's variant of Critical Theory, and the self-referentiality of Niklas Luhmann's sociological systems theory,[7] was this theme abandoned. The reasons for the turn away from nature are familiar enough, namely a suspicion of *any* fundamental grounding of the ethical or political in a reference to the natural. (This suspicion was thus shared by Habermas and Luhmann with Derrida, despite their other differences.) As the introductory chapter demonstrates, however, there was a very high cost to be paid for this move.

This book will argue that a reconsideration of nature need not necessarily imply a return to invariant biologically-grounded essentialism or other sorts of ontological fundamentalism.[8] Beyond even the history of modern German literary nature, traced here in four exemplary cases, the book seeks to re-evaluate nature as an object worthy of renewed philosophical and critical investigation. For nature in the wake of technocracy is anything but a self-evident matter. If it were simply a question of a "rational choice" on the part of our civilization not to behave self-destructively — as Posner and, to some extent, Diamond imply — one wonders why it is that we continue not to make that choice. We cannot understand why that is so without grasping what it is about a certain kind of modernity that forbids our considering the problem of nature. It is this blindness of modernity that is the real subject of the present book's critique.

The first chapter seeks to redefine the idea of nature itself at the intersection of several theoretical discourses, including the usually opposed perspectives of sociology and psychoanalysis. The eclecticism of this approach is due to more than the outsider status of literary theory, and in no way seeks to repeat the now-familiar deconstructivist gesture of reducing all truth claims to textual or rhetorical surface. The rationale for referring alternately to Luhmann and Lacan is that neither of these discourses is capable in itself of formulating the problem of nature as this book seeks to do. Rather, both sociological systems theory and Lacanian psychoanalysis have in different ways marginalized nature. The cross-disciplinary or cross-theoretical approach used here is required to formulate a new "question concerning nature" in the theoretical environment of these discursive and interpretative systems.[9] In this respect, this approach is very much in the tradition of Critical Theory, without, however, returning to the nostalgia for metaphysics typical of Adorno and Horkheimer. If Habermas titled one of his books *Post-Metaphysical Thinking*,[10] then the subject of the following must also be a post-metaphysical nature.[11]

This is at first encounter not at all a self-evident, but rather a paradox formulation. To avoid falling back onto the metaphysical or transcendental horizon of nature, the first chapter, as its title (*The Limits of Technocracy*) implies, must proceed critically or negatively.[12] After an introductory sketch of how recent theories of aesthetic modernity have elided nature *in toto*, the chapter then goes on to propose a critique of the technological sublime. The sublime has indeed been one of the crucial tropes of modernity, from Kant to Adorno. Yet as this section shows, the late-modern reformulation of the sublime made by Lyotard, taken here as exemplary of a certain technocratic aesthetic, elides important aspects of the sublime. Lyotard's aesthetics of sublime self-reference is then, in a second interpretative move, seen as related to the theoretical self-reference of Niklas Luhmann's systems theory, which elevates self-referential observation to the foundation of all perception of reality.

To show how internally unstable this self-referentiality is, a third interpretative move is necessary, namely to psychoanalysis. In other words, the sublime self-reference found in Lyotard's aesthetics and Luhmann's systems theory is read symptomatically, as informed by anxiety. This is an interpretative combination familiar from Critical Theory, which moved freely (and often rather riskily) between anthropology, sociology, and psychoanalysis. Even further, however, this shift to psychoanalysis implies a potential link to feminist criticism of a certain type of technocratic mastery. (As will become clear, though, this does not mean a return to the essences of ecofeminism, nor even the strategic essences of Diana Fuss.)[13] The section concludes with the re-examination of one of modernism's most famous allegories of technocratic mastery, Fritz Lang's *Metropolis*, along with an extension of Andreas Huyssen's influential commentary on the film.

The following section is the most difficult part of the chapter. Here Kant's original formulation of the problem of the sublime is extended. Put in the simplest terms, Kant's Critique of Judgment describes a moment where theoretical reason encounters its own limits and necessarily breaks down. In Kant's version of this, moral agency must step into the void or groundlessness left by this ultimate (metaphysical) inadequacy of theoretical reason. The sublime thus becomes not only an aesthetic figure, but also a moral or ethical one. Thus Slavoj Žižek has frequently and rightly insisted on the kinship between Lacan's ethics of psychoanalysis and this Kantian diagnosis of the sublime.[14] In Lacan's late-modern, existentialist-influenced version of the ethics of the sublime, the subject deserted by his or her reason must make an absolute and theoretically ungroundable (thus "absurd") Leap into moral agency. (Lacan's *Seminar VII* reads Oedipus and Antigone as allegorical figures of this ethical heroism.) The kinship of this with decisionism, whether right (Jünger) or left (Sartre), is obvious.

Here the current book breaks from the Kantian or Lacanian interpretation of the sublime. Rather than see the sublime as an ethical imperative to act for no reason — which one may interpret as, quite precisely, the technological imperative of mastery! — we may see it as an injunction to reflect. In this, *The Technological Unconscious* transfers a concept of *reflexive modernity* long known in sociology (Ulrich Beck) to aesthetics.

This injunction is already contained in a suggestive formulation of Adorno's that, through its universalization in modernity, the sublime becomes latent. What Adorno means here is not only that the sublime is the accompaniment to modernity in its technological guise, but also that it is a blind spot of subjectivity. The sublime was paradoxical from its inception. On the one hand, it was meant to be a protest of authenticity against the inauthentic calculation of the rhetorical tradition. On the other, it became itself the most effective, since the most invisible, form of rhetoric. As rhetoric, the sublime both perpetrates and conceals subjective agency. The most omnipresent form of rhetorical concealment in current society is the mass media, with its rhetoric of presence and information eliding any chance at subjective reflection. The sublime of technological mastery similarly conceals the subjectivity that produced it in seemingly endless effects of power. (That a great deal of "theory" merely echoes and reinforces these effects will also emerge from this first chapter.)

Nature is redefined in this section as a paradoxical domain of in-between: both between the subject and the objects that continually elude its mastery, and an interstice between the social subsystems of science, art, and economics. The methodological pluralism of approach taken here turns out to be the only way to grasp this intermediary domain.[15] Again, though, rather than postulate it as a positivity — hybrid, for instance, which means little — this domain is here seen as related to Lacan's Real. The Real, for Lacan, has nothing at all to do with empirical reality, with any supposed factual given or datum. It is rather precisely what cannot be grasped or controlled by language (the Symbolic) or imagined in fantasy. It thus has some kinship with Adorno's unreachable or noumenal *das Andere* — although it is most often figured in art in relation to Kristeva's abject. The book's first chapter tries to give this idea a concrete illustration from the history of modern art (Max Ernst).

The aforementioned paradox of contemporary nature is then restated in stronger form, putting forth an imperative that the concept of aesthetic modernity itself needs a further reflexive reformulation.[16] Once again, the continued persistence of nature even in contemporary literature, is evoked with reference to the work of Elfriede Jelinek. The last two sections then situate what has been defined as the *Technological Unconscious* relative to extant culturalist reformulations of Freud, such as those of Rosalind Krauss and Fredric Jameson, and then in relation to Derrida and Critical Theory again. The conclusion must necessarily return once more to Kant and his idea of a mutual constitution of nature and culture (an idea also familiar from Bruno Latour).

Chapters 2 to 5 are devoted to single authors. The second chapter sets the stage for what will follow with the example of Rilke and turn-of-the-century *Jugendstil* poetics. As Adorno and others repeatedly insisted,

Jugendstil was a phenomenon offering a key to all of modernity *in nuce* (to the point where Wagner's libretti and Husserl's phenomenology were also seen as *Jugendstil*), and nowhere is it more of a key than in its peculiar presentation of high artifice as second nature. Rilke's introduction to his 1900 volume on the Worpswede painters is something of a manifesto as regards *Jugendstil*'s relation to nature. That relation was an ambivalent one, given that the Worpswede group were at once living a programmatic pastoral withdrawal from industrial society to rural peasant life, and also pursuing a high style within their artistic technique. Rilke's introduction is not only aware of this tension, but also cannot help betraying an additional level of anxiety — *the* Expressionist affect *par excellence* — in his discussion. (The visionary aspect of the Worpswede landscape, its floating and timeless suspension, was inseparable from its oneiric quality.) The second chapter reads this anxiety in psychoanalytical terms and goes on to find traces of it in Rilke's later poetry, including not only landscape poems but also the so-called *Dinggedicht* or thing-poem, once read by Paul de Man as an allegorical emblem of modernist self-reference. In a sense, this chapter reads de Man's allegory "in reverse" (to borrow Andreas Huyssen's familiar description for his reading of Adorno). As the first chapter has already suggested, the sublime failure of Rilke's technique, which de Man sees as an ethical imperative to allegorical self-reference, is here read as the index of an unrepresentable (Real) Natural remnant. This would have to hold true even of Rilke's most famous poem, "Archaischer Torso Apolls" ("Archaic Torso of Apollo"), with its familiar command to "change one's life" at the end. Rilke's unnatural "thing-poetics" emerges as one of perverse denial (*Verleugnung*) of nature, even of a fetishistic blocking off of nature. This is an aspect in which he is quite typical of *fin-de-siècle* aesthetics (Wilde, Mallarmé).

The third chapter, devoted to Gottfried Benn, continues the psychoanalytical concerns of chapter two, perhaps unsurprisingly given the number of Freudian readings of Benn. As with Rilke, too, the foreclosure of nature required by a high modernist poetics of self-referential artifice cannot help but be pursued by a guilty conscience. This emerges through a close reading of Benn's long wartime ode, "Ikarus," a poem roughly contemporary with the poet's Rönne novellas (*Gehirne*, 1916), arguably the acme of Benn's modernist experimentalism. "Ikarus," the unhappy cousin of Joyce's Stephen Dedalus, is read here against the German ode tradition to which it refers and which (as David Wellbery has argued at length) constitutes a primal scene of German poetic subjectivity. Between Goethe's "great odes" and Benn there also lie the "Dionysios Dithyrambs" of Benn's beloved Nietzsche, and these too must be considered as poetic ancestors. Both Goethe's and Nietzsche's odes are, like Benn's, narrative stagings of the sublime (hence the chapter's title). Nature becomes here a medium for the staging of the subject's failure, in the course of which the rhetorical underpinnings of sublime mastery are exposed. This becomes even clearer through a comparison of Benn's poetics of artifice with that of Mallarmé. The chapter concludes with a reading of one of Benn's most well-known poems, "Poplar," showing how the poem stages a confrontation between the sublime and an irony inherited from Heine. As in many poems by Heine, or as in Mallarmé's "Afternoon of a Faun," Benn's poem depicts an oscillating "relationship between nature and man in language" (Hans-Jost Frey). In other words, it "invents a hetero-reference" outside of its own enclosure (as was suggested in the first chapter with reference to Renate Homann). The conclusion of the chapter proposes that Benn's overall body of work has been falsely judged, with too much praise going to poetry from the 1920s that has in fact not always well stood the test of time. Against these well-known song-like (or sing-song-like!) poems, with their predictable shock techniques confronting Romantic clichés with urban or technological slang, the poems discussed here are in fact more complex, thus even ultimately more perdurably modern.

Chapter 4 is concerned with two earlier novels about nature by Alfred Döblin, famous largely for his later (1929) *Berlin Alexanderplatz*. Like Benn, Döblin is thus associated with the literature of urban modernity. Yet at the same time, at the height of the New Objectivity of the 1920s, Döblin was centrally concerned with rethinking the inheritance of Romantic *Naturphilosophie* (such as F. W. Schelling and Franz Baader). In 1927 he devoted an entire book to this topic, titled *Das Ich über der Natur* (*The Ego Over Nature*);[17] his epic poem "Manas" is a narration of natural history in the allegorical guise of Hindu myth, and as late as 1948 he returned to the conceit of nature's rebellion against human domination in his *Märchen vom Materialismus* (*Fairy Tale of Materialism*). These concerns are central to the two novels discussed here, the Expressionist *Drei Sprünge des Wang-lun* (*Three Leaps of Wang-lun*, 1913), which had a considerable influence on the younger Brecht, and *Berge Meere Giganten* (*Mountains Seas and Giants*, 1924), a wild science-fiction fantasy of the world's destruction and regeneration through natural catastrophe. As with Rilke and Benn, nature is in Döblin massively overdetermined in psychoanalytic terms, to the point where it is almost too easy to see the gendering and mother-father instances. (Like Benn, Döblin was a trained doctor and psychiatrist quite familiar with Freud.)

Given Döblin's complex personal situation as the descendant of Polish Jews who had only recently moved to Berlin, the chapter reads his novel of Chinese peasant revolt as an allegory of *Ostjudentum*. Such a reading inevitably places itself in the vicinity of scholarship about Orientalism and postcolonialism, a matter further reinforced by the historical proximity of the novel's composition to real revolts in then-contemporary China against their European seaport occupiers (and to the end of the Manchu Ching Dynasty in 1911). However, as many Germanists have pointed out, Germany was unfortunately a gaping lacuna in Said's *Orientalism,* and German Orientalism itself hardly matched the patterns of imaginary domination typical of its British and French counterparts. Since Germany itself had to be seen as somewhat "Eastern" in relation to these more advanced colonial and imperial powers, the German relation to the East had to be a more reflected one. This is certainly the case with Döblin.

The fifth chapter moves from Weimar to the end of the 1930s and the early 1940s, the period known in German literary history as exile.[18] In this case, the exile writer in question is Bertolt Brecht. After his early, anarchic period (of *Baal* and the early poems) was replaced by the satiric vein of the *Hauspostille* and the politically engaged works of 1930 and afterward, Brecht found himself returning, in his Danish and Finnish exiles, to the very tradition of *Naturlyrik* he had earlier proclaimed dead. (This was also the period when he was in close contact with Walter Benjamin.) The reasons for this are more complex than the mere biographical fact of his having moved from Berlin to the Scandinavian countryside. Nature poetry became, for Brecht, a vehicle for the redeployment of natural law. In the absence of the concrete context of political struggle through which his work had defined itself in Germany, nature became at once stage and addressee of a work that would otherwise have fallen into the very monologic solitude Brecht abhorred.

Here, however, a reduction to rhetoric — typical of a great deal of work in the burgeoning field of law and literature studies — must be avoided. The implicit proximity to ethical questions earlier mentioned is also evident in the context of law and literature, which tend to get stuck in a sterile opposition between pure rhetoric and an inexpressible ethics of justice or engagement. (Derrida's later writings on law are characterized by just such an opposition.) Instead of this, this fifth chapter prefers to see Brecht's exile poetry in the larger sociological context of the relation between the art system and the legal system. These two had been in close relationship (or, in Niklas Luhmann's terms, structural coupling) since the advent of aesthetic modernity, namely in copyright and publishing law. Brecht himself had been involved in what he called the "sociological experiment" of the Threepenny Trial in the last years of Weimar. What that trial proved, beyond Brecht's own financial loss to the film company responsible for the cinematic version of his and Weill's opera, was that bourgeois individual authorship — as exemplified in Enlightenment ideas of genius — was no longer legally protected in the age of mass media, or of "art's technological reproducibility," in Benjamin's famous phrase. Brecht's nature poems only make full sense against the background of their author's critical relation to law, and his tactical appeal to nature in an exile situation of real and complete political powerlessness.

In addition, though, a proper understanding of Brecht requires rethinking some of Luhmann's own terms regarding art. For in emergency situations like that of Brecht's exile from Nazi Germany, the modern differentiation between social subsystems that is so central to Luhmann's sociology itself breaks down (as it has also been doing recently in the United States). The coupling between nature and art effected by Brecht's poetry is an example of such a breakdown. Here the sublime failure of reason already mentioned in the context of Kant acquires a direct political urgency, being a response to very specific historical circumstances. Once again, this book's insistence on the need for a reflection on nature directly contradicts the ethical decisionism still so popular even now. In this case, we must contrast Brecht's turn to nature in the strongest terms with Carl Schmitt's, and also with Benjamin's, *theological* response(s) to the collapse of parliamentary law.

These four chapters imply, by their chronological order alone, at least the outline of a history of modernist nature. In fact, the original project was defined by a theoretical figure historically contemporary with the literary works discussed here, namely Adorno's deliberately paradoxical idea of *Naturgeschichte*. That idea was to be brought into tension with other models drawn from poststructuralism, in particular Lacan, in order to unfold it: such a combination of Frankfurt and France was typical of the early 1990s.[19] However, the book's development saw a gradual abandonment of both history and nature in their older, metaphysical sense, in favor of a critical position that finally became post-metaphysical (without, however, the now predictable deconstructive gesture of attacking "Occidental metaphysics"). The reading of Kittler and Luhmann during the final redaction certainly influenced this. With that abandonment of metaphysics went also an abandonment of the metaphysics of language that may be one of the strongest links between Adorno and Lacan, and one that they shared with the inheritance of German poetry discussed here.

Thus the implication of a history of modernist nature must be in a sense resisted, for if there is a history here, it is not one of decline and fall, or any other larger telos, but only a set of four variations or case studies. What was preserved from the original link to Adorno is the philosophical ambition, the wish to do justice to the deeper conceptual content of the German philosophical aesthetic tradition, and an attention to close reading inherited from hermeneutics.

The internal pragmatism of method preferred here, which was, as already noted, necessitated by the subject of nature itself, means that different chapters receive different theoretical emphases. Common to all of them is the tension between the hermeneutical and philosophical tradition and more recent anti-hermeneutical methods (Lacan, the Foucault-influenced projects of postcolonialism and Kittler, Luhmann). The advantage of this is variety: each of the single authors is not simply put into the same mill or grinder to prove the same theses. There is a deeper reason for it as well. As Harro Müller has pointed out, hermeneutical perspectives and the external, rhetorical perspectives adopted by poststructuralism stand in complementary relation to each other. Neither can function as an ultimate meta-language, nor is there any central perspective from where they can be unified or synthesized. There is no way to avoid the pragmatic risks taken by any particular interpretation.[20]

The final chapter's displacement of psychoanalysis by sociological systems theory may still come as a surprise. The reason for this was at first (if not only) pragmatic: the original attempt at reading Brecht's exile poetry through psychoanalysis came up with only rather thin and forced results. Nature, in these exile poems, is already rather impersonally functional instead of subjective or metaphysical; in this respect, these last nature poems could already be seen as a transition to the postwar period. The last chapter thus documents a change in the "nature" of the technological unconscious under the pressures of war, pointing ahead to the "cybernetic" paradigm that would dominate from 1945 to the 1970s. A richer reading of Brecht's poems required the methodological shift.[21] What has resulted from this is also implicitly a history of theory itself, viewed through the lens of a shift in the definition (or location) of nature, from the turn-of-the-century origins of psychoanalysis, to Lacan's ties to 1920s high modernism, and the tensions between system and culture, sociology and anthropology, that have defined so many postwar debates (e.g. Parsons vs. Geertz, Derrida and Lacan vs. Foucault, or current discussions on Luhmann and cultural theory).

This study thus does not take theory as something simply given *ab ovo*, but rather tests it against the specific historical and literary material to see where it may (or may not) be appropriate. This means that theory itself becomes experimentally testable, extendable, and not merely applied (although, conversely, the boundary between the theoretical and the literary is not therefore blurred, in the familiar deconstructivist fashion). If this approach is not without difficulties, these last may well be constitutive of literary criticism itself, insofar as it seeks to be neither mere thick description, nor connoisseurship, nor even merely a branch of applied philosophy. *Non ancilla nisi libera,* as the Schoolmen had it on philosophy: criticism cannot arrive at philosophical insight without being free.

The present choice of authors does still imply a historical periodization of the problem. Why end discussion of literary forms of the technological unconscious at the onset of the Second World War? Implicit in this choice is the definition of an epoch, the circumscription of the question between roughly 1900 and 1940–1945. In other words, the ongoing reference to nature found beneath the surface of high modernism would seem then to vanish at last with the beginning of postwar society. The death of nature disputed at the opening of the introduction would then only have been postponed for a half a century.[22]

This is still a little too simplistic. In a sense, the end of natural history Wolf Lepenies once placed in the mid-eighteenth century — that key moment in nascent modernity so often referred to by figures as otherwise distinct as Habermas, Luhmann, and Koselleck — is as infinite as the ageing of the modernity that has ever sought to replace it.[23] Nature as referent can never *entirely* vanish from either definitions of society, anthropology or art (as the end of the present work's third chapter suggests). To suggest it could — as so many discontinuously sublime phase-models do (following the example of Foucault) — is to yield to a terrible simplification. In opposition to these sorts of simplifications, we might apply Luhmann's characterization of social evolution to the period after 1945:

> The higher complexity of the newly-achieved stage of development makes it possible to give older elements a new meaning insofar as they can be integrated. New achievements do not necessarily bring with them a compulsion to renounce the old, but probably a compulsion to recombine [*Rekombinationszwang*].[24]

So too we can still find isolated instances of nature poetry even after 1945, most notably in the somewhat more conservative context of the German Democratic Republic, in the poetry of Johannes Bobrowski and Peter Huchel.[25] It must be admitted that for all its traditional beauty, GDR poetry is no longer as concerned with the central problems of modernism as the authors discussed here. (Celan would be the prominent exception to this.)[26]

Postwar forms of the literary avant-garde were arguably to be found in France more than in Germany, which after the exhaustion of modernism's Fascist perversion took solace in the moderate forms of Grass and Böll's humanist "rubble literature." (As George Steiner pointed out, the aesthetic technique of Grass is a recapitulation of Döblin's Weimar aesthetic — and in particular of Döblin's most accessible novel, *Berlin Alexanderplatz*.)[27] Postwar German experimental writers such as Heissenbüttel seem oddly epigonal and derivative relative either to their German predecessors or their French contemporaries. So Andreas Huyssen noted that "the center of avant-gardism in Germany in the 1950s was neither in literature nor in the visual arts, but in music experiment."[28] By the 1960s, Hans Magnus Enzensberger could claim to be beyond the infantile leftism of the old avant-garde.[29] Only French writers such as Robbe-Grillet,

Ponge, and Sollers continued the pattern of modernist experiment on into the late 1960s or early 1970s.

In Robbe-Grillet's *Pour un nouveau roman,* one finds one of the very last literary manifestos (its successor being Sollers's "Telquelist" program, *Logiques* of 1968). Here, more programmatically than in the work of any German writer after 1945, the postwar paradigm, with its central shift from metaphor to metonymy, is defined. (This is why so many writers outside France, from Handke to Cortazar, continued to take their programmatic cues from the New Novel.) In the book's central theoretical statement, "Nature, humanisme, tragédie," that paradigm is defined through the explicit rejection of nature. The technical correlative of nature in literature is metaphor. "Metaphor is in fact never an innocent figure." Metaphors, as "anthropomorphic analogies, are too often repeated, with too much consistency, not to reveal an entire metaphysical system" that supports them.

Robbe-Grillet's essay opposes this idea of a secret sympathy between the human and the natural with cinematic flatness and calculating technological exteriority. The essay provides thus the ideological justification for postwar literature's move away from the metaphors of metalanguage typical of earlier modernism (especially surrealism, with its visionary subjectivity) to a New Novel of metonymy. Implicit here also is a shift from a literary paradigm centered on lyric poetry to one centered on narrative prose. Interestingly, the real object of Robbe-Grillet's polemic here is the idea of human nature, especially as defined in the humanism of his existentialist literary adversaries Sartre and Camus. "The belief in a nature reveals itself thus as the source of all humanism in the habitual sense of the word. [. . .] The idea of a nature leads infallibly to that of a nature common to all things, that is to say *superior.*"[30]

The translation here again is: nature leads to metaphysics. What Robbe-Grillet is rejecting here is not only metaphor and analogy, but also any idea of dialectics, of hermeneutical dialogue or of mediation between man and nature. The Marxist materialism of Sartre, for instance, is here denounced as being theological (an accusation made also by Lacan). In opposition to all "myths of depth," whether of humanism, tragedy or nature, Robbe-Grillet puts forth an aesthetic of the flat, unpathetic exteriority of the look.

That such exteriority, such elision or suppression of subjectivity (or, specifically, of any psychoanalytic domain: the kinship of Robbe-Grillet to Husserl's phenomenological *epoché*[31] has often been remarked) is in fact impossible[32] would take the present discussion too far afield — as would the interesting relations to other media besides literature (i.e. film) implied by this aesthetic. What is important is that Robbe-Grillet has put forth here what a recent German commentator has called a *Cybernetic*

Anthropology.[33] This does not mean only yet another variant of literature as mimicking (the objectivity of) science — something already familiar from Naturalist poetics of the 1880s. It is much rather a poetics of linguistic and cultural self-reference — of the feedback circuit, if one will. Within this poetics, the old "natural" unconscious of Freud is displaced by what has been called "the unconscious of machines."[34] The earlier-mentioned "displacement of psychoanalysis by sociological systems theory" turns out to have a basis in literary history itself.

This "cybernetic" paradigm of late modernism would remain effective from the 1950s until the now-eclipsed postmodernist debates of the 1980s. At that point the question of nature began to emerge with renewed force, both in criticism and in actual artistic production. So Hartmut Böhme found Adorno's old dialectic of nature and history again in the elegiac ruined landscapes of Andrei Tarkovsky.[35] One might see the same phenomenon in Wim Wenders's long melancholic traveling shots in *Kings of the Road*. As chapter 1 states, it is hard not to sense Böhme's return to an Adornian aesthetics as a very unwitting form of postmodernism. What has become visible since the 1980s can be better described without a nostalgic return to metaphysics.

Several times, Luhmann noted an interesting central failure of late modernity, one he described in his characteristically value-neutral fashion as semantic. Luhmann's work is itself one of the best descriptions of the cybernetic society that produced it. In a cybernetic society, the metaphysical grounding function once taken by God and then by Nature is taken by system self-reference itself. Thus, for instance, media must deliver the trust or confidence once given by religion or morality. One of the side effects of this is that the functional system trust encouraged by communications media usurps the place of cultural and moral norms and thereby makes the stabilization of any unitary culture unlikely. As Habermas pointed out, complex, differentiated societies have difficulty forming a "rational identity," for their culture cannot be formed "exclusively in prospective terms," or in those of technical planning, without remaining "abstract."[36] Luhmann shares this skepticism: "functionally differentiated systems . . . have such a novel form . . . that up to now no semantics adequate to them has been able to develop."[37]

The conclusion to be drawn from this is an interesting one. It is implied that the bracketing out of nature is ultimately linked to one of *semantics*, in the word's most emphatic sense.[38] Semantics always lag behind structural development, are thus necessarily conservative, and need to be viewed with a certain mistrust (here Luhmann is quite close to both Lacan's and Derrida's distrust of signification). Semantics — to pursue the line of argument put forth in section three of chapter 1 — requires an interruption (or asymmetrizing) of social self-reference, what Renate Homann calls the invention of a hetero-reference. The exclusion of semantics — which are always historically coded, always bearers of memory — exposes in turn Luhmann's multiple blind spots: to the life-world, to protest movements, to the women's movement, and to nature.

The return of interest in nature thus coincides with a return of the theme of memory (i.e. cultural semantics), another topic marginalized by technological modernity. At the same time that nature was again thematized in the 1980s, Ulrich Beck's *Risk Society*[39] became an unexpected bestseller, and its thesis was drastically confirmed by the disaster of Chernobyl. The underside of the cybernetic society became visible as catastrophic; the unacknowledged complement to Luhmann became René Thom, whose catastrophe theory, originally developed in the 1960s, gradually became better known in the following decade.[40] Beck's diagnosis of risk society, wherein "the commonality of anxiety takes the place of the commonality of need,"[41] links up quite directly with the present book (see "The Anxiety of Observation" in chapter 1, which is also the anxiety of the technological unconscious itself). So does his idea that "nature can no longer be understood outside of society, or society outside of nature" (80), and that therefore "in advanced modernity, society with all its subsystems of the economy, politics, culture and the family can no longer be understood as autonomous of nature" (81). Chapter 1's plea for an aesthetic of *heautonomy* (following Renate Homann) only draws the consequences of this for literature and art.

Such an aesthetic, or redescription of modernity, cannot evade some tentative dimension of the programmatic, no matter how unrealized Beck's suggestions for a reflexive modernity have remained in the twenty years since the appearance of his book.[42] As this is a book concerned with the aesthetic, it is appropriate to conclude with an immediate and intuitive image taken from one of the latest, most contemporary forms of aesthetic modernity. For Nature had made its most literally spectacular returns in film and then in video. Already in the films of Tarkovsky and Wenders one may see the melancholy remnants of natural history, of landscapes of memory. Nature is the central actor in these films, yet in a sense far more complex than the "ceremonies of innocence" of which Leo Braudy once accused filmic Nature.[43] (In German film, the Hunsrück landscape in Edgar Reitz' *Heimat* (1984) embeds its "German chronicle" back not only in the periodic seasonal rhythms of regional agriculture, but also of nature itself.)

Even more than in film, though, we may find the constellation of nature and the technological sublime so central to this book in the videos of Bill Viola. The massive slowness and panoramic immensity of natural rhythms and space are dwelt on in Viola's work to the edge of kitsch (and, in the view of some critics, perhaps even beyond); here, as already in

Stockhausen's electronic Orientalism of the 1960s, or Wenders's fascination with the Chinese character for "nothing" on Ozu's grave, the technological unconscious appears to open directly onto mysticism and nature regained. The paradox is only an apparent one.[44] One of Viola's videos is particularly appropriate to this book, since it is one of an unresolved threshold. In it, a single human figure (of the artist himself) walks in slow-motion flat frontality toward the viewer, then stops. On one side of the screen, the figure is gradually consumed by water, and on the other by fire (recalling a proverbial poem on the end of the world by Robert Frost),[45] until the human figure entirely disappears, absorbed by images (and sound images) that are at once primitive forces of nature and also — precisely in the perfect transparency of their photographic reproduction, both eliding and reinforcing the rhetoric of the sublime — allegories of technological power. So, too, we cannot decide whether this elision of the human in the natural is apocalyptic or utopian. Viola's images are trying to take us beyond that "passion for the Real" Alain Badiou has recently seen as characteristic of the last century: the fascination with trauma and sublime violence to the point of self-destruction, a fantasy which now appears frighteningly near to realization.[46] The video, dating from 1996, is titled *Crossing*.

Notes

[1] Jared Diamond, *Collapse: How Societies Choose to Fail or Succeed* (New York: Viking, 2004). The earlier work is *Guns, Germans and Steel: The Fates of Human Societies* (New York: Norton, 1997).

[2] Bertolt Brecht, "Vom armen B.B.," *Gesammelte Werke 8: Die Gedichte 1* (Frankfurt: Suhrkamp, 1970), 262.

[3] Posner, *Catastrophe: Risk and Response* (Oxford: Oxford UP, 2004).

[4] Fredric Jameson, *Post-Modernism: Or The Cultural Logic of Late Capitalism* (Durham, NC: Duke UP, 1991), 48.

[5] Jonas, *The Imperative of Responsibility: In Search of an Ethics for the Technological Age* (Chicago: U of Chicago P, 1985); Habermas, *The Future of Human Nature* (Cambridge: Polity Press, 2003). One might also compare Derrida's later ethical turn, which has been interpreted by some as a farewell to postmodernity: see, for instance, in addition to chapter 1 of this book, Francois Debrix, "Specters of Postmodernism: Derrida's Marx, the New International and the Return of Situationism," *Philosophy and Social Criticism* 25, 1 (1999): 1–21. As Debrix points out, Derrida's return to an ethics of responsibility depends on a compromise between postmodernity and its reformist self-reflection, or between Marx and liberal individual rights. Debrix calls this "retro-postmodernism" (5).

[6] This is the subject of Ernst Bloch's *Natural Law and Human Dignity* (Cambridge, MA: MIT Press, 1987).

[7] Readers unfamiliar with Luhmann's work may consult the appendix of this book for a brief outline of his theory and its reception.

[8] A much-discussed instance: Steven Pinker's *The Blank Slate: The Modern Denial of Human Nature* (New York: Viking, 2002), which asserts (416) that "the dominant theories of elite art and criticism in the twentieth century grew out of a militant denial of human nature." What follows will, instead of throwing out the modernist baby with the anti-naturalist bathwater, as Pinker does, argue that there were other strands of modernism along with this. Pinker takes the utopian claims of modernism too much at their word, in order to reduce modernism to a straw man of "elitist" contempt for purportedly "natural" aesthetic desires — which then turn out to be a neat restoration of nineteenth-century bourgeois middle-brow taste.

[9] Compare the "transdisciplinary" work of Steven A. Moore on sustainability in architecture and urban planning (cf. *Technology and Place: Sustainable Architeture and the Blueprint Farm* [Austin: U of Texas P, 2001]).

[10] Habermas, *Postmetaphysical Thinking: Between Metaphysics and the Critique of Reason* (Oxford: Blackwell, 1992).

[11] The aesthetician Martin Seel has recently tried to put forth a non-metaphysical aesthetics of nature (*Eine Ästhetik der Natur* [Frankfurt: Suhrkamp, 1996]): as will become clear, there are marked differences between Seel's project and the present book.

[12] In the terms of systems theory, which has been famously skeptical about the "old-European" rhetoric of the "critical," this would be a *reformulation of paradox*.

[13] The most famous instance of this would be Carolyn Merchant, *The Death of Nature: Women, Ecology and the Scientific Revolution* (New York: Harper, 1990); "deep ecology" would probably belong in this camp as well (cf. Bill Devall and George Sessions, *Deep Ecology* [Layton: UT: Gibbs Smith, 1985]). Diana Fuss, *Essentially Speaking: Feminism, Nature and Difference* (London: Routledge, 1990) argues for a qualified "strategic essentialism" for political purposes.

[14] On this, see now Alenka Zupančič, *Ethics of the Real* (London: Verso, 2000), esp. 149–60.

[15] In Adorno's theory, this would be designated by the Hegelian term *Vermittlung*, or mediation (meaning the object's mediation through the subject, or the mediation of aesthetic experience through the historical). It is ironic that much of current *media theory* proceeds precisely through blocking off this aspect of mediation.

[16] There are signs that such a reformulation may be underway in the art world itself: see for instance the idea of art as "transfer discipline" in *TRANSFER: Kunst Wirtschaft Wissenschaft*, ed. Klaus Heid, Ruediger John (Baden-Baden: Verlag für kritische Ästhetik, 2003).

[17] Döblin, *Das Ich über die Natur* (Berlin: S. Fischer, o.J., 1927).

[18] To add literary "inner emigration" would have exceeded the limits of a book. In fact, this project began its life as a study of the nature poetry of Oskar Loerke, which will have to be published separately.

[19] Two examples: Peter Dews, *Logics of Disintegration* (London: Verso, 1987), for Adorno with Lacan; Christoph Menke, *Die Souveranität der Kunst* (Frankfurt: Athenäum, 1988), for Adorno and Derrida.

[20] Harro Müller, "Hermeneutik oder Dekonstruktion? Zum Widerstreit zweier Interpretationsweisen in der Moderne," in *Giftpfeile* (Bielefeld: Aisthesis, 1994), 108–29; here 121–22.

[21] As David Caudill has noted, Lacan has very little resonance in legal theory, even Critical Legal Theory (*Lacan and the Subject of Law* [Atlantic Highlands, NJ: Humanities Press, 1997]).

[22] This would tally with Fredric Jameson's differentiation of modernity from postmodernity through the latter's complete elimination of nature: "In modernism . . . some residual zones of 'nature' . . . still subsist . . . Postmodernism is what you have when the modernization process is complete and nature is gone for good" (*Postmodernism, Or, The Cultural Logic of Late Capitalism* [Durham, NC: Duke UP, 1991], ix). There has, however, never been any agreement on when this caesura took place, whether after 1945 or 1980; Jameson's own suggestion of the 1973 oil crisis seems the most persuasive. This means that there are late modernist works from 1945 to 1973 where nature indeed plays little role.

[23] As in the suggestive title of Ulrich Schönherr, *Das unendliche Altern der Moderne* (Vienna: Passagen-Verlag, 1994). See also Lepenies, *Das Ende der Naturgeschichte* (Munich: Hanser, 1976).

[24] "Das Problem der Epochenbildung und die *Evolutionstheorie*" in *Epochenschwellen und Epochenstrukturen im Diskurs der Literatur- und Sprachgeschichte*, ed. Hans Ulrich Gumbrecht and Ursula Link-Heer, 11–33 (Frankfurt: Suhrkamp, 1985), here 20.

[25] Oliver Schütze, *Natur und Geschichte im Blick des Wanderers: Zur lyrischen Situation bei Bobrowski und Hölderlin* (Würzburg: Königshausen und Neumann, 1990) (= Epistemata, Würzburger Wissenschaftliche Schriften, Reihe Literaturwissenschaft, vol. 47).

[26] For a discussion of Celan and nature, see Rochelle Tobias, *The Discourse of Nature in the Poetry of Paul Celan* (Baltimore: Johns Hopkins UP, 2006). For a detailed demonstration of how one of Germany's most prominent postwar poets stood in somewhat marginal relation to modernist problematics, see Neil H. Donahue, *Karl Krolow and the Poetics of Amnesia* (Rochester, NY: Camden House, 2002).

[27] One can see a similar retreat from modernism in post-1945 Russian literature, which never returned to the experimentalism of Khlebnikov, Mayakovsky, or Platonov. It is interesting that Germany remained the European center for *musical* experimentalism after 1945.

[28] Andreas Huyssen, *Twilight Memories* (New York and London: Routledge 1995), 202.

[29] So most famously in the idea that "Der Begriff der Avantgarde bedarf der Aufklärung" (*Einzelheiten* [Frankfurt: Suhrkamp, 1962], 290–315; here 296). Enzensberger accused avantgardism of being nothing more than a mask for the commodity — a truism since Benjamin's Baudelaire essay of the 1930s; yet

Enzensberger fell backwards behind the insights of Benjamin and Adorno into a stance of mere moralizing.

[30] Robbe-Grillet, "Nature, humanisme, tragédie," in *Pour un nouveau roman* (Paris: Gallimard, 1963), 63, 65.

[31] This term refers to Husserl's "bracketing out" of a phenomenon's surrounding circumstances, whether historical or psychological.

[32] Already in 1963, Philippe Sollers noted the impossibility of eliding all reference to tragedy from language ("Sept Propositions sur Alain Robbe-Grillet," in *L'Intermédiaire* [Paris: Seuil, 1963], 149–56).

[33] Stefan Rieger, *Kybernetische Anthropologie* (Frankfurt: Suhrkamp, 2003).

[34] So Henning Schmidgen, *Das Unbewusste der Maschinen: Konzeptionen des Psychischen bei Guattari, Deleuze und Lacan* (Munich: Fink, 1997). The difference between these two conceptions of the unconscious could be described as one between the *repressed* and the *latent*. Their meeting point would be in Lacan's second *Seminar* of 1954/55, with its famous discussion of information theory, later taken up by Friedrich Kittler.

[35] Hartmut Böhme, "Zum Verhältnis von Naturgeschichte und Allegorie in den späten Filmen von Andrej Tarkowskij," in *Natur und Subjekt* (Frankfurt am Main: Suhrkamp, 1988).

[36] Habermas, "Können komplexe Gesellschaften eine vernünftige Identität ausbilden?" in *Zur Rekonstruktion des historischen Materialismus* (Frankfurt: Suhrkamp, 1976), 92–128; here 118–19).

[37] Luhmann, "Das Problem der Epochenbildung und die Evolutionstheorie," 23. See also his *Die Gesellschaft der Gesellschaft* (Frankfurt: Suhrkamp, 1997), 963.

[38] Urs Stäheli has discussed the problematic status of semantics in Luhmann's theory in detail ("Zum Verhaltnis von Sozialstruktur und Semantik," *Soziale Systeme* 4, 2 [1988]: 315–40), and reaches the conclusion that semantics are not in fact merely *ex post facto* — as ideology or superstructure in Marxism — but rather play a constitutive role in defining communication as action. Thus the entire distinction between semantics and structure becomes problematic. In the context of this essay, this means that the "old-European" semantics of nature is not merely a side effect of a now-obsolete, pre-modern social structure, but helped to constitute the latter; so also nature's exclusion contributes to the constitution of more modern self-referential social structures. "With displacements in semantics . . . 'real' system problems are created."

[39] Ulrich Beck, *Risikogesellschaft: Auf dem Weg in eine andere Moderne* (Frankfurt: Suhrkamp, 1986); trans. by Mark Ritter as *Risk Society* (London: Sage, 1992).

[40] Thom's book *Stabilité structurelle et morphogenèse*, first published in 1972, was translated into English by David Fowler in 1975 as *Structural Stability and Morphogenesis* (New York: Wesley, 1975). Practical extensions of the theory were suggested by E. C. Zeeman in his *Catastrophe Theory, Selected Papers* (London/Reading, MA: Addison-Wesley, 1977). Dirk Baecker has referred to the post-Communist transformation of Eastern Europe in terms of Thom's catastrophes in his *Poker im Osten* (Berlin: Merve, 1998).

[41] Beck, *Risk Society*, 49.

[42] Instead, one sees the fulfillment of Beck's direst prediction — that of "re-industrialization" (224–28) — and worse still, of a "scapegoat society" based on "denial from fear" (75) of the real threat of environmental and social catastrophe: the renascence of fundamentalist religious extremism in the US and the Muslim world may be interpreted as just such a denial, as one of Beck's "interpretative diversions of stirred-up insecurities and fears" to absorb the massive instability of world society's self-destruction.

[43] In Nick Browne, ed., *Refiguring American Film Genres* (Berkeley: U of California P, 1998).

[44] On the peculiar relation between New Age holistic mysticism and metaphysics on the one hand, and nanotechnology and brain research on the other, see the suggestive article by Barbara Maria Stafford, "Leveling the New Old Transcendence: Cognitive Coherence in the Era of Beyondness," *New Literary History* 35 (2004): 321–38. Viola's work has also been seen as an aesthetic of post-traumatic shock, which would link back to this book's chapter 1 on Real Nature as traumatic (Deirdre Boyle, "Post-Traumatic Shock: Bill Viola's Recent Work," *Afterimage* 24 [Sept.-Oct. 1996]: 9–11).

[45] "Fire and Ice," *The Poetry of Robert Frost,* ed. Edward Connery Lathem (New York: Holt, 1979), 220.

[46] Badiou, *Le Siècle* (Paris: Éditions du Seuil, 2005). See also Žižek's political reading of this idea in *Welcome to the Desert of the Real* (London: Verso, 2002).

1: The Limits of Technocracy

After Nature?

NEAR THE END OF HIS LIFE, in the 1990s, Niklas Luhmann[1] was shocked at the sight of the Brazilian *favelas,* a sight that appeared to shatter the confines of theoretical explanation or even simple description. For a moment, Luhmann was forced to step out of the jumbo jet of high theory and adopt the low-level eyewitness perspective of an ethnographer:

> Anyone who dares to make a trip to the favelas of the big South American cities and succeeds in leaving them alive can attest to this. [. . .] Even a trip to the settlements left behind as a result of the shut-down of the mining industry of Wales will convince you of this. Empirical description is not necessary. Anybody who trusts his eyes can see this — to such a degree of intensity that every explanation fails.[2]

Although the present book will not abandon all theory for anthropology, it will still attempt to do justice to this very real experience of shock, the encounter with what so many theories of modernity have refused to include. In this late-modern "domain of exclusion, humans are grasped no longer as people, but as bodies"[3] — that is, as what Giorgio Agamben[4] called "bare life," as part of an extra-social state of nature. Not by chance, Luhmann evokes in the same breath as this terrible spectacle of subhuman poverty the bleak industrial wasteland of South Wales (a landscape that has now become a World Heritage Site in Blaenafon's Big Pit), for this state of nature is the unacknowledged complement to modernity. Nature has been the subject of precisely the same exclusion as the global poor. One wonders, however, if wastelands like the Big Pit of Blaenafon will continue to be such museum rarities that they need to be preserved.

Luhmann's surprise had more than personal causes. The exclusion of Nature typical of his thought was characteristic of most of his generation after 1945. From the increasingly technified and self-sufficient project of modernism, Nature has apparently been elided without a trace, less the "accursed share" Bataille saw as excluded from the capitalist economy of utility and thrift than merely forgotten. No longer dynamically repressed as Marx's alienated species-being or Freud's unconscious, nature is now stripped even of the utopian potential it had borne from the Enlightenment to the beginning of the twentieth century. The concept of nature itself conjures up so quick a suspicion of metaphysics or essentialism, along with memories of its instrumental use by National Socialism, that it hardly appears to deserve serious consideration. Nature seems less repressed than simply marginalized, made invisible, rather like the working poor — a self-evidence that ought, one imagines, to be cause for reflection. Yet this exclusion is only repeated and reinforced, not reflected, by most literary historiographies of modernism.

The representation of nature had at best a marginal part in postwar definitions of the modernist project. Within the restorative context of 1950s Cold War Germany, where aesthetic modernity often fostered an apolitical hermeticism, nature poetry emerged from its shadowy existence during the Nazi period as the so-called "nature-magical school" of Lehmann and Krolow. Yet the work of this group has not stood the test of time well.[5] The politicization of the 1960s effectively dismissed it outright with a sweeping reference to Brecht's famous wartime strictures against any "conversation about trees" (*Gespräch über Bäume*). Even Paul Celan (hardly an overtly political poet) joined in this rejection, mocking the conventions of the nature poem in a witty parody of Brecht:

> Ein Blatt, baumlos
> für Bertolt Brecht:
>
> Was sind das für Zeiten,
> wo ein Gespräch
> beinah ein Verbrechen ist,
> weil es soviel Gesagtes
> mit einschliesst?[6]
>
> [A leaf, treeless
> for Bertolt Brecht:
>
> What times are these
> where a conversation
> is nearly a crime,
> because it includes
> so much that is said?]

Celan's poem ironically elides not only any reference to nature, but also the whole of the hermeneutical notion of meaning that had fed the nature-lyrical tradition from its beginnings. In the idea that a "conversation" could be a crime, we may hear an ironic refusal of Gadamer's idea of "the conversation that we are," that is, of hermeneutical dialogue as such. Yet one should not overlook the fact that the loss of nature here goes hand in hand with a loss of faith in speech: Celan's poem is not simply an apology for deconstructivism *avant la lettre*. In still highmodernist fashion, the irony of the poem is inconceivable without the background of the meanings (nature, conversation) it declares lost.

From the strictures of the 68ers, whether political or modernist, German literary Nature would never completely recover.[7] For the not very "new" subjectivity of the 1970s — the turn away from politics by authors such as Peter Handke, Rolf Dieter Brinkmann, and Ulrich Plenzdorf, and whose central representative in poetry was Sarah Kirsch — hardly entailed any fundamental rethinking of the categories of *Naturlyrik*. Instead, this movement preferred most often to recur to older traditional patterns of nature as backdrop or projection screen for a subjectivizing depth psychology.[8] The more emphatic attempts of Handke at a restoration of natural aesthetics (*Über die Dörfer/Walk about the Villages,* 1982) remained isolated and without imitators. The 1980s' environmentalist debates suggested a return to critical theory's central indictment of the domination of nature (*Naturherrschaft*), but an eclectic theoretical blend of Foucault with a mix of Schelling, Jakob Böhme, Paracelsus, and other hybrid forms of Romantic *Naturphilosophie* undermined their theoretical weight.[9] Both postmodernism and ongoing re-evaluations of modernism had thus little difficulty in relegating literary nature to the historical dustbin; as a representative German critic, Karlheinz Bohrer, put it:

> If one wants a central category of modernity, as it has been defined since 1800, [...] then the concept of artifice (*Künstlichkeit*) offers itself. Artifice means a definitive farewell to Nature as it is immediately experienced, as it speaks of God or the gods. We live, since the end of the eighteenth century, *without* this nature, *after* this nature.[10]

To add insult to injury, Bohrer's argument is even made with specific reference to lyric poetry (Hölderlin, Benn), the very genre once so intimately associated with nature. Yet for all of Bohrer's self-declared modernity, his rhetoric does little other than update *topoi* well known since Wordsworth and Schiller. An essay proclaiming the demise of all philosophies of history cannot avoid producing such a philosophy itself. Bohrer ends up giving Schiller only a slight new twist: the loss of nature, experienced by a collective subject ("*das* moderne reflexive Subjekt") fitted out with the rhetoric of historical irreversibility, results in the promotion of a purely imaginary subjectivity decoupled from its traditional anthropological ground of nature and history.

The problems with Bohrer's premature exequies for nature do not end here. His claim that the loss of nature was the condition for a modern myth of the city[11] ignores the fact that the latter was, precisely, a naturalizing of the city, obvious in titles such as Brecht's *In the Thicket of Cities* (*Im Dickicht der Städte*) and countless Expressionist images and poems.

Most importantly, the crude binary opposition between the eighteenth century and the present (typical of many Foucauldian phase-models, with their disjunctive breaks between epistemes) excludes many important intervening mediations. The claim that modernity is defined by a paradigmatic shift of subjectivity from a "subject of reason" to one of imagination ignores the constitutive role of imagination in the defining theoretical text of subjective rationality, Kant. There can be no "historical leap from a subject of reason to one of imagination" (224) since the two are interdependent in their very constitution. Just as the promotion of rationality was always compensated for by that of imagination, so the aesthetic representation of nature was, from the beginning, a response to the loss of immediately lived nature — nature as experience and environment; and one may wonder whether that "loss" might itself have been in part imaginary, thus part of a particular strategy of nostalgic desire.

Bohrer's construct of a purely imaginary "protest-ego" and evocations of "primary identity" (225) remind one more of the ambivalent rhetoric of Benn, of Nietzsche's monologic art, than of the language of theoretical reflection. The evocation of an imaginary subjectivity never refers to any psychoanalytical theory of the imaginary. The survival of subjectivity after nature, according to Bohrer, depends on the fact that, in modern poetry, "speaking seems to make itself autonomous," so that "despite the recognizable ties of the speaking subject to given discourses, an infinite element, the Imaginary, which [...] was invented by Early Romanticism, has become detachable" (226). What has been conveniently forgotten here is psychoanalysis's critical mistrust of the imaginary and its regressiveess, which is anything but the expression of subjective autonomy. Just as the faculty of the imagination was inextricably bound up with that of reason in Enlightenment epistemology and anthropology, so in psychoanalysis is the imaginary inseparable from its symbolic matrix.

In his promotion of a subject supposedly severed from any mere natural anchoring, and his resulting aporetical and sterile opposition between essentialism and constructivism,[12] Bohrer's work shows how the marginalization of nature is also a side effect of a late-modern (or postmodern)[13] popularizing of self-referentiality. This popular variant of postmodernism must be distinguished from the more rigorous poststructuralism pursued by Derrida, for instance.[14] Popular self-referentialists like Bohrer promulgate what this book will designate as Imaginary Theory: namely the Icarian delusion that the fanciful flights of literary *rhetoric* may dispense with differentiated *conceptual* arguments that take hold of anything real. Imaginary Theory is academia's answer to performance art: while loudly proclaiming its own subversiveness, it is in fact the purest expression of the university system's self-reference — just as the neo-Dadaist gesture of attacking the "bourgeois institution of art" has now become that institution's most well-subsidized and harmless rehearsal.[15] Historically, one would have to see Imaginary Theory as a late-modern, popular recapitulation of *Jugendstil*, which Adorno saw as paradigmatic for modernity in all its aspects. One might even ironically suggest that Imaginary Theory was academia's inflated New Economy of information-without-production, of investment and speculation without underlying resources. Within film theory, for instance, the practice of so many proclaimedly "subversive" and "contestatory" readings has already been criticized as an often institutionally self-justificatory and projective *circulus vitiosus*.

Caveat lector, however: the answer proposed here is not a "post-theory," nor a reversion to any stable grounding in nature as substantial totality. To believe that a return to hale and hearty positivism, to the evidence of common sense, were the only answer to the excesses of "theory" would be only to take the reductions and simplifications of popular Imaginary Theory at face value and thereby reproduce its own aporia. We need not choose only between pure self-reference and so-called "naïve" empiricism. Instead, one might recognize that much of popularized academic "theory" has long been deeply complicit with the windmills of positivism at which it so quixotically tilts. Many North American imports from "Continental theory" have unwittingly reduced the latter to precisely the empiricism they purported to oppose. (One obvious instance would be the reduction of Lacan's Other — a transcendental instance of address, and nothing factual — to the empirical "others" of postcolonialism.) Reconsidering a by now routine exclusion of any consideration of nature can offer one way to break out of sterile oppositions, such as that of supposedly ideological science versus constructivism (to take one example).

There are in fact already signs of dissatisfaction with some of these theoretical clichés. Terry Eagleton has recently pointed out the blindnesses caused in cultural theories by the complete theoretical elision of nature:

> Culturalists are afraid that unless we keep reminding ourselves that we are cultural animals, we will slip back into the insidious habit of naturalizing our existence, treating ourselves as inalterable beings. Hence their protests against essentialism, which would have been commended by such doyens of bourgeois thought as John Locke and Jeremy Bentham. In fact, one can be just as essentialist about culture as one can about Nature.
>
> If you play down the material species-being of humanity, you may be left assuming that human beings exist only at the level of meaning and value. And that is a common mistake for intellectuals to make . . . Anti-essentialism is largely the product of philosophical amateurism and ignorance.[16]

Similarly, Elaine Scarry's recent plea for beauty as bound up with "the experience of 'being in error'"[17] implies the idea that beauty, or aesthetic experience as such, cannot be conceived of without a margin felt beyond the closure of "meaning and value," thus beyond the normal functioning of social conventions. Scarry's discussion takes place in the context of the very conversation about trees Brecht saw as politically unacceptable. It is Brecht's criterion of the political — of function and usefulness — that Scarry seeks to call into question. The individual subject of beauty is one which must be, in a sense, "incorrect" within the larger social system of meaning, or the smooth functioning of technocratic aesthetics. Although the present argument will not follow Scarry's defense of beauty against the domination of the sublime, it is nonetheless as such an "incorrectness" that Nature will be conceptualized here. The closed, circular self-reference of cultural "meaning and value" — of "social construction of reality," as the popular mantra has it — must in fact be interrupted for the endless play of academic rhetoric to have a chance at referring to anything outside itself. Thus the critique of culturalism requires also a break with the descriptive, immanent, anti-structural methodology of cultural studies as well. Yet simply to postulate Nature again, as some grandly indefinable Other to meaning, would be only another variant of the mystical theories of law and justice propounded not long ago by Derrida: that is, a new form of theological aporia. We cannot begin to conceive of nature again without a closely argued criticism of what has excluded it.

One way to open up a criticism of the hubristic delusions of Imaginary Theory, with its peculiar rhetorical claims to technocratic omnipotence, is to view it as a late, perhaps even the last, form of the sublime;[18] hence, the main argument of this chapter must begin with a critique of the sublime. This critique will proceed in several phases: firstly, a rereading of Lyotard via systems theory and psychoanalysis, culminating in a fresh look at one of the emblematic representations of modernist technocracy, Lang's *Metropolis*. The analysis of Lyotard and Lang exposes the modernist self-referential sublime as an aesthetics of deliberate *Angst*. Secondly, Kant's fundamental discussion of the relation of art to nature in the *Critique of Judgment* will be returned to, again with an eye to how this might help one to revise long-held sociological views on the art system's relation to its environment. Renate Homann's reading of Kant's Critique will be extended to reconsider how art may reflect on the consequences of social differentiation.

The continued relevance of nature to modernity will, thirdly, be illustrated with an example from modern art, namely Max Ernst's Surrealist nature of trauma. Finally, the idea of a *technological unconscious* will be programmatically limned in. Here a proposal will be made for a "crossing of the fantasy" of technocratic omnipotence, exemplified in a play of

Elfriede Jelinek, and a definition of the technological unconscious found in Freud. In closing, the mutual constitution of the human and the natural is discussed, again with reference to Kant (although some readers may be reminded of Serres's natural contract or Latour).

The Anxiety of Observation

In the *Aesthetic Theory,* Theodor Adorno had already seen the sublime as a defining moment of modernity:

> to put it gently: after the collapse of formal beauty, throughout modernity, the sublime was the only traditional aesthetic idea remaining . . . The ascendancy of the sublime is one with the demand of art not to hide its defining conflicts, but fight them out within itself; reconciliation is no longer the resolution of their conflict; the only thing that matters is that such conflict find a language. With this however the sublime becomes latent.[19]

Within Adorno's own thought, this unresolved conflict paradoxically figured by the sublime is complemented by passages which serve to limit or mediate that conflict. Unlike the postmodern sublime, Adorno's philosophical variant emphatically does not liquidate all subjectivity as such, nor is it a triumph of pure artifice or self-reference for its own sake. Instead, the sublime appears as a "trembling oscillation (*Erzittern*) between nature and freedom," or an awakening to humanity's irreducible anchoring in nature: experiences which lead to the affective release of tears.[20] This continued mediation of the sublime is tied to Adorno's preservation of the tension between the hermeneutical and that which defies it, between historical memory and the modernist quest for absolute presence.

From Lyotard's influential reformulation of the sublime, however, all such dialectical qualifications have completely vanished, leaving nothing but empty and frozen aporia in its place. With a shift in the sublime from modernism to the avant-garde, Lyotard reduces the question to nothing more than that of pure predication, of the modality of an event.

> The avant-gardist attempt inscribes the occurrence of a sensory now as what cannot be presented and which remains to be presented in the decline of great representational painting. Like [Adorno's] micrology, the avant-garde is not concerned with what happens to the "subject," but with: "Does it happen?," with privation. This is the sense in which it still belongs to the aesthetics of the sublime.[21]

There is more than one way to read Lyotard's sublime. Many commentators have linked it back to Kant and the relation of art to ethics, others, in more postmodern fashion, to Heidegger.[22] The difficulty of this passage is due to its debt to Heidegger, in whose later work "event" (*Ereignis*) was a key term, and this term "event" has been influential in the reception of Lyotard. For Heidegger, the "event" is where thinking (*Denken*) meets being (*Sein*).[23] Since this occurrence is opposed to discursive rationality (which must, in Heidegger's view, be complicitous with technocracy), it can only be stated in paradoxical or apophatic manner. Lyotard's particular appropriation of the term takes it out of the context of Heidegger's ontology (a move common to many French followers of Heidegger); it has thus something in common with Foucault's discontinuous, groundless "condition of possibility" of statements (*The Archaeology of Knowledge*). Ironically, Heidegger's notion of "event," often tied to an investigation of mediation such as the copula *ist* (is), was subjected to harsh criticism in the very same work Lyotard here cites, namely *Negative Dialectics*.[24]

What is curious here is Lyotard's aversion to any sort of aesthetic or formal realization, which leads him to a lopsided and reductive understanding of Cézanne (the promulgator of the famous doctrine of the *réalisé*, in the letter to Vollard of 9 January 1903) as an avant-gardist who was not interested in "finding his 'style.'"[25] The sublime of the Event is so ineffable that it appears to defy any specific aesthetic realization. This may be the precise moment where Lyotard's aesthetic tips over from modern to postmodern. Even beyond the high modernist disinterest in style — a matter shared by Adorno as well — Lyotard's reading of Cézanne emphasizes an attempt to paint "perception 'before' perception," an urge "to make seen what makes one see, and not what is visible" (Lyotard 207).[26] This avant-garde position, which must always relate itself to a horizon of that which does not yet exist, stands in sharp contradiction to the closed, hard materiality on which Cézanne insists with his idea of formal *realization*. (It was just Cézanne's solid materiality, his close observation of nature which was emphasized by contemporary observers such as Rilke, who termed him "a masterer of reality" and asserted that "all of reality is on his side.")

Moreover, Lyotard's anti-hermeneutic bent means that he neglects questions of aesthetic production, the inner logic of artworks (which are the true micrology meant by Adorno at metaphysics' fall), in favor of reception aesthetics alone (203). Little wonder that all that remains of art for Lyotard is that his question of the event should be reduced to "information" about it (210) — what Lacan would call the *discours courant*, the production of academic and journalistic discourse that "does not cease to write itself" — or that his sublime should be subject (as Jameson saw) to veer over into self-parodying camp.[27]

Most important for the present argument is Lyotard's insistent use of the term *privation*.

> The event [of the sublime] happens as a question mark "before" happening as a question. *It happens* is rather in the first place *is it happening, is this it, is it possible?* [. . .]
>
> An event, an occurrence — what Martin Heidegger called *ein Ereignis* — is infinitely simple, but this simplicity can only be approached through a state of privation. [. . .]
>
> But the mark of the question is "now," *now* like the feeling that nothing might happen: the nothingness now. [. . .]

It is this privative question from which Lyotard derives the terror of the sublime:

> Terrors are linked to privation: privation of light, terror of darkness, privation of others, terror of solitude; privation of language, terror of silence; privation of objects, terror of emptiness; privation of life, terror of death. What is terrifying is that the *It happens* does not happen, that it stops happening. (197–98, 204)

Viewed in psychoanalytic terms, the term privation offers a perspective distinct from extant philosophical, political or sociological critiques (i.e. Adorno, Habermas, and Jameson)[28] of this peculiar form of the sublime. This particular rhetoric and pathos of the sublime occurs again and again in otherwise seemingly divergent theoretical figures, whether the old "death of Man" or the latter's reincarnation in Friedrich Kittler's subjectless media machines, or the endless deconstructivist rehearsals of the impossibility of meaning and their attacks on the straw man of "Occidental metaphysics," or perhaps even in certain forms of systems theory's "sublime" rejection of mediation between divergent partial systems. All of these models share the pathos of privation Lyotard found in the sublime. We will describe this privation now, in a formulation that draws on elements of psychoanalysis and systems theory, as the Anxiety of Observation.

In the terms of Niklas Luhmann's sociological systems theory, the move from the modern to the postmodern sublime is an intensification of second-order observation, that is, of reflexivity. (Second-order observation simply means "observing the observer," whether the latter is oneself or someone else.) If traditionally mimetic art sought to hide the observer in a semblance of the "natural," modernity instead exposed precisely the artifice of observation, as reflexivity.[29] Yet Lyotard's sublime goes even further, in that it seeks for another form of primary, undiscursive, incommunicable "event" beyond this reflexivity. It does so by appearing to undo the structural coupling between first- and second-order observation, between immediate consciousness (or perception) and intersubjective communication, that is normally effected by art.[30] (This cutting of connections is of course linked to Lyotard's anti-hermeneutical impulse, a larger tendency he shared with many other late-modern theorists.) This combination of perception and communication is similar to the binary function in other aesthetic systems: play and fantasy in Freud, mimesis and construction in Adorno, or the traditional opposition between the intuitive and the discursive. In each case, art requires that *both* aspects of the binary be involved: *both* the immediate and vivid perception, which is always individual, and its reflective mediation by artistic language, which is intersubjective. Lyotard's sublime, by contrast, seeks to leap out of this dialectical tension into an absolute Beyond. It can only do so at the cost of severing its connection to concrete aesthetic form.

In Luhmann's terms, the structural coupling of perception and communication "guarantees that something at all [*überhaupt etwas*] is indeed observed, when observation takes place in second-order mode."[31] That is, this coupling roots the linguistic or communicative aspects of art in the specificity of perception, and forbids art from ever becoming purely self-referential, from being only discursive. Precisely this specific "something" is what is elided by Lyotard's frightening privation. As a result, the observer of the postmodern sublime is left staring at nothing other than the ultimately unobservable blind spot of his or her own paradoxical reflexivity. The severing of this coupling of reference and reflection means also that art ceases to refer to anything outside itself, anything beyond its immaculately pure and ultimately empty Event. Put otherwise, an art which has been reduced to pure (academic!) "self-reference," cut off from the structural couplings with other social systems on which it normally depends (for instance, politics, law or science),[32] undoes itself altogether and has nothing left to say but tautology. This emptiness is only thinly veiled by a heroic moral pathos that seeks to stylize this "observation-unto-*Angst*" as somehow an index of authenticity.

Little wonder the result is the terror of which Lyotard writes. For this form of endlessly self-reflexive sublime is decodable as a form of anxiety or *Angst*. To do so helps to break apart the seeming purity of this sublime, its lofty inaccessibility to mere discursive criticism, and show that its abstraction draws on more concrete sources. If we map Lyotard's anxious worry about whether the Heideggerian Event will or will not happen — a worry that virtually guarantees it will not — onto the genesis of the psychoanalytic subject, we find anxiety to be characteristic of a stage *before* the full (castrating) installation of the Symbolic. This may seem at first somewhat surprising, given the sublime's traditional association, from Kant to Lacan's *Ethics of Psychoanalysis,* with the moral Law of the Father. Yet the anxiety of Lyotard's endless reflexiveness is such as to undo that law, pulling the subject back into an undifferentiated and pre-symbolic domain.

Anxiety has been a notoriously hard phenomenon to define in clinical terms. Psychoanalysis itself has always been uncertain as to where to assign a cause for it. The later Freud had (in *Hemmung, Symptom und Angst* of 1926) abandoned his early diagnosis of anxiety as tied to castration fear, coming to recognize it as bound rather to a lack of object, to an excessive turning backwards upon itself. Instead of being the direct conversion of repressed libido, anxiety is one of the ego's forms of reflexivity, indeed the chief discontent of a developed conscience. "The ego is the actual place of anxiety (*Das Ich ist die eigentliche Angststätte*)."[33] Furthermore, Freud now sees anxiety as tied to the loss of the mother, even before the advent of any (castrating) paternal instance.[34]

Lacan continues this shift of anxiety toward the mother. In Lacan's extension and rereading of Freud, anxiety becomes neither fear of the father and his castrating instance of the Law, nor of the mother's loss, but rather of too great a proximity to a mother perceived as overwhelming and devouring. The object relations of the child become legible as defenses or bulwarks against this anxiety. The exemplary horse phobias of Freud's famous child patient Little Hans, for example, thus function as an "outpost" against the outbreak of his anxiety.[35] Anxiety happens when the affective investment usually made in an object is turned back upon the subject, disturbing the latter's normal stability and producing a sense of anxious expectation, of suspense.[36] In particular, anxiety is bound up with a disturbance in the subject's narcissistic ideal ego (*moi-idéal*, Freud's *Ideal-Ich*, algebraically written by Lacan as "i(a)"). Unlike the ego ideal, which is tied to the symbolic, the ideal ego "originates in the specular image of the mirror stage" and "is a promise of future synthesis towards which the ego tends," continuing "to play a role as the source of all secondary identifications."[37] When the ideal ego is disturbed or occluded in anxiety, its expectant futurity is, as it were, left hanging without object. We have seen this anxious waiting already in Lyotard's characterization of the "event." In the case of the sublime, this waiting is a strange form of, or strange relation to, desire, but it is a desire without an object other than the subject's simultaneously endless and truncated self-reflexivity.

> In brief, anxiety is correlative to the moment where the subject is suspended between a time where he no longer knows where he is, and a [future] time where he will be something where he can never again find himself.[38]

Lyotard's unanswerable question *is it happening, is this it, is it possible?* is thus also *is it me who am still perceiving this?* or *will it still be me that perceives it?* The identity of the observing subject is here put literally into question. Rilke once concluded one of his most famous poems, "Archaic Torso of Apollo," with a severe ethical imperative delivered by the artwork to its observer: *You must change your life*. Here, it is as if Lyotard has inverted the message of art from Rilke's confident imperative into a frightening interrogation. The question art poses to its observer is now not so much "Will you be able to change your life?" as "Will you be able to keep it (and yourself) the same?" It is hardly surprising, given this perceived fragility of the subject, that anxieties about "identity" have now become so current.

One may go even further and correlate this anxiety of observation to a deliberately cultivated and paradoxical "experience" of frustration. To do so is to work out further the implication of Lyotard's insistently repeated word *privation*, a term which means something quite specific in psychoanalysis, and particularly in the Lacan of the mid-1950s, engaged as he is in a debate with Winnicott and object relations theory. At that time, Lacan was engaged in opening up the pre-Oedipal domain of fetishism governing the relation of mother and child. Lacan's privation, however, refers to the path followed by the specifically feminine subject, a feminine counterpart to castration. Prior to both of these two lies the moment of frustration, and it is this to which Lyotard's endlessly unsatisfying and irresolvable sublime is correlated. (As will become clear, this need not mean eliding the implications of Lyotard's argument in terms of the assumption of sex.)

Frustration is, for Lacan, prior to the entry into the Symbolic, and thus bound up with still-Imaginary dualisms (child-mother, child-phallus) and the irresolvable aggressions which such dualisms must sustain. Lacan goes even further and says that frustration "is only thinkable as a refusal of the Gift, inasmuch as the Gift is symbol of love." That is, "frustration is thus not the refusal of an object of satisfaction."[39] It is the refusal of the symbolic debt to language, to the mother who gives the gift of love. Could not Lyotard's endless "question" be decoded as just such a refusal, namely to let the Event — the particular object, the specific artwork — happen? For if we suspend or postpone any specific realization in the infinite self-reflection of anxious reflexivity, we keep all possibilities open, not needing to be bound by any particular object. (So also the critical ritual of endless perorations on "deconstructing Occidental metaphysics" appears as a refusal of any metaphor of meaning.) A great deal of late- or postmodern attacks upon Art are an angrily frustrated refusal of Art as realization, as symbolic gift, or as beauty. Against this, the endlessly self-reflecting subject can only oppose aggression. Yet the result of such a refusal of metaphor and meaning, of exchange, can only be anxiety, an anxiety which is moreover now felt to be pleasurable — or even somehow sublimely true. It is the willful sustaining and prolonging of what would otherwise be, in the traditional history of subject formation, only a "vanishing moment."[40] (If one refuses the metaphor or symbolic gift, one remains in the endlessly mechanical clicking on and off of presence and absence, like the alternation of heads/tails or odds/evens: *does the Event happen or does it not? am I still here or am I not?* This position of frustration has, Lacan notes, "an absolutely vanishing character, and one that is *literally impossible to satisfy.*").[41]

Unsurprisingly, this domain of frustration and anxiety is also in close relation to that fetishism which dominates the pre-Oedipal. Lacan correlates frustration with the Symbolic Mother, a term which has recently become an object of renewed discussion.[42] At this junction, high modernism interposed its central figure or fantasy of technocracy. Thus the ambivalent relation to the symbolic mother constructed by the sublime bears directly on the question of the human relation to nature.

The problem of the symbolic mother returns in a well-known example of the conjunction of technocracy and sexuality, namely Fritz Lang's *Metropolis* (1928). Andreas Huyssen has read this film as a specifically gendered form of Adorno and Horkheimer's domination of nature, one where "technological man" performs the "ultimate task" of reproducing, and thus rendering superfluous, Woman herself, through a modern variant of Pygmalion or Frankenstein.

> By creating a female android, [the scientist] Rotwang fulfils the male phantasm of a creation without mother; but more than that, he produces not just any natural life, but woman herself, the epitome of nature. The nature/culture split seems healed. The most complete technologization of nature appears as re-naturalization, as a progress back to nature.[43]

This is indeed a figure of modernist discourse central to the present book. Again and again high modernism's megalomaniacal fantasies of technocratic omnipotence are revealed as always accompanied by such fantasies of re-naturalization. Such a re-naturalization was in fact a necessary accompaniment to technocracy, something like its "return of the repressed." Huyssen's reading, however, should be expanded and extended to make this clear. In particular, we need to correct a long-lived tendency in literary and film studies to reduce psychoanalytic readings to theories of fantasy alone. Thus in Huyssen's view, the "threat" of technology becomes merely a "male phantasm," a "projection" and thus something "imaginary . . . that does violence to a real woman."

> On this plane, then, the film suggests a simple and deeply problematic homology between woman and technology, a homology which results from male projections . . . (71)

The technocratic fantasies of male subjectivity are, in other words, here exposed as paranoid. Huyssen is certainly correct to point out the fantastic investments made by male sexuality in the technological, a central feature of much modernism, not only Fascist. Yet the term "projection" is too common-sensical; not only Lacan, but even Freud himself, in the Schreber case, warned against it.[44] It reduces psychoanalysis to a dualism of "imaginary" fantasy and merely empirical "reality," a dualism which is itself imaginary. In "projection," the Symbolic has been forgotten, and the traumatic, impossible quality of the Real flattened out to factual given. Thus Woman can be reduced to a merely empirical "difference" from male fantasy, one surely deserving of more decently liberal respectfulness:

> But neither technology nor woman can ever be seen solely as a natural extension of man's abilities. They are always qualitatively different and thus threatening in their otherness. It is this threat of otherness which causes male anxiety and reinforces the urge to control and dominate that which is other.

It is easy to slip from this "urge to control" into a moralizing simplification. If only men would just be more ethical, more tolerant of otherness, and stop dominating it, one might be tempted to think, forgetting that this "other" has nothing to do with psychoanalysis any more. In a move that we will see repeated again and again in recent interpretation,[45] Huyssen's Theweleit-inspired critique of "male fantasies" risks falling back behind Lacan to an old-Freudian idea of woman as repressed Nature, as a "threat" of female sexuality *in toto* which must be gotten "back under control" (81). The result of this totalizing of Woman can become somewhat confusing:

> Woman, nature, machine had become a mesh of significations which had all one thing in common: otherness; by their very existence they raised fears and threatened male authority and control (70).

This is a very broad, "culturalist" generalization of Lacan's Other, and also a very widely held one. Yet such a vast, overarching "otherness" exists, in fact, as little as does Woman. To generalize Lacan's Other into a broad, empirically given cultural fact, or a collective fantasy, is to restore precisely that totalizing master signifier that Lacan wanted to criticize with his concept. The reduction of psychoanalysis to binary alternatives ("real woman," in the empirical sense of real, versus "imaginary male fantasy") risks falling into the trap of Imaginary Theory. (How, for instance, can a "threat of technology" which must be ultimately that of castration — i.e. symbolic! — *also* be an "imaginary projection"?) We can draw out more productively the insights of Huyssen's pioneering reading through differentiating more carefully the pre-Oedipal domain he has marked out.

The way to do so lies in working out in more detail the role of the mother; and rather than making the latter the repository of a Kristevan semiotic *chora*, or the source of some supposed *écriture féminine*, recent writers have tried to develop the symbolic role of the mother in the symbolic exchange of gifts with the child. This has the advantage of moving away from older models wherein woman is seen to be mere object of fantasy towards an understanding of the active and primary role of the mother. As Lacan noted, the symbolic mother is in fact original. It is only when the oblative relation of gift and exchange between mother and child is broken by frustration that she becomes real.

> The mother is first of all a symbolic mother, and it is only in the crisis of frustration that she begins to realize herself, by dint of a certain number of shocks and particularities which are produced in the relations between mother and child. The mother as object of love can be at any moment the real mother, inasmuch as she frustrates this love.

There can be thus no question of "male fantasies" at this stage, when symbolic and imaginary have not properly been defined and the subject has not yet precipitated its fundamental fantasy. Lacan makes this clear in rejecting Freud's idea of infantile (or primitive) "omnipotence of thought." Mother Nature can thus no longer be simply the object of "ambivalent" pre-Oedipal narcissistic projections of dependency versus power, to be controlled by "male fantasies."

> At this moment which I am now describing to you, of the realization of the mother, it is she who is all-powerful and not the child. It is a decisive moment where the mother passes into reality from a completely archaic symbolization.[46]

What Lacan means by "archaic symbolization" is the propping (Freud's *Anlehnung*) of Symbolic language onto the Real of Nature.

> That which is originally natural or biological never stops referring to the symbolic level, where it is a question of subjective assumption, inasmuch as the subject is itself taken up in the symbolic chain.[47]

This is a dense passage requiring careful attention to semantics. Lacan's "assumption into the symbolic" almost echoes the Feast of the Assumption of the Virgin, which is especially appropriate given that he is here discussing a specifically feminine subject. His term for "refer to," *se reporter sur*, is worth looking at more closely, since it seems to imply that nature, in itself, "refers ahead" to human language. Yet the French *reporter* (as a non-reflexive verb) has richer connotations, implying also a lithographic transfer, a carrying-over in a mathematical calculation, and a contango in finance (i.e. where delivery prices for futures exceed spot prices). If natural symbols refer, in this sense, to the human symbolic, it is almost as if nature were straining for language (an idea one would not normally associate with Lacan). Yet this is not illogical, given that Lacan asserts that "behind the symbolic mother, there is the symbolic father."[48] In other words, rather than there being a relation of absolute discontinuity between mother and father, one where "male violence" and symbolic artifice arbitrarily impose themselves on the innocent wholeness of Mother Nature, there is a secret relation of mutual solicitation between the two. Thus the traditional claim made by poststructuralism that language or culture completely effaces any precedent traces of nature must be modified: as Lacan notes, the natural real is taken up in and "becomes an element in" the symbolic.[49]

To illustrate this with a more familiar example: the domain of the symbolic mother, of the anaclitic propping of language on nature, is that of Freud's *fort-da* ("le plan de la première connotation présence-absence," as Lacan calls it).[50] It is, if one will, something like the mechanical chain of odds and evens, heads or tails which Lacan discussed in the second *Seminar*, but one where the subject has not yet "precipitated out" into a relation of fantasy ($S <> a$ in the "Lacanian algebra" developed from 1955 onward), since not yet forced to give up its *jouissance* by castration. It is precisely this irreal alternation which one may see at work in Lyotard's sublime doubt of privation: *is it happening, is this it, is it possible? Does it happen or does it not? is it I who am still perceiving this? or will it still be I who perceive it?*

It now becomes possible to draw out the full implications of Huyssen's reading of *Metropolis* and its mechanical vamp: the vamp is the Symbolic Mother of Technocracy, ambivalently holding the empty place between nature and culture, impotence and omnipotence, passivity and activity, melancholia and mania. The technological sublime then becomes legible as a particular relation to Woman. The anxiety and frustration, the endless and ultimately sterile conceptual aporias that characterize it are bound up with this relation. Even further: one may see the technological sublime's denial of any natural substratum as close to psychotic. If, according to Lacan, modern science itself depends upon a paranoiac foreclosure (or *Verwerfung*) of Nature,[51] this foreclosure becomes even more extreme in the technocratic delusion of total self-reference.[52] Little wonder such delusions are accompanied by a constant Anxiety of Observation.

"The Un-Form of Reason"

The ever-more suffocating and sterile enclosure of the technocratic sublime has thus put us in a position which is opposite to that of the Ape in Kafka's "Report to an Academy." If Kafka's Ape sought desperately for a "way out" of the imprisonment of nature, we must now find a way out of the prison-house of language, of the monotony of endless self-reference and self-observation. Yet any affirmation of a positive alternative is doomed to futility, including "nature" as whole or wholly "other": the gates to Eden are no more open to us now than they were to the Romantics. Nature cannot be made into an all-encompassing maternal Other again; and the attempts of theorists since the 1970s, beginning with Lyotard, Deleuze, and Guattari, to posit an anarchic domain of "desire" which would be extra-linguistic have only led back into imaginary delusion, to a "simple prioritization of the unconscious over the conscious" which "can scarcely be seen as a liberation."[53]

Renate Homann has offered an interesting critique of the technocratic tendencies of both deconstructivism and systems theory which may be extended in the present context. Her *Theorie der Lyrik*[54] works also with the Kantian sublime, but in a way diametrically opposed to Lyotard: rather than dwelling on the fascinating technological violence of the sublime, like the latter, she sees Kant's conception as a way out of the split (*Kluft*) between knowledge and morality, between theoretical and practical reason, thus between different subsystems of modern differentiated society itself. This phenomenon of differentiation (into independent systems of law, art, economy, politics, and religion) has, according to Luhmann, rendered obsolete the once over-arching claims of a concept such as nature to provide any larger universal grounding for social or aesthetic practice; with this even Habermas would not disagree. Yet rather than seeing that phenomenon of differentiation as an implacable and insurmountable fate (as does Luhmann), Homann sees it both as an ongoing process and also as a challenge which modern poetry must answer with the invention of an "inter-systemics" that points society towards a possible reformulation of its constitution (*Verfassung*). (Here her work is comparable to that of other systems theorists like Richard Münch or Hellmut Willke.) In Kant's sublime, according to Homann's rereading, there appears the possibility

> which is unthinkable for systems theoreticians like Niklas Luhmann: namely, the possibility that in the case of the acute failure of one subsystem, another system may become active for it, without copying or occupying the ordering principle of the system which has failed. (95)[55]

To restate the familiar problem: in Kant's sublime, theoretical reason and understanding (*Verstand*) fail, and practical reason (normally associated with morality) must step in. This is of course precisely what the technological sublime sketched in here refuses to do, waiting and watching anxiously on the threshold of its older metaphors of (moral) agency and meaning, to see whether or not the event of a subject might take place. Yet Homann does not simply revert back to a traditional Kantian position. In her rereading, poetry (*Lyrik*) appears to take the decisive place formerly assigned by Kant to practical reason. For Homann, modern poetry as self-reflexive aesthetic practice must heuristically invent a hetero-reference (*Fremdreferenz*) to fill in the gap produced in the ultimate failure of self-reference or autopoiesis. In other words, Homann suggests taking a step beyond Lyotard's Anxiety of Observation, beyond the bad infinity of the self-reflexive sublime, the self-consuming dead end of a late modernist *l'art pour l'art,* or a rhetorically self-performing avant-gardism without material substrate. Art must re-link up with something outside itself to renew itself. What could or should this external reference of art then be?

In Homann's conception, this hetero-reference is occupied by the whole of other literature (in an expanded version of intertextuality), by a variant of Russian Formalist *literatur'nost* which has now taken the place of the Kantian faculty (*Vermögen*) of reason. Kant's key tactic, in the *Critique of Judgment,* of subsuming the individual faculty of judgment (*Urteilsvermögen*) under the faculty of judging "in general" (*überhaupt*) has been here transposed to literariness "in general." If, in Kant, the aesthetic subject uses the failure of concepts to turn back and reflect on its own faculties, in Homann, literature reflects on its own status as literary. Like Kant, Homann is concerned to provide a transcendental grounding for her subject. Kant, concerned to limit the arbitrary subjectivity of aesthetic judgments, sought to ground them in the larger, anthropological generality of human judgment in general. So, too, individual humans are grounded for Kant in the larger concept of humanity.[56] Literature or the literary system occupies, for Homann, this same systematic place as Kant's humanity or judgment in general. Thus Homann may claim that the closure of the constitution of poetic language paradoxically implies "a transgression beyond this closure to a hetero-reference" (61). For a literary work to be valid, it must open out beyond itself.

Yet Homann's arguments have even larger potential implications than her work carries out: if, for her, "other poems" must function as an "environment" (*Umwelt*) for modern poetry (465), could one not extend her idea to a still larger *Umwelt,* namely that of nature? The relation of nature to culture was, after all, one of the central concerns of Kant's *Critique of Judgment,* the work on which Homann's is an extended commentary. (Homann herself expressly rejects such a reference to nature, 105–6.) Homann's use of "literariness" as poetry's hetero-reference is not without difficulties, for it depends upon a totalizing closure of literature, a systemic compulsion (*Systemzwang*) that is opposed to the concrete individuality of the artwork. The modern poem must, she claims, "reflect on the agreement of all other literatures" (212) to effect the new constitution (*Verfassung*) of its language. Yet even if one recognizes that this totality is not necessarily meant as an empirical summa, the generality of "*all* other literatures" remains nonetheless problematic. There are other aspects of Homann's work that may be more helpful here, though, in solving the problem of how modern literature may break out of the prison-house of self-reference. One of her glosses on the introduction to the *Critique of Judgment* is particularly suggestive:

> The heuristics of practical reason implies, as discussed, no immediate "goal-directedness" [*Zweckmässigkeit*] of the form of nature for the form of reason (i.e. of empirical knowledge), but rather the *break* with the immediacy of such a relation: namely the invention of the "goal-directedness" of the non-form [*Un-Form*] of nature, even more precisely: of the non-form of empirical understanding [*Verstand*], for the invention of a form of reason as a whole. And this latter is no longer to be described with the category of "form," but only with that of an inter-systemic "constitution." (167)[57]

This is a passage rich with larger implications. We may try to unpack a few of its dense conceptual formulations. To begin with, we might signal the paradoxical idea of a "goal-directedness of a non-form," which will remind the reader of the idea of a necessary "incorrectness" or "signifying dysfunction" attached to nature (see the earlier discussion of Elaine Scarry). The idea of an "un-form" here clearly resonates with the historical origin of aesthetics in the valorization of perceptions that could not be subordinated to the ideal of *clara et distincta perceptio*. "Un-form" means specifically: that which cannot be readily absorbed by normal discursive reason, by cultural convention. It is thus un-intuitive, before distinct perception, like Lyotard's sublime event. But we need not aporetically oppose this "un-form" to perception and absolutize it in splendid isolation, as Lyotard does. For here, in Homann's Kantian context, "un-form" is at once mediated (via the inter-systemic constitution), goal-directed, and also definable as the irreducibly intuitive "something" which art must observe to be art at all.

There is still more involved here. Art entails "the invention of the form of reason as a whole": hardly a modest claim. We must re-narrate the process of aesthetic invention to understand this. To rephrase Kant's process again: aesthetic imagination (*Einbildungskraft*) perceives a sublime *Unform* of nature which theoretical reason cannot grasp, and to which it cannot assign a goal or purpose (*Zweck*). The answer to this failure of understanding — which is inseparable from a break in normal discursive communication — must lie in between the distinct, differentiated social systems (of morality, or practical reason, and knowledge, or theoretical reason). In the terms already mentioned earlier, we might see this "event" of the break with goal-directedness, of the invention of a purposeful un-form, as a break in the normal (self-referential) functioning of communication that produces a new aesthetic perception. Not by chance, Kant must specify the pleasure of reflexive aesthetic judgment, of the un-form of nature, as "according to the concept of freedom," *zufolge dem Freiheitsbegriffe*.

In Homann's rereading of Kant, this is given form through a heuristic reference to literariness as such, to "all other literature" as the hetero-reference of the self-constituting modern literary work. Reference to larger, general literariness helps stabilize an individuality that would otherwise collapse in on itself. Yet one could draw this out further by seeing Homann's heuristic hetero-reference as similar to the "asymmetrizing," "conditioning" or interruption of tautological self-reference Luhmann had already seen as necessary for all meaning.[58] As Luhmann stressed, all social systems must interrupt their self-reference in order to produce meaning. It is just this interruption of tautological self-reference which Lyotard's sublime refuses to perform. Indeed, Luhmann had even discussed Homann's idea that "in the case of the acute failure of one subsystem, another system may become active for it": this is nothing other than the phenomenon of structural coupling.[59] In structural coupling, different social systems may share the same element: law and economics are coupled by contracts, law and politics by the constitution. No single social system can exist entirely independently, without such links to other systems: this is as true of art as it is for politics, economics or science. Yet this fact is consistently blocked out by sublimely technocratic theorists of the late- or postmodern avant-garde, or those of self-sufficient culturalism, who can only conceive of aesthetic modernity as the impossible stance of Icarus. In contradistinction to these theories, one may see that what lies outside technocratic self-sufficiency, outside the prison-house of culture, is what Kant and Homann termed "the un-form of nature." This un-form of nature need no longer pose the threat of fundamentalism or essentialism, for it is inseparable from the workings of society and culture, since found in the interstices (Kant's *Kluft*) left *between* differentiated and self-referentially closed social systems, Conceived thus, nature is these social systems' paradoxical product, remnant, or fallout.

We may remind ourselves here that "technology" as such has been, historically, nothing but a structural coupling between the science system on the one hand and the economic or political system on the other.[60] In other words, technology already entails the coupling between theoretical reason and understanding and practical reason which Homann is claiming for modern poetry. The difference is that technology — especially under the all-too-willingly fascinated "gaze" of its academic interpreters — has tended to conceal this structural coupling under the semblance of scientistic omnipotence.[61] In doing so, technology — or even more so in the form of technocracy, which forgets the origins of technology in social differentiation — reproduces the very nature it appears to conceal and deny in the form of naturalistic adaptation to its environment (as commentators as different as Adorno and Heidegger have variously signaled). The result is theories which, for all their claim to being up to date, are at bottom deeply naturalistic.

Worse still, these theories prove unable to account for the fact that *technocracy cannot ultimately work*. The attempt at closing technology off in a completely self-referential loop cannot but break down, as countless literary allegories such as Kafka's penal colony have shown. This ultimate failure of technocracy is a matter of some current (environmental) urgency, yet it must be understood in terms more precise than broad and loud assertions of ethical imperatives. (In this, the present discussion partly agrees with Heidegger, who asserted in "Die Kehre" that humanity cannot see *Technik* from the outside, since *Technik* itself helps constitute human subjectivity.)[62] As Lang's *Metropolis* already knew, the technocratic illusion must break down, precisely because it forecloses and denies the very subjective agency on which it is blindly based. Even Luhmann himself was extremely sanguine about modern differentiated society's ability to become, in Ulrich Beck's terms, reflexive about its own limits, especially as regards the ever more marginalized natural environment. In light of the preceding psychoanalytic discussion of the technocratic subject, technocracy breaks down because it overlooks the irreducible remnant of subjectivity that cannot be incorporated into the symbolic (linguistic, technological) order. This remnant of the subject is what Lacan once called the "object little a." Put differently: the technocratic subject, fixed at a stage of anxious frustration relative to the symbolic mother, refuses to acknowledge that the mother could have a lack, could be wanting and thus desiring. Technocracy is the true Phallic Mother, complete unto itself, wanting nothing, thus omnipotent. As a totalizing fantasy it must always generate the anxiety of observation along with itself, along with the abject (Kristeva) of what it refuses.[63]

Nature in the Wake of Trauma

In light of this, it becomes possible to reconceptualize nature as no longer the fantasy of maternal wholeness it was from the eighteenth century on — Rousseau's "douce voix de la nature" of the woman and mother — but rather as precisely this fallout of differentiation, as unsymbolizable remnant of the subject, as an object a. If "the symbolic order . . . produces something, in the course of its autonomous organization, that goes beyond itself,"[64] then this must be true also for the technological order which is itself a form of the symbolic. Nature is thus one of the forms of "the "real" of our civilization which returns as the traumatic kernel in all social systems."[65] It is here where one may situate the anaclitic propping of language on nature already mentioned, in the "extimacy" of the object, which is "in us more than we ourselves." It is also here where one may reformulate that mediation between nature and history that Adorno imagined in an early (1931) lecture on the idea of natural history, as a point where it might be possible

> to grasp historical Being in its most extreme historical definiteness — there where it is most historical — as a natural Being [*als ein naturhaftes Sein*], or where it could be possible to grasp nature as a historical Being there where it seems to rest most deeply in itself as nature.[66]

To be sure: we cannot simply yoke these two fine old master signifiers of nature and history together in the familiar metaphysical paradoxes beloved of Adorno himself, and so richly suggestive of endless horizons of hermeneutical meaning. Yet that such a mediation was still very much a part of aesthetic modernity is immediately evident in art history, where modernity is by no means equivalent to pure techne-for-techne's sake: the *Jugendstil* illustrations for Erich Haeckel's *Die Natur als Künstlerin* (*Nature as Artist*, 1914), republished in the Surrealist periodical *Cahiers d'Art* as late as 1934, continued to fascinate Kandinsky on into the 1930s, and Klee wrote, while at the Bauhaus in 1923, an essay entitled "Wege des Naturstudiums" (Paths of Studying Nature); even after the war, in the late 1950s, Dubuffet worked dried leaves and flowers into his series *Éléments botaniques* (as Anselm Kiefer would do again in his landscapes of memory much later). Georges Bataille devoted an article in the 1929 issue of *Documents* to an enthusiastic review of Karl Blossfeldt's plant photographs, titled "Le Langage des fleurs."[67] Much of this work may be understood as an ironical commentary on Darwin's natural history, an attempt to "grasp nature as a historical Being," as Adorno suggested.

This is not to forget that much of the Surrealists' refunctioning of natural imagery was done in a spirit of ironic parody of eighteenth-century Encyclopedism wherein an unleashed imagination displaced older Renaissance ideas of *ekphrasis* or description of nature. (Adorno's proposed link of nature and history may have been better figured in Surrealist irony than he would have liked to admit.) In the process, Enlightenment notions of nature's ordered rationality were displaced by a deliberate strangeness that might recall Foucault's pre-Enlightenment discourse on nature as cabinet of curiosities or speculative hermeneutics. (This last had already been revived in German Romanticism's idea of *Natursprache,* a conceit that would persist well on into twentieth-century nature poetry.) In a sense, Surrealist "nature" is allegorized nature, a nature bearing the stamp of history, much as that of Benjamin's German tragic drama. In Surrealist natural allegory, Kant's "un-form" of nature appears to have been violently cut loose from its larger organic embedding.

Even within Surrealism, however, there are important differences in the response to nature. The artist who contributed most substantially to a specifically modern depiction of nature was Max Ernst, in his *Histoires Naturelles* of 1926. Already his pluralization of "natural histories/natural stories" takes one beyond the unitary *grand récit* of nature the Enlightenment had seen in this term. Even further, though, Ernst himself claimed this series as a "Copernican Revolution" taking him "beyond art."[68] This "beyond" was, however, a paradoxical one since it entailed something different from the usual avant-garde sublation: Ernst's beyond was paradoxically also a *before*. Similarly, that before was now no longer the claim of traditional mimetic practice to be only a transparent referent to its natural signified. It affected the referent nature itself.[69] In Ernst's *frottages*, nature appears to revert to *nature morte*, a fossil state before the difference of organic and inorganic: it is a nature which is "not yet differentiated (*noch nicht ausdifferenziert*),"[70] and which thus points *ex negativo* to the fact that "nature" in its modern form is itself the product of social differentiation. Ernst's lithographs could be seen an illustration of how nature "transfers itself" (*se reporte sur*) to the symbolic, in Lacan's earlier-cited terms. The peculiarly ambivalent quality of these lithographs, in a no-man's land between living and dead, reminds one of Adorno's observation on Celan that nature in his work is always still life (*nature morte*).

It should straightway be noted that such a pre-differentiated nature is strictly speaking an ideal construction, and thus unrepresentable. Like another great unknowable construct of modernity, it is, if one will, the unconscious primal scene (*Urszene*) of nature. As Whitney Davis has recently written of the "psychoiconography" surrounding Freud's Wolf-Man case, where drawings and diagrams play so important a role:

> ... it is, almost by definition, the site of what we could call the *manifestation* of latency: a picture is the formation in which mental memory- and fantasy-images become, at the moment of production and observation, nominations or predications, symbols or "meanings."[71]

Davis is here referring not only to the Wolf Man's own famous drawing of the phobic "wolves in the tree," but also to the "domains of graphic imagination, conception and notation" that accompanied and defined Freud's own conception of science, including "Haeckel's comparative embryology," the subject of the still-popular illustrations just mentioned here.

In technical terms, Ernst's Real Nature can only be represented as paradox: so in his analysis of Number 6 from the *Histoire naturelle* series, "Les pampas," Ralf Konersmann points out that the peculiar fascination of the image lies in its being simultaneously read as raw wood-grain — as *datum* — and as the image of a landscape, as *factum*.[72] The image oscillates between two semantic levels of literal and metaphorical. In the terms of the present argument, these are also the levels of history and nature, material and fantasy, or even consciousness and communication. Ernst's artwork thus presents a paradoxical form of art's normal structural coupling between these last two: rather than hiding the artifice of his work behind a mimetic illusion, thus hiding the artwork's dependency on second-order observation behind a program, he exposes the underlying paradox of art as both made and imagined, material and sign. Yet Nature is *not therefore simply elided,* as it ought to be according to the falsely teleological arguments of modern apologists for self-sufficient technocracy, rather it is preserved alongside its artistic or artificial complement.

In this respect, Ernst's work anticipates the "return of the Real" that Hal Foster found a decade ago in the neo-avant-garde, and which he designated as a form of "traumatic realism."[73] Foster also notes the paradoxical nature of a Real which can never be directly represented (unlike "reality" which must, in Lacanian terms, be seen rather as an Imaginary formation), and ties its location in visual art to Lacan's idea of the random encounter (*tuche*) or Barthes's momentary *punctum:* "a confusion of subject and world, inside and outside."[74] In other words, an extimacy, to borrow Lacan's punning term for the object a. "Traumatic realism," in Hal Foster's sense, presents a Real Nature that remains in the wake of the failure of all imaginary utopias, including that of technocracy. Thus it is important to keep in mind that Ernst's turn to Real Nature followed shortly upon his break with the avant-garde of his day (Dadaism). Real Nature is not, properly speaking, an avant-garde concern: it is, perhaps, a reflection on trauma in the wake of the avant-garde, and thus not an object of conscious nostalgia. Rather than postulate any substantive domain of lost wholeness to which one must return, or absolutizing technology as nature's total negation, the reflection on Real Nature recognizes that "technology . . . is itself an ecological entity."[75] Such a recognition might prove a way out of endless postmodern repetitions of an avant-garde gesture which has finally become parasitical[76] on the institution of art it once claimed to destroy, and thus itself only just such another institution.

Reformulating the Paradox

We may now return to a broader sociological perspective to see what consequences the rehabilitation of nature might have for a larger theory of art. Even Real Nature cannot ever escape the inevitability of second-order observation, in Luhmann's terms. Nature can never become again what it was for the classical and romantic period — that is, a way for society to observe the unity of its own distinctions, a whole within the whole; nor can blurry appeals to a purported "environmental ethics" offer anything more than further paradoxes disguised at best in rhetorical appeal. Instead of such rhetoric, the present work prefers "insight into the structures of modern society and the consequences thereof."[77]

Luhmann himself was the first to stress that — in sharpest contradistinction to the naïve aesthetizing fantasies of literary scholars — technocracy could never be a solution to its own problems, and yet its loop of endless self-reference cannot simply be broken without catastrophic consequences. As Luhmann explains,

> Technology turns back upon itself in a fatal loop.
> The most common expectation seems to be that one should be able to control this problem through organisation. This only repeats the same problem on another level. Society itself is no organisation.[78]

No end appears possible other than a catastrophic one: "technology has no limits, it is a limit; and in the last resort it may fail not due to nature but to itself."[79] Like the widespread poverty produced simultaneously with immense wealth by global markets, nature is now less dynamically repressed (in Marx' and Freud's old sense) than simply marginalized, made "latent" or invisible by system self-reference.[80] For it is the very "form of technology" itself which "becomes a problem"[81] — namely its paradoxical nature as exclusionary, as a strict coupling which paradoxically produces increasing amounts of risk and chaos through what it cannot observe. To reconsider that form requires a further recognition of paradox, thus the "reintroducing of the difference of system and environment within the system."[82] The strangely inconclusive end of Luhmann's late essay "On Nature" almost grudgingly admits as much: "When a resolution of paradox no longer functions satisfactorily, one must go back to the original paradox and re-paradoxify it, try out another schema for resolving it [Auflöseschema]."[83]

What follows is an attempt to work out such a reformulation of paradox. For the excluded third of all binary codes, the blind point inevitably produced by all observation, is the observer him- or herself, but precisely as a part of Real Nature, and *thus already nonidentical*. (Here Adorno's favorite notion of the non-identical can be given specific reference.) This blind spot may be correlated with the extimate object a of psychoanalytic fantasy. The reformulation of paradox is thus also a reconfiguration of fantasy, even what the later Lacan called the "crossing" or "traversing of fantasy."[84] In the traversing of fantasy, the subject recognizes the object of its fantasy (the object a) to be its own production and assumes it as such, thereby offering the chance to alter that fantasy, or at least the subject's position relative to its own desire. Bruce Fink has described this process as

> a "crossing over" of positions within the fundamental fantasy whereby the divided subject assumed the place of the cause, in other words, subjectifies the traumatic cause of his or her own advent as subject,

coming to be in that place where the Other's desire — a foreign, alien desire — had been.[85]

With this, we have again respecified the connection between fantasy and technocracy suggested by Huyssen (among many other commentators). Rather than simply "critique" this fantasy as a projection, as inadequate to an empirically "real" woman or nature, we may see that this fantasy of mastery is born of "trauma as the child's encounter with the Other's desire"[86] and thus inevitably implicated in the structure of subjectivity (and perhaps not only male at that). To cross over "beyond" this entails an assumption of responsibility for the cause of one's own desire. (It is interesting that Fink believes this should also entail "a separation from language itself" that takes the subject "momentarily out of discourse, split off from discourse," Fink 66.) This moment of crossing is closely related to anxiety, to a doubt about where one is as a subject: but unlike Lyotard's anxiety of observation, it is not pleasurably protracted for its own sake. Instead of enjoying one's sublime helplessness, the subject who crosses must give up the enjoyment of being subjected to the Other (to a desubjectified science, or to delusions of technocracy) and take on the cause of desire as its own. In this sense, crossing of fantasy is a crossing beyond the sublime.

To subjectify the fantasies of technocracy, reformulating the paradox of scientific subjectivity (or observation), would be just such a step. The massive overproduction of catastrophic blindness by technology's "fatal loop" produces the anxiety of observation, an anxiety which apologists of the postmodern, paralyzed by fears of any metareflection, can only helplessly reproduce and reinforce.

One of the reasons technocratic problems have been so difficult to formulate — thus tempting many to the facile appeal to "ethics" — is that the problem of technocracy is not only, or even primarily, a purely scientific one. As Luhmann notes in *Risk*, "In the fields of ecology and technological consequences,"

> Science finds itself driven into territory it would never (or only in exceptionally rare cases) have entered for theory-controlled research reasons of its own. Problems occur here that do not arise within the framework of the research itself, so that it remains unclear exactly how such problems are to be formulated; which discipline they should be assigned to; what efforts, what time should be assigned for the research; and whether it will be possible to gain useful knowledge within the meaning of the task set.[87]

That is: technology is not a problem within any single social system, because it is the effect of a structural coupling between the scientific system and the economic system (and in some cases, the political system as well). This is why the risk incurred by technology goes so far beyond the risk of scientific research: it is a speculative risk dependent ultimately on that of the economic and banking systems. Within the latter, an increasing system self-reference or autopoiesis has come to be the norm: "Speculation takes its cue from speculation. In other words, the observation of observation of the market is guided more and more by the prognoses of others and not only by the form in which it calculates its own business results" (85).

This is the origin of the "transcendental illusion" of postmodernity, of the New Economy of information (which may already have seen its apogee and end in the Wall Street scandals of the new millennium's beginning). The economic system is "guided more and more by the prognoses of others" to the exclusion of any consideration of industrial production, or even of its own form of observation, and thereby takes on what one could only call Imaginary or delusional aspects.

Thus, as Luhmann notes, "Research does not operate in the headlights of its own vehicle; it is carried on in the lateral shadows." This book seeks to investigate these lateral shadows. The lateral shadows of every social system's autopoietic self-reference are its dependency on structural couplings, which its normal operation cannot see. Luhmann himself noted that in light of the "structural crisis" of late modernity, "it may be wise to proceed . . . to an ecology of ignorance, that is, to steer the description toward the form behind which lies unmarked space."[88]

Recognition of this "unmarked space" of the natural environment outside the autopoietic reproduction of communication is a way to avoid falling into what Klaus Eder has called the "theoretical naturalism" of systems theory, which Eder believed is due to the latter's disregard not only for natural conditioning, but also for the mediation of culture as well. As Eder noted, one cannot grasp nature except as (paradoxically) the result of human work and history: nature must be understood as mediated through culture. This recognition exposes the covert naturalism informing so much systems-theory work, with its borrowings from evolutionary theory and biology:

> A reformulation of the forms of social differentiation in terms of cultural theory reveals the secret logic of the theory of social differentiation: it provides a secondary naturalization of the social differences among people. Social differences are explained with the aid of an evolutionary theory . . . In more recent functionalism, this naturalism becomes conceptually visible in the increasing borrowings from biological explanatory models. Society, like nature, is viewed as an autopoietic system that maintains itself by the regulation of contingency . . . The naturalism of fundamental theoretical assumptions wreaks its revenge in the treatment of the phenomenon of culture

... The "cultural ignorance" of functionalism in the social sciences ultimately consists in not seeing the non-instrumental aspects of the social construction of nature and thus losing sight of the constitutive function of culture in the social evolution ...[89]

In the process of its functional simplification, sociology has reduced what Moscovici called "the human history of nature" to "the natural history of a society which culminates in European modernity."[90] Against this, Eder suggested a "cultural sociology of nature" (20) that would re-open nature's relation to culture and to history. Eder's own approach to this, however, followed a Habermasian model of "communicative interaction" which the present work will not imitate. Instead, it will seek to open up the presumed self-reference and autonomy of aesthetic modernity to its own "ecology of ignorance"[91] or "unmarked space," namely the continued persistence of nature even in the mid-twentieth century. For art, too, as any other social system, is constitutionally dependent on structural couplings with other systems, be they economic, political or scientific. To open up and expose these structural couplings may also offer a chance at opening up the structural coupling of consciousness and communication through which humans are socialized, namely language; and to see how this latter functions historically may be a way out of the "prison-house" of its eternal self-sufficiency. Such a way out might in turn also offer us that chance at changing the concept of art itself in which Adorno saw the sole chance at the latter's survival.[92]

As a contribution to this project of changing the concept of art, what follows will offer four paradigmatic case studies of the persistence of nature in modernity. These studies imply a larger history of that persistence, yet such a history cannot be in any way teleological or definitively closed; thus one could imagine other chapters to add to those present. The fate of representations of nature after the Second World War would require another book. Very broadly, nature was occluded by programmatic statements such as (in France) Robbe-Grillet's refusal of "nature, humanism, tragedy," or (in Germany) by Adorno's claim that in Celan's poetry, "the last rudiments of the organic are put aside," leaving only a "deobjectivization of the landscape" into purely linguistic processes.[93] Nature in its older, more emphatic (metaphysical) sense had to be occluded by the cybernetic anthropology[94] that prevailed between 1945 and at least the 1980s, which marked a sharp break between nature and culture, thereby rendering irrelevant their traditional mediation in *Naturgeschichte*. In the work of 1950s nature poets such as Günter Eich or Karl Krolow, nature becomes an oddly positivist escape from the nightmare of recent history into abstraction.[95] By contrast, in the poetry of Peter Huchel or Johannes Bobrowski, or in the frozen Alpine descriptions of early Thomas Bernhard (e.g. *Frost*), nature serves as an allegory of history and its mourning or anamnesis. This mourning would turn up again in the long traveling shots of the East/West German border in Wenders's *Kings of the Road*. Most recently, David Barison's and Daniel Ross's *Der Ister* (2004) is a filmic meditation on nature and history in the landscape of the Danube, as commented on by Hölderlin, Heidegger, Hans-Jürgen Syberberg, and Philippe Lacoue-Labarthe. These works are (to borrow Simon Schama's title) landscapes of memory, therefore of historically indexed loss, and not representatives of any promise of redemptive wholeness. Such a promise had to have politically ambivalent connotations. Thus the attempts of Handke to return to a more substantive poetics of nature in the 1970s promptly provoked a satirical response from Elfriede Jelinek (*O Wildnis, o Schutz vor ihr* [Oh Wilderness, Oh Protection from It]; see also the landscape descriptions of *Gier*), directly attacking the political and gender restoration implied by this. The same criticism as Jelinek's of Handke would not be hard to make of the role played by the Hunsrück landscape in Reitz' *Heimat,* performing "ceremonies of innocence"[96] which are crucial to the ambiguous politics of the entire film.

Yet even the same Jelinek who had been so sharp a critic of 1970s radical feminist claims to Nature regained (Verena Stefan) cannot help but refer to natural landscape as late as her 1998 Robert Walser monologue, *Er nicht als er (He not as he)*. In this more lyrical than dramatic stage piece, Nature comes alternately to stand for the poet's nonviolence, nonidentity, and finally even his death. Kant's and Schiller's eighteenth-century walk out of the enclosure of culture into nature is repeated as an exodus from humanity, subjectivity, and life itself; it is the artifice of Walser's writing that opens up this way out. Nature seems here to be asleep, a fairy-tale figure still awaiting the awakening kiss.

> Here in the forest interior it is quiet as in a happy human soul, from which the work has come, or as in a temple or magic castle or dreamt-of fairy tale palace, like Sleeping Beauty's castle, where everything sleeps and is silent for hundreds of long years.[97]

The poet's room, a metaphor for his work, releases him to the room of nature and death:

> It lets me, needy one that I am, even out into the woods at any time, under a dripping fir tree, to friendly houses, into the jubilation of birds and the most beautiful glow of evening! (28)

At the very end, just as for Sade, whose work she has so carefully studied, nature promises Jelinek a liberating disorder, a way out of society into chaos, into that absence of *clara et distincta perceptio* in which aesthetics had its historical origin:

Thus. Earth and sky flow and fall together into a flashing, blurrily shimmering fog-form that rolls over itself in waves. Chaos begins, and the orders disappear. Wearily the shaken one seeks to retain his senses: he succeeds in doing so. Later, he walks confidently on further. (35)

Jelinek here does not yield to Lyotard's postmodern sublime, the sublime that "is a stranger to consciousness . . . is what dismantles consciousness, what deposes consciousness."[98] For the "shaken" Robert Walser succeeds in preserving his conscience here and walks confidently on. Without preserving some trace of reflective consciousness, there is no way out of the monotonous monad of self-reference. It is striking that Jelinek should have discovered this natural world of fairy tales as a last repository of hope in her late work. By contrast, the sublime is, for Jelinek, a lie with dangerous political implications: its violent purity is inseparable from a purity of race (the theme of her play *In den Alpen*).[99]

"O Inch of Nature!"

This continued persistence of nature in the absence of its once-unified concept suggests a reformulation of the latter. Luhmann, noting the relation of the semantics of nature to aristocratic privilege, remarked that

> around the middle of the nineteenth century, the concept of nature had to be newly formulated from the concept of energy, and energy conceived as work. One could almost surmise that even the upper classes, and they in particular, now have to work. Therefore nature too.[100]

So also, as Friedrich Kittler has shown, women began to work circa 1900; once Woman did not exist, Nature could not either, at least not as the same master signifier it had been in the classic-romantic period. Yet if Nature ceases to speak with the "gentle voice" of Rousseau's maternity, as the *Autre grand A*, this does not mean it ceases entirely, rather that it has changed place. In very schematic terms, one might say that Nature has, under pressure from social differentiation and technological invention, moved from the Imaginary to the Real, and from A to a: from silent source of language to senseless (part-)object, from harmonious whole to traumatic and unsymbolizable remnant. The paradoxical formulation "technological unconscious" describes this change.

The title itself bears clear historical resonances or traces that ought, in closing, to be addressed. the technological unconscious may be read as a dialogical answer to two other preceding works, each one a decade apart: Fredric Jameson's *The Political Unconscious* (1981) and Rosalind Krauss's *The Optical Unconscious* (1993). As in these prior works, the present book engages with the material historicity of psychoanalysis. With Jameson, and against the rhetoric of Imaginary Theory, it insists that "history is *not* a text," although it would prefer to see history (no longer capitalized as in Jameson) as less itself a Real "absent cause" than one of the latter's effects.[101] With Krauss, the present book shares an impulse to "map onto the modernist logic only to cut across its grain, to undo it, to figure it otherwise."[102] If, for Krauss, "high modernism established and then fetishized an autonomous realm of the visual" (124), this holds true of the larger project of modernism's *technocratic* autonomy as well. Krauss's book shows how, for instance, Max Ernst's Surrealist ready-mades exposed the anaclitic propping of desire onto need, of language onto natural givens, producing an impression of "both-at-once," of "being caught inside the illusion and . . . looking on nonetheless from without," which Krauss then analyzes as "a model both of vision's claims and of vision's failure" (209, 74). The following pages will find in the modernist poetics of Rilke, Benn, Döblin, and Brecht a similar ambiguity of claim to and failure of sovereignty over nature, of both claiming the place of the sovereign, sublimely technocratic Beholder of Nature, and also betraying the technological unconscious as Krauss formulates: "inside consciousness, undermining it from within, fouling its logic, eroding its structure, even while appearing to leave the terms of that logic and that structure in place" (24).

The concept of a technological unconscious is, to be sure, not without its difficulties.[103] At one point in her book, Krauss cites Benjamin's evocation of an optical unconscious materially specific to photography,[104] and compares this to Freud's discussion, in *Civilization and Its Discontents,* of "technological advances . . . as a set of "prosthetic limbs" that expand the power of the individual." Here though the comparison runs aground for Krauss:

> Freud, however, is clear that the world over which technical devices extend their power is not one that could, itself, have an unconscious. It may have a microstructure that lies beyond the range of the naked eye, but that structure is neither conscious/unconscious nor can it be in conflict with consciousness (179).

Yet a look back at Freud leaves one less convinced of this than Krauss:

> These things that, by his science and technology, man has brought about in this earth, on which he first appeared as a feeble animal organism and on which each individual of his species must once more make its entry ("oh inch of nature!") as a helpless suckling — these things do not only sound like a fairy tale, they are an actual fulfilment of every — or almost of every — fairy-tale wish. All these assets he may lay claim to as his cultural acquisition. Long ago he formed an ideal conception of omnipotence and omniscience which he embodied in

his gods. To these gods he attributed everything that seemed unattainable to his wishes, or that was forbidden to him. One may say, therefore, that these gods were cultural ideals. Today he has come very close to the attainment of this ideal, he has almost become a god himself. Only, it is true, in the fashion in which ideals are usually attained according to the general judgment of humanity. Not completely; in some respects not at all, in others only half way. Man has, as it were, become a kind of prosthetic God. When he puts on all his auxiliary organs he is truly magnificent; but these organs have not grown onto him and they still give him much trouble at times.[105]

Against Krauss, it is not hard to find the implication of a technological unconscious in this passage. So Lacan also, with similar pessimism, re-translated Sophocles' famous chorus ("Many are the wonders"), of which Freud must surely have been thinking as he wrote the preceding passage, as an early (441 B.C.) diagnosis of the technological unconscious. Lacan quotes the opening of the chorus (*Polla ta deina*), with its conventional translation, "Many are the wonders," but rapidly begins to pull the text away from its traditional humanist exegesis as an encomium of mastery. As opposed to the usual translation of *ep' ouden erchetai to mellon* as "being never without resources," Lacan reinterprets: "He advances toward nothing that is likely to happen, he advances and he is *pantoporos*, 'artful,' but he is always *aporos*, always 'screwed.' He knows what he's doing. He always manages to cause things to come crashing down on his head."

Even Sophocles's line, "escape from hopeless diseases / he has found in the depths of his mind"[106] must be rewritten by Lacan as an anticipation of a "dialectics of enlightenment": "He [man] hasn't managed to come to terms with death, but he invents marvelous gimmicks in the form of sicknesses he himself fabricates."[107]

The paradox of the technological unconscious is that these "unnatural" sicknesses themselves replicate the "original" inadequacy of the human to nature. This perennial inadequacy, Freud's "inch of nature," prevents technology from ever being able to close as a self-sufficient whole — thus from ever becoming a total replacement for nature itself.

The Mutual Constitution of Nature and Techne

This last notion of nature as limit links with Drucilla Cornell's development of an "ethics of the limit" from Derrida's "logic of the parergon" and the notion of an unknowable excess to any system.[108] In Cornell's reading of Derrida, "the very establishment of the system as system implies a *beyond* to it, precisely by virtue of what it excludes" (1). This notion of system can, in our current context, mean both systems of meaning and systems of technology. Cornell goes on to add that this "beyond" is "a materiality that persists *beyond* any attempt to conceptualize it." Yet the idea of nature as traumatic Real goes "beyond" even this, because it specifies what is outside systems and interpretation, rather than leaving them as sublimely incomprehensible (e.g. a mystically unattainable "Other"). While not simply falling back into older ideas of objectivist metaphysics, or a premodern philosophical anthropology, this notion of nature is a differential notion, one which exposes that it is technocracy which is the most powerful form of metaphysics.[109] What follows will not seek to work out any fully fledged modern *aesthetic* of nature, as was attempted by Martin Seel's *Eine Ästhetik der Natur*.[110] Seel's book, with its deliberate exclusion of any metaphysical dimensions of nature, ends up, however, being Epicurean: it is a nature aesthetics of the Ego, of the pleasure principle. Against this, the present book presents nature as akin to what Adorno, in his critique of Kant's moral subject in *Negative Dialectics*, termed "das Hinzutretende," or the supervenient, which is the moment of nonconceptual somatic innervation without which no freedom or will can be conceived.

> To philosophical reflection it appears absolutely other [*ein schlechthin Anderes*], since the will, once reduced to pure practical reason, is an abstraction. The supervenient is the name for that which was eliminated by that abstraction; in reality, will could not exist at all without it.[111]

As also for Lacan, "das Hinzutretende" is for Adorno tied to a break or rupture in the discursive: "The subject's decisions do not proceed along the causal chain, and there is a leap [*ein Ruck erfolgt*]."[112] The proximity of this to Lacan's idea of the subject as a jump or break in the signifying chain is evident. Adorno's "Hinzutretendes" is itself thus bound up with his critique of the closure of the conceptual. We may extend that critique to one of the technocratic sublime. Against the latter's monotonous refrain of self-fascinated narcissism, the only aesthetic of nature here proposed is an aesthetic of supervenience.[113]

The reader may, finally, wonder in what way the version of nature proposed here differs from the construct of "second nature" familiar from Lukács's *Theory of the Novel* and its utopian-allegorical descendancy in Benjamin and Adorno. Have we only reverted back from the linguistic Unconscious of Lacan, or Habermas's distinction between work and interaction, to an old-Freudian Nature, one before philosophy's linguistic turn?

This can only be avoided by preserving a distinction between the unconscious of the individual psyche and that of communication, which sociology has, since Robert Merton, termed *latency*. (In strictly systems-theoretical terms, the idea of a "technological unconscious" would be impossible, since it appears to violate this distinction. The individual unconscious can only be an *environment* to the social *system* of communication.) To collapse these two together would be to risk positing a collective unconscious (as Benjamin did in the 1930s), or to fall back into the fatal Freudo-Marxist nexus of *Dialectics of Enlightenment*. Yet to separate them too neatly — as both Luhmann and Habermas have done — is to produce precisely the massive blind spot of the technological unconscious.[114] With Lacan's earlier-mentioned idea of the propping of language on nature in mind, we might say that the technological unconscious — collective, phylogenetic — props itself on the individual, ontogenetic one. The social and historical cathexis of technocratic power, with its massive and fatal blindness to its own limits, props or leans itself on the individual subject's sensual and perceptual blind spot, namely his or her inability to observe the act of observing. This explains the origin of the sexual investment, even overdetermination, of technocratic fantasies in cases such as that of *Metropolis* analyzed earlier here.

Systems theory has not been able to address the effects of this propping of (communicative) latency onto the (perceptual) unconscious. Yet it is not hard to find traces of an awareness of the problem in Luhmann's work. Thus, on the one hand, Luhmann dismisses what he terms "the specter of a scientifically based, technocratic domination,"[115] a specter that had been conjured up for the New Left by Marcuse and discussed by Habermas (in *Technology and Science as Ideology*). Indeed, as we have seen here, it makes no sense to blame technology in itself for the effects of its coupling to the economic system (in capitalism) or to the state (in Stalinism). And yet this specter of technocracy is nonetheless very real. The wide success of the popularized theories of self-reference evoked at the beginning of this chapter would otherwise be inexplicable. Some pages earlier in the same book Luhmann explained its genesis:

> In functionally differentiated societal systems the relation of a subsystem to the whole is determined by a specific *function;* while relations to the other subsystems can be designated as *performances* and described in terms of input/output models. It is important to separate function and performance carefully, because otherwise one eliminates the possibilities of analyzing the consequences of functional system differentiation. The conflation of function and performance is a typical mistake of "technocratic" theories of society that view society as a kind of recipient of performances although the performance carriers themselves are a part of society.[116]

Luhmann's disdain for such "technocratic theories" is justifiable, and yet they are no less real for being erroneous. Through this error, the functional relation of social system to natural environment is modeled after, and hidden behind, the performance-relation of the scientific to the economic or political systems. It is just this blurring of function with performance that is the transcendental illusion of modernity.

In this regard, the subculture of information technology, and even of science fiction, where such illusions are most well nourished, has already begun to acknowledge the existence of a technological unconscious. (Media theories' play on the multiple meanings of *medium* refers to the same phenomenon.) The formulation may be found in Erik Davis's *TechGnosis: Myth, Magic and Mysticism in the Age of Information*.[117] Davis's book (which has been popular among a cult or New Age subculture) opens the gates to a "spiritualist" understanding of *techne*, and constitutes the perfect complement to the inability of theories of modernity (like Luhmann's) to grasp the unconscious investment in the technological. Unlike both unreflective modernization theory and its shadowy double of New Age "spiritualism," the present book would argue for a further stage in Enlightenment.

One way to formulate this, and the key to the difference between post-technocratic nature and the old-utopian historico-philosophical construct of nature, lies in a reinterpretation of the term *Verfassung*, constitution, already mentioned here (see earlier on Homann). *Verfassung* has been an important term in the history of aesthetics and epistemology as well as of political thought. Within the hermeneutical tradition, it has been associated with modes of *Verstehen*, specifically with the latter's empathetic mode (as *Einfühlung*),[118] a matter important from Schleiermacher's "divinatory method" through Dilthey to Husserl. Heidegger uses the term *Verfassung* to mean constitution, whether of Being (in the introduction to *Sein und Zeit*), or that of metaphysics (in the lecture on the latter's "onto-theological *Verfassung*" of 1957). Most pertinent to the present context is, unsurprisingly, Kant, who in the *Critique of Judgment* (§83) links the realization of nature's purposefulness to human political constitution:

> Skill [*die Geschicklichkeit*] cannot be developed in the human race except by means of inequality among men; for the great majority provide the necessities of life, as it were, mechanically, without requiring any art in particular, for the convenience and leisure of others who work at the less necessary elements of culture, science and art. In an oppressed condition, they have hard work and little enjoyment, although much of the culture of the highest classes gradually spreads to them. Yet with the progress of this culture . . . their calamities increase equally in two directions, on the one hand from violence from without, on the other hand through internal discontent; but still this splendid misery [*das glänzende Elend*] is bound up with the development of the natural capacities of the human race, and the purpose of nature itself, although not our purpose, is thus attained.

Thus far, Kant is still very much the ancestor of the sublime aesthetics of technocracy we have been criticizing here: the "splendid misery" of Nature's undemocratic, inhumane purpose, which we can only imitate, is not far from Sade's magnificent and cruel Nature. Yet here Kant makes a turn that is too often forgotten by theoreticians of the sublime.

> The formal condition under which nature can alone attain this its final design is that arrangement of men's relations to one another by which lawful authority in a whole, which we call a *civil community* [*bürgerliche Gesellschaft*], is opposed to the abuse of their conflicting freedoms; only in this can the greatest development of natural capacities take place.[119]

Kant's recognition of this need for civil society takes place *without* the now-fashionable and bathetic overlay of "ethics" tinged with natural law that Alain Badiou has rightly criticized.[120] Civil society here is born not of the moralizing denial (in Freud's sense) of real existing human evil, but rather of its acknowledgement. Yet the idea of opposition to "the abuse of freedoms" means that Kant is no simple apologist for *le capitalisme sauvage,* either. Civil society means a form of reflexive modernity, in Ulrich Beck's sense: it is a correction to the political sublime of savage individual "conflicting freedoms." Here we have returned to this chapter's point of departure, in Luhmann's shocked encounter with Brazilian slums and the empty Welsh mines as a state of nature, where the poor and nature are both rigorously excluded from modern functional differentiation. Kant's comment on inequality reads like an anticipation of Durkheim on the division of labor and resultant anomie — or even of the "dialectics of enlightenment." So Adorno, too, had, in a sarcastic commentary on Hegel's *Philosophy of Law,* noted that "the constitution [*Verfassung*], name of the historical world that mediated all immediacy of nature, inversely determines the sphere of mediation — precisely that of history — as nature."[121] To clarify Adorno's extremely abstruse paradox: because Hegel sees human history, in the constitution, as mediating nature, history itself becomes naturalized.

Adorno's comment underlines a passage wherein Hegel claims one must see the constitution, a product of history, as divine. Yet Adorno's paradoxical unity of nature and history is almost too tidy, too compact, too — paradoxical, one is tempted to say, allowing its two component parts to circle around each other in endless negativity. Kant's reflection on the mediation of nature and history in the *Verfassung* leaves its paradox more open.

Kant begins by noting both the inevitability and the increasing injustice of the division of labor — even, one would now say, of modern social differentiation. He goes on to consider the sobering prospects of social evolution, which tend to produce both progress and violence, yet then makes the surprising comment that social development forwards the ultimate purpose of nature, even if this last "is not right away our own." (The peculiar sonority of Kant's *gleich nicht* is important to this passage, and almost — almost, for philosophy is not literature and rhetoric alone! — exceeds conceptual meaning, much as the word "gar" does in Hölderlin's "Winkel von Hardt.")[122] The fulfillment not only of human potential, but also that of nature itself, depends upon a civil society that will restrain the violence of competing interests from causing "damage" (*Abbruch*) to each other's freedom. Civil society, in Kant's image, is almost like a forcing box or trellis imposed upon natural impulse to train it.

The key is that, for Kant, nature itself depends upon the human constitution for its ultimate self-realization, cryptic as the latter may remain. Today one would have to add that it depends upon the human constitution for the mere continuation of its existence, as of our own — that is, for the continuation of that peculiar equation or constellation of nature and history upon which the human as such has depended. Without a redefining of the constitution (*Verfassung*) between the human and the natural,[123] there will ensue only serious damage (*Abbruch*) to freedom. Unlike theories of evolution such as Luhmann's, or Habermas's theory of law (*Faktizität und Geltung*), which completely decouple the human constitution from its natural embedding — indeed, make the human as such synonymous with a severing from it — Kant preserves this latter as an object of reflection. Unlike Adorno, who views this natural embedding of human history as a fateful and mythic nexus (one would say, in German, a *Schuldzusammenhang*), Kant treats it as a more fluid and mobile relation. And although the purpose of criticism is not right away (*gleich nicht!*) a prognostic or even a normative one, this study would like to contribute to keeping open that necessary mobility.

Notes

[1] As already noted in the introduction, readers unfamiliar with Luhmann's work may consult the appendix of this book for a brief outline of his theory and its reception.

[2] Luhmann, "Jenseits von Barbarei," *Gesellschaftstruktur und Semantik* (Frankfurt: Suhrkamp 1995), 4:147; translated by Friedrich Balke as "Tristes Tropiques," *Soziale Systeme* 8.1 (2002): 31. The end of Luhmann's *Soziale Systeme* (Frankfurt: Suhrkamp 1984, 661) had famously metaphorized systems theory as a risky, high-tech "night flight," nonetheless equipped with adequate observation instruments.

[3] Luhmann, "Inklusion und Exklusion," *Soziologische Aufklärung 6: Die Soziologie und der Mensch* (Opladen: Westdeutscher Verlag, 1995), 245.

[4] Giorgio Agamben, *Homo Sacer: Sovereign Power and Bare Life*, translated by Daniel Heller-Roazen (Stanford: Stanford UP, 1998).

[5] Recent scholarship has shown postwar German nature poetry's continuities with the Nazi period: see most recently Neil H. Donahue, *Karl Krolow and the Poetics of Amnesia in Postwar Germany* (Rochester, NY: Camden House, 2002), and Glenn Cuomo, *Career at the Cost of Compromise: Günter Eich's Life and Work in the Years 1933–1945* (Amsterdam: Rodopi, 1989).

[6] Celan, *Gesammelte Werke in drei Bänden* (Frankfurt: Suhrkamp, 1983), 2:285.

[7] For an overview, see Hermann Korte, *Deutschsprachige Lyrik nach 1945*, 2nd ed. (Stuttgart: Metzler 2004), chapter 3.1 (1960s) and chapter 4.4 (1970s).

[8] Judith Ryan, in her article "Das Motiv der inneren Landschaft," called the *Naturlyrik* of the 1970s "ein ganz traditionell anmutendes sich-Hineinprojizieren des Dichters in die Natur" (In *Im Dialog mit der Moderne*, ed. Roland Jost, et al. [Frankfurt: Athenäum 1986], 139). See also Alexander von Bormann, "'Manche Wörter lockern die Erde, später vielleicht.' Romantische und zeitgenössische Naturerfahrung/Naturdichtung," *Der Deutschunterricht* 38 (1986): 90–100; Helmut Scheuer, "Die entzauberte Natur — Vom Naturgedicht zur Ökolyrik" in *Literatur für Leser* 1 (1989): 48–73; here 67: "die moderne Ökolyrik ist vorrangig Gedankenlyrik."

[9] Hartmut Böhme's attempt to re-situate art "in die praktische Aufgabe einer ästhetischen Einrichtung der Erde" in his *Natur und Subjekt* (Frankfurt: Suhrkamp, 1988), 32, falls back to a pre-aesthetic level of applied and decorative art combined with abstract aesthetizing utopianism: "im gespensterhaft wiederkehrenden Geist des Jugendstils, am Ende im ideologischen Glauben, es lasse von der Kunst her die als schlecht . . . erfahrene Realität sich wenden, nachdem die reale Änderung verbaut ist" (Adorno, "Parataxis," *Noten zur Literatur, Gesammelte Schriften* 11, 453). The suggested poetics of "the body" ignores the critical recognition of Marx and psychoanalysis that "*the* body" is no basis for any *prima philosophia*, but itself a social and historical construct. Gernot Böhme's plea, in *Für eine ökologische Naturästhetik*, for a "*humane* Umwelt" and "Erfahrungs-möglichkeiten *des Menschen*" merely repeats old bourgeois aporias of "humanity" in a New Age key (Frankfurt: Suhrkamp, 1989), 15. For similar reasons, the considerable body of Anglo-American ecocriticism, with its links to environmental ethics, is not relevant here. A fairly recent survey noted how "highly Americanized" such criticism remains, precisely in its individual moral imperatives and calls to immediate praxis (Sally Eden, "Environmental Issues: Nature versus the Environment?" *Progress in Human Geography* 25, 1 [2001]: 2). These are aspects that would not easily fit in with the theoretical design of this book. The terminological choice of *nature* over *environment* nonetheless marks the difference from environmentalist literary criticism. "Nature" will emerge here as something different *both* from systems theory's "environment" (hence Luhmann's continued irritation with the term, an irritation to be made productive here) *and* from that of ecology. The advantage of nature as concept is precisely that, in difference-theoretical terms, it does not respect environmentalism's distinction of human/nonhuman or systems theory's distinction of system/environment. Instead, nature is that distinction's parasite (Michel Serres) or trans-classical rejection value (Gotthard Günther). The use of the term nature points *ex negativo* to the historical origins of the term environment circa 1800, that is, in conjunction with the modern differentiation of society (see on this connection

Luhmann, "Über Natur," *Gesellschaftsstruktur und Semantik* [Frankfurt: Suhrkamp 1995], 21). For an alternative, Habermasian critique of environmentalism, see Robert J. Brulle, *Agency, Democracy, and Nature: The U.S. Environmental Movement from a Critical Theory Perspective* (Cambridge: MIT, 2004).

[10] Karl Heinz Bohrer, *Nach der Natur* (Munich: Hanser 1988), 210.

[11] Bohrer, *Nach der Natur*, 310.

[12] Tim Dean, *Beyond Sexuality* (Chicago: U of Chicago P, 2000), 87.

[13] Critiques of postmodernity abound, and such a critique is not the main purpose of the present book, which prefers to follow Luhmann's suspicion of the "post-modern" as such. The blurring of culture and theory is certainly a feature of so-called postmodernity. The present book takes a two-pronged approach, showing how Imaginary Theory misrepresents or simplifies both its theoretical origins and its reading of modern German literature. Lyotard's view of Cézanne, or Kittler's of Benn, are both inadequate as theories of modernity and as interpretations of art. Rather than pointing out historical inaccuracies or providing historical contextualization, this book argues against a one-sided concept of modernity.

[14] Rodolphe Gasché pointed out long ago that "deconstructionist criticism is the offspring of a heritage that has little in common with that of Derrida's thought" (*The Tain of the Mirror* [Cambridge, MA: Harvard UP, 1986], 3); the popularizing extensions of deconstructionism into anthropology and other fields are even more removed from this properly philosophical dimension. What follows here is thus less a criticism of poststructuralism than of its facile misappropriation. As Jameson pointed out in his *Post-Modernism: Or The Cultural Logic of Late Capitalism* (Durham, NC: Duke UP, 1991), "fantasies about the salvational nature of high technology" are common to both "theory" and pop culture (46): the link between them may be one feature of what I will call Imaginary Theory.

[15] Benjamin Buchloh, "The Primary Colors for the Second Time: A Paradigm Repetition of the Neo-Avant-Garde," *October* 37 (Summer 1986): 41–52.

[16] Terry Eagleton, *After Theory* (New York: Basic Books, 2003), 163, 120–21.

[17] Elaine Scarry, *On Beauty and Being Just* (Princeton, NJ: Princeton UP, 1999), 28.

[18] On the relation between the sublime and deconstruction, see H. Silverman and G. Aylesworth, *The Textual Sublime: Deconstruction and Its Differences* (Albany, NY: SUNY Press, 1990). The idea of a "rhetoric of the technological sublime" was first formulated by Leo Marx in *The Machine in the Garden: Technology and the Pastoral Ideal in America* (Oxford: Oxford UP, 1964). It was taken up again by Mario Costa in *Il sublime tecnologico* (Rome: Castelvecchi 1998; 1st ed. Salerno: Edisud, 1990), albeit in more celebratory form than in the present project. Sanford Budick has recently suggested, in his *The Western Theory of Tradition*, that the "cultural sublime" is the form in which traditions renew themselves (New Haven: Yale UP, 2000): this already implies a critical re-inserting of the sublime into the cultural context against which it was once a protest.

[19] Adorno, *Asthetische Theorie, Gesammelte Schriften* 7 (Frankfurt: Suhrkamp 1997), 293–94.

[20] Adorno, *Ästhetische Theorie*, 172, 295, 410.

[21] Lyotard, "The Sublime and the Avant-Garde," in *The Lyotard Reader,* ed. Andrew Benjamin (Oxford: Blackwell, 1989), 208.

[22] For Kant: Serge Trottein, "Lyotard: Before and After the Sublime" in *Lyotard: Philosophy, Politics, and the Sublime,* ed. Hugh Silverman (New York: Routledge, 2002), 192–200; for Heidegger, Hugh Silverman, "Lyotard and the Events of the Postmodern Sublime," ibid., 222–29. The present book argues in a sense against the Heideggerian reception of Lyotard, and for Kant.

[23] A key text here is *Identität und Differenz* (Pfüllingen: Neske, 1975; now in the *Gesamtausgabe,* vol. 11 [Frankfurt: Klostermann, 1976–]).

[24] Adorno, *Negative Dialektik, Gesammelte Schriften* 6: 107–111. Heidegger's "event" is itself not opposed to nature (in fact, Heidegger's own criticism of technocracy, in his Nietzsche lectures or "The Question Concerning Technology," make him rather an advocate of the anamnesis of nature, albeit in very different terms than Adorno's).

[25] Lyotard, "The Sublime and the Avant-Garde," 206.

[26] Behind Lyotard's discussion here is Lacan's evocation of Cézanne in *The Four Fundamental Concepts of Psychoanalysis,* where he states that "that which I gaze at is never what I want to see" (*Le Séminaire XI: Les Quatre concepts fondamentaux de la psychanalyse* [Paris: Seuil, 1973], 118). Lacan, however, is in some ways closer to Adorno in his dialectical idea that the artist definitively puts down his or her gaze in the brushstroke (in an "acte de la déposition du regard," ibid., 130).

[27] Jameson, *Post-Modernism: Or The Cultural Logic of Late Capitalism* (Durham, NC: Duke UP, 1991), 34.

[28] For an overview of critiques of the sublime since the 1970s, from Paul de Man to Frances Ferguson, see Martin Donougho, "Stages of the Sublime in North America," *MLN* 115.5 (2000): 909–40. Donougho notes the same tendency mentioned here for *theories* of the sublime to mimic the latter's poetic *effect;* one might add that the sublime's critique has accompanied it from the beginning as well, given its inherent reflexivity.

[29] Luhmann, *Unbeobachtbare Welt* (Bielefeld: Haux, 1990), 9; see also his *Die Kunst der Gesellschaft* (Frankfurt: Suhrkamp, 1995), 140. Jean Clam has interestingly compared Luhmann's basal concept of *operation* to Heidegger's *Ereignis,* yet notes that unlike the latter, Luhmann's operations "can never stop operating," that is, their "event" cannot be arrested in the radicality of Lyotard's sublime. Operation's "difference can never attain the status of an in itself quiescent unity" (Jean Clam, "System's Sole Constituent, the Operation: Clarifying a Central Concept of Luhmannian Theory," *Acta Sociologica,* 43, 1 [March 2000]: 63–79; here 74). Here Derrida is closer to Heidegger than Luhmann.

[30] Luhmann, *Die Kunst der Gesellschaft,* 36, 76. This severing from consciousness was already described in Jameson's well-known diagnosis of the "postmodern sublime' as "an impossible imperative" to a "mutation in what can perhaps no longer be called consciousness" (*Postmodernism,* 31). Another analogy would be Paul de Man's "madness of words" or the inevitable circularity of reading processes (*The Rhetoric of Romanticism* [New York: Columbia UP, 1984], 122).

[31] Luhmann, *Die Kunst der Gesellschaft,* 94.

[32] On this, see (paradigmatically) chapter 4 on Brecht and the law. Luhmann, interestingly enough, has as little faith in the possibility of purely "self-referential art" as Adorno (*Die Kunst der Gesellschaft*, 458, 505).

[33] Freud, "Hemmung, Symptom und Angst," *Studienausgabe* (Frankfurt: Fischer, 1970), 6:238.

[34] Freud, "Hemmung," 277.

[35] Lacan, *Séminaire IV: La relation d'objet* (Paris: Seuil, 1994), 22.

[36] Lacan, *Séminaire VIII: Le transfert* (Paris: Seuil, 1991), 424, 428.

[37] Dylan Evans, *An Introductory Dictionary of Lacanian Psychoanalysis*, London: Routledge, 1996), 52.

[38] Lacan, *Sém. IV*, 226.

[39] Lacan, *Sem. IV*, 181. This is, as will be seen in chapter 1, directly relevant to Rilke, whose rewritten Prodigal Son notes stubbornly at the end of *Malte* that he *did not yet want to be loved*.

[40] *Le Séminaire IV: La relation d'objet* (Paris: Seuil 1994), 99.

[41] Lacan, *Sém IV*, 131, emphasis added. I have elsewhere ("Zufall und Subjekt. Erwägungen zu Cage," in *Mythos Cage*, ed. C. S. Mahnkopf [Hofheim: Wolke 1999], 203–22) shown how this sort of frustration works in John Cage.

[42] Lacan, *Sém. IV*, 199; see Luisa Muraro, *Die symbolische Ordnung der Mutter* (Frankfurt: Campus, 1993).

[43] Huyssen, "The Vamp and the Machine," *After the Great Divide* (Bloomington: Indiana UP, 1986), 71. Lang's mechanized Woman is of course the predecessor of a more recent technophile fantasy, Donna Haraway's cyborg; for feminist critiques of Haraway, see the last chapter of Carol Stabile, *Feminism and the Technological Fix* (Manchester [England] and New York: Manchester UP, 1994) and Elaine L. Graham, *Representations of the Post/Human: Monsters, Aliens, and Others in Popular Culture* (New Brunswick, NJ: Rutgers UP, 2002).

[44] Freud, "Psychoanalytische Bemerkungen über einen autobiographisch beschriebenen Fall von Paranoia," *Studienausgabe* (Frankfurt: Fischer, 1970), 7:198; see also Samuel Weber's criticisms of "projection" in his introduction to Schreber's *Denkwürdigkeiten* (Frankfurt: Ullstein, 1973), 48.

[45] See for instance the discussion of Klaus Scherpe's reading of Döblin in chapter 4. This error of confusing Lacan's Real with empirical "reality" was already made by Althusser. Jameson grasps Lacan's Real as absent cause better than Althusser, yet seeks to put History in its place; thus his assertion that "the Real in Lacan . . . is simply History itself" ("Imaginary and Symbolic in Lacan," in *Ideologies of Theory*, vol. 1 [Minneapolis: U of Minnesota P, 1988], 104). For Lacan, History with a capital H was an Imaginary illusion. Jameson wants to refigure History as Real rather than Imaginary. A similar move will be argued here with Nature.

[46] Lacan, *Sém. IV*, 223, 69.

[47] Lacan, *Sém. IV*, 96. Cf. also p. 95 on the "ambiguity between natural and symbolic relations" which Lacan claims is precisely the domain of "the analytic dimension." This idea of the "propping" of symbol on nature is also discussed in *Seminar II*.

[48] Lacan, *Sém. IV,* 223.
[49] Lacan, *Sém. IV,* 175.
[50] Lacan, *Sém, IV,* 69.
[51] See Lacan, "La Science et la vérité," *Écrits,* 855–77.
[52] See the discussion of postcolonial theory in chapter 3, below.
[53] Peter Dews, *Logics of Disintegration* (London: Verso, 1987), 142.
[54] Renate Homann, *Theorie der Lyrik* (Frankfurt: Suhrkamp, 1999).
[55] See chapter 4 below for an instance of how this is worked out in a close reading of Brecht.
[56] See Kant, *Kritik der Urteilskraft,* section 28.
[57] The passage from Kant that Homann is discussing is in the *Kritik der Urteilskraft* (Leipzig: Meiner, 1922), 29 (A XLVII).
[58] Luhmann, *Soziale Systeme* (Frankfurt: Suhrkamp, 1984), 431.
[59] Luhmann, *Die Gesellschaft der Gesellschaft* (Frankfurt: Suhrkamp, 1997), 66 and 446.
[60] For a detailed analysis of this coupling, see Nathan Rosenberg, *Exploring the Black Box: Technology, Economics, and History* (Cambridge: Cambridge UP, 1994); *Inside the Black Box: Technology and Economics* (Cambridge: Cambridge UP, 1983). The present discussion thus follows a definition of "technology as system" rather than "technology as hardware," since "it is not clear that hardware outside of human context of use and understanding really functions as technology" (Val Dusek, *Philosophy of Technology: An Introduction* [Malden, MA: Oxford Blackwell, 2006], 32). Neil Postman, too, refers to management practice in defining what he calls "technopoly," a formulation more dramatically totalizing than the present book's (*Technopoly* [New York: Vintage, 1993], 50).
[61] In Jameson's terms: "technology ... seems to offer some privileged representational shorthand for grasping a network of power and control even more difficult for our minds and imaginations to grasp" (*Post-Modernism,* 38). Taken at face value, "technology" thus becomes a form of what Jameson called the schizophrenia of postmodernity (25–26): namely the *forclusion* (foreclosure) of any reference to anything outside its own artifice.
[62] See Heidegger, "Die Kehre," in *Bremer und Freiburger Vorträge, Gesamtausgabe* vol. 79 (Frankfurt: Klostermann, 1994), 68–77. Heidegger rejects a political-ethical response to ecological problems as being merely another form of metaphysics, of subject-philosophy. The present book does not follow Heidegger in seeing technology's danger as "das in der Wahrheit seines Wesens sich gefährdende Seyn selbst" (69), that is, as an ontological "Geschick."
[63] This has been pointed out by Helmut Lethen in his study *Verhaltenslehren der Kälte,* which shows how 1920s *Neue Sachlichkeit* generated a complementary thematics of fallen, natural "Kreatur" and melancholy (Frankfurt: Suhrkamp, 1994).
[64] Bruce Fink, *The Lacanian Subject* (Princeton, NJ: Princeton UP, 1995), 27.
[65] Slavoj Žižek, *The Sublime Object of Ideology* (London: Verso, 1989), 50. Tim Dean's comments on this passage, refuting Judith Butler's false accusation of

Lacan as ahistoricist, should be recalled here (*Beyond Sexuality*, 211–12). A similar argument for reformulating nature as a Lacanian Real has been made by Iannis Stavrakakis in "Green Fantasy and the Real of Nature: Elements of a Lacanian Critique of Green Ideological Discourse," *Journal for the Psychoanalysis of Culture & Society* 2, 1 (Spring 1997): 123–32. This tendency to see nature as not unitary is already there in later Lacan in formulations like "nature specifies itself to be not one" (*Le Séminaire XXIII: Le Sinthome* [Paris: Seuil 2005], 12; see also Adrian Johnston, "Ghosts of Substance Past: Schelling, Lacan and the Denaturalization of Nature," in *Lacan: The Silent Partners*, ed. Slavoj Žižek (London: Verso, 2006), 34–55.

[66] Adorno, "Die Idee der Naturgeschichte," *Gesammelte Schriften* 1 (Frankfurt: Suhrkamp, 1997), 354–55.

[67] References in the exhibition catalogue *Die Erfindung der Natur: Max Ernst, Paul Klee, Wols und das surreale Universum*, ed. Karin Orchard and Jörg Zimmermann (Freiburg im Breisgau: Rombach, 1994), 12 (Kandinsky, Dubuffet, Bataille), 131 (Klee).

[68] See the Max Ernst issue of *Cahiers d'Art* (nos. 6–7, Paris 1937), with Ernst's "Au-delà de la peinture." A re-evaluation of the aesthetics of nature in relation to musical high modernism has recently been undertaken by Julian Johnson in *Webern and the Transformation of Nature* (New York and Cambridge: Cambridge UP, 1999).

[69] The *Histoires Naturelles* were the didactic and serial illustration of the newly discovered technique of *frottage* or rubbing, wherein Ernst literally traced or transferred the grainy surface of wood to the canvas, subsequently amplifying the aleatoric forms seen in the wood grain into more determinate shapes. Ernst compared it to Leonardo's famous recommendation (in the *Trattato*) that artists stimulate their imagination through "reading" forms into cloud or wood-grain shapes; yet in Ernst, the mediating function of Leonardo's imagination has been elided in favor of direct material transfer.

[70] *Die Erfindung der Natur*, ed. Orchard and Zimmermann, 146.

[71] Whitney Davis, *Drawing the Dream of the Wolves: Homosexuality, Interpretation and Freud's "Wolf-Man"* (Bloomington: Indiana UP, 1995), xxiii.

[72] Ralf Konersmann, "Max Ernst und die Idee der Naturgeschichte," in *Die Erfindung der Natur*, ed. Orchard and Zimmermann, 159–76; here 160.

[73] Hal Foster, *The Return of the Real* (Cambridge: MIT Press, 1996), 130.

[74] Foster, *Return of the Real*, 134.

[75] Luhmann, *Risk: A Sociological Theory* (New York: Aldine De Gruyter, 1993), 95.

[76] In the sense of Michel Serres: *Le Parasite* (Paris: Grasset, 1981).

[77] Luhmann, *Risk*, 212. One of the most articulate critics of "environmental ethics" or political ecology has been Bruno Latour: see most recently *Politics of Nature: How to Bring the Sciences into Democracy* (trans. Catherine Porter [Cambridge, MA: Harvard UP, 2004]). Latour has also shown how so-called "social constructivists" remain prisoners of the very dichotomy of nature and politics they claim to attack (32–33).

[78] Luhmann, "Über Natur," *Gesellschaftsstruktur und Semantik* (Frankfurt: Suhrkamp, 1995), 4:24.

[79] Luhmann, *Risk*, 95.

[80] Luhmann, *Soziale Systeme*, 464–65.

[81] Luhmann, *Risk*, 90.

[82] Luhmann, *Ecological Communication* (Chicago: U of Chicago P, 1989), 138.

[83] Luhmann, "Über Natur," 30.

[84] See Fink, *Lacanian Subject*, 72: "The crossing of fantasy thus involves a going beyond of castration and a utopian moment beyond neurosis."

[85] Fink, *Lacanian Subject*, 62.

[86] Fink, *Lacanian Subject*, 62.

[87] Luhmann, *Risk*, 205.

[88] Luhmann, *Observations on Modernity* (Stanford: Stanford UP, 1998), 83.

[89] Klaus Eder, *The Social Construction of Nature* (London: Sage, 1996), 18.

[90] Eder, *Social Construction*, 19.

[91] Luhmann's term: the title of the last chapter of *Observations on Modernity*. The phrase is now gaining popularity among sociologists (see Paul Rabinow's "Assembling Ethics in an Ecology of Ignorance," closing plenary lecture given at the First Conference on Synthetic Biology, MIT, 10–12 June 2004; see also Will Medd, "What is Complexity Science? Toward an Ecology of Ignorance," *Emergence: Journal of Complexity Issues in Organisation and Management* 3, 1 (2001): 45–62).

[92] Adorno, *Ästhetische Theorie*, 97.

[93] Robbe-Grillet, "Nature, humanisme, tragédie," in *Pour un nouveau roman* (Paris: Minuit, 1963); Adorno, *Ästhetische Theorie*, 477.

[94] Stefan Rieger, *Kybernetische Anthropologie* (Frankfurt: Suhrkamp, 2003), offers a Kittler-inspired history of this historical moment, with its reliance on Shannon and Weaver's model of the mathematical theory of communication. The absolute split between nature and history found in Lévi-Strauss would be adopted by his friend Lacan as well.

[95] For a more detailed discussion of Krolow, see Donahue, *Karl Krolow and the Poetics of Amnesia in Postwar Germany* (see note 5 above), especially page 243, where he cites Krolow's Büchner Prize–speech, which asserts that "das Gedicht" had, after 1945, to rediscover its "alte, alterslose Fähigkeiten und Fertigkeiten," such as how to "*zaubern*" with nature magic. Donahue contrasts the "vague existentialism" (247) of Krolow with Celan's working through historical trauma. On Eich, Sabine Buchheit has written that "in dieser Metaphorik" — that is, of nature — "drückt sich der Wunsch aus, die Faktizität der Welt aufzuheben und die Leere . . . als einzigen möglichen Bereich einer freien Existenz aufzuwerten" (*Formen und Funktionen literarischer Kommunikation im Werk Günter Eichs* [St. Ingbert: Röhrig, 2003], 131). Christian Kohlross confirms this: "Auch bei Günter Eich gerät die zeitliche Vermittlung von natur und Gedicht zu einer allgemeinen, vor allem aber zu einer abstrakten Angelegenheit" (*Theorie des modernen Naturgedichts* [Würzburg: Königshausen und Neumann, 2000], 159). In both cases,

Nature's timeless abstraction was a way to repress historical trauma. On nature in Ernst Meister, see Christian Soboth, "Die Un-Natur der Natur: Zu einigen Gedichten Ernst Meisters," *Text und Kritik* 96 (Oct. 1987): 75–84.

[96] The phrase is Leo Braudy's (see his article with this title in *Reconfiguring American Film Genres*, ed. Nick Browne [Berkeley: University of California, 1998], 278–309).

[97] Elfriede Jelinek, *er nicht als er* (Frankfurt: Suhrkamp 1998), 11.

[98] Lyotard, "The Sublime and the Avant-Garde," 197.

[99] Elfriede Jelinek, *In den Alpen* (Berlin Verlag, 2002).

[100] Luhmann, "Über Natur," 19. Latour, again, has argued for letting go of the old unitary concept of "nature" altogether (*Politics of Nature*, 25–32).

[101] Jameson, *The Political Unconscious* (Ithaca, NY: Cornell UP, 1981), 35.

[102] Krauss, *The Optical Unconscious* (Cambridge, MA: MIT Press, 1993), 24.

[103] For a recent example of a cognate attempt, see Thomas Khurana, *Die Dispersion des Unbewussten: Drei Studien zu einem nicht-substantialistischen Konzept des Unbewussten. Freud — Lacan — Luhmann* (Giessen: Psychosozial Verlag, 2002).

[104] Benjamin, "Das Kunstwerk im Zeitalter seiner technischen Reproduzierbarkeit," *Gesammelte Schriften*, vol. I:2 (Frankfurt: Suhrkamp, 1991), 500; compare also Siegfried Kracauer, "Das Ornament der Masse," in *Das Ornament der Masse* (Frankfurt: Suhrkamp, 1977), 50.

[105] Freud, *Civilization and Its Discontents*, trans. Strachey (New York: Norton, 1989), 43–44 (*Das Unbehagen in der Kultur, Studienausgabe* 9:222).

[106] Trans. David Grene, *Sophocles I* (Chicago: U of Chicago P, 1991), 174–75.

[107] Lacan, *Le Séminaire VII: L'Éthique de la psychanalyse* (Paris: Seuil, 1986), 320–21; in English, *Seminar VII*, trans. Dennis Porter (New York: Norton, 1992), 274–75.

[108] Cornell's *The Philosophy of the Limit* (New York: Routledge, 1992) argues for a link between her reading of Derrida and Luhmann's systems theory; see also her "Enabling Paradoxes: Gender Difference and Systems Theory," *New Literary History* 27.2 (1996): 185–97. If any variant of ethics could link up to this book, it would be Cornell's. Her description of how gender as difference acquires semantic meaning would be applicable to nature as difference as well.

[109] This (originally Heideggerian) idea has been taken up again by Charles Shepherdson in *Vital Signs: Nature, Culture, Psychoanalysis* (London: Routledge, 2000).

[110] Martin Seel, *Eine Ästhetik der Natur* (Frankfurt: Suhrkamp, 1991).

[111] Adorno, *Negative Dialektik, Gesammelte Schriften* 6, 228.

[112] Adorno, *Negative Dialektik, Gesammelte Schriften* 6, 226.

[113] This has little to do with analytic philosophy's notion of supervenience, for Adorno reverses the latter's idea that mind "supervenes" on physical and biological nature: here it is body that supervenes onto the social and artificial construct of language.

[114] So Peter Fuchs's attack on psychoanalysis's concept of the unconscious ("Blindheit und Sicht: Vorüberlegungen zu einer Schemarevision," in Fuchs and Luhmann, *Reden und Schweigen* [Frankfurt: Suhrkamp, 1997], 178–208) systematically (!) misunderstands Freud; Luhmann himself, although no Freudian, is

more guarded, and more aware of the potentially catastrophic consequences of systemic blindness (see the section on latency in *Soziale Systeme* [Frankfurt: Suhrkamp, 1984], 456–65).

[115] Luhmann, *Political Theory in the Welfare State*, trans. John Bednarz, Jr. (Berlin: de Gruyter, 1990), 107.

[116] Luhmann, *Political Theory in the Welfare State*, 73.

[117] Erik Davis, *TechGnosis: Myth, Magic and Mysticism in the Age of Information* (New York: Three Rivers Press, 1998).

[118] Cf. Dilthey, *Gesammelte Schriften* (Stuttgart: Teubner; Göttingen: Vandenhoeck & Ruprecht, 1961–2006), 7:214 on this.

[119] Translation J. H. Bernard (New York and London: Hafner, 1968), 282.

[120] *Ethics: An Essay On the Understanding of Evil*, translated and introduced by Peter Hallward (London and New York: Verso, 2001).

[121] Adorno, *Negative Dialektik*, 350.

[122] Hölderlin, *Werke und Briefe*, ed. F. Beissner and Jochen Schmidt (Frankfurt: Insel, 1969), 1:134: this is itself a poem centrally concerned with the allegory of *Naturgeschichte*.

[123] This idea of a renewal of the human-natural constitution has also been taken up by Bruno Latour (*We Have Never Been Modern*, trans. Catherine Porter [Cambridge: Harvard UP, 1993]).

2: Rilke's Unnatural Things: From the End of Landscape to the *Dinggedicht*

The Fading Landscape

> ... nature, in the form it presents
> itself to man, as it adapts itself to
> him, is always profoundly denatured.
> — Lacan, *Le Séminaire IV*

> What Rilke calls Nature is not cut
> off from History.
> — Heidegger, "Wozu Dichter?"

THE BREAKTHROUGH INTO painterly abstraction around 1900 is associated with the concrete names of local natural places: L'Estaque, Murnau, and earliest of all, Worpswede. In the wide open space of Worpswede's heather and moor, nature itself seemed to strain toward its expression in pure abstract spaces of light and color, spaces whose bareness suggest the subjectivity of *Stimmung* or mood. "For a few years around the turn of the century, it seemed as if nature painting and avant-garde modernism could enter into a productive liaison."[1] The liaison took the form of what Adorno would later call a *Kulturlandschaft*, a landscape reflecting nature's own imprint by human history.[2] The promise of epochal renewal felt in those landscapes was inseparable from the primeval quality of heather and moor, their literally antediluvian quality: this was a landscape that had been drained and colonized from flooded marshland only in the eighteenth century. The affect of *Angst* so typical of the turn of the century, had specific historical origins. Worpswede around 1900 was thus a landscape of memory, painted "around . . . moments of recognition . . . when a place suddenly exposes its connection to an ancient and peculiar vision of the forest, the mountain, or the river."[3] This melancholy or fearful anamnesis was inseparable as well from a moment of hope: these natural landscapes have become the visual embodiment of modernity's birthplace. This is why, at modernity's end, a painter like Anselm Kiefer would return to the iconography of these landscapes with a further intensification of irony and ambivalence.

The historical signature of Worpswede was already legible to Ernst Bloch, looking back at the landscape of *Jugendstil* on the eve of the National Socialists' coming to power in 1932. As in the Expressionist controversy that would break out in the 1930s between Bloch and Brecht on the one hand and Lukács on the other, Bloch defended the merely bourgeois rebellion of *Jugendstil* against criticism from the left. In the fascinating emptiness of the North German moor and heath, Bloch finds both allegories of oceanic prehistory, historical memories of urban life, and the nascent abstraction of the modernist sublime. Even in 1932 the promise of this natural landscape remains undiminished for Bloch.

> All such images, in fact pre-images, persist longer than their time and have wider implications than the place where they were found. Moor and heath are not the least among such a broader circle of perceived meetings with self and world; indeed, they finally persist precisely because in their image, in the "Jugend" image of autumn, swampy moor and heath, also from the sooty factory plain that was then popular, there is a content that has not yet been fully experienced.[4]

For Adorno, too, similarly looking back on the whole of modernism from the vantage point of the 1960s, *Jugendstil* contained in itself the secret of aesthetic modernity as a whole. Even philosophical modernity had an affinity with Jugendstil, most particularly in Husserl's phenomenology.[5] Yet in Adorno's version, this exemplary nature of *Jugendstil* lay not in its relation to nature, but rather in its emphatic pursuit of the religion of art, of art's metaphysical claims to redemption. In this, modernism had finally to reenact the myth of Icarus. "Jugendstil, as its name betrays, is the self-declared permanence of puberty: a Utopia that its own unrealizability."[6]

The two aspects of *Jugendstil* brought out by Bloch and Adorno are in fact not incompatible. Just as the serpentine ornaments of Art Nouveau prefigured the functionalism of high modernism, as the stylized solitude of *Jugendstil* and Expressionism had in it already the collectivism of the 1920s, so the hesitant, ambivalent landscape discovered specifically by the turn of the century contained the technological artifice of modernity. In a late and highly civilized variant of the old millennial Pauline motif of nature groaning in travail for redemption (Romans 8:22), it was as if the very natural landscape, around 1900, held forth to young artists the promise of a new culture, one which would be reconciled with nature, whether the nature outside or that of their own sexuality. Bloch's evocation of the "sooty factory plain" together with the heath implies that this dis-covery of a new landscape need not mean a flight from political and urban problems. The political consciousness of Camille Pissarro, who went out of Paris to paint the unspectacularly flat *vexin Normand* with the young Cézanne in the 1870s, including prosaic factory chimneys and steamboats in his river landscapes, bears this out. The *Jugendstil* painters of Worpswede were also conscious of the social embedding of landscape.

The German painters — Fritz Mackensen, Otto Modersohn, Heinrich Vogeler — who founded the artists' colony of Worpswede near Bremen in the 1880s and 1890s exemplified the utopian project of Adorno and Bloch. The Worpswede painters' project was at once technical and social: "to reject both the classical landscape tradition and the contemporary tourist convention by climbing down from elevated vantage points . . . and immersing themselves in . . . close-up views."[7] The decision to live among the local peasants was not merely a sentimental move "back to nature" but entailed a critique of the classical landscape's rational *veduta* perspective. Significantly, the Worpswede group included a number of women painters — Rilke's future wife Clara Westhoff and Paula Modersohn — as well. The descent from the lofty vantage point of classical landscape art was also tied to a diminishing of male privilege. The young Rilke arrived in Worpswede in 1900 at the time of his own self-definition as an artist. Rilke's short book, entitled simply *Worpswede*, of 1903 is thus not only a book on painting and the visual arts but a manual for artists on how to live and a narrative of his own self-discovery as a poet,[8] as well as an essay on the relation of nature to aesthetic artifice, and thus one of the earliest manifestoes of modernism.

The introduction to *Worpswede* programatically addresses the poetic production of natural landscape at the turn of the century. Although Rilke is ostensibly writing about painting, the work marks an important stage on the path from the still musically inward poetics of his early collection, *Das Stunden-Buch* (*The Book of Hours*), to the optically centered poetics of the *Neue Gedichte*. Beneath the definitions of painterly genres, one senses the proximity of poetry and novel, lyric, and narrative. The profiling of landscape painting against portraiture also attempts to redefine the genre of the lyric against Naturalist aesthetics, and bears the stamp of an antipsychologizing impulse, just as Cézanne's increasingly abstract landscapes, much admired by Rilke, would mark the transition to a painterly modernity of similarly objective intent. Rilke contrasts the history of portraiture (whose imaginary author "müßte nicht allein Historiker sein, sondern auch Psychologe")[9] with that of landscape, and then leaps from the history of the genre (*Landschaftsmalerei*) into the internal history of the object itself, its individual subjective experience:

> Those undertaking to write the history of landscape would find themselves at first helplessly exposed to the strange, the unrelated, and the ungraspable. We are used to reckoning with forms [*Gestalten*], and the landscape has no form; we are used to concluding from movements to acts of the will, and the landscape does not *will* [*will nicht*], when it moves . . . Landscape stands there with no hands and no

face, — or it is all face and has, through the unsurveyable size of its traits, a fearful and oppressive effect on human beings. (308)

The strangeness of nature is no longer the magical *schöne Fremde* of Eichendorff. Rilke's discomfort is defined by a loss both of the relation between nature and society, and of the ability to personify. On the one hand, the nervous calculation typical of the modern citydweller has here no object to reckon with; on the other, the facelessness of nature resembles the urban anonymity from which Rilke's Malte Laurids Brigge would suffer, dissolving the personal identity of the individual.[10] With this the sovereign panoramic perspective from which natural landscape had earlier been viewed, metaphorizing the historical distance between Eden and the present, is lost. Where the Schiller of "Der Spaziergang" (1795) (or, at roughly the same time in 1798, Wordsworth in "Tintern Abbey") could enjoy a friendly conversation with ancestral nature, Rilke no longer knows with whom, or from where, he is talking. The face of nature is too close for comfort, and its instability suggests an allegorical dimension.

A sense of uncanniness had been present at least since the eighteenth century in nature poetry. One may take Schiller's post-Hellenic, depantheized nature as an instance: "Does this saddened silence / Announce to me my Creator?"[11] A Kantian deity has no more immediate, intuitive contact with nature, and thus cannot be reached via the pleasure principle but only through renunciation: "Obscure, like Him, is His Veil, / And my renunciation [*Entsagen*] — that which honors Him." Such a renunciation was the condition of the subject's participation in sublimated ideal beauty; yet it has become problematic in Rilke. The former innocence of nature, the traditional ally of individual subjective claims against social mediation, has been replaced by an implication of the viewer in an ambivalence and anxiety which would become the historical signature of Expressionism. Neither Goethe's sovereign poetics of the eye nor the Romantic notion of *Natursprache* operates for Rilke. Nature will not remain still, encouraging the production of poetic language, nor is it decodable as a mystic book which would re-alphabetize the poet in an initiation of maternal meaning (Kittler). All imaginary fantasies of natural wholeness have broken down before the immediate threat of something very real, something not far from what Malte will later simply call *das Grosse* ("the Big Thing").

However, although nature has lost the dimension of proleptic futurity that once grounded the subject of lyric in favor of an archaic, prehistoric recurrence of the uncanny, Rilke's text still proceeds on the assumption of nature as teacher once pioneered by Rousseau and Kant: only nature's lesson has changed, not its exemplary position. This lesson is the real object of Rilke's introduction, which does not touch on specifically painterly questions of composition or technique.[12] The variety of his approaches to the problem belies any reading of German literary history that would see

Naturlyrik as neatly superseded by the late-industrial, post-Symbolist *Artistenmoral* and "monologic art" of George and Benn. For Rilke describes in his Worpswede monograph the rediscovery of nature he is delineating as nothing less than an "Umwertung aller Werte" (318); one might paraphrase this as a *denaturing of nature*. This transformation suggests a reading at once historical and also psychoanalytically informed, as the historical background to Rilke's refiguring of landscape will reveal.

The subject of lyric, figuring the relation of the collective subject Man with nature, had been defined, in the eighteenth and nineteenth centuries, by two larger discursive formations: those of history and of science, meeting in the Enlightenment project of *histoire naturelle*, and the Romantic one of a metaphysical *Naturgeschichte* (which Lukács and Benjamin would soon reactivate around the beginning of the First World War).[13] Rilke's text, however, describes the failure of just this mediation, thus breaking with the *Kulturlandschaft* so central to Goethe.[14] Rilke's project cannot fulfil Hegel's dictum that landscape painting's "particular objective situations" should produce moods [*Stimmungen*] in the viewer's temperament [*Gemüt*] "that correspond to the moods of Nature."[15] However, both natural history and Newtonian science continue to haunt Worpswede: for the complete absence of any mediation between nature and the human subject is, as Rilke is well aware, literal madness.

Regarding history, Rilke writes that the normative embedding of humanity in Darwinian *Naturgeschichte* is no comfort:

> Admittedly, many could call on our relation to Nature, from which we all are descended as the last fruits of a great family tree. Whoever does that cannot deny that this family tree, if we follow it back from us, twig by twig and branch by branch, quickly gets lost in a darkness inhabited by extinct giant beasts, monsters full of enmity and hatred; and that the further back we go, the more we come to ever stranger and more cruel beings, so that we have to assume we will find Nature itself to be the most cruel and strange of all in the background (308–9).

Natural genealogy, far from granting humans a legitimate pedigree, rapidly loses its path in a thicket of myth. Man no longer has his old supremacy over the rest of nature, nor may he take for granted that he is an integral part of it; that integration must now first be achieved, through passive submission. This is best understood, according to Rilke, by

> Poets or painters, composers or architects, fundamentally lonely people ... who, since they can't convince Nature to take part in their lives, see their task in grasping [*erfassen*] Nature, in order to insert themselves somewhere into its great contexts [*Zusammenhänge*]. (311)

Reconciliation with nature is no longer a scientific (or political) question, but one resolved only by artists, who alone may represent the universality of mankind: "with these individuals, all of humanity approaches Nature" (311). Since this reconciliation is no longer under the primacy of practical action, it need no longer be just one for adults either: thus Marx' idea of the humanization of nature (via the famous *Stoffwechsel* or exchange of material), or Darwin's great Tree of Life,[16] take on mythic connotations of family fantasms, even incest. For Rilke, the eye turned on landscape in the present of contemplation cannot help seeing therein its mythic past:

> ... is there a landscape without figures that isn't entirely occupied with narrating about the person who saw it? [...] sometimes man appears to go forth out of the landscape, and at others, landscape comes forth out of man, and then again they behave connaturally, like siblings [*ebenbürtig und geschwisterlich*]. Nature seems to approach at moments, by giving even cities the appearance of a landscape, and with centaurs, mermaids and old men of the sea in the manner of Böcklin, humanity approaches Nature: but it is always a question of this relation [*Verhältnis*] ... (312)

Rilke here anticipates a central topos of modernity: the mythic naturalization of the metropolis via narrative. Yet even this mythic nature, far from offering a metaphorical alternative to culture (as it had from the eighteenth century down at least to Storm's *Oktoberlied*) can only allegorically refer back to the latter: anxiety and the instability of allegory are corollaries.

Scientific Nature depends on a silencing of nature as subject, which has become impossible to maintain. Rilke's writing constantly veers away from the objectivity he is ostensibly seeking to a mythic dimension which acknowledges nature's own form of "subjectivity." One of the chief figures of this latter is the minatory face of nature already referred to in the opening quotation, which Rilke's text desperately denies. Human work and houses may have faces, but nature either has none at all or too much of one, dangerous to look into, as were the faces of Medusa or Moses' God. Alone among the German Romantic painters, Philipp Otto Runge had, like the later painters of Worpswede, "ihr [der Natur] ins Gesicht gesehen" (317); of the peasant inhabitants of the surrounding countryside, Rilke observes:

> There is no family resemblance among these people; the mother's smile does not get passed on to her sons, for the mothers never smiled. All have only *one* face: the hard, tense face of work, whose skin has been so stretched out by these efforts, that it becomes too big with age, like a long-worn glove. (321)

This lack of family resemblance among the peasants recalls the confused monsters of the Darwinian *Stammbaum;* and as with nature, their one monotonous face has something eerie and minatory about it. Despite Rilke's denial, the facial analogy is omnipresent in his text, much as one can often find concealed traces of the human body in a Cézanne landscape. Science's normative replacement of nature's animistic "face" with the intelligible and logical system of Cartesian spatial coordinates — a desperate battle in Cézanne as well — no longer functions.

Thus *Worpswede*'s most frequently used term for nature is *teilnahmslos,* impartial — surely a characteristic of scientists' Nature.[17] This word also tellingly occurs in the description of the Gioconda (314), thereby undermining its supposed neutrality. We may recall Rilke's somewhat desperately emphatic italics in the earlier quotation: "the landscape does not *will,* when it moves . . ." What kind of a subject is a nature which "does not will," which has no desire? One suspects it could only be a dead one.

Nature's impartiality and indifference extend even to ignorance: of Millet, one of nature's greatest painters, nature "has . . . known nothing" (317). (Such ignorance is traditionally associated more with fathers than with omniscient Mother Nature.)[18] Nature is thus neither a helpful supporter of the human subject nor actively hostile to it. It is paradoxically both a personified subject and one with neither the desire nor the knowledge which normally defines subjectivity. This subject position will define Rilke's later poetics.

Rilke's own text repeatedly contradicts the claim of nature's impartiality. Nature constantly shifts its aspect at the beginning of the essay, moving from the neutral, desubjective indifference of landscape to a lack of "relationship" (*Verwandtschaft*), and then to a mythic Earth which is actively, subjectively hostile to human civilization and language:

> But again and again through the centuries, the forces [of Nature] shake off her names and rise up, like an oppressed class, against its little overlords, indeed, not even *against* them, — they just rise up, and cultures fall from the shoulders of the earth . . .
>
> What does it mean, that we alter the external surface of the earth . . . if we recall besides this one single hour when Nature acted above us, above our hopes, as if over the heads of our lives, with that sublime loftiness and indifference with which all of its gestures are filled. She knows nothing of us. And whatever men may have achieved, none of it was so great that Nature took part in their pains, or agreed with their joys. At times, she accompanied great and eternal hours of history with her powerful, roaring music . . . but only in order to turn away a moment later and leave that person high and dry, with whom she had seemed to share everything. (309–10)

This is a sublime less reminiscent of Kant's Lisbon than of Sade's nature.[19] The fickleness and caprice suggest not only the feminine, but also frustration with the mother.[20] As will be evident in the poetics of the *Dinggedicht,* personification is a ghost Rilke must work hard to exorcise.

This instability of the sublime — once, in the eighteenth century, the marker of virile distance and self-control — is evident in another synonym for nature, the turn-of-the-century topos of "das Leben." That life, however, no longer the unitary matrix or collective subject of nineteenth-century biology, has the uncanniness of death:

> One is hardly as vulnerable when alone with a dead person as when alone with trees. For however enigmatic death may be, a life that isn't our life is even more enigmatic, a life that doesn't take part in us and, as if blind to us, celebrates its own festivals, at which we are onlookers, watching with a certain embarrassment, like guests who have come by chance and *who speak another language.* (308, emphasis added)

The loss of any remnant of Romantic *Natursprache,* of the semiotic legibility or decipherability of nature, is here programmatic. And if life does not tend to its opposite, it tends to become the attribute of the feminine and the somatic. So in the implicitly feminine *demi-monde* of Renaissance portraiture, to which Rilke compares the landscapes of Worpswede, the historian is "umlächelt von berühmten Lippen und festgehalten von Händen, die ein eigentümlich selbständiges Leben führen" (307). Like the high society of the Mona Lisa, Rilke's nature is a matter of ambiguous and ultimately indifferent feminine wiles.

Near the end of Rilke's introduction a temporary foothold outside the claustrophobic delusions of the anxious subject seems to appear:

> Landscape is determined, it is without chance, and every falling leaf fulfils, by falling, one of the great laws of the cosmos. This lawfulness makes nature such an event [*Ereignis*] for young people. For that is precisely what they seek, and when they look for a master in their confusion, they don't mean one who constantly intervenes in their development . . . they want an example. They want to see a life beside them, above them, around them, a life that lives without concern for them. Great figures of history live so, but they are invisible, and one must close one's eyes to see them. (319)

Here at last the vague, either faceless or too proximate blur of nature is overcome in definitude. In the sublime "event" of Nature, Rilke overomes the Anxiety of the Event we saw in Lyotard's discussion of Heidegger in chapter 1. Unlike the capricious Earth who may abruptly leave her children "high and dry," this form of nature is reliable and regular. Yet although Rilke first reverts to a scientific paradigm of nature, the "lawfulness" of Newton and Kant, what concerns him in the law is its "Ereignis," again under the sign of the eye (unlike invisible history, which Rilke likes as little as Goethe did) and correlated to the adolescent search for authority. That authority, however, is not simply the paternal Law, which would have to "intervene" (*eingreifen*) in their development. (The authority of nature as "Meister" is thus not one of explicit command and imperative, but only one of example, less an imperative to practical reason than an illustration for the faculty of judgment.)[21] The falling leaf, although it first serves as an allegory of the order of that Law, implicitly shifts to a metaphor for the observing subject's gesture of surrender to the overwhelming vastness of Nature, an imaginary and sovereignly indifferent power enjoyed in a relation of spectatorship.

The instability of Rilke's solution is evident in the curious sound of the singular "*ein* Leben," which undermines the (metaphoric) biological universalism of the subject of nature by putting it into a (metonymic) relation of historical uniqueness with the autobiographical *Ereignis* of "junge[n] Menschen." The pleasure of identification with the *Leben* in the falling leaf is thus mitigated: it is both the same as one's own and not so. If the life in the falling leaf is one's own, it implies also an identification with death in that of the leaf. Thus nearly two decades later the last *Duino Elegy* would close:

> Aber erweckten sie uns, die unendlich Toten, ein Gleichnis,
> siehe, sie zeigten vielleicht auf die Kätzchen der leeren
> Hasel, die hängenden, oder
> meinten den Regen, der fällt auf dunkles Erdreich im Frühjahr. —
>
> Und wir, die an *steigendes* Glück
> denken, empfänden die Rührung,
> die uns beinah bestürzt,
> wenn ein Glückliches *fällt*.[22]
>
> [But if the endlessly dead woke a symbol in us,
> see, they would point perhaps to the catkins,
> hanging from bare hazels, or
> might intend the rain, falling on dark soil in springtime. —
>
> And we, who think of *ascending*
> joy, would feel the emotion,
> that almost dismays us,
> when a joyful thing *falls*.]

The *Worpswede* introduction, not yet protected by the mantle of a developed high style, specifies more openly who is falling and dead here: it is Nature herself, and not only, as is better known, the Great God Pan.[23]

The Adolescent Sublime: Nature as Sister

The familial and gendered subtexts which Rilke's aesthetics of nature cannot help betraying emerge in the poetry written during the stay at Worpswede. The same half-formed subjectivity sketched into Rilke's nature figures in a pair of poems entitled "Von den Mädchen," written at Worpswede in September 1900. Most people cannot leave the poet in peace, but

>fragen immer irgendwen,
>ob er nicht einen hat singen sehen
>oder Hände auf Saiten legen.
>Nur die Mädchen fragen nicht . . .
>
>[always ask someone
>If he hasn't seen someone singing
>Or putting hands to strings.
>Only the girls do not ask . . .]

The Girls take the place of impartial Nature here, and the poet will speak for them as he once did for the Mother Nature of Romanticism. This proves less easy than the Romantic project, however:

>Mädchen, Dichter sind, die von euch lernen
>das zu *sagen*, was ihr einsam *seid*;
>und sie lernen leben an euch Fernen,
>wie die Abende an grossen Sternen
>sich gewöhnen an die Ewigkeit.
>
>Keine darf sich je dem Dichter schenken,
>wenn sein Auge auch um Frauen bat;
>denn er kann euch nur als Mädchen denken . . .[24]
>
>[Girls, poets are those who learn from you
>To *say* that which you *are* alone;
>And they learn to live from you distant ones,
>as evenings get used to eternity
>from the great stars.
>
>None of you may ever give herself to the poet,
>even if his eyes asked for women;
>for he can only think of you as girls.]

The unattainable distance of the Girls has taken over Kant's once-virile starry metaphor for "the moral law within me." The Law here in question is one of a teasing denial of desire, not of the latter's sublimation. Girls are not to be possessed, but identified with. Their fullness of being still renders speech superfluous to them, leaving the poet a place to speak. The traditional superiority of the sublime subject to nature has been lost in Rilke's ambivalent identifications.

"Women circa 1900 are no longer the Woman, who, without writing herself, made men speak, and they were no longer feminine consumers, who at best wrote down the fruits of their reading."[25] Rather they were Sisters:[26] the same "emancipated women" known to both Nietzsche and Rilke — who tried nonetheless to configure them as Girls. His Girls are themselves half-human, half-thing; so Rilke's Thing will in turn be half-natural, half-artificial. In the words of Rilke's later exegete Heidegger: "We call a young girl who faces a difficult task a thing still too young [*ein noch zu junges Ding*], but only because we miss humanity in a certain sense and find rather that which makes up the thingness of things [*das Dinghafte der Dinge*]."[27]

As Rilke's poem shows, this lack of full humanity (or developed sexuality) is what the poet wants from the Girls, which makes them the perfect object for the operation of poetic naming; thus also Rilke's perennial androgynous identification with them. His own looking into the landscape is identical with that of girls as painters (Clara Westhoff, Paula Moderssohn), who are "half knowing, that is, painters, half unconscious, that is, girls . . . This is why they look so long into the landscape . . ."[28]

Rilke's Girls are as imaginary, and thus charged with ambivalent affect, as was Nature, but have a new function for the poet. The importance of the Girl suggests a historical analogy from the annals of contemporary psychoanalytic case-studies. Rilke's *Mädchen* seem less related to Schreber's chattering Girls than to the mythic Sisters of Little Hans, who was born only a year after the publication of *Worpswede*. Although Freud wanted to see him as a paradigm of Oedipal normality, Little Hans's assumption of the paternal Law was, for Lacan's later rereading, less complete than Freud might have wanted.

> To be sure, Little Hans will love women, but . . . he will never stop being wary of them. If one may say so, they will be his mistresses. They will be *the daughters of his spirit* [*les filles de son esprit*], and . . . ravished away from the mother. (emphasis added)

Hans, like Rilke, had an "extraordinary awe of women."[29] Women in the plural are no longer any more to be mastered than Nature. At best, one may hope to *divide et impera* — at the cost, however, of splitting oneself in the process. The Girls (like angels) are thus (metonymic) allies against the Mother, a means both to preserve and deny her power and one's own identification with it. Through his imaginary children, "Hans has substituted himself for the mother, and he has children like her . . .

Woman will never be anything for him but the fantasy of these little sister-girls [*soeurs-filles*] ... *He will have children structured in the mode of the maternal phallus.*"[30]

Thus also Rilke's Girls are Things, imaginary children ravished from the implacable hostility of Mother Nature and yet also substituting for her.[31] Through the comparison with Little Hans (a generation younger than Rilke, it should be admitted), something like a phenotype emerges, highlighting a specifically historical aspect of subjectivity. If neither Rilke nor Hans is homosexual, they are not precisely strong male egos, either. A closer look at Rilke's poetic vocabulary may offer more hints as to how this subjectivity is formed.

The oddly faltering semblance of neutrality in Rilke's word *teilnahmslos* (indifferent), in the denial of knowledge of or interest in the nature of Worpswede, suggests Freud's *Verneinung* (denegation) or *Verleugnung* (denial): a negation that simultaneously admits what it refuses to acknowledge (namely the anatomical difference of the sexes) and which produces a split in the ego as its result.[32] For the *Worpswede* introduction opens up the place where the poetry of the *Ding* will develop; where nature was, there Thing will be.[33] The Thing, impartial and indifferent, thus takes over the place of the desiring subject of Classical and Romantic nature poetry. Rilke's *Dinggedicht* is a response to the failure of nature in the form of its received poetic, as is evident in the insistent fading[34] of Worpswede's landscape, a fading written into the fantasy of Nature from its origin:

> Aug', mein Aug', was sinkst du nieder?
> Goldne Träume, kommt ihr wieder?[35]
>
> [Eye, my eye, why do you sink down?
> Golden dreams, will you return?]

Lyrical address is doomed to missing totality, which is then perennially produced (retrospectively) as nature. What is new is Rilke's response to this loss.

Only in the *Dinggedicht* will Rilke gain the chiastic identity as lyrical subject[36] that nature as landscape could not offer. Chiastic inversion, in older lyric such as Goethe, allows for dialogic exchange between desiring subject and desired addressee. In Rilke's mature work, it will come to stand for an exchange between human subject and inhuman Thing. The structure of the *Ding* is a fetishistic one, which rewrites the maternal plenitude that post-Goethean nature had opened to lyric. For the Thing cannot occupy the place of nature in the older metaphoric fashion of symptom and symbol. Even when it treats of nature, Rilke's mature poetry is strictly speaking no longer *Naturlyrik,* any more than the "totgesagter Park" (death-said park) of his Symbolist contemporary George. Merely to point out the artificial constructedness of Rilke's work, as opposed to any Diltheyan reflection of *Erlebnis,* is, however, still too unspecific. The particular relation of the lyric subject to nature and artifice is a historical formation, legible in psychoanalytic terms.[37]

The lyric paradigm of the *Goethezeit* is a fundamental structuring fantasy. "The voice of Nature from which the lyric (conceived as the primordial form of all poetry since Herder) emerges is the fantasy of oneness, wholeness, and erotic union within the mother/child dyad."[38] However, this fantasy is not (as older Freudian readings would have had it) a matter of regression to a pre-symbolic (or pre-Oedipal) unity; rather fantasy ensues as a response to loss and absence. Fantasy is the product and complement of separation from original unity, and not its literal recovery (which would be psychosis). Romantic poetry heightens this dimension of absence even beyond Classical lyric.[39]

In the Worpswede introduction, Nature is, in every sense, *not wanting:*[40] *teilnahmslos,* impartial, designates Nature's absence of desire, even of need. This necessitates a refiguring of the fundamental fantasy of lyric, since its object has changed. The absent object of fantasy (in Lacan's terms, the *object a,* configuring the desire of the mother) is replaced with the fetishistic one of the Thing. The move from nature poetry to the *Dinggedicht* emerges forcefully in several poems from 1900–1908.

"Zu wenig Ding und doch noch Ding genug"

> *Things are homely [heimlich]. See,*
> *our heart too is a homely thing.*
> — Rilke[41]

The poems Rilke wrote contemporary with *Worpswede* betray traces of nature's growing displacement by the nascent poetics of the *Dinggedicht.* At first this may take the form of just the sort of personification *Worpswede* had criticized as naïve. The landscape poems of this period are few indeed, albeit nonetheless telling, even when they seem rather much under the aegis of Art-Nouveau preciosity.

"Abend in Skåne" (1904, from the *Buch der Bilder*) is still formed by elements both of Goethean alliance with painting and of the elegiac narrative by which Schiller's walking Exodus from culture to nature was effected.[42] Yet the step out from the Symbolist artifice of one of George's parks into the open plain, historic signature of the *Jahrhundertwende*[43] leads not out of the house to freedom, but only back inward to prehistory.

> Der Park ist hoch. Und wie aus einem Haus
> tret ich aus seiner Dämmerung heraus
> in Ebene und Abend. In den Wind,

> denselben Wind, den auch die Wolken fühlen,
> die hellen Flüsse und die Flügelmühlen,
> die langsam mahlend stehn am Himmelsrand.
> Jetzt bin ich auch ein Ding in seiner Hand,
> das kleinste unter diesen Himmel. — Schau:
> Ist das Ein Himmel?:
>
> [The park is lofty. And as out from a house
> I step out of its twilight
> Into plains and evening. Into the wind,
> the same wind that the clouds feel,
> the bright rivers and the mill arms,
> which stand slowly churning on the edge of the sky.
> Now I too am a thing in His hand,
> the smallest under this sky — Look:
> Is that One Sky?]

Rilke has walked into his own imaginary landscape, the same as Millet's described in *Worpswede:*

> And there came unexpectedly with the herds the shepherd himself into the pictures, the first human in the vast solitude. Silent as a tree he stands there in Millet's paintings, the only upright thing in the great plains of Barbizon. He doesn't move; like a blind man he stands among the sheep, and his clothes are sure as the earth and weathered as stone. *He has no own, particular life. His life is that of that plain* . . . He has no memory . . . (314–5, emphasis added)

The minatory aspect of the poem's amnesic plain is sensed only at its edges, in the slow grind of the mills at the horizon. What the narrator of "Abend in Skåne" finds refuge in is the sense that 'I am His Thing, His Toy'; this early poem presents the poetics of the fetish in simpler, more candid terms than later work.[44] The poet is playing dead in God's hand (recalling several other poems from the *Buch der Bilder* and also the Gospel of Matthew),[45] as if he had fallen from the sky into that hand. The security of being a thing is promptly followed by an echoing question, the desire for visible unity (so central to post-Kantian aesthetics). The answer to this question can hardly be other than tautological.

> Selig lichtes Blau,
> in das sich immer reinere Wolken drängen,
> und drunter alles Weiß in Übergängen,
> und drüber jenes dünne, große Grau,
> warmwallend wie auf roter Untermalung,
> und über allem diese stille Strahlung
> sinkender Sonne.

> Wunderlicher Bau,
> in sich bewegt und in sich selbst gehalten,
> Gestalten bildend, Riesenflügel, Falten
> und Hochgebirge vor den ersten Sternen
> und plötzlich, da: ein Tor in solche Fernen
> wie sie vielleicht nur Vögel kennen . . .[46]

> [Blessed light blue,
> into which ever purer clouds are pressing,
> and below, everything white in transitions,
> and above, that thin, great grey,
> warmly swelling as if on a red background,
> and above all this silent streaming
> of a sinking sun.

> Wondrous building,
> moving in itself and by itself held,
> forming shapes, giant wings, folds,
> and high mountains before the first stars,
> and suddenly, there: a gate into such distances
> as are known perhaps only by birds . . .]

Rilke's poem collapses in answering the vocal demand for unity. In these two answering strophes, nature appears not only as architecture (*Bau*) — recalling, in admittedly much weaker form, Baudelaire's familiar nature as animistic temple — but also as a static, autopoietic machine, nonetheless leaving a "gate" open at the end, analogous to the implicit door by which the speaker earlier left the park's "house." The birds are metempsychotic messengers of the soul's survival of its death, continuing the narrative exodus at the end beyond the limits of the poem itself. Yet Rilke has not really gotten out of the "Haus" of family fantasm at all, since the poem only reassimilates nature to the "building" of its civilized other. (Schiller's culture-critical *Spaziergang* has here been taken back into culture and thus not happened at all.) The only way out is death, but a death here unfortunately reduced to a *Jugendstil* ornament of the metaphoric door. The Thing will close off this door with a Cézanne-like insistence on the *réalisé*.

Thus the poems of middle-period Rilke absorb even such narrative elements as remain in "Abend in Skåne" (still suggesting a neo-Romantic metalinguistic horizon at the poem's trailing end) more completely into what has usually been read as a law of metaphor. In "Eingang" (1900, *Buch der Bilder*)[47] the face of nature, still threatening, as it was in Worpswede, is controlled by the sovereign activity of the poet, whose Adamic naming the poem narrates.

Wer du auch seist: am Abend tritt hinaus
aus deiner Stube, drin du alles weißt;
als letztes vor der Ferne liegt dein Haus:
wer du auch seist.
Mit deinen Augen, welche müde kaum
von der verbrauchten Schwelle sich befrein,
hebst du ganz langsam einen schwarzen Baum
und stellst ihn vor den Himmel: schlank, allein.
Und hast die Welt gemacht. Und sie ist groß
und wie ein Wort, das noch im Schweigen reift.
Und wie dein Wille ihren Sinn begreift,
lassen sie deine Augen zärtlich los . . .[48]

[Whoever you may be:
come evening, step out of your room,
wherein all is familiar;
your house stands as the last thing before the distance:
whoever you may be.
With your eyes, which, tired,
barely free themselves from the worn threshold,
you raise very slowly a black tree
and place it before the sky: slender, alone.
And have made the world. And it is great
and like a word, still ripening in silence.
And as your will grasps its sense,
your eyes let it gently go . . .]

If "Abend in Skåne" ended with the dissolution of the subject in the self-regulating order of nonhuman nature and overtones of metempsychosis, "Eingang" succeeds in blocking off the sky in deliberate activity, in giving the Law to nature. The solitary tree presented "before the sky" has aspects of apotropaic magic, of warding off a threat — at once addressed to the sky and turned against it. The final triumph verges on paranoia: having made the entire world, which then swells strangely large, the poet's eyes may drop the world from which they have sucked out the sense (thus once again letting it fall).

"Eingang" displays in paradigmatic fashion how nature is exorcised from the world of Things. The structure of the *Dinggedichte*, wherein specific objects are gradually effaced in favor of linguistic self-referentiality, is already here present *in nuce*.[49] The developed type of the *Dinggedicht* completes the displacement of nature in favor of culture, of artificial objects. The metaphoric and appellative structures that control this are, however, often fragile. For the Thing is — like the fetish to which it may be correlated — at once nature and culture, living and dead; like the drives themselves, or the partial and transitional objects of the child, *das Ding* is on the border between inner and outer, subjective and objective. (Lacan's witty formula for this was "extimacy," the subject's being outside itself in its cathected objects.) This border appears read in exemplary fashion in "Der Ball" (1908).

> Du Runder, der die Wärme aus zwei Händen
> im Fliegen, oben, fortgiebt, sorglos wie
> sein Eigenes; was in den Gegenständen
> nicht bleiben kann, zu unbeschwert für sie,
>
> zu wenig Ding und doch noch Ding genug,
> um nicht aus allem draußen Aufgereihten
> unsichtbar plötzlich in uns einzugleiten:
> das glitt in dich, du zwischen Fall und Flug
>
> noch Unentschlossener: der, wenn er steigt,
> als hätte er ihn mit hinaufgehoben,
> den Wurf entführt und freiläßt —, und sich neigt
> und einhält und den Spielenden von oben
> auf einmal eine neue Stelle zeigt,
> sie ordnend wie zu einer Tanzfigur,
>
> um dann, erwartet und erwünscht von allen,
> rasch, einfach, kunstlos, ganz Natur,
> den Becher hoher Hände zuzufallen.[50]
>
> [You round one, who flying above, gives away
> the warmth of two hands, careless, as
> its own; that which in objects
> cannot remain, too weightless for them,
>
> too little thing and yet still thing enough,
> from all that which is lined up outside
> to slide suddenly into us:
> that slid into you, between fall and flight
>
> still undecided; who, when it climbs,
> as if it had carried it upwards,
> abducts the throw and releases it —, and then inclines down
> and pauses and shows at once a new place
> from above to the players,
> ordering it as into a dance figure,
>
> in order then, expected and desired by all,
> quickly, simply, artlessly, wholly nature,
> to fall back to the cup of raised hands.]

This is unquestionably a high piece of linguistic virtuosity, a demonstration of poetry's Cratylic capacity to enact the very process it describes. The entire poem is one single sentence composed of multiple subordinate clauses without any main verb. The ball's hanging in mid-air is thus directly mimicked by the weightlessness of the verbless sentence itself. Instead of a definite predicate form of the verb, one has, as the poem's literally "cadential" last word, the infinitive *zuzufallen*, designating a temporal immanence or futurity that is always as if about to happen before the reader's eye. The intricacy of syntax here could be described, with an art-historical term typical of the turn of the century, as an *arabesque*. One is reminded of Heidegger's comments on the relation of *das Ding* to syntactic structure: "Who would undertake to rattle these simple relations between thing and sentence, between sentence structure and thing structure [*Satzbau und Dingbau*]?"[51]

Rilke has exposed just these simple relations. Even God Himself had been embodied, as "thing of things," in the throw of a ball in the *Stunden-Buch*.[52] In the penultimate line, the ball gains a crescendo of attributes: "simply artless, wholly nature," the last two words rhyming doubly with the "dance figure" designating the artifice of Rilke's own linguistic production. What fades and vanishes here is not Nature, but Art. Herein lies precisely the problem with the *Dinggedicht*.

Rilke's ball is at once a model of his most self-referentially modern manner and the paradigmatic *Jugendstil* poem. Beauty is here what falls, just as it had been with the Worpswede landscape's falling leaf. Its *Jugendstil* ornament was, for Adorno, one of the cruxes of modernity:

> Beauty, impotent to define itself, which definition it would only gain from its other, is as if a root in the air, and is caught in the fate of the invented ornament.[53]

The waiting hands at the end figure this Other of Rilke's absolute Art, from which the latter could gain its self-definition. (As Lacan half-jokingly noted: "le style, c'est l'homme même . . . à qui l'on s'adresse" [Style is the man himself . . . the one being addressed].)[54] Whose hands are catching the ball? If the ball itself has changed nature in the course of its flight, might its recipient also not be the same as the thrower?

This recalls a passage from *Malte*, which so many recent readers[55] have preferred to the poetry. The fear of falling is omnipresent in the novel; equally central to the famous passage before the mirror is the child Malte's (admittedly quite retrospective) mastering practice of throwing and letting himself fall:

> I became bolder and bolder; I threw myself ever higher, for my skill in catching was beyond all doubt.[56]

The origin of the poetics of the *Dinggedicht* thus becomes legible as the overcoming of a phobic seizure.[57] In fact, the wholeness of "wholly Natur" at the end of "Der Ball" is not complete, for it does not include the "new place" at the apex of the ball's flight, which has been simply thrown off and expended into the air. "Nature" is only available once subjectivity has been thrown away and gotten rid of.[58] This desubjectivized remnant of nature is diametrically opposed to the dynamic *natura naturans* of classical and romantic nature.

Key here is not only the replacement of physical activity with abstractions of intentionality ("warmth" and "throw," as if independent of any individual subject or of the ball's materiality and endued with a pathos anticipating later *Existenzphilosophie*), but also the abrupt passage from a dialogic naming *Du* to an objective *er*. The throw or cast of "Der Ball" figures the ostension of pronominal address and then arrives at the discursive confirmation of the third-person pronoun (*er*) in which the poem itself, the poet's own act, returns to him in "natural" confirmation. Thus we have the affirmation of "simply, artlessly, wholly nature," which can then fall safely into a cultic "cup of high hands" at the end, in a figure also representing the poem's eventual arrival in the reader's hands. The poem's tenuousness is due in part to the dangerously decorative and personifying "dance figure" in which the ball's gradual separation from human agency culminates. Even more risky, though, is the abruptness of the shift from *Du* to *er* at line 9, most artfully bridged over by another intentional abstraction (*you* between fall and flight / still undecided one: *who*, when *he* climbs . . ."). The result is an allegory concealing a pathetic fallacy of personification at its origins.[59]

One could scarcely find a better instance of the fragility of a poetics of pure tautological self-referentiality, of allegory in de Man's sense. The ball is the figure of answered desire, its unity being slowly added up from a set of partial attributes, and dependent on a functional *Stelle* in the linguistic structure which generates it.[60] At the end, however, nature must inevitably return for there to be the illusion of wholeness. "Wholly Nature" here means the subject's reflexive re-constitution through the return of language to itself.

What the artificial closure of the *Dinggedicht* had to exclude is exposed even more directly in the Expressionist desperation of "Römische Campagna" (1908), one of the very few larger landscapes in the *Neue Gedichte*.[61]

> Aus der vollgestellten Stadt, die lieber
> schliefe, träumend von den hohen Thermen,
> geht der grade Gräberweg ins Fieber;
> und die Fenster in den letzten Fermen

sehn ihm nach mit einem bösen Blick.
Und er hat sie immer im Genick,
wenn er hingeht, rechts und links zerstörend,
bis er draußen atemlos beschwörend

seine Leere zu den Himmeln hebt,
hastig um sich schauend, ob ihn keine
Fenster treffen. Während er die letzten

Aquädukten zuwinkt herzuschreiten,
geben ihm die Himmel für die seine
ihre Leere, die ihn überlebt.[62]

[From the filled city, which would rather
sleep, dreaming of lofty therms,
the straight grave-path goes into fever;
and the windows in the last farms

look after it with an evil gaze.
And it has them always on its neck,
when it goes on, destroying right and left,
until it, imploring breathlessly outside,

raises its void to the skies,
hastily looking around, to be sure no
windows hit it. While it gestures

to the last aqueducts to stride toward it,
the skies give it, in exchange for its own,
their void, that will survive it.]

Here Rilke has produced the sort of *Kulturlandschaft* that Worpswede had rejected (and that the poet had nonetheless himself produced in his many park poems). Yet far from being "sharpened (*gebeizt*)" only by "real past suffering," as in Adorno's elegiac model,[63] Rilke's landscape of culture is still enacting that pain in the present, unto the edge of madness and death. It is hardly clear from where the mortal threat originates (it is apparently the city, the evil eye of the windows, which is hunting the road). An Expressionist inversion of humans and objects nearly bursts the formal closure of the familiar sonnet form. That form is here particularly unstable, and produces an odd selection of rhymes (as soon as lines 1–2, the word "lieber" given strange emphasis by its rhyming position). Personification turns against the poetic subject rather than assuring its triumph: the feverish *Gräberweg* tends less to assume the menace of space within dematerialized significance than aggressively to write it back onto the subject (e.g. the "Genick" of line 6). Thus the personification is extended to such length that the reader eventually imagines a person walking along the path, and not the path itself, to be the subject.

At the end, instead of a confirmation of the identity of narrator and object in the chiasmic exchange of linguistic signification and perception, there is helpless dissolution (the futile and unexplained gesture to the aqueducts "herzuschreiten," as in a Klee painting of 1937 entitled *Arches of the Bridge Break Ranks*) and death: the plural skies' "Leere" survives the road's end and the narrator's extinction almost as shame does Kafka's Josef K. The "Leere" at the end is also a grammatical one, that of the unresolved "er" which has not succeeded in objectively detaching itself from the writer's merely private phobia (baldly personified in the *Gräberweg*), but cannot directly name the latter either, remaining suspended between speaker and object. Unlike the ball's transfigured "neue Stelle," that place cannot be filled here. The poem's lack of semantic closure is at the opposite pole from the final triumphant affirmation of "Der Ball." Although the final rhyme (überlebt/hebt) closes on the implied death of the "Gräberweg," the raising (*heben*) of the skies' emptiness (*Leere*) over that death opens up an endless horizon of ambiguous meaning, comparable to the empty spaces of promise and anxiety Rilke had seen earlier in Worpswede.

Within the various approaches tried out in the type of the *Dinggedicht*, the particular objects selected for poetic treatment "share a similar fundamental structure"[64] to the point of being virtually interchangeable: the obsessively repeated fundamental structure actually robs the poetic subject of that concreteness it ostensibly seeks, and thus what is enacted in these poems appears as a ritual of renunciation and self-discipline. The Thing does not exist — any more than Woman or Nature; only things do. Yet the aesthetic of Rilke's *Dinggedicht* is a desperate denial (*Verleugnung*) of precisely this: thingliness is subsumed in thinkliness, and the plurality of things is refused as insistently as the non-unity of Woman. De Man's statement that "metaphor can be thought of as a language of desire and as a means to recover what is absent" (47) must be modified here: metaphor is rather the means to produce unsatisfiable desire.[65] The narrator of the *Dinggedicht* has taken the dead place of nature in *Worpswede*, which "*will* nicht, wenn sie sich bewegt" and which "steht ohne Hände da und hat kein Gesicht." This mimesis of death could then be tied to a denial of desire, with the aesthetic fragility of these poems thus correlatable to their attempt to transform older strategies of lyric subjectification and sublimation, but now without the collusion of unreliable Mother Nature.

What has irritated so many readers — most notably Adorno and Brecht — in Rilke is the lack of concretion, the constant and monotonous reduction to *Innerlichkeit*. This brings to mind Hegel's symbolic art, driven by "das stets gesteigerte Hinaufschrauben zu dieser äußersten Abstraktion selber, in welcher nicht nur der gesamte konkrete Inhalt, sondern auch das Selbstbewußtsein untergegangen sein muß."[66] Characteristic of this sort of art is a murky blurring of "das schlechthin Unsinnliche, das Absolute als solches, die Bedeutung schlechthin" with "die Einzelheiten der konkreten Wirklichkeit" in a confusion which only leaves the two "in um so grellerem Widerspruch" (Hegel I 436). (The most intolerable of these contradictions would be Rilke's personifications [Hegel I 441], which are due to the allegorical instability of subject and object, namer and named.)

However, rather than accusing Rilke of a restoration of metaphor as vehicle for imaginary plenitude or maternal symbiosis, we may see the *Dinggedicht* as linked to the operation of the fetish. Fetishism is characterized by a temporal structure of arrest and a logical one of simultaneous denial and acknowledgment. In "Der Ball," the moment where the ball stops and hesitates at the top of its trajectory might be this time of arrest. The instability of "Der Ball" is one between a metaphor become intolerably decorative, thus insubstantial and unconvincing (the positivity of the "Tanzfigur" and the rhyming "ganz Natur" affirmed at the end), and the metonymic acknowledgement of the non-identity of language and world in the empty and referentially undecidable "neue Stelle" — an emptiness which is the place of Rilke's sublimation of desire. "Dans toute forme de sublimation, le vide sera determinatif."[67]

Beyond any individual depth-psychological "explanations" of the genesis of poetry, the suggestion of a perverse moment at the heart of Rilke's mature poetic helps understand its particular historical signature, its relation to a *Jugendstil* aesthetic that still causes some discomfort even today. It is no longer so simple to link Rilke's well-known apolitical conservatism with his poetics of the fetishized Thing, as Adorno once tied Heidegger's philosophy to his politics. For recent opinion differs on the politics of the perverse; several commentators have sought to link it to a (non-Marxist) left.[68] Interestingly, however, both Freud and Lacan are more sanguine. For the latter, neurosis alone is innovative, as contrasted with the conservatism of the perverse: "Et le cercle se ferme, la perversion apportant des éléments qui travaillent la société, la névrose favorisant la création de nouveaux éléments de culture"[69] (And the circle closes, perversion bringing elements that work on society, neurosis favoring the creation of new elements of culture).

The expression "travailler la société" is ambiguous; and suggests "working society" as one "works the land": a form of patient cultivation, more than a sudden creation *ex nihilo*. In contrast, Lacan states elsewhere unmistakably that the (neurotic) creation of new meaning must always be metaphoric.[70]

Such speculations on the politics of the perverse remain, however, still too far removed from specifically literary questions; more interesting might be to recall Kristeva's attempt to claim Mallarmé as revolutionary, in obvious contradiction to the latter's disdain for direct political *engagement*. For the return of Rilke's ball to the nature it had abandoned in the artifice of the cast (*Wurf*) is cognate with the nodded greeting the severed head of Mallarmé's Saint John offers at the end of its fall in *Hérodiade*.[71] In both poets, only the passage through the subject's extinction renders possible its redemption or release.

For Kristeva, Mallarmé's change in "signifying practice" meant also a restructuring of the subject — that is, an opening of the latter's normal closure to the margins of madness.[72] Recent Rilke exegetes (Kittler, Huyssen) have suggested that Malte works with just such a destabilization of the subject, the traces of which have also been found in *Worpswede*'s view of nature. As the present chapter has argued, the poetics of the *Dinggedicht* prefer rather to conceal this instability with a fetishizing of language and self-referentiality. Despite this, Rilke was able to do without nature much less comfortably than Mallarmé: the specter of nature was, for one writing within the tradition of German poetry, not easy to exorcise. For the loss or fall of nature characteristic of the turn of the century seems to have been as little liberating as was the death of God.[73] And if art, rather than being merely endless self-referential play, must gain renewal of continued meaning from its specific other (cf. Adorno earlier on beauty as "root in the air"), then the historical complement to turn-of-the-century Artifice is Nature.

"Wozu Dichter?" Rilke and the Modernist Canon

Common to most major late-twentieth century readings of Rilke — whether deconstructive, psychoanalytic, or discourse- and media-theoretical — is an accent on the fragility and instability of the authorial and poetic subject. Against earlier existentializing readings, Rilke's modernist authenticity appears to later critics as verified with reference either to his historical witness to the end of the Subject (Kittler, Huyssen) or to a deconstructive revamping of the old high modernist autonomy of the signifier (de Man).

Only the last tactic, however, has been used in defense of the poems, which de Man terms "primarily successes of language and of rhetoric."[74] This conception runs into an aporia. Although de Man is aware that "the notion of a language entirely freed of referential constraints is properly inconceivable" (49) — in this not far from Adorno's complaint in the *Jargon der Eigentlichkeit* that such exclusive self-reference makes for bad poetry — he ultimately admires Rilke's exploitation of "a potential inherent in language," his meta-metaphor or "metaphor of a metaphor" (37). His only solution to this tension lies in a claim for Rilke's intermittent admission of the fragility of his project. Thus his reading closes with the

"Horseman" sonnet from the *Sonnets to Orpheus* read as a "failure of figuration" (de Man 54). Rilke's authenticity, once more, must depend on his failure (as, in different fashion, it does for Huyssen's reading of *Malte*).[75] Modernity is not compatible with the finished work of art.

Has the present discussion, terminating as it does with the "failure" of *Römische Campagna,* not followed the same pattern? Such a reading would still fall short of explaining the continued presence of Rilke — as opposed to, for instance, Stefan George — in the canon as more than mere kitsch. One of the most famous of the *Neue Gedichte* compelled even Benjamin and Adorno to grudging admiration.[76]

> Wir kannten nicht sein unerhörtes Haupt,
> darin die Augenäpfel reiften. Aber
> sein Torso glüht noch wie ein Kandelaber,
> in dem sein Schauen, nur zurückgeschraubt,
>
> sich hält und glänzt. Sonst könnte nicht der Bug
> der Brust dich blenden, und im leisen Drehen
> der Lenden könnte nicht ein Lächeln gehen
> zu jener Mitte, die die Zeugung trug.
>
> Sonst stünde dieser Stein entstellt und kurz
> unter der Schultern durchsichtigem Sturz
> und flimmerte nicht so wie Raubtierfelle;
>
> und bräche nicht aus allen seinen Rändern
> aus wie ein Stern: denn da ist keine Stelle,
> die dich nicht sieht. Du mußt dein Leben ändern.[77]
>
> [Never will we know his fabulous head
> where the eyes' apples slowly ripened. Yet
> his torso glows: a candelabrum set
> before his gaze which is pushed back and hid,
>
> restrained and shining. Else the curving breast
> could not thus blind you, nor through the soft turn
> of the loins could this smile easily have passed
> into the bright groins where the genitals burned.
>
> Else stood this stone a fragment and defaced,
> with lucent body from the shoulders falling,
> too short, not gleaming like a lion's fell;
>
> nor would this star have shaken the shackles off
> bursting with light, until there is no place
> that does not see you. You must change your life.][78]

What can the preceding considerations contribute to the understanding of this so-often-commented-on poem? Beneath the virtuosity, the poem's internal instability has not, perhaps, been sufficiently noticed: in particular, the oddness of its addressee, its change of shifters from *wir* to *du*. Here, unlike the ball, the Thing is no longer being addressed, but rather passed back and forth between unspecified pronominal addressees. The central identificatory device of lyric, the "thou" of *Erlebnis* becoming the "I" of readerly *Verstehen*, is prominent here. In fact the pronoun *Du* constitutes the real agency of the poem, and no longer the Thing, animate as the latter may be; for the reality of perception depends upon the *Du*.[79] Right at the beginning the collective *wir* is negated as subject of knowledge. The *dich* in line 6 is uncomfortable: here, as with the pronominal shift of *Der Ball*, the familiar Rilkean *Wandlung* is underway, yet the seams are showing. The elided reference to the genitals, veiled in the embarrassed *Lächeln* of the statue's *contrapposto*, depends in fact on the discomfort over the *dich*, which is the true Symbolic *pudendum* here. In the timid *Lächeln*, in the "blinding" which the "bend of the breast" effects, one senses that the observing *Du* is somehow guilty as a *voyeur*. Vision thus cannot offer any way out (thereby obviating any need to discuss the by-now banal gaze). The imaginary plenitude of the body, its head cut off from the neck, cannot remain stable within itself, but must speak. What sort of change is demanded at the end, at precisely the "neue Stelle" of transformation where the ball changed in falling, the reader-receptive *Leerstelle* of interpretation?

The end is a classic instance of what de Man diagnoses as the tendency of Rilke's pure play with language to overextend itself into a "messianic" appellative reading (51). In de Man's case this is due to the inherent Imaginary implications of all language ("meaning" being part of the domain of the Imaginary). From a psychoanalytic perspective, Rilke's surprising conclusion — far from being a tacked-on bit of *Jugendstil* rhetoric — is the eruption of a Symbolic instance of address which the preceding lines have done their best to evade. The subject, which the poetics of the Thing would elide, has been constantly hammering away at the apparent descriptions in the form of the contrary-to-fact subjunctive mood and of the constant negations[80] — indices that, once again, the object is fading, to be replaced by the imperative of the final sentence. Rilke obtains from the Thing — or rather from its fading, enacted in the poem and not preceding the latter (as in Mallarmé) — the Voice he could not find in Nature. In this Voice, the fetishistic Thing must finally be abolished in favor of anthropological renewal. As Carsten Strathausen has shown, Rilke's poems demand from the reader a particular interpretative effort to complete their form and meaning. Rilke "calls upon the reader to actually feel the words and listen to them rather than only reading them. [. . .] The goal is to stop reading and close the semiotic gap between sign and reference."[81] Here this must take place through the reader's "changing" his or her own life, as the poet himself did in order to "learn to see." The voice uttering the command to change one's life at the end may be that of Freud's instance of conscience itself, the superego. In other terms, this poem of Rilke's has attained a form of poetic stability through its reconquest of the Law, as if the poem spoke to the author: 'Thou art my Father, in whom I am well pleased; see, what has been written is very good.'

That voice is, by means of the "change" it demands, also addressed to the reader — so that the praxis in question is, via one last self-referential chiasmus, bent back upon the poem itself, as if the latter's virtuosic language, its *Wandlung,* were already the *vita nuova* impending. The open frailty, even unlikelihood, of this, however, undermines its inevitable deceit. As Adorno wistfully wrote, looking back at modernism: "Das Neue ist die Sehnsucht nach dem Neuen, kaum es selbst, daran krankt alles Neue."[82] These distortions of the poetic subject illustrate both the historic signature of a logics of disintegration and also the chance at a looser, less disciplinary form of subject. The perverse woundedness of Rilke's poetic bears witness to just this paradox.

Notes

[1] Nina Lübbren, *Rural Artists' Colonies in Europe, 1870–1910* (New Brunswick, NJ: Rutgers UP, 2001), 97.

[2] Adorno, *Ästhetische Theorie, Gesammelte Schriften* 7, 101–2.

[3] Simon Schama, *Landscape and Memory* (New York: Alfred Knopf, 1995), 16.

[4] Ernst Bloch, *Literarische Aufsätze* (Frankfurt: Suhrkamp 1984), 447.

[5] Adorno, *Negative Dialektik, Gesammelte Schriften* 5 (Frankfurt: Suhrkamp 1997), 202.

[6] Adorno, *Ästhetische Theorie, Gesammelte Schriften* 7, 404.

[7] Lübbren, *Rural Artist's Colonies,* 85.

[8] On the fictional aspects of the book, see David Reynolds, "'Es handelt sich hier um Werdende': The Fiction of the Artist in Rilke's *Worpswede,*" *Seminar* 35:1 (1999): 55–68.

[9] Rilke, "Worpswede," *Werke in 4 Bänden* (Frankfurt: Insel 1996), 4:307.

[10] See for instance the description of the facelessness of the inhabitants of Paris (*Die Aufzeichnungen des Malte Laurids Brigge, Werke* 3:457–58).

[11] Friedrich Schiller, "Die Götter Griechenlands," first version (*Sämtliche Werke in 5 Bänden* [Munich: Hanser, 2004], 1:166). Compare Hegel's commentary (*Ästhetik,* II. Teil [Frankfurt: Suhrkamp, 1970], 114). This nostalgia for *saturnia regna* may be dated back to Virgil or even Hesiod.

[12] How much more concrete was, by contrast, Goethe's unfinished essay "Landschaftliche Malerei" of 1818 (*Werke*, Hamburger Ausgabe [Munich: DTV, 1998], 12:216–23).

[13] On the relation of *Naturgeschichte* and *histoire naturelle*, cf. Foucault, *Les mots et les choses* (Paris: Gallimard, 1966), 288; also Lepenies, *Das Ende der Naturgeschichte* (Munich: Hanser, 1976). An earlier and shorter essay of Rilke's from 1902, titled *Von der Landschaft* (*Werke in 4 Bänden*, [Frankfurt: Insel 1996], 4:208–13), embeds the genre in a historical *grand récit* that *Worpswede* omits; the first paragraphs are a recapitulation of *Über naïve und sentimentale Dichtung*, and Rilke's reading of "die christliche Kunst" anachronistically recalls the educational system preceding Kittler's "discourse network" of 1800, where *Buchstaben* had as yet no *Geist* (ibid., 209).

[14] On *Kulturlandschaft*, see Adorno, *Ästhetische Theorie*, 101.

[15] Hegel, *Ästhetik* III, *Werke* 15 (Frankfurt: Suhrkamp 1970), 60. This subjectivization of nature was the very condition by which Ruysdael could be, for Goethe, a *Dichter* (*Werke*, Hamburger Ausgabe [Munich: DTV: 1998], 12:138–42).

[16] Charles Darwin, *The Origin of Species* (Harmondsworth: Penguin, 1985), 172.

[17] So Darwin, *Origin of Species*, 132–33.

[18] "Pour être un père . . . il y a assurément des choses qu'il faut ferocément ignorer" (Lacan, *Le Séminaire XVII: L'Envers de la psychanalyse* [Paris: Seuil, 1991]: 157).

[19] Elsewhere Rilke writes of nature's "erhabene Gleichgültigkeit (welche wir Schönheit nennen)" (*Worpswede*, 315): in this last phrase one hears anticipated the beginning of the first Duino Elegy.

[20] On this, see T. Rittmeester, "Heterosexism, Misogyny and Mother-Hatred in Rilke Scholarship: The Case of Sophie Rilke-Entz," *Women in German Yearbook* 6, ed. J. Claussen and H. Cafferty (Lansdale, MD: UP of America, 1991); also "Rilke und die namenlose Liebe: Eine vorläufige Bestandaufnahme," in *Rilke-Rezeptionen/Rilke Reconsidered*, ed. S. Bauschinger and S. Cocalis (Tübingen: Francke, 1995), 201–14. Compare the discussion of this frustration in the previous chapter (in the context of Lang's *Metropolis*). As will become evident, the present essay sketches in a less definite place for Rilke does Rittmeester, who claims him for gay identity.

[21] "So sind Beispiele der Gängelwagen der Urteilskraft" (Kant, *Kritik der Urteilskraft*, *Werkausgabe*, ed. Weischedel [Frankfurt: Suhrkamp, 1976], 3:185).

[22] Rilke, *Werke*, 2:234.

[23] Rilke's dying Nature might be seen in relation to the *fin-de-siècle* fantasy of aestheticized dead women (cf. Elisabeth Bronfen, *Over Her Dead Body: Death, Femininity and the Aesthetic* [Manchester, UK: Manchester UP, 1992]).

[24] Rilke, *Werke*, 1:260.

[25] Kittler, *Discourse Networks 1800/1900* (Stanford: Stanford UP 1990), 199.

[26] Thus an early poem of Oskar Loerke is significantly titled "Unterm Schwesternamen" (Loerke, *Die Gedichte* [Frankfurt: Suhrkamp, 1984], 22); Gerhard Neumann has read this poem in the context of the escape from the Name of the Father which Deleuze and Guattari saw in Kafka ("Einer ward Keiner: Zur

Ichfunktion in Loerkes Gedichten," *Marbacher Loerke-Kolloquium 1984* [Mainz: Hase und Koehler, 1986], 223). Rilke's Girls are thus part of a larger phylogenetic shift in family codes.

[27] Heidegger, *Der Ursprung des Kunstwerkes* (Stuttgart: Reclam 1982), 12.

[28] Worpswede diary, quoted in Stefan Schank, *Rainer Maria Rilke* (Munich: DTV, 1998), 59. The identification with girls is evident also in "Mädchen-Klage," from the *Neue Gedichte*, where the girl of the title suffers from Malte's phobia: "Plötzlich bin ich wie verstoßen, / und zu einem Übergroßen / Wird mir diese Einsamkeit" (Rilke, *Werke*, 1:450).

[29] Helen Sword, *Engendering Inspiration: Visionary Strategies in Rilke, Lawrence and H.D.* (Ann Arbor: Michigan UP, 1995), 34. Sword's interesting investigation of "the gender dynamics" of Rilke's poetics finds them often "almost hopelessly complex" (36); since so much of gender definition is in fact composed of *imaginary fantasy*, the present attempt at a *structural description* of the poetic subject may serve to complement Sword's essay.

[30] Lacan, *Sém. IV*, 385, 338, 414, my emphasis.

[31] So Alkestis says of herself: "Ich bin Ersatz" (Rilke, *Werke*, 1:505).

[32] Freud, "Die Verneinung"; "Fetischismus"; "Die Ichspaltung im Abwehrvorgang" (all in Freud, *Studienausgabe* [Frankfurt: Fischer, 1970], vol. 3).

[33] In Heidegger's words again: "Insofern das Offene von Rilke als das Ungegenständliche der vollen Natur erfahren ist, muß sich ihm dagegen und in der entsprechenden Weise die Welt des wollenden Menschen als das Gegenständliche abheben" ("Wozu Dichter?" 268).

[34] "Fading" is the subject's disappearance in every speech act (*énoncé*), which opens up a diachronic moment in the subject (Lacan, *Écrits* [Paris: Seuil, 1966], 835). Speech acts inevitably leave an unexpressed remnant behind, which is retrospectively felt as precedent to speaking. (It is bound up with what Lacan terms alienation, the subject's failure in the face of the Other's demand; and it is followed by separation, Freud's *Ichspaltung*; cf. Lacan, *Le Séminaire XI: Les Quatre concepts fondamentaux de la psychanalyse* [Paris: Seuil 1973], chapters 16–17).

[35] Goethe, "Auf dem See," *Werke*, Hamburger Ausgabe (Munich: DTV, 1998), 1:102.

[36] David Wellbery, *The Specular Moment* (Stanford: Stanford UP, 1996), 51. This chiastic process of generating lyric identity will be discussed again in chapter 3.

[37] For an individual "depth-psychological" reading — which the present chapter is *not* attempting, although it has often been undertaken with Rilke — the most telling material would be the odd sexual imagery of the last poems of the *Stunden-Buch*.

[38] Wellbery, *Specular Moment*, 71.

[39] Compare a psychoanalytic formulation in Fink, *Lacanian Subject*, 53–54.

[40] In the same sense, then, as the translation of Lacan's *manque-à-être* as "wanting to be."

[41] Rilke, *Sämtliche Werke* (Frankfurt: Insel, 1955), 2:240 (cited in R. Eppelsheimer, *Rilkes larische Landschaft* [Stuttgart: Verlag Freies Geistesleben, 1975], 27).

[42] Elegiac narrative may thus here be understood in Yuri Lotman's sense (in *Die Struktur literarischer Texte*, trans. R.-D. Keil [Munich: Fink, 1972]) as the crossing over of the topographic and semantic.

[43] Ernst Bloch, "Herbst, Sumpf, Heide und Sezession," *Literarische Aufsätze* (Frankfurt: Suhrkamp, 1984), 439–47; Thomas Koebner, "Der Garten als literarisches Motiv: Ausblick auf die Jahrhundertwende," in *Park und Garten im 18. Jahrhundert* (Munich: Winter, 1978), 144.

[44] This passive surrender to thinghood may be implicitly one to violence also, as in "Der Schauende": "ließen wir, ähnlicher den Dingen, / uns *so* vom großen Sturm bezwingen, — / wir würden weit und namenlos" (Rilke, *Werke*, 1: 332).

[45] "Herbst" and "Strophen" (*Werke*, 1:282–83, 288); *Matt.* 10:29.

[46] Rilke, *Werke*, 1:286.

[47] That the poem is dated to 1900 shows that the Rilkean development sketched here is no genetic, linear-teleological "maturation," but rather a process of selection from various coexisting poetic possibilities; the ideal scale along which poems may be arranged does not strictly coincide with temporal sequence.

[48] Rilke, *Werke*, 1: 257.

[49] De Man comments on this poem in his Rilke essay (39); from a viewpoint different from Lacan's, he also rejects ideas of subjective "projection" onto the "real": "The notion of objects as containers of a subjectivity which is not that of the self . . . is incomprehensible so long as one tries to understand it from the perspective of the subject" (37).

[50] Rilke, *Werke*, 1: 583–84.

[51] Heidegger, "Wozu Dichter?," 15.

[52] Rilke, *Werke*, 1: 167.

[53] Adorno, *Ästhetische Theorie*, 352.

[54] Lacan, *Écrits* (Paris: Seuil, 1966), 9.

[55] On this, see Andreas Huyssen, "Paris/Childhood: The Fragmented Body in Rilke's *The Notebooks of Malte Laurids Brigge*," in *Modernity and the Text*, ed. David Bathrick and Andreas Huyssen (New York: Columbia 1989), 113–41. One might suggest alternatives to Huyssen's reading of Malte's trauma before the mirror: the knocking over and smashing of glass recalls Helen Keller's smashing her doll just prior to her entry into the Symbolic, which R. Boothby has seen as a form of castration (*Death and Desire* [New York/London: Routledge, 1991], 156–57). Huyssen reads Malte through Mahler and Klein's "pre-Oedipal"; the present essay's preference for the fetish, if not normalizing, nonetheless cannot avoid reference to Oedipal structures.

[56] Rilke, *Die Aufzeichnungen des Malte Laurids Brigge* (Frankfurt: Suhrkamp, 1978), 527; compare Huyssen's discussion of this and similar passages in "Paris/Childhood," 125–28; a similar passage also in Kittler, *Discourse Networks*, 321.

[57] On this, see *Rilke, The Alchemy of Alienation*, ed. Frank Baron, Ernst S. Dick, Warren R. Maurer (Lawrence: Regents Press of Kansas, 1980); David Kleinbard, *The Beginnning of Terror* (New York: New York UP), 1995; Friedrich Loock,

Adoleszenzkrise und Identitätsbildung: zur Krise der Dichtung in Rainer Maria Rilkes Werk (Frankfurt/New York: P. Lang), 1986.

[58] So the earlier poem on God as Ball had had it: "Dort hätte ich gewagt, dich zu vergeuden" (1966: 21).

[59] Compare the criticisms of Adorno (*Jargon der Eigentlichkeit, Gesammelte Schriften* 6, 468–69) and Wellbery ("Zur Poetik der Figuration beim mittleren Rilke: Die Gazelle," in *Zu Rainer Maria Rilke*, ed. Egon Schwarz [Stuttgart: Klett, 1983], 132), which point out that a process of artificial linguistic invention is being here passed off as metaphysical or natural.

[60] That place (*Stelle*) is literally empty, the object's absence and negation taking its place, recalling the vacancy of psychoanalysis's transitional object, "qui n'est en fait que la présence d'un creux, d'un vide, occupable ... par n'importe quel objet" (Lacan, *Sém. XI*, 201; cf. also *Sém. VII*, chapters 9 and 10, on this void in the object).

[61] The Roman Campagna, home to the painterly Uncanny of Poussin, was in Antiquity a border zone both religious and political (since it impinged on culturally distinct peoples whom Rome had prolonged difficulty in dominating, among them the Etruscans, mentioned in the Eighth Duino Elegy); Rilke does not make this explicit. (The present reading arrives at diametrically opposed conclusions to those of Eppelsheimer, *Rilkes larische Landschaft*, 61.)

[62] Rilke, *Werke*, 1: 549.

[63] Adorno, *Ästhetische Theorie*, 102.

[64] Paul de Man, *Allegories of Reading* (New Haven: Yale UP, 1979), 40.

[65] "Das Begehren des dichterischen Subjekts richtet sich nach etwas, das es nicht erreichen kann" (Wellbery, "Zur Poetik," 127).

[66] Hegel, *Ästhetik* I (Frankfurt: Suhrkamp, 1986), 433.

[67] Lacan, *Sém. VII*, 155. One might read this also as the *Leerstelle* familiar from reader-reception theory, e.g. Iser.

[68] Cf. Emily Apter and William Pietz *Fetishism as Cultural Discourse*, ed. E. Apter and W. Pietz (Ithaca: Cornell UP, 1993); more carefully argued, but still open to contestation, is Joel Whitebook, *Perversion and Utopia* (Cambridge: MIT, 1995).

[69] Lacan, *Le Séminaire VIII: Le Transfert* (Paris: Seuil, 1991), 43.

[70] *Sém. IV*, 378; compare *Sém. III*, 91, 226. In this, Lacan follows Freud's idea that Oedipus is the motor of history ("Die Psychologie des Gymnasiasten," *Studienausgabe*, vol. 4, 1970). This is backed by Jacques-Alain Miller's reading of perversion ("On Perversion," in *Reading Seminars I and II*, ed. R. Feldstein, B. Fink, and M. Jaanus [Albany: SUNY 1996], 306–20; here 308): "perversion is, in no sense, a subversion."

[71] Mallarmé, *Oeuvres complètes* (Paris: Gallimard, 1945), 49: in the last lines, John's severed head "penche un *salut*," meaning at once a greeting and salvation; this theological dimension conceals artifice less than Rilke's "ganz Natur." (Charles Bernheimer describes John's head as also a fetish: cf. "Fetishism and Decadence: Salome's Severed Heads," in Apter and Pietz, 71.)

[72] Kristeva, *Revolution in Poetic Language*, trans. M. Waller (New York: Columbia, 1984), 226.

[73] "La mort du père, pour autant qu'elle fait écho . . . à cette bonne nouvelle, que Dieu est mort, ne me paraît pas, loin de là, de nature à nous libérer" (Lacan, *Sém. XVII*, 138).

[74] De Man, *Allegories of Reading*, 45.

[75] For an alternative view, see Neil H. Donahue, "Fear and Fascination: Rilke's Use of Georg Simmel in *The Notebooks of Malte Laurids Brigge*," *Studies in 20th Century Literature* 16: 2 (Summer 1991): 197–219.

[76] Adorno, *Ästhetische Theorie*, 172.

[77] Rilke, *Werke*, 1: 513.

[78] Trans. C. F. Macintyre, *Rilke: Selected Poems* (Berkeley: U of California P, 1957), 93.

[79] Cf. Lacan, *Sém. III*, 313, on the "relation which exists between the superego, which is nothing else than the function of the *thou*, and the sentiment of reality." "If the subject does not doubt what it hears, this is in function of this character of strange body presented by the delirious *thou*."

[80] On the key function of the negation (*ne*) as implying the instance of the "sujet de l'énonciation," see Lacan, *Écrits* (Paris: Seuil, 1966), 800–801.

[81] Carsten Strathausen, *The Look of Things: Poetry and Vision around 1900* (Chapel Hill, NC: U of North Carolina P, 2003), 228.

[82] Adorno, *Ästhetische Theorie*, 55.

3: Nature on Stage: Gottfried Benn — Beyond the Aesthetics of Shock?

THAT THE PLEASURES OF NATURE may have been, in the German case, guilty ones was overtly acknowledged in Gottfried Benn's *Morgue und andere Gedichte* (1912). This first published collection, which established his literary reputation straightway, begins with a famously sardonic burial of a little aster inside a human corpse during an autopsy.

> Ein ersoffener Bierfahrer wurde auf den Tisch gestemmt.
> Irgendeiner hatt ihm eine dunkelhellila Aster
> Zwischen die Zähne geklemmt.
> Als ich von der Brust aus
> unter der Haut
> mit einem langen Messer
> Zunge und Gaumen herausschnitt,
> muss ich sie angestossen haben, denn sie glitt
> in das nebenliegende Gehirn.
> Ich packte sie ihm in die Bauchhöhle
> zwischen die Holzwolle,
> als man zunähte.
> Trinke dich satt in deiner Vase!
> Ruhe sanft,
> kleine Aster![1]

> [A drowned beerwagon driver was loaded onto the dissecting table.
> Someone had stuck a darkly bright lilac aster
> Into his teeth.
> When I, proceeding up from the chest
> Cut out his tongue and gums
> From under his skin
> With a long knife,
> I must have bumped into the flower, for it slipped
> Into the neighboring brains.
> I packed it into his belly
> Between wood shavings,
> when we sewed him up.

> Drink deeply in your vase!
> Rest in peace,
> Little aster!]

The Blue Flower of Romantic Nature is here ritually laid to last rest, together with the subject of humanist autonomy revealed as dissected anatomy, all to the ironized tones of an implicitly liturgical ceremoniousness: the concluding invocation, *Ruhe sanft, / kleine Aster!* invoking the words of the *Requiem*. Irony and artifice are here inseparable; nature, at least to the classicising aesthetic of the later nineteenth century, was not known for its humor.

The shock of these poems immediately made Benn's name; yet *Morgue* was more than a frontal attack on the poetics of nature that had been in effect since the Classic-Romantic period. For the deeper irony of *Morgue* is that there is, ultimately, no escape from poetic language, and thus from the imperative of self-reference: the humor of the poems, their sarcastic evocation of theological *topoi* of earthly transience and vanity, ends up by re-integrating their grotesque and shocking imagery and narratives of death and its cynical dissection into a poetics of parody. As we know since Freud, humor may often have a paradoxically sublimating function.[2] Benn's sick jokes here oscillate between a sublimating bravado and that ambivalence of black humor later beloved of André Breton.[3] Even the most disruptive images cannot help being re-incorporated into a larger half-ironic, half-pathetic discourse which owes as much to religion as to science. The result is a form of parodic sublime that lives parasitically off the now-clichéd metaphysics it mocks. In his irony, Benn reactivates a literary vein which had lain largely dormant since Heine. The ceremonious burial of Nature carried out in *Morgue* is thus far from unambiguous.

Like Heine, too, Benn saw himself in a tradition formed by French example. As heir to the artificial paradises of Symbolism and of George's Latinate notion of *métier*, Benn was an explicit and polemical practitioner of a poetics of self-reference,[4] continuing the movement away from older Classical and Romantic natural and experiential paradigms of lyric seen in the previous chapter's discussion of Rilke. Those paradigms had become suspect by the early twentieth century, as would be made clear in Benjamin's attack on Dilthey.[5] Most recently, Friedrich Kittler has seen Benn's work, precisely at its most radical (as in the Rönne novellas), as emblematic of the epochal displacement, after Nietzsche, of nature by technological media, and characterizes Benn's work as follows.

> Verbal transmission as neurosis, without any basis in a transcendental or creative Poet's ego; medial selection without reference to the real, to the incomprehensible background of all media . . . The word that had always reached people operates at a certain psychic reaction

threshold, which was called the discourse of nature and the nature of discourse. [Rönne's] Psychophysics does away with both of them.[6]

It is hardly surprising that Kittler should have chosen Benn as one of his patron saints, for in many ways Kittler reproduces Benn's stylistic — and above all rhetorical! — tactics within the discourse of the university. In Kittler, as in Benn, one may find a preference for grandiose historical and even anthropological "phase-models," for the deployment of an "imperative world view" via a rhetoric of crisis, and above all an "interdiscursive aesthetic imperialism,"[7] which, in Kittler's case, subjects not the political but the scientific to an aesthetic model, namely that of the sublime. For all of Kittler's anti-hermeneuticism, there is a deep hermeneutical complicity between his seeming historical "materialism" and the Nietzschean rhetoric of Benn. One can thus as little overlook the hyperbolic gesture at the root of this theoretical sublime in Kittler as one can in Benn. Not surprisingly, Kant, the originary theorist of the sublime, forms one of the chief blind spots of Kittler's history, and is disposed of hastily in *Discourse Networks*:

> Whereas Kant, a transitional figure, played the double game of lecturing on an outdated ontology and writing its critique, the new philosophy shortcircuited production and consumption. Fichte accomplished an act as revolutionary as that of Faust. Realizing that reading and particularly lecturing can indeed be tiresome, Fichte did not base his first lecture source on a textbook or the work of other philosophers; rather, he lectured on his own book. (155–56)

This is simply inadequate. Did not Hegel, too, play the game of lecturing on "the work of other philosophers," specifically on the "transitional figure" of Kant? In fact, Kittler's elision of Kant from his sublimely discontinuous history allows him to rewrite that history itself under the figure of the sublime. We may here recall Kant's text:

> For this reason the pleasure of the sublime in nature is only *negative* ... namely the feeling of a deprivation of the freedom of the imagination by the imagination itself insofar as it is purposefully determined according to another law than that of its empirical use. In this way it acquires an expansion and power which is greater than that which it sacrifices, the ground of which, however, is hidden from it, instead of which it *feels* the sacrifice and the deprivation and at the same time the cause, to which it is subjected.[8]

This could also be a description of the theoretical sublime of Kittler, whose negative pleasure lies in dethroning subjectivity so that it may enjoy its own determination by the law of technological media, all the while concealing the actual ground of this pleasure — namely the continuing affective investment in sublimely enjoyed negativity.

That affective investment in the modern sublime was, in Benn's case, correlated to a poetics of depersonalization and ambivalent ego-loss (*Ich-Verlust*), and has been, appropriately enough, subjected to psychoanalytic examination.[9] What is important for the present discussion is the inherent and manic instability of this self-referential sublime, its constant alternation, right to the end of Benn's poetic career, with a depressive sense of helplessness, even a sentimental recourse to the most predictable *topoi* from the lyrical tradition, including evocations of nature in its most Goethean sense. If anything, these lapses into sentimentality increase toward the end of Benn's career (the period to which Kittler refers in his work on Benn and the radio). The omnipresent figure of irony serves less to undo this paradox than simply to contain it as a *principium stilisationis*.[10] Benn's frame of reference included not only the radio singled out by Kittler, but also, and prominently, "Rosen" and tears — which last were the common element linking "Melodien" and the persistence of nature. It would be short-sighted merely to overlook Benn's perennial outbursts of sentimentality as peripheral moments of weakness in an otherwise heroically modernist *oeuvre*, for they are in fact inseparable from the modernist fantasy of total self-reference, of aesthetic autopoiesis. Technology can never be entirely affectively neutral, as Andreas Huyssen pointed out in his rereading of Lang's *Metropolis*.[11] Technology thus cannot help but continue to bear along with it historical traces of the subjective agency on which it continues to depend. This persistence of subjectivity, albeit in a degraded and wounded form, defines Benn's relation to nature.

From Prometheus to Ariadne

The sublime configuration of *techne* and nature is represented most acutely in Benn's early work by a poem contemporary with the Rönne novellas, and which rewrites a myth central to the history of technology: "Ikarus." Unlike Joyce's victorious artificer Stephen Dedalus, Benn's Icarus is an exemplum of the ultimate unhappy conscience of artifice. With its classical associations, "Ikarus" may seem less immediately shocking, perhaps even less superficially modern than the "Morgue" poems written three years earlier. Yet it makes use of its Antique references to rewrite the tradition of lyric subjectivity in more complex fashion than did "Morgue"; to see how this is so will require a look back at its poetic predecessors. In the form most appropriate to the sublime, the ode, the poem is an answer, across almost a century and a half, to German poetry's primal scene of technological autonomy, namely Goethe's "Prometheus." And one should also keep in view a crucial intervention within the semantic field of the sublime: Nietzsche's "Dionysios-Dithyramben," which were already a rewriting of the poetics of Goethe's great odes. What follows will read Benn's poem through reference to these two key poetic predecessors.

In his exhaustive study of Goethe's early lyric, David Wellbery has shown how odes such as "Prometheus," "Mahomets Gesang," and "Harzreise im Winter" founded the "hermeneutical standpoint" of lyric humanity, narrating a "movement from the state of 'childhood' . . . to 'manhood,'" thereby configuring "the fundamental historico-philosophical schema of the Enlightenment," and even, as speech acts, themselves realizing "the emancipatory program of Enlightenment."[12] Benn's poem is located within this same poetic tradition, with its scarred and sublime landscape, its use of invocation and address, and even the daring of its neologisms (one may recall the "Knabenmorgenblütenträume" of "Prometheus"). In this, Benn's work is at the end of a long tradition of mythological rewriting that extends from Winckelmann, Karl Philipp Moritz, and the "new mythology" proposed by the *Ältestes Systemprogramm des deutschen Idealismus* (1796/7), through Schelling and Nietzsche.

Central to Goethe's odes, such as "Prometheus," is the deployment of mythic narrative as a means to establish subjective reflexivity. Myth here at once projects a program of individual autonomy which is potentially unlimited, as is *Aufklärung,* and also grounds that program in an elite knowledge, as a sensibility or taste not accessible to all.[13] This defensive moment (of myth) would remain a component part of the German lyric tradition until 1945; it is thus a key figure of German *Bildungsbürgertum.*

Parallel to this dimension of social paradox is the paradox of the poetic subject's own constitution, which both symbolically subordinates its speaker to the Law and also produces a realm of imaginary omnipotence and maternal plenitude alongside it. In other words, it socializes or acculturates while at the same time preserving (or producing) a reserved domain of "nature" for the subject. ("Nature" is thus legible both sociologically, as a trace of "irrational" aristocratic privilege and hierarchy, and psychoanalytically, as the emblem of the Mother's Voice.) The instability of this position is reflected in the theatricality and heightened rhetoric of Prometheus's position.

> The individual . . . may take itself as its point of departure. Without an adequate concept of individuality (or even of individuality that may be enhanced), the individual already finds itself outside the social order which is still to be accepted as before. It is no longer in any condition to bear that order. It emphasizes it — and also withdraws from it [. . .] stratification is now reconstructed within society as a mere assignment of roles.[14]

This combination of defiance and obedience, although arguably a common feature to (post-1789) bourgeois subjectivity, was particularly acute in the German case. If, in Luhmann's terms, this type of individual subjectivity was a "transitional semantics" serving to bridge between Old European high cultures and functional modernity, then this was a very protracted transition indeed, since it extended from the eighteenth to the early twentieth centuries. As we will see with natural law in chapter 5, such "transitional semantics" play a more important role than Luhmann often credits them with. Luhmann's concept of the "role" or of "role-playing" helps also to understand the function of Prometheus as a recoding of the artist, a recasting of the role of aristocrat as genius; the theatricality of this role will be central for Nietzsche and Benn as well. It is a further paradox of the German lyric tradition that it combines claims to intimacy (Luhmann's term) with a peculiar theatricality in staging those claims.

One of the literary and rhetorical techniques by which this process of simultaneous socialization and exclusion of the individual, of paradoxical boundary-marking and mediation between nature and culture, is accomplished, concretely, in Goethe's poem is of particular interest in the present context, namely the poem's structure of rhetorical questions which become reflexive, as do also its series of metaphors (Wellbery, 294, notes the key set *Erde, Hütte, Herd* → *Herz*). Through these self-answered questions, the poem manages to turn its lack, its fragility, into final plenitude, and to produce metaphorical master signifiers which bring its narrative to a conclusive end in the triumph of hard-won autonomy. At the same time, however, the very emphasis of Prometheus's final peroration reminds one that he has, at last, succeeded only in attaining the position of the Absolute Master himself, a position so extreme it forecloses women altogether from the act of procreation. In this, Prometheus reiterates an archaic male fantasy which will periodically return to haunt the margins of Enlightenment autonomy (cf. Hoffmann's Sand Man).

If Prometheus yet manages to enact his theatrical assumption of male autonomy, Nietzsche's poetry — which clearly situates itself as a parodic descendant of Goethe's *große Hymnen* — would seem to undo this position altogether. (The parodic moments in Nietzsche reactivate those at work in "Prometheus" itself, as Wellbery notes [324–26].) This is most especially evident in the "Klage der Ariadne," which exposes the rhetorical underpinnings of mythic subjectivity as performance.[15] Common to Nietzsche and Goethe is the rewriting of myth as a form of subjective reflexivity, as observation of observation, thus an anthropological foundation. Shared also is the long German tradition of rewriting Christian *topoi* through the allegorical mask of Hellas, suggested not only by the obvious reference to St. Paul's *agnostos theos* (Acts 17:23), but also, in the idea of the lover's midnight visit, to the Song of Songs (3:1, 5:2), and to the suffering posture of St. Sebastian or St. Teresa. The result is a subject who is almost nothing but lack and want, who cannot find a way into the symbolic without a voice from outside.[16]

[*Ariadne:*]
O komm zurück,
mein unbekannter Gott! mein *Schmerz!*
    mein letztes Glück! . . .

Ein Blitz. Dionysos wird in smaragdener Schönheit sichtbar.

Dionysos:
Sei klug, Ariadne! . . .
Du hast kleine Ohren, du hast meine Ohren:
steck ein kluges Wort hinein!
Muss man sich nicht erst hassen, wenn man sich lieben soll? . . .
Ich bin dein Labyrinth . . .

[O come back,
My unknown god! *My pain!*
    My last happiness!

Lightning. Dionysios becomes visible in emerald beauty.

Dionysios:
Be clever, Ariadne!
You have small ears, you have my ears:
Put a clever word into them!
Must people not first hate themselves, if they are to be in love?
I am your labyrinth . . .]

Described in the psychoanalytic terminology with which lyric subjectivity has often been analyzed (as in Wellbery's reading of Goethe), Ariadne might be the figure of precisely what Prometheus had to give up to attain his autonomy: a non-phallic *jouissance,* which may be available to men as well as women, and which is tied to an absence of knowledge (what Bataille would call *non-savoir,* and what Irigaray's figurative language may be reaching for as well). Thus the insistence of Nietzsche's Ariadne on her ignorance:

Wer wärmt mich, wer liebt mich noch?
[. . .]
Unnennbarer! Verhüllter, Entsetzlicher!

[Who warms me, who still loves me?
[. . .]
Unnameable one! Veiled one, fearful one!]

Unlike Prometheus, Ariadne cannot answer these (rhetorical) questions herself. Where Prometheus may still assume his own subjectivity through the device of rhetorical questions, Ariadne has hers broken open through the staged theophany of Dionysios, which bursts the confines of lyric intimacy by externalizing its "inner" ground. Ariadne has made the Unconscious God speak as Prometheus never could.

> . . . it is only from where the dear woman is whole, in other words, from the place where the man sees her, that the dear woman can have an unconscious.
> And what does it help her do? It helps her, as everyone knows, make the speaking being, who is reduced here to man, speak . . .[17]

The "specular moment" Wellbery saw at the origin of modern lyric has here been reversed: rather than a moment of seeing, of privileged control of the look, it is a moment of being given to see, almost of exhibitionism. If you see me I am whole, I can have a soul, Ariadne admits; if you speak to me, I may know my own desire. This is the opposite of the Promethean position of silencing the Other in order to assume its speech, its instance, within oneself (via introjection). Rather than acquiring the Voice of Conscience, of the internalized superego, Ariadne hallucinates her Other as a theophany. So also the question of Freud — what does Woman want? — is here, in Nietzsche's poem, addressed to the God:

> Du Blitz-Verhüllter! Unbekannter! sprich!
> Was willst du, Wegelagerer, von — *mir*? . . .
> Wie?
> Lösegeld?
> Was willst du Lösegelds?
>
> [You lightning-veiled one! Unknown one! Speak!
> What do you want, you road-bandit, of — *me*?
> What?
> Ransom?
> Why do you want ransom?]

The effect is as if we were overhearing one end of a phone conversation, since we cannot hear the God, only his quasi-analytic silence. You want ransom? Ariadne asks, presumably to ransom herself from her exile, having being abandoned by Theseus, on Naxos. Yet Ariadne does not want freedom, but rather to be possessed. She desires the very lightning Prometheus scornfully claims cannot touch him at all.

> Verlange viel — das rät mein Stolz!
> und rede kurz — das rät mein andrer Stolz!

> Haha!
> *Mich* — willst du? mich?
> mich — ganz? . . .
>
> [Demand a lot — so advises my pride!
> And be brief — so advises my other pride!
> Haha!
> You want — me? Me?
> Me — entirely?]

The place where she is possessed is the place where, in Lacan's words, Ariadne could "be whole" or "be all."[18] Ariadne is daring the God, seducing him, suggesting sexual possession to him: mere freedom would not be enough. Yet her desire is as unassuagable as the hysteric's.

Thus Dionysios appears in order to bring Ariadne back to reflectiveness, to assume her own agency as author of her desire ("sei klug!"). He is virtually in the position of the analysand's *object a*, forcing the hysteric to recognize herself in her own symptom. His attitude even approaches that of an evangelist, a bearer of the Word as *kerygma* (proclamation) — "steck ein kluges Wort hinein!" Ariadne can do this because she has herself the "small ears" of Dionysios, which implies not only cunning selectiveness, but also a form of imaginary kinship. The God may be less unknown, less unfamiliar (*unheimlich*), than she thinks.[19]

Nietzsche has here exposed the mythic foundations of poetic-lyrical subjectivity. If, as Peter Sloterdijk claimed, Nietzsche's philosophical dramatizing of history "is staged not in terms of narrative but in terms of theater,"[20] this is especially true of his poetic texts, which externalize the narrative tensions typical of myth[21] into theatricality. The theater, against which Nietzsche polemicized in his anti-Wagnerian broadsides as "feminine" and addressed to the rabble, becomes, in this poem, a means of opening up the monadological Subject of lyric. (In this preference for an *invisible* theater, Nietzsche is close to his contemporary Mallarmé and to the tradition of "closet theater" Martin Puchner[22] has seen as a constant accompaniment to modernist anti-theatricality.)

This staging of the subject has also made Ariadne into one of the patron saints of deconstructivism, most emblematically in Derrida's *Éperons*:[23] in this model, Ariadne becomes an allegory of *différance* itself, resistant to any definitive allegories, including the psychoanalytic one just sketched in.[24] In the terms of the present argument, Ariadne would become a (paradoxical) figure for the basal paradox of self-reference implied in all meaning. For Derrida, there can be no way out of this, out of the infinity of *différance*, of which Nietzsche's labyrinth must then become an allegory. Any attempt at an assignment of meaning would be liable to its eventual and inevitable deconstruction.

Kittler's reading of Ariadne merely transposes *différance* to the typewriter keyboard. The material conditions of Nietzsche's Ariadne are given as follows: "It was first necessary to write with and about typewriters; the act of writing had first to become a blind incidence from and upon a formless ground before speech could be directed toward the unanswering conditions of speech itself."[25]

What arrives at the end of Ariadne's lament is thus the direct opposite of the conclusion of Goethe's "Prometheus": where Goethe's mythic hero had moved from raw individual, material perception to socialized, symbolic communication (in Wellbery's terms, from the Imaginary to the Symbolic, Kittler 388), Ariadne breaks out of speech into pure light. The lightning of Dionysius "sends a dark and assaulting light, which transposes speech into its other medium" (Kittler 198). Little wonder that Ariadne's hallucinations anticipate Schreber's, or that she could be seen to personify McLuhan's dictum that "there is no difference between occult and technological media" (229).

The problem is that, once again, media are here, for Kittler, much less material and historical than merely another figure of the theoretical sublime. The anti-hermeneutical model here operates with typically Derridean binaries, tracing a movement from symbolic meaning (coded here by Kittler as hermeneutic, bureaucratic, and male) to a sublime, incomprehensible hallucination (coded as female). In the language of systems theory, this movement is an attempt at breakout from communication to consciousness (*Bewusstsein*).

This is less shockingly new than Kittler would like us to believe. The pathos of this impossible anti-hermeneutical sublime, shared by Nietzsche, Benn, Derrida, and Kittler, turns out to live parasitically on the very metaphysics and meaning it endlessly negates. Benjamin Marius and Oliver Jahraus have suggested a way out of this false infinity, namely by "drawing a distinction" (in Spencer-Brown's terms) into Derrida's difference yet again, this time the distinction we have just mentioned between consciousness and communication.

> Because it cannot see this distinction between consciousness and communication, thought [e.g. of deconstruction] remains attached to . . . the difference of meaning and meaninglessness. This has as a consequence that deconstruction always stays on the side of communication, but has no possibility of tying this, its own communication, its linguistic form of expression, *to anything outside of itself*.[26]

If one exposes the difference of consciousness and communication that deconstruction ignores, one arrives at the rhetorical mediality of expression, the mediality that in fact links the two. (Kittler had to elide this mediality to arrive at his anti-hermeneutical sublime.)

> Whoever speaks of consciousness and communication ... must also speak of media (and vice versa), and whoever speaks of media must speak of culture, of language and signs and (symbolic) order, also about reality and conceptions of reality ... (Marius/Jahraus, 77)

In this sentence, Marius and Jahraus summed up the direction that recent German systems theory has taken, namely a move from self- to hetero-reference (emblematized in Siegfried Schmidt's recent *Geschichten und Kulturen*). We may here take "reality and conceptions of reality" to refer to society's physical environment, the complement to its basal operation of communication.

More importantly, this reopening of the medium allows one to overcome the anti-hermeneutical sublime invented by Nietzsche and then repeated by his successors. "It is a question of not letting the movement of reflection end in an aesthetization of theory" — as in Derrida and Kittler — "but to make it productive for concrete research" (Marius/Jahraus, 77). Where Kittler had elided the material medium as a mere "formless ground" so that he could oppose meaning (or communication) and perception, man and woman in a sublime and aporetical enmity — and turn speech back onto itself in a movement of heroically endless reflection (or iteration) on its own "unanswering conditions" — a systems-theoretical approach recognizes that "media exist because both consciousness, on the one hand, and communication on the other, are both operatively closed" (Marius/Jahraus, 76) and can only be medially coupled. There is no escape from communication: meaning and reflection are thus inevitable. Unlike Kittler, Luhmann stresses that no system can be self-sufficient without meaningful couplings to its environment (to other systems). Self-reference and hetero-reference, distinction and designation, are two inseparable sides of the same coin.

Our look at Ariadne and her interpreters has shown that Nietzsche's poem indeed exposes some of the rhetorical underpinnings of both of Kittler's discourse networks: that of the Goethean subjectivity of 1800 and that of the more modern, decentered network of 1900. This does not, however, simply mean the elision of all meaning or reference in favor of "a blind incidence from and upon a formless ground." As Wellbery pointed out, the narrative process of "Harzreise im Winter" was one of a generation of symbolic metaphor on which lyric subjectivity depended: the poem proceeded from "snow-crowned peaks" to the final abstract "Altar of sweetest thanks," which omits the tenor (in I. A. Richards's terminology) in favor of a symbolic self-referentiality (Wellbery 386–88). Wellbery centrally invokes Hegel's *Phenomenology* in this discussion (368–69), for the discourse being founded here is that of modern functional poetic autonomy, as later defined by Niklas Luhmann — whom more than one recent commentator has linked to Hegel.[27] Both the "ascent" of the

"Harzreise" and of the Hegelian movement of sublation and Luhmann's favorite image of the "blind flight" (*Blindflug*) participate in the same rhetoric of ascension Bachelard described in *L'Air et les Songes*.[28] That all these ascensions to sublime meaning depend on particular rhetorical figures does not justify the anti-hermeneutical gesture of leveling them to Kittler's "formless ground," however. The deconstructive insight into this function of rhetoric needs to be worked out in careful attention to textual specifics, where historical distinctions may be uncovered.

Nietzsche may be seen to turn this movement of ascension back onto its origins in personification and prosopoia. The movement de Man read in his work, wherein metaphor is exposed as "blind metonymy"[29] (1979: 102), is found in exemplary form in Ariadne's Lament, where the "lightning" (*Blitz*) once associated with the anti-rhetorical, uncalculated spontaneity of sublime authenticity now unmasks the latter as another form of rhetoric. De Man elucidates Nietzsche's peculiar rhetoric in terms that are still useful:

> What is here [in Nietzsche's 1872–3 Basel course on rhetoric] called "language" is the medium within which the play of reversals and substitutions ... takes place. This medium, or property of language, is therefore the possibility of substituting binary polarities such as before for after, early for late, outside for inside, cause for effect, without regard for the truth-value of these structures (108).

One might add to this list the substitution of the woman Ariadne for the male Magician. We need only generalize *medium* from a "property of language" to a description of it to find here the movement sketched in by Marius and Jahraus, wherein deconstructivism "tips over" into media theory. In the media-theory terms of Luhmann, Nietzsche's poem exposes the (linguistic) medium of metonymy underlying the (meaningful) form of metaphor. If, for Kittler, Nietzsche was the "mechanized philosopher" whose work exposed the material media on which the production of meaning depended, Dionysios and Ariadne reveal the rhetorical underpinning of technology. "The word technology is to be understood here essentially, so that its meaning matches the title: the fulfillment of metaphysics."[30] Benn's retelling of the Icarus myth situates itself relative to this problem.

Anthropological Negation: "Ikarus"

In many later poems of Benn, fantasized technocratic omnipotence and a depressively helpless acquiescence in a maternally coded Nature alternate according to a static binary model stylized by irony. "Ikarus" works out this opposition in more narrative fashion, according to an underlying model of myth, which has its historical origins back in the "New Mythology" of German Idealism. This mythic narrativity (more than any simple external "natural reference"), along with the scenic and theatrical dimension this narrative entails, brings Benn's poem within the purview of *Naturlyrik*. Other poems such as "Morgue" or even the later "Palau" may work with natural imagery — as do crucial sections of the Rönne novellas. Yet their internal instability, which deliberately relativizes the natural discourse of German poetry via ironic interferences from scientific and medical discourse ("Morgue") or the system of economics (advertising, in "Palau"), prevents them from settling within the frame of nature lyric. The mythic figure of Icarus, by contrast, anthropologically grounds the narrating subject of this poem as a natural subject, a subject within nature. To do so, the poem must work with a "simultaneity of different contexts" (Wellbery 359, citing Stierle) as complex as that of "Prometheus" or the "Harzreise" — or of "Ariadne's Lament" after them. However, that situation within nature is anything but as stable as a Classical or Romantic one.

I.

O Mittag, der mit heißem Heu mein Hirn
zu Wiese, flachem Land und Hirten schwächt,
daß ich hinrinne und, den Arm im Bach,
den Mohn an meine Schläfe ziehe —
O du Weithingewölbter, enthirne doch
Stillflügelnd über Fluch und Gram
Des Werdens und Geschehns
Mein Auge.   8

Noch durch Geröll der Halde, noch durch Land-aas,
Verstaubendes, durch bettelhaft Gezack
Der Felsen — überall
Verwehn der Sonne, überall
Das tiefe Mutterblut, die strömende
Entstirnte
Matte
Getragenheit.   16

Das Tier lebt Tag um Tag
Und hat an seinem Euter kein Erinnern,
Der Hang schweigt seine Blume in das Licht
Und wird zerstört.

Nur ich, mit Wächter zwischen Blut und Pranke,
Ein hirnzerfressenes Aas, mit Flüchen
Im Nichts zergellend, bespien mit Worten,
Veräfft vom Licht —   24

O du Weithingewölbter,
Träuf meinen Augen eine Stunde
Des guten frühen Voraugenlichts —
Schmilz hin den Trug der Farben! Schwinge
Die kotbedrängten Höhlen in das Rauschen
Gebäumter Sonnen, Sturz der Sonnen-sonnen,   30
O aller Sonnen ewiges Gefälle. —

II.

Das Hirn frißt Staub. Die Füße fressen Staub.
Wäre das Auge rund und abgeschlossen,
Dann bräche durch die Lider süße Nacht,
Gebüsch und Liebe.
Aus Dir, Du süßes Tierisches,
Aus euern Schatten. Schlaf und Haar,
Muß ich mein Hirn besteigen,
Alle Windungen,
Das letzte Zwiegespräch. —

III.

So sehr am Strand, so sehr schon in der Barke,
Im krokosfarbnen Kleide der Geweihten
Und um die Glieder schon den leichten Flaum —

Ausrauscht Du aus den Falten, Sonne,
Allnächtlich Welten in den Raum —
O eine der vergeßlich hingesprühten
Mit junger Glut die Schläfe mir zerschmelzend,
Auftrinkend das entstirnte Blut —[31]

[I.
O midday, weakening with hot hay my brain
to field, flat land and herdsman,
that I flow out, my arm in the stream
I draw the poppy to my brow —
still winging over curse and grief
of growth, great arched one
de-brain my eye.
Yet through mountain scree, through dusty carrion,
through beggarly serration
of the rocks — everywhere
the passing of the sun,
the deep mother-blood, the streaming

decapitated
gestation.
Animals live day for day
And forgets the udder,
the slope holds out in silence to the light its flower
and is destroyed.
But I, with watchman between blood and claw,
brain-consumed carrion, curses
hurled in the void, bespat with words,
aped by the light —
O great arched one
let drop into my eyes one hour
of the good early light before the eyes —
melt away colors' deception, brandish
the mud-crushed lairs in the thunder
of the prancing suns, plunge of the double suns,
O all suns' ceaseless falling.

II.

The brain eats dust. So do the feet.
If the eye were round and finished,
Then there would break sweet night through the lids,
Bushes and love.
From you, you sweet animality,
Your shadow, sleep and hair,
Must I ascend my brain,
All its twists and trails,

III.

So on the beach, already in the barque,
In the crocus-colored garment of the dedicated
And already the light seam around the limbs —

You roar out of the folds, sun,
Every night worlds into space —
O one of the forgetfully sprayed-off ones
Melting my temples with young glow,
Drinking up the debrowed blood —]

"Ikarus" is a wartime poem, and contemporary with Trakl's war ode "Grodek"; one may also remember Norbert von Hellingrath's then-still-recent rediscovery of Hölderlin. But if Trakl's poem, like Hölderlin's great odes, projects its form of the sublime onto the tragedy of history, maintaining a severe and epic distance from the narrated events, "Ikarus," much like the Rönne novellas from the same period, brackets out any such topical reference to move the conflict into the narrating subject itself and its primal scenes of family prehistory.

That conflict is organized around a reworking of myth, in which the title figure is combined with evocations of Phaeton (the hippic "gebäumter Sonnen"), Orpheus's death (the final vampire-like dismemberment and sacrificial blood-drinking), and Charon (the "Barke" of part 3). Common to all of these myths is a central figure of ecstatically desired sacrifice. Mythic is also the landscape of affect, but one less "inner" (as has been maintained of Rilke, for instance)[32] than drastically and metonymically externalized: the sun uses hot hay to weaken the brain into meadow, flatland and shepherds, and the "bettelhaft Gezack" of the rocks is a metonymy for the narrator's own pleading with the sky, as the trash-hill (*Gehalde*) and carrion are for his loathed mortality. The despairing "Nur ich" of line 20 is a speaking pronoun which has not the universality of representing humanity (unlike the preceding *Gattungswesen* of "Das Tier"). The constitution of a landscape sublime does not result in any stable symbolic moral subject. Despite the dominance of the visual and the exclusion of any social reference from the absolutely isolated *Ich*, the entire poem is still a form of address or invocation, a request or demand: the long hypotactic sentences ache with an unrealizable desire closely related to Rönne's. For in the place of Prometheus's metaphorized "Herz," which condenses within it the "Herd" of patriarchal domesticity and the "Erde" of mortality, Benn's poem works rather with the same stubbornly literal bodily metononymies of the Rönne novellas (*Stirne, Schläfe*), while excluding those prose works' reference to scientific language; in fact, the entire poem extends Rönne's plaint: "he felt himself exposed to a breathless sky."[33] As in the prose-poetry of Rönne, many of the devices used in the poem are traditional for the ode and the lament; among these latter, Linda Austin lists

> the elemental "O" of trauma . . . Disconnected, halting utterance without conjunctions (asyndeton), signaling agitation or surprise; accumulating figures (anaphora and polyptoton); apostrophe; verbal condensation; and syntactical inversions (hyperbaton) . . . Paratactical lines (asyndeton), inversions, and great imagistic condensation, in addition to ejaculations and lapses in grammar . . .[34]

Yet Benn is using the classical mythic and elegiac tradition for purposes drastically opposed to those of Goethe's fundamental texts. Wellbery (295) has described the illucutionary temporality of "Prometheus," of its parodied command to the gods to try to destroy him, as follows: "Go ahead and do it! You can't hurt me." The command of Benn's Icarus, by contrast, could be summed up as: "You won't do it, even though I ask you, and therefore I can be hurt." If Prometheus's command is "a response to an antecedent threat," Icarus must face a future which will not happen because he desires it; and if Prometheus finally attains insight by discarding his earlier delusions, Icarus can find none.

This indefinite quality of the poem depends on its loose and composite formal structure, which moves from an ode-like beginning to second and third parts wherein pentameter, hints at quatrains, and even rhymes suggest an approach to forms closer to song. This formal shift itself mirrors the poem's narrative of mystic ritual integration of its main figure into a dimly implicit community, and it also recapitulates the history of German poetry from the virility of the classical sublime to the maternal dissolution of the Romantic *Lied* — thereby also seeming to look ahead to many of Benn's own later poems from the 1920s. Thus the unnamed interlocutor, the poem's *Du*, shifts from a masculine (Apollinian?) "Weithingewölbter" to the feminine associations of "süßes Tierisches," "Schatten, Schlaf und Haar" in the second part, only to return to the sun at the end.

Yet the conclusion — Icarus's resocialization, the answer to his plea — is anything but definite.[35] The very last sentence sounds like an upbeat, an appoggiatura, with its concatenation of participial verb forms (another device familiar from Rönne). The poem may restrain its structural openness by means of semantic and thematic condensation, and yet the recurrent figures of *Auge, Blut,* and *Hirn* do not settle into stable metaphors. The very last word, *Blut*, is particularly unstable, recalling the bloody flow of other Benn poems such as "Der junge Hebbel" (1913), or the *Parsifal*-like "Wunde / auf meiner Stirn" of "Mutter" (1913), or with the flowing blood Klaus Theweleit found in so many Fascist narratives.[36] "Blood is a very special juice," as *Faust*'s Mephistopheles drily noted, and Nietzsche had famously aspired to write in "blood and epigrams." What is important here is that this blood blocks the narrative production of metaphor which organized Goethe's poem; yet it does not appear to turn around on itself in the double affirmation Deleuze heard in "Ariadne's Lament" either.[37] If ever there were a "blind metonymy" (de Man), this mute blood, which both rhymes with and stops off the "young burning" (*junge Glut*) of the preceding line, is it. Like Nietzsche, Benn is here reversing the movement of sublime ascension to symbolic meaning typical of Goethe's primal scene of the lyric. The blunt literality of "blood" here is also related to the ironic debunking of the Blue Flower seen earlier in "Aster."

Similarly, if Prometheus, through his rhetorical questions, opens up a metonymic space which he himself (his own heart) will then metaphorically fill,[38] Benn's Icarus is, from the beginning, defined by weakness ("O Mittag, der mit heißem Heu mein Hirn . . . *schwächt*, / Daß ich *hinrinne*"), and thus unable to stage any narrative of hard-won reflexivity. Nor does he have the mad assurance of Nietzsche's Ariadne, who is able to arrive, by the end of Nietzsche's poem, at a hallucinatory epiphany of her desired God. In place of such a triumph, Benn's "Icarus" trails off with an uncertain dash and an implied death of the narrating subject.

With Goethe and Nietzsche, Benn shares the impulse to use myth as form of reflexivity, of self-constitution. As Wellbery noted of Prometheus, "the negation of the prior belief in an external source of support and comfort [e.g. Zeus] *enables the subject to accept its suffering as the irrefutable evidence of its own inner resources.*"[39] In Nietzsche's poem, this reversal is suggested by Dionysios's words: "Muß man sich nicht hassen, bevor man lieben soll?" Nietzsche's poem does not complete the move into symbolic, social integration as securely as does Goethe's. Icarus attains this sort of definitive self-confirmation even less. Even the opening lines of the third part, "So sehr am Strand, so sehr schon in der Barke," which imply a temporal dimension lacking in the agonized plea of the first part — and also imply that something of that plea has "already" been achieved — nonetheless seem almost to come *too soon:* "*so sehr schon,*" as if to imply: *so much already* that it cannot hold, that something must be wrong. The "so sehr" has a connotation of "however much, however already," and thus seems conditional as much as conclusive. Where Rilke's "Ball" concluded its long string of subordinate clauses with a cadential verb confirming the union of subject and object, here the conditional arrives at no conclusion at all. The process of subject formation central to the lyrical tradition is here left open-ended.

These internal tensions of the lyrical subject confronted with nature may be brought out further through a comparison with one of Benn's predecessors, Mallarmé. The peculiarity of the German classical and romantic tradition will emerge more clearly in the process.

Benn has often been grouped together with his French predecessors under the aegis of a larger shared modernity: this construct dates back, even more than to Benjamin, to Hugo Friedrich, and was not disputed by Kittler, either. Yet the differences are as significant as the common traits. Edgar Lohner[40] evoked, in connection with "Ikarus," the *Afternoon of a Faun;* but one might also contrast Benn's poem with Mallarmé's even more closely related "L'Azur,"[41] an early poem of 1864.

> De l'éternel Azur la sereine ironie
> Accable, belle indolemment comme les fleurs,
> Le poète impuissant qui maudit son génie
> A travers un désert stérile de Douleurs.
>
> Fuyant, les yeux fermés, je le sens qui regarde
> Avec l'intensité d'un remords atterrant,
> Mon âme vide. Où fuir? Et quelle nuit hagarde
> Jeter, lambeaux, jeter sur ce mépris navrant?

Brouillards, montez! Versez vos cendres monotones
Avec de longs haillons de brume dans les cieux
Que noiera le marais livide des automnes,
Et bâtissez un grand plafond silencieux!

Et toi, sors des étangs léthéens et ramasse
En t'en venant la vase et les pâles roseaux,
Cher Ennui, pour boucher d'une main jamais lasse
Les grands trous bleus que font méchamment les oiseaux.

Encor! que sans répit les tristes cheminées
Fument, et que de suie une errante prison
Eteigne dans l'horreur de ses noires traînées
Le soleil se mourant jaunâtre à l'horizon!

— Le Ciel est mort. — Vers toi, j'accours! donne, ô matière,
L'oubli de l'Idéal cruel et du Péché
A ce martyr qui vient partager la litière
Où le bétail heureux des hommes est couché,

Car j'y veux, puisque enfin ma cervelle, vidée
Comme le pot de fard gisant au pied d'un mur,
N'a plus l'art d'attifer la sanglotante idée,
Lugubrement bâiller vers un trépas obscur.

En vain! l'Azur triomphe, et je l'entends qui chante
Dans les cloches. Mon âme, il se fait voix pour plus
Nous faire peur avec sa victoire méchante,
Et du métal vivant sort en bleus angélus!

Il roule par la brume, ancien et traverse
Ta native agonie ainsi qu'un glaive sûr;
Où fuir dans la révolte inutile et perverse?
Je suis hanté. L'Azur! l'Azur! l'Azur! l'Azur!

[The serene irony of the eternal Azure,
Its languid beauty like that of the flowers,
Overwhelms the impotent poet who curses his talent
Across a sterile desert of Griefs.

Fleeing, eyes closed, I sense it watching,
With the intensity of a dreadful remorse,
My empty soul. Flee where? And cast what hostile night,
    what scraps,
On this terrible contempt?

Arise, fogs! Let your dull ashes fall
With long trails of mist in the heavens
That the pallid autumnal marsh will swallow up.
Arise and build a great silent cover over me!

And you, dear World-weariness, leave Lethe's pools
And as you come, gather their mud and pale reeds,
To block with a hand never weary
The large blue holes that the birds spitefully create.

Again! May the sad chimneys smoke without respite
And a wandering prison extinguish
In the horror of its black trails of soot
The yellowish sun, dying on the horizon!

— The sky is dead. — I run toward you! O matter,
Let this martyr who comes to share the bed
Where the contented cattle of men lie,
Forget the cruel Ideal and Sin.

For there, since in fact my brain, empty
Like the grease-paint pot lying at the base of a wall,
No longer has the skill to dress up the sobbing idea,
I want to yawn gloomily toward an obscure death.

In vain! The Azure triumphs and I hear it singing
In the bells. My soul, it gives voice to frighten us more
With its wicked victory, and
Living metal comes out as blue Angelus bells.

Ancient, it rolls across the mist, traversing
Your native agony like a sure sword;
Where can I flee in useless and perverse revolt?
I am haunted. The Azure! the Azure! the Azure! the Azure!]

Like the narrator of "Ikarus" (or Rönne), Mallarmé's poetic narrator confronts "De l'éternel Azur la sereine ironie," which stares him down as one immense Evil Eye. Although both the dramatic setting and the fundamental stance (the aphasic "experience") of the two poems are closely related,[42] Mallarmé's poem lacks the mythical primitivism, the jagged, sublime ode form, and the dialogic-appellative *Du* of Benn. Instead of the breathless stammering of Benn's hymnic parataxis, Mallarmé has retained the regularity of rhymed quatrains and the poise of the Alexandrine — a classicism as yet undisturbed (formally at least) by Nietzsche's Dionysios.

These technical differences between the two poems translate into the difference between a politics of aggression and one of identification. Unlike Benn's protagonist, Mallarmé's does not seek to go to the sacrificial, decapitating end of aphasia and panic. (For that fascination with sacrifice, French literature would have to wait until the esoteric speculations of Caillois and Bataille's *Acéphale* of the 1930s; even the decapitation of John in *Hérodiade* is calmer than this.)[43] Instead, he asks with what "nuit hagarde" or fog or smoke he could block off the inimical sky, and desires the figurative death of a descent into crude materialism, since his brain is void, incapable of producing an "idée." Unlike Benn's desperately self-decapitating Icarus, Mallarmé's narrator rebels, albeit helplessly (in a "révolte inutile et perverse"), since he understands the failure of the discursive (devoid of ordering master signifier) or of metaphor to be behind his perceptual disturbances: the aphasic hostility of the sky is still mediated by more narrative and syntactic stability than is Benn's loosely associative and paratactic figuration, mimesis of a primitivist "acting out." Yet the relative increase of seeming linguistic autonomy in Benn is paid for with a loss of autonomy for the speaking subject. The theatrical role of Icarus, unlike that of the Faun which Mallarmé would adopt soon after "L'Azur," is not one of sovereign artifice, but of agonizing failure. Benn's Icarus turns his aggression not against the sky, but against his own body, desiring to extend the voiding of the discursive, the failure of language, into the literal loss of the brain, into an imaginary biological transmutation. Icarus, like Nietzsche's hysterical Ariadne, is still enthralled unto death by the power of the sun even if it will not answer; the existence of a solar authority, however inaccessible to dialogue, is an immutable condition of the poem's Antique ode conventions. The precedent of Goethe's odes appears here as an obstacle to the process of poetic modernization.

Thus Mallarmé's sonorous Azure is the polar negation of Benn's favorite Antique-Mediterranean *blau* and *Südkomplex* (his shorthand symbolic terms for the imaginary realm of poetry): rather than supporting any fantasized investment, it is the latter's undoing. Benn, however, ends with the raw shock of sacrificial blood, deadly serious and primitively literal, devoid of Mallarmé's urbane irony. In both cases — *pace* Nietzsche — "la mort du Père . . . ne [me] paraît pas, loin de là, de nature à nous libérer"[44] (The death of the father does not seem to me liberatory — far from it). The specifically visual emphasis of the German ode tradition, even its hostility to the aural or musical element which allows Mallarmé his ironic close, seems here bound up to a stubborn attachment to paternal authority. Rather than ironize this latter, the German sublime prefers to enjoy the pathos of the sacrifice of its own (male) subjectivity.

Like Benn in the literary-historical models of Kittler and Friedrich, Mallarmé has sometimes been glossed as representing an absolute break with any poetics of nature or of referentiality. So Benjamin, in his own "monumental history" of modernity, had already understood Baudelaire.

Yet Paul de Man warned against this sort of dramatic or sublime phase-model of history precisely in the context of Mallarmé. Against Karlheinz Stierle's "assertion that a language of representation is immediately replaced by an allegorical, figurative language" in Mallarmé, he insisted that "Up to a very advanced point, not reached in this poem ["Tombeau de Verlaine," LP] *and perhaps never reached at all,* Mallarmé remains a representational poet . . ."[45]

In case the reader might object that the problematic of representation is not equivalent to that of nature, de Man then adds that "Stierle prematurely allegorized a Mallarmé who knew himself to be forever trapped in the deluding appearance of natural images" (77).

Both "L'Azur" and "Ikarus" narrate this entrapment, and it is answered by an acknowledged failure of poetic technique. Deconstructive criticism was more sensitive to this inevitable failure than media-theoretical criticism has been. As Barbara Johnson has noted, Mallarmé's final outcry of "L'Azur!" is equivalent to "cliché!" or: "I have failed to produce a fresh metaphor."[46] For all their apparent semantic opposition, Mallarmé's Azure, iterated with helpless literality, and the dull "blind metonymy" of Benn's *Blut* function similarly, namely to cut off the production of poetic meaning and to prevent the closure of self-referential artifice.

Nature as Medium

The natural sublime, of which "Ikarus" worked out the narrative and discursive tensions at extended length, appears to be condensed into a more traditionally intuitive (*anschaulich*) lyric form in "Pappel"; yet here, too, similar tensions between different aspects of the poetic inheritance are at work.

> Verhalten,
> Ungeöffnet in Ast und Ranke,
> Um in das Blau des Himmels aufzuschrein —:
> Nur Stamm, Geschlossenheiten,
> Hoch und zitternd,
> Eine Kurve.
>
> Die Mispel flüchtet,
> Samentöter,
> Und wann der Blitze segnendes Zerbrechen
> Rauschte um meinen Schaft:
> Enteinheitend,
> Weitverteilend
> Baumgewesenes?
> Und wer sah Pappelwälder?

Einzeln,
Und an der Kronenstirn das Mal der Schreie,
Das ruhelos die Nächte und den Tag
Über der Gärten hinresedeten
Süßen aufklaffenden Vergang,
Was ihm die Wurzel saugt, die Rinde frißt,
In tote Räume bietet
Hin und her.[47]

[Restrained,
Unopened in twig and vine,
In order to cry out into the sky's blue —:
Only bole, closednesses,
High and trembling,
A curve.

The medlar flees,
Seedkiller,
And when did the blessed shattering of lightning
Rush about my shaft:
Deunifying,
Widely dispersing
What was once a tree?
And who ever saw poplar forests?

Individual,
And on the brow the mark of cries,
That restless through the nights and day
Over the gardens mignonetted away
Sweet torn-open perishing,
Which sucks at its root and eats its bark,
Offering into dead spaces
To and fro.]

One of Benn's most canonical poems, "Pappel" works with many central figures from the classical tradition of *Naturlyrik,* and yet it is precisely in its traditional resonances also exceptional, compared with the rest of Benn's production from 1915 through 1917 ("Morgue," "Söhne," "Alaska," and the much-anthologized urban poems "Nachtcafé" and "D-Zug"). The poem shares its dynamics of controlled explosivity with the overtly classicizing "Karyatide," with its imperative commands:

> Entrücke dich dem Stein! Zerbirst
> Die Höhle, die dich knechtet! Rausche
> Doch in die Flur . . .

> [Wrench yourself out of the stone! Break apart
> The cave that enslaves you! Rush ecstatically
> Out into the plains . . .]

and thus is distantly related to the familiar imperatives of Rilke's Torso of Apollo to "change one's life." But the poem's resonances with poetic tradition do not end there. Recent Benn scholarship has tended to correct older readings' postulate of originality with a stress on Benn's relation to his immediate predecessors at the turn of the century;[48] this relation extends further back as well. As Luhmann has put it, "art permits observation to oscillate between astonishment and recognition,"[49] and this oscillation is central to "Pappel."

So in this poem one may find traces still of Goethe's effort at finding "ein Paar große Formeln" to give the effect of intuitive immediacy,[50] as also of the reflexive self-sufficiency characterized in "Mächtiges Überraschen,"[51] where "Ein Strom entrauscht" from its source, only to be inhibited by mountains into forming a lake in which the stars are then mirrored. The chiastic structure, by which subjectivity is figured, dates back to "Auf dem See," and becomes programmatic with "Das Sonett" and its paradigmatic combination of "Natur und Kunst."[52]

In Benn, however, heroically self-contained individuality is interrupted or displaced by ironic personification, evoking in turn another subtradition in Romantic poetry, that of Heine:

> Ein Fichtenbaum steht einsam
> In Norden auf kahler Höh.
> Ihn schläfert; mit weißer Decke
> Umhüllen ihn Eis und Schnee.[53]

> [A fir tree stands alone
> In the North on a bare peak.
> It feels drowsy; with a white blanket
> Do ice and snow surround him.]

The oscillating tension of "astonishment and recognition," Expressionist *Schrei* and restraint, traditional meter and graphic visuality,[54] involves also one between different strains in German nature poetry.[55]

All this was long subsumed under the sort of hermeneutical meaning effect which has traditionally represented itself as natural; the concluding "hin und her" would then sum up the poem's intuitive self-representation of its own internal signifying movement. But there are details, especially in the central stanza, which need to be explained more closely, most particularly the question marks.

Rhetorical questions are a familiar technique of the sublime: in "Harzreise im Winter," the question "Aber abseits, wer ist's?" marks off a sub-section within the poem and has the effect of a *mise-en-scène*, a command to the reader to see the dramatic staging of nature which is to follow. In "Prometheus," questions also play a crucial role:

> Wer rettete vom Tode mich,
> Von Sklaverei?
> Hast du nicht alles selbst vollendet
> Heilig glühend Herz?
>
> [Who saved me from death,
> From slavery?
> Did you not accomplish all yourself,
> Holy glowing heart?]

Wellbery comments that in these questions, Prometheus enacts "an initiation . . . into autonomy," reinterpreting a suffered past in "a moment of hermeneutic anagnorisis, the recognition that the heart, as the center of Promethean subjectivity, was the sole agency of the antecedent process."[56] (In psychoanalytic terms, this would be the subject's assumption of responsibility for its own desire, what Lacan would call assuming the "cause" of desire and thus subjectifying it.) This answering of the subject's own rhetorical question is a central aspect of traditional lyric structure.

The questions of Benn's poplar are, however, not so easy to read as confirmations of subjectivity. As with Goethe's Prometheus, Benn's "der Blitz segnendes Zerbrechen" evokes Zeus the Thunderer, whose destructiveness is welcomed, not defied (as in the desire for death of Nietzsche's Ariadne). If Prometheus's questions are easy to answer, with a yes or no, Benn's "When?" is less readily answered. Rhetorical questions normally assume their answer as already given. Here it is not even certain what the question is. Matters are complicated by the colon at line 10 (after "Schaft"),[57] which would imply that "wann" is not a question, but an assertion. "And when lightning rustled its blessed shattering around my shaft: [was it] de-unifying, wide-strewing, what was a tree?" That is, through the colon, the question becomes not when did this happen, but rather: was it de-unifying and wide-strewing, and was it ever a tree in the first place? Was I a tree, asks the personified narrator, as if after death, or at least an Ovidian metamorphosis.

The next line, "Und wer sah Pappelwälder?" is the shortest sentence in the entire poem, and the most syntactically regular. It has been traditionally read as an evocation of heroic Expressionist solitude — poplars do not congregate in forests — and yet the rhetorical question implies the answer: no one. The absence of observer links up with, and strengthens, the negation of the tree's existence in the previous lines.

The final strophe is perhaps the most complex of all, both syntactically and semantically. The stigma (or mole) of screams offers, above the sweet gaping perishing of gardens, and in dead spaces, that which sucks its roots and eats its rind: that is, its own eventual future end, to which it gives form. To whom or what is this offering or bid (*bieten*) made? The "dead spaces" imply that even the Zeus of the second stanza, liberator via destruction, is no longer present.

If Classical and Romantic nature poetry moved through a chiastic structure of reversal transforming deprivation into gift, solitude into community, death into life, and lack into plenitude — a metaphoric process meant to imitate the internal workings of nature itself — Benn's poem, for all its symmetries, cannot effect this transformation. The impression earlier commentators had that the content had been absorbed, almost elided, is connected with this palpable inconclusiveness. This is why Buddeberg could write: "Hier von 'Metapher' zu sprechen ist im strengen Sinne kaum erlaubt" (It is strictly speaking not permissible to speak of "metaphor" here). What presents itself here as nature is thus no longer any plenitude of meaning, but rather the latter's absence. There is here no enigmatic Romantic "Rauschen," none of Trakl's musicality, no metalinguistic horizon implied. The graphic presentation of the poem, in contradistinction to any lullingly melodious *Lied*-form or *Knittelvers* (used, for instance, in the famous "Gesänge"), insists on being read literally, unmetaphorically. The telegraphic shortness of most of the poem's lines is an almost gestic interruption. The appearance of the poplar is thus defined by its non-belonging to any larger natural context, its splitting away from a hermeneutical relation of part to whole.

It would be too simplistic, however, merely to cut the Gordian knot here and assert that the poplar is no more than allegory for poetic self-reference, and nature merely a nostalgic mask. Self-reference and unnatural artifice are thematized much more overtly in other poems of the period such as "Reise" (1916), "Synthese" (1917), or "Strand" (1920); in fact, the tactic of absolutizing the "Ich-Begriff" and the "astrales Monoton" of sheer verbal identity was to reach its apex *after* the silence of 1917 to 1920. In poems like "Dynamik" from 1925, or "Trunkene Flut" of 1927, Benn's irony must intervene to frame what is an insoluble address. The second stanza of the Heine poem quoted earlier shifts, in accordance with Napoleon's famous dictum which Heine himself quoted elsewhere,[58] from the solitary sublime to a (ridiculously) sentimentalized topos from love poetry:

> Er träumt von einer Palme
> Die, fern im Morgenland,
> Einsam und schweigend trauert
> Auf brennender Felsenwand.

> [He dreams of a palm tree
> That, in the distant Orient
> Mourns in solitary silence
> On a burning wall of mountains.]

If Heine could already parody this Romantic topos of the solitary tree, one wonders how Benn could take it seriously a half century later — as many commentators have implied by overlooking the irony here.[59] So the second stanza of Benn's poem seems almost embarrassed by the Expressionist heroism of its opening, and deflates its own bathetic pretension with deliberately wisecracking exaggeration and even an element of absurdity (what Adorno called *das Alberne*). The tone of "Und wer sah Pappelwälder?" has something improbable about it. Benn's poplar thus stands right at the crossroads of the modern revision of the sublime.

> Wird jedoch Geist selber auf sein natürliches Maß gebracht, so ist in ihm die Vernichtung des Individuums nicht länger positiv aufgehoben. Durch den Triumph des Intelligiblen im Einzelnen, der geistig dem Tod standhält, plustert er sich auf, als wäre er, Träger des Geistes, trotz allem absolut. Das überantwortet ihm der Komik.[60]

The theatricality of Benn's poplar, which undoes the myth of traditional lyrical *Innerlichkeit* by exposing its primal scene, carries out just this (tragi)comedy. Hegel had seen early on this hidden theatricality of lyric subjectivity:

> The less the lyrical material and content has autonomy and objectivity for itself — being, on the contrary, primarily inward and only rooted in the subject as such, while it still needs an external anchor for its communication — the more it demands a decisive outwardness for its delivery. Because it remains inward, it must become externally more exciting.[61]

Benn's poem continually refers to this performative externalizing with unanswerable questions, its imagery of emptiness, of a central void: "Enteinheitend," "aufklaffend," "tote Räume," and even the final endless oscillating "hin und her."

Here we may refer again to the distinction of medium and form already mentioned in the discussion of Nietzsche. Luhmann has referred to this in the specific context of representations of nature circa 1900:

> Where the severity of the intervention in nature (Cézanne's railway cutting) is shown and contextualized in nature, then nature itself can become a medium by making apparent that technology is one (but only one) of its possibilities. In contrast to everyday primary experience nature is dissolved into elements that can be differently com-

bined, and for this reason it is exposed (but not completely) without resistance to the intervention of technology and also art. In its own way modern science has discovered nature as a medium for the intervention of theories: as a medium that is open to different (but not arbitrary) possibilities of synthesizing.[62]

Careful qualifying parentheses differentiate Luhmann's soberly theoretical discourse from the sublime neo-Nietzschean aestheticization of Kittler. (Cézanne is the artist on whom Lyotard had called as a chief witness for his conception of the technological sublime.) Luhmann is most likely thinking of Cézanne's 1870 painting "La tranchée du chemin de fer" (The Railway Cutting), in the Neue Pinakothek in Munich: hardly one of the artist's better-known works. Cézanne's painting is a remarkably American landscape, showing a path slashed brutally through a hill in the manner of American highways that do not follow any well-worn cart-tracks or lay of the land.[63] In this sense the painting portrays a traumatized landscape. (So André Breton had already seen Cézanne in *L'Amour fou:* as a painter of traumatic "halos" or auras attached to nature.)[64]

Benn's poplar, like Cézanne's railway cutting, depicts the exposure of nature as a medium. Instead of concealing the old hermeneutical paradox of "the individualized generality" (Manfred Frank), that is, the individual who is also a representative of nature, Benn's poem makes this paradox external and theatrical in unresolvable, unanswerable questions. "And who saw poplar forests?" means also: the medium of nature is, like all media, unobservable except through the specific forms of history. Kittler's idea that Benn's poetic was one of "medial selection without reference to the real" (see the first section of this chapter) is applicable only to a part of Benn's production. As Luhmann shows, the "cuttings" of technology are not completely arbitrary, and this is as true of the neuronal "breaching" or "clearing" (*frayage, Bahnung*)[65] of Freud's 1895 *Project* as it is of Cézanne's railway cuttings in the landscape. *Écriture* does not, cannot, take place in a void any more than Ariadne's speech could refer only to a "formless ground." Benn's paradoxical and impossible poplar forest occupies here the place of the Dionysian labyrinth in Nietzsche's poem. As in Nietzsche, the poplar forest marks a "blind metonymy" ("who saw . . ."), or the impossibility of any transcendent metaphor of meaning, but (again paradoxically) within nature itself.

So also Mallarmé's Faun had been "preoccupied with the relationship between the real tree and the metaphorical tree" of his meaning, in Hans-Jost Frey's commentary.[66] Frey continues: "The Faun is the tree that becomes the metaphor of the horror of man faced with the opaqueness of meaningless nature" (148). We have seen this same horror already in Rilke's Symbolist *Worpswede,* where solitude in nature was compared with that of a corpse. Frey continues: "Mallarmé's Faun is the suspense between tree and man. He is the relationship between nature and man in language.[. . .] The Faun has neither ceased to be a tree nor has he become man, but he is the tree that has become man's language" (148–49).

The Faun is also the mute, prelinguistic "solicitation" (Lacan) of nature towards language, or the "propping" (Freud's *Anlehnung*) of language on nature, as proposed in the first chapter of this book. Just as, in de Man's deconstructive allegory (or, for that matter, Derrida's ever-incompleted escape from metaphysics), representation can never be entirely elided from modernist artifice, neither can a painful kernel of nature. The poetics of unattainable self-reference will thus have to circle around this inelidable natural trace. As Mallarmé and Nietzsche did before him, Benn puts Nature on stage as a means to dramatize this problem. At precisely the moment when Expressionist theatre banishes reference to nature as external scene,[67] the poetry of nature must become theatrical.

The later Benn, in contrast, will attempt to close off this wounded fragility with a New Mythology of the Technocratic Absolute Subject, an "armored character" translating, in terms of concrete poetic practice, into routine gestures of ironic sentimentality and an updated version of *Gedanken-* or *Weltanschauungslyrik*. This returns us to our opening problematic of the theoretical sublime. Is it an accident that Kittler bases his argument for Benn's dependency on radio, for the entirely self-referential artifice of his work, on some of Benn's worst poems?[68] In his discussion of two versions of a poem, "Schöpfung" (1929) and "Ein Wort" (1941), Kittler sees the later version as due to wartime radio technology's having replaced nature as source of poetic production. On the second strophe, Kittler comments that it is a "lyrical anticipation of a radio voice, whose completely unnatural, namely discrete on- and off-switching pleases memories once again with their recently discovered Zeigarnik effect" (122–23). The disproportion between the grandiose rhetorical claims made by Kittler's interpretation and the actual literary quality of lines like the following is, however, unintentionally comical:

> Ein Wort — ein Glanz, ein Flug, ein Feuer,
> ein Flammenwurf, ein Sternenstrich —
> und wieder Dunkel, ungeheuer,
> im leeren Raum um Welt und Ich.[69]

> [A word — a gleam, a flight, a fire,
> a flame-throw, a falling star —
> and again darkness, monstrous,
> in the void space around world and I.]

Kittler reads topical wartime references into "Flammenwurf" and "Chiffre," although they are in fact familiar *topoi*. The Zeigarnik effect (disovered in 1927) is the psychological phenomenon of unfinished tasks remaining in the memory longer than completed ones, one well known in broadcast media. Evidently Kittler thinks the dashes and list of apposite nouns ("gleam, flight, fire, flame-throw, star-line") are a Zeigarnik effect interrupting the sentence. One might as easily see them as an instance of the rhetorical device of apposition, however, and the dash was not precisely invented by Benn or connected to the radio. Kittler's citing of the Zeigarnik effect only continues Benn's own fondness for the novelty value of technical terms: it is an aesthetic device, not analytically illuminating. The self-reference of "Sternenstrich" back to the poem's own *Gedankenstriche* (dashes) is in fact neo-Romantic, and links the poem back to an aesthetic of autonomy rather than war technology. But there is nothing metrically or syntactically complex or rich about this poem; its limping *Knittelvers* and monotonous iambs are little more than a convenient scheme on which to hang the images.

So, too, Bernhard Dotzler, in a recent article on Benn's relation to the media, astonishingly asserts that "Chopin" is Benn's "most beautiful poem."[70] The banal sentimentality of both thought and form in "Chopin" hardly support this:

> Wer je bestimmte Präludien
> von ihm hörte,
> sei es in Landhäusern oder
> in einem Höhengelände
> oder aus offenen Terrassentüren
> beispielsweise aus einem Sanatorium,
> wird es schwer vergessen.[71]
>
> [Whoever has heard certain
> Preludes of his,
> whether in country houses or
> on a high terrain
> or from open terrace doors,
> for example, from a sanatorium
> will not easily forget them.]

Benn's lines, flat, shapeless, and as clichéd as the "Lyrik für Leser" of the 1970s[72] are little more than a blank assertion ("Whoever heard . . . won't forget"). Nothing is said about Chopin's music in itself, which is left unspecified ("certain preludes"), but only about the occasional locations where it may have been heard, about Benn's un-objectified and arbitrary reaction to it, which may as well be attached to pure kitsch like Sibelius's *Valse triste* (as it is in "Melodien").[73] The most important line is the mawkish *pointe* of "beispielsweise aus einem Sanatorium," referring not to the music but to Nietzsche's condition of the suffering person, a "condition ... in which one cannot hear music without crying" (*Morgenröte* no. 114). Chopin is here functionalized as Muzak for the poet's self-staging. An encomium to Chopin — a composer beloved of governesses and salons, and a favorite kitsch emblem of genius's tragic mortality (as in the Hollywood weepie *A Song to Remember,* exactly contemporary with Benn's poem) — is less emblematic of modernity than its sentimental complement. Benn's poem is second-hand *Stimmungslyrik.* One wonders why a media-theoretical approach must deafen one to questions of poetic quality. Kittler's own odd sentimental affection for the adolescent lyrics of Pink Floyd would strengthen such a suspicion. Here Karl Kraus's famous critique of Heine's "kleinen Witz der kleinen Melancholie" and second-hand imagery acquires a new applicability, for Benn's weaker poems exemplify just that "Einkleiden fertiger Stimmungen" (re-clothing of readymade moods) Kraus found in Heine.[74]

Against the generalizing tendency to subsume all modern poetry from Baudelaire to Celan under blanket categories, which is palpable in Kittler's ongoing reference to Hugo Friedrich, one should insist on specific distinctions within modernity, here within different stages of Benn's own career. After about 1920, Benn brings the anarchic verbal inventions of his earlier period back into the sing-song *Knittelvers* and *Liedform* he had earlier parodied.[75] Little wonder these later poems were such an immediate "hit" (Kittler's word) with German readers. The absolute subject of the technological sublime turns out, in terms of concrete poetic quality, to be merely a rehashing of old *topoi* of *Innerlichkeit,* which is why technocracy is so easily married, in Benn (and not only in Benn), to the old lofty apoliticism of German poetry.

Such lofty apoliticism is echoed in Kittler's own "technocratic" reading of Benn, with its emphasis on the later work, and even on later revised versions of earlier poems. Yet in place of Kittler's preference for the later, revised versions of Benn's poems, many other writers have seen greater freshness and spontaneity in the first published variants.[76] Kittler's preference aligns him with the first "Benn Renaissance" of the 1950s, and not by chance.[77] The 1950s were also the epoch of Concrete Poetry, the first programmatic and collective attempt by German literature to come to terms with real existing communications media.

The preceding discussion of poems from various stages of Benn's career compels one to differentiate further Kittler's model of Benn as media poet. Such a differentiation allows one, moreover, to evaluate Benn's real poetic achievement in more sensitive and less sweeping terms. Rather than the Media Age's simply displacing all at once the Age of Goethe with Nietzsche's typewriter and Edison's inventions at the end of the nineteenth century — a model which leaves no space at all for the gradual social dissemination of technological inventions — it is more productive to stress the historical *hiatus* between liberal bourgeois humanism and the media influence on culture in the 1920s and — even more — in the 1930s. If the early Benn of Rönne, "Ikarus," and "Pappel" is indeed working within a context of medical discourses on neurasthenia (and not yet neurosis in Freud's sense), this is a very different position than that of the later mass-mediated Benn. For the early Benn, rather than simply switching over from one discourse network to another, has fallen out of his discursive representation altogether: the Rönne novellas thematize nothing else but this. The self-stylization of the 1920s, a kind of poetic *bricolage* of varying Romantic and modern *topoi*, was the style not only of the *entre-deux-guerres*, but also of an interregnum between two discourse networks, hung instably in a void. One may see this model in a poem like "Der späte Mensch" (1921), which ironically manages to naturalize history into a static and senseless cyclic panorama forbidding any rational agency.

This happens, it must be reiterated, under the aegis of the sublime — that is, precisely the stylistic principle that would be so central to Benn's grandiose constructions of history and art (as also to Kittler's after him). The sublime was indeed the one element of Classical and Romantic aesthetics that survived into modernity, albeit in transmuted form,[78] and we have seen how important it was for the constitution of the nature-lyrical subject in Goethe's odes, as also for their rewriting in Nietzsche and in Benn's "Ikarus." In its modern form, however, the sublime has an inherent tendency to veer over into either melodramatic bathos and depressiveness, or kitsch (as is evident, for instance, in cinematic melodrama and in Jameson's critique of postmodernity). Such a kitsch form is the perfect complement to sublime delusions of absolute self-reference and self-sufficient artifice. The oscillation between irony and sentimentality, sarcasm and bathos, staged public role and depressive isolation, *Artistentum* and nature would inform Benn's entire *oeuvre*; in early poems like "Poplar" it is contained in its most concise and lively form. The paradoxical quality of Benn's modernity is inseparable from its unresolvable and perennial *odi-et-amo* relation to the inheritance of *Naturlyrik*. To ignore this, reducing Benn's work to only one side of this characteristic binary opposition, is only to misread it.

Notes

[1] Gottfried Benn, "Morgue," *Sämtliche Werke* (Stuttgarter Ausgabe), ed. Gerhard Schuster in Verbindung mit Ilse Benn (Stuttgart: Klett-Cotta, 1986–2003), 1: 11.

[2] Freud, "Der Humor" (1927), *Studienausgabe* (Frankfurt: Fischer 1970), 4:275–82.

[3] André Breton, *Anthologie de l'humour noir* (Paris: Éditions de Sagittaire, 1940).

[4] Cf. Harro Müller, "Ästhetischer Absolutismus II: Gottfried Benn," in *Giftpfeile* (Bielefeld: Aesthesis, 1994), 202–20.

[5] This political context marks the crucial differences between Benn's variant of poetic autonomy and that of, say, Mallarmé before him — differences often glossed over in scholarly literature since at least Hugo Friedrich.

[6] Kittler, *Discourse Networks 1800/1900* (Stanford: Stanford UP, 1990), 243; cf. also "Benns Gedichte — Schlager von Klasse," in *Drakulas Vermächtnis* (Leipzig: Reclam 1993), 105–29.

[7] Müller, "Ästhetischer Absolutismus II," 207–12. ("Phasenmodelle," 207; "imperatives Weltbild," 210, Benn as "Krisenrhetoriker," 212; "Ästhetisierung der Politik," 209).

[8] Kant, *Kritik der Urteilskraft* (Frankfurt: Suhrkamp, 1974), 195; see Wellbery, *The Specular Moment*, 391.

[9] Among others: Oskar Sahlberg, *Gottfried Benns Phantasiewelt: "wo Lust und Leiche winkt"* (Munich: Text und Kritik, 1977); Jürgen Schröder, *Gottfried Benn und die Deutschen* (Tübingen: Stauffenburg, 1986).

[10] Within a larger European and comparativist context, this alteration reminds one of the later Verlaine, who continually played the game of alteration (*Parallèlement, Jadis et Naguère*) between modernist transgressive bad boy and born-again Catholic (Catholicism occupying, within the French tradition, the normative place taken by nature in German); this binary alternative may already be found in Baudelaire.

[11] Huyssen, "The Vamp and the Machine: Fritz Lang's *Metropolis*," in *After the Great Divide* (Bloomington: Indiana UP, 1986), 65–82, esp. 71–72: see the discussion of this in the section titled "The Anxiety of Observation" in chapter 1 of this book.

[12] Wellbery, *The Specular Moment: Goethe's Early Lyric and the Beginnings of Romanticism* (Stanford: Stanford UP, 1996), 291–93. Wellbery's study is so detailed that the present discussion will only briefly summarize some of its most salient points.

[13] I refer here to Niklas Luhmann, "Individuum, Individualität, Individualismus," in *Gesellschaftsstruktur und Semantik*, vol. 3 (Frankfurt: Suhrkamp, 1989), 149–238, esp. 200–208 on the role of aesthetics as both referring to the *Sozialdimension* of an educated elite and also undermining that caste's authority by an appeal to the intuitive, unformulable aspects of taste. This is one of the central paradoxes of German classicism. Classicism serves, in Luhmann's terms, as a *program* to specify the general code of art (see *Soziale Systeme*, 434). In Talcott Parsons's terms, one might see this as a combination of universalization and specification.

[14] Luhmann, "Individuuum, Individualität, Individualismus," 193.

[15] In Bianca Theisen's formulation, "Die Autorschaft des Dionysos, der seine Dithyramben signiert und autorisiert, bricht die bedeutungskonsolidierende Intentionalität des Performativen, der Geste des Unterzeichnens . . ." ("Die Gewalt des Notwendigen: Überlegungen zu Nietzsches Dionysios-Dithyrambus 'Klage der Ariadne,'" *Nietzsche Studien* 20 [1991]: 191).

[16] One is reminded of Irigaray's reading of Ariadne as in a state of "dereliction" relative to the symbolic, to sublimation (see *Ethique de la différence sexuelle* [Paris: Minuit, 1984], 70, 122–23; also Margaret Whitford's comments in *Luce Irigaray: Philosophy in the Feminine* [London: Routledge, 1991], 77–78).

[17] Lacan, *Encore*, trans. Bruce Fink (New York: Norton, 1998), 98–99.

[18] Fink's translation has "be whole" — e.g. be one subject — but the French "être toute" could mean "be all" (e.g. all, entirely, a woman).

[19] This ambivalence of Dionysios's identity emerges in the cycle of myths around Ariadne, Theseus, and Minos. According to Robert Graves's commentary, "Cretan Dionysius, represented as a bull — Minos, in fact — was Ariadne's rightful husband" (*The Greek Myths* [Harmondsworth: Penguin, 1960], 347); yet Ariadne was also Minos's daughter.

[20] Sloterdijk, *Thinker on Stage*, trans. J. Daniel (Minneapolis: Minnesota UP, 1989), 20.

[21] Cf. Yuri Lotman, "The Origin of Plot in the Light of Typology," trans. Julian Graffy, *Poetics Today* 1.1–2 (1979): 161–84.

[22] Martin Puchner, *Stage Fright: Modernism, Anti-Theatricality, and Drama* (Baltimore: John Hopkins UP, 2002).

[23] Jacques Derrida, *Éperons: Les Styles de Nietzsche* (Paris: Flammarion, 1976); see Luce Irigaray's mythopoeietic response, *The Marine Lover of Friedrich Nietzsche*, translated by Gillian Gill (New York: Columbia UP, 1991), which has itself spawned yet further commentaries; also Teresa de Lauretis, *Technologies of Gender* (Bloomington: Indiana UP, 1987), 31–33.

[24] See Theisen's criticism of Adrian Del Caro for precisely such an unambiguous assignment of meaning ("Die Gewalt des Notwendigen," 198): this would by extension have to apply as well to Kittler's media-theoretical reading of Ariadne (as none other than, *mirabile dictu*, Nietzsche's *stenotypist*) (Kittler, "The Mechanical Philosopher," *Looking After Nietzsche*, ed. Lawrence Rickels [Albany: SUNY, 1990], 195–208).

[25] Kittler, *Discourse Networks*, 196.

[26] Marius and Jahraus, *Systemtheorie und Dekonstruktion*, 34, emphasis added.

[27] On Luhmann's relation to Hegel, see Lutz Ellrich, "Entgeistertes Beobachten. Hegel und Luhmann im Vergleich," Gerhard Wagner and Peter Merz-Benz, eds., *Die Logik der Systeme* (Konstanz: Universitätsverlag, 2000), 73–126.

[28] Gaston Bachelard, *L'air et les songes; essai sur l'imagination du mouvement* (Paris: José Corti, 1943).

[29] De Man, *Allegories of Reading*, 102.

[30] Heidegger, *Vorträge und Aufsätze* (Pfüllingen: Neske, 1954), 76. Cf. also the comment of Reiner Schürmann: "The spirit of technology is the god Janus, the spirit of the *ianuae* and the *iani*, doorways and thresholds" (*Heidegger on Being and Acting: From Principles to Anarchy* [Bloomington: Indiana UP, 1987], 87).

[31] Benn, *Gedichte* (*Werke* 1): 39–40 (this is the first of two slightly different versions given, which I have chosen for its greater clarity of form; the second version is continuous, without the articulation of stanzaic breaks).

[32] See above, chapter 2. Rilke's own "Orpheus. Eurydike. Hermes," written in 1904 but only published in 1907, offers a much stabler mythic narrative than Benn's. It is possible that Benn could have known the Rilke poem (there may be a faint echo of Rilke's "fraß sein Schritt den Weg" in Benn's "Die Füße fressen Staub").

[33] Benn, "Gehirne," *Sämtliche Werke,* vol. 3: *Prosa 1* (Stuttgart: Klett-Cotta, 1987), 32.

[34] Austin, "The Lament and the Rhetoric of the Sublime," *19th Century Literature* 53.3 (Dec. 1998): 279–306; here 283, 288–89.

[35] This emerges in the objections raised by Rainer Rumold, *Gottfried Benn und der Expressionismus: Provokation des Lesers, Absolute Dichtung* (Königstein: Scriptor, 1982), 153, to Edgar Lohner's earlier reading of the close as conclusive (*Passion und Intellekt: Die Lyrik Gottfried Benns* [Neuwied: Luchterhand, 1961], 210).

[36] Theweleit, *Männerphantasien* I (Reinbek: Rowohlt, 1980), 235; Benn's mother-complex was the favored topic of Oskar Sahlberg, *Goffried Benns Phantasiewelt: "wo Lust und Leiche winkt"* (Munich: Text und Kritik, 1977).

[37] Gilles Deleuze, *Nietzsche and Philosophy,* trans. Hugh Tomlinson (New York: Columbia UP, 1983), 186–89.

[38] Peter Brook, "Freud's Masterplot: Questions of Narrative," in *Literature and Psychoanalysis,* ed. S. Felman (Baltimore: Johns Hopkins UP, 1982), 280–300; here, 295.

[39] Wellbery, *Specular Moment,* 320. Luhmann has noted the central function of negativity in the discourse of early modern anthropology in which "Prometheus" participates (cf. "Frühneuzeitliche Anthropologie: Theorietechnische Begriffe für ein Evolutionsproblem der Gesellschaft," *Gesellschaftsstruktur und Semantik,* 1:162–234).

[40] Lohner, *Passion und Intellekt* (see note 35).

[41] Mallarmé, *Oeuvres complètes* (Paris: Gallimard, 1945), 37. The same idea of celestial hostility is taken up again in Francis Ponge's later "Notes sur un Ciel de Provence."

[42] Thus an older commentator referred to Mallarmé's poem as *"ce poème — ou plutôt ce drame à deux personnages, l'azur et le poète"* (This poem — or rather, this drama for two characters, the Azure and the poet; Paul Surer, "Explication de texte: 'l'Azur,' *L'Information littéraire 19* (1967): 96, italics author's). Kristeva generalized this scenic aspect in her comment that "l'idée mallarméenne est une 'mise en scène' ou 'dramatisation spéculative'" (Mallarmé's idea is a "performance" or a "speculative dramatization"; *La Révolution du langage poétique* [Paris: Seuil, 1974], 537).

[43] As one commentator has written, "Mallarmé has divested the beheading of all but its plastic homologies" (J. D. Hubert, "Representations of Decapitation: Mallarmé's *Hérodiade* and Flaubert's *Hérodias,*" *French Forum* 7[3] (Sept. 1982): 247); like Flaubert in his contemporary Herodias, Mallarmé insists on a geometric and structural impersonality light years removed from Benn's *affective* hyperbole. As Mallarmé wrote in a famous letter to Cazalis, "l'azur torture l'impuissant en général" (The azure tortures the impotent in general; cited in Henri Mondor, *Vie de Mallarmé* [Paris: Gallimard, 1941], 105).

[44] Lacan, *Le Séminaire XVII*, 138.

[45] De Man, "Lyric and Modernity," in *Stéphane Mallarmé*, ed. Harold Bloom (New York: Chelsea House, 1987), 74, emphasis added.

[46] Barbara Johnson, "Les fleurs du mal armé," in *Stéphane Mallarmé*, ed. Bloom, 211–27; here 216.

[47] Benn, *Gedichte*, 1:35.

[48] Cf. Hugh Ridley, *Gottfried Benn: Ein Schriftsteller zwischen Erneuerung und Reaktion* (Opladen: Westdeutscher Verlag, 1990).

[49] *Art as a Social System*, trans. Eva Knodt (Stanford: Stanford UP, 2000), 141.

[50] "Einfach bleibt die Gestalt der ersten Erscheinung," states Goethe in the "Metamorphose der Pflanzen" (*Werke*, Hamburger Ausgabe 1:199); "große Formeln," letter to Sartorius, July 19, 1810.

[51] Goethe, *Werke*, Hamburger Ausgabe 1:294.

[52] Goethe, *Werke*, Hamburger Ausgabe, 1:245.

[53] Heine, *Buch der Lieder* (*Werke*, vol. 1 [Frankfurt: Insel, 1968], 43); other poetic antecedents of Benn's poplar might also include Droste's "Die Linde" (from the cycle "Der Weiher") or C. F. Meyer's "Der verwundete Baum," both allegories of suffering individuality.

[54] The poem's composition on the page, its one-word lines, bring it also into the vicinity of Stramm, Apollinaire, and Dada experiment, of the visual dimension which would later be exploited by Concrete Poetry (on this, see most recently Klaus Schenk, *Medienpoesie* [Stuttgart: Metzler, 2000]).

[55] This type of near-Expressionist tension between construction and contemplation was already found in Rilke's "Eingang" (see chapter 1 above).

[56] Wellbery, *The Specular Moment*, 317, 320–21; cf. also 265–66 for discussion of rhetorical questions in "Der Fischer."

[57] In the later *Gesammelte Gedichte* of 1956, this colon is removed (see Schuster's editorial comments in the apparatus, *Werke* 1: 365).

[58] So in chapter 11 of *Ideen. Das Buch Le Grand*, Heine, *Werke in 4 Bänden*, ed. W. Preisendanz [Frankfurt: Insel, 1968], 2:211).

[59] Instances of this cliché are legend, but one could cite Lenau ("An einen Baum"), Droste ("Die Linde"), C. F. Meyer ("Der verwundete Baum") and a particularly egregious example in Liliencron, for whom a "mächtige deutsche Pappel" becomes, in most Wilhelmine fashion, an "alter Hüne" (Liliencron, *Werke*, ed. B. von Wiese [Frankfurt: Insel, 1977], 1:37). Théophile Gautier had parodied this same topos in "Nostalgies d'obélisques" (1851) a poem very close to Heine's and possibly indebted to it (*Émaux et Camées* [Paris: Gallimard, 1981], 60–65).

[60] Adorno, *Ästhetische Theorie*, 295.

[61] Hegel, *Ästhetik* III, *Werke* (Frankfurt: Suhrkamp, 1970), 15:449–50.

[62] Niklas Luhmann, "The Work of Art and the Self-Reproduction of Art," *Essays on Self-Reference* (New York: Columbia UP, 1990), 220.

[63] It was this aspect of the American landscape that Adorno would notice in *Minima Moralia*, part 1, #28.

[64] "Un tel halo existe aussi bien, autour d'une pomme . . . Tout se passe comme si l'on était en présence d'une réfraction particulière où le milieu non transparent est constitué par l'esprit de l'homme" (Halos of this sort exist around apples, too. . . . Everything happens as if we were in the presence of a particular refraction where the human spirit constitutes the transparent medium; *L'Amour fou* [Paris: Gallimard, 1937], 157). Here too we may replace Breton's "milieu" with medium.

[65] See the familiar discussion of these "breachings" in Derrida, "Freud and the Scene of Writing" (in *L'Écriture et la différence* [Paris: Seuil, 1972]).

[66] "The Tree of Doubt," in *Stéphane Mallarmé*, ed. Bloom, 141–49; here 143.

[67] "Abgetan ist die Natur auf der Bühne," proclaimed Lothar Schreyer in 1916 in a programmatic statement in *Der Sturm* (cited in Dieter Harth, "Die Bühne als Labotorium der Gefühle," *IABLIS* 2003, no page number).

[68] Kittler, "Benns Gedichte — Schlager von Klasse," in *Draculas Vermächtnis* (Leipzig: Reclam, 1993), 105–29. The poems are found in Benn, *Gedichte*, 2:66 and 1:198.

[69] Benn, *Gedichte*, 1:198.

[70] "Benns Woyzeck," *Deutsche Vierteljahresschrift* 78.3 (September 2002): 482–98; here 492.

[71] Benn, *Gedichte*, 1:181.

[72] See Hermann Korte's devastating criticism of this now-forgotten movement (*Deutschsprachige Lyrik nach 1945* [Stuttgart: Metzler, 2004], 164–65): with a name change, Benn's poem is not far from Delius's equally sentimental "Einsamkeit eines alternden Stones-Fans."

[73] Benn, *Gedichte*, 1:257.

[74] "Heine und die Folgen," *Untergang der Welt durch schwarze Magie* (Frankfurt: Suhrkamp, 1989), 193, 197.

[75] As Brian Holbeche put it, a "much more traditional poetry . . . began to predominate from the mid-twenties," "Benn's 'Palau,'" *Seminar* 22, 4 (November 1986): 312–23, here, 323.

[76] So for instance Helmut Heissenbüttel ("Der entfirnißte Gottfried Benn," in *Über Gottfried Benn*, ed. Bruno Hillebrand [Frankfurt: Fischer, 1987], 2:240–44).

[77] On the elements common to various Benn Renaissances, cf. Wolfgang Rothe, "Benn-Renaissancen," in Hillebrand, ed., *Über Gottfried Benn*, 251–60.

[78] Cf. Adorno, *Ästhetische Theorie*, 293–94.

4: The Limits of Violence: Döblin's Colonial Nature

> *A machine has no sex. Nature, on the other hand, always has a sex.*
> — Luce Irigaray, *Sexes and Genealogies*

Imaginary Theory?

FEW MODERN GERMAN WRITERS have been as extensively occupied with non-European cultures as Alfred Döblin. From the Expressionist China of *Die drei Sprünge des Wang-lun* (1915) to the Marinetti-influenced African passages of *Berge Meere und Giganten* (1924), the rewriting of Indian myth in *Manas* (1927), and the explicitly colonial epic of *Amazonas* (1937/8–1947/8), along with countless literary and philosophical essays drawing on Asian religious traditions, Döblin transformed the exoticist and Orientalist inheritance of the turn of the century into a specifically historical investigation of other cultures, in their relation to European and technological modernity. Moreover, this tension is one in which Nature is a central actor, an actor repeatedly allied with the struggles of colonized peoples against occupying powers. Nowhere is this role of Nature more crucial than in *Wang-lun*, Döblin's first published novel, and one which was important not only for his own subsequent development, but also for that of Brecht. It would thus make sense to bring the question of modernist Nature into relation with discussions of colonial history, which have in recent years begun to include German literature within their purview.[1]

Many of these discussions, however, bring as much confusion as they do clarity to the question, an impression going far beyond the usual heavy poststructuralist reliance on rhetoric, to serious doubts about internal theoretical coherence. Nowhere is that coherence more open to question, in a movement self proclaimedly "committed to theory,"[2] than in postcolonial theory's relation to psychoanalysis. Given that film theory's synthetic reliance on the latter has recently come under scrutiny, and not only from a neo-empiricist perspective,[3] one may ask whether postcolonial theory is really as psychoanalytic as it claims to be. A strong suspicion persists that beneath the rhetorical mask of Lacanian phraseology — which serves largely as a means of institutional legitimacy — the difficult and counter-intuitive conceptual substance of psychoanalysis has been reduced to common sense, even to that ultimately empiricist standpoint which postcolonial theory most loudly disavows. Ironically, such common-sense flattening has greatly eased the reception of this theory in the USA, where nothing succeeds so well as the reduction of Continental theory to the instrument of familiar North American moral crusades.[4] It will not be possible, therefore, to propose a reading of Döblin's Chinese novel without first clearing the ground of theoretical confusions, which requires that one "draw . . . a line of separation between Theory proper and its jargonistic imitation."[5] To do this means not a return to hale and hearty empiricism, as so many post-theorists advocate, but rather a recognition of a historical causality beyond textuality and fantasy. That causality will come to be defined as, in Lacan's term, Real: a term we may render less portentous by linking it concretely with trauma, a paradoxical "experience" that cannot be reducible to text or fantasy. As will emerge, Döblin's peculiar version of fictional historiography shares certain common "traumatic" traits with other famous early-twentieth-century writers, including Daniel Paul Schreber and Freud himself. Like these last, Döblin's writing works through multiple traumas of ethnic, sexual, and linguistic displacement in a peculiar form of part-fictional, part-autobiographical historiography; what this writing work ultimately addresses will turn out to be a form of the technological unconscious.

The sheer consistency of the current American academic jargon of subversiveness is such that it would ultimately need a linguistic critique as lengthy as Adorno's still little-read *Jargon of Authenticity* (the work so rarely referred to when discussing Heidegger's politics). Much of Adorno's broadside against the pseudo-religious tone of this now-extinct German jargon is fully relevant to much current American university discourse, if one replaces the existentialist pathos of authenticity with a rhetoric of armchair politics and self-styled subversion.

> Before any specific content it [the jargon] models thought so as to adapt it to submission, even where it claims to resist the latter . . . Thus the character of the jargon is thoroughly formal: it makes sure that what it intends is largely sensed and accepted through delivery [*Vortrag*], without regard to the content of the words. The preconceptual, mimetic element of language is used to reach desired effects.[6]

It would thus be ineffective only to quibble with individual inconsistencies: a critique according to mere logic cannot explain the perdurability of such a jargon, indeed its paradoxical function within the guild. (If such a critique were adequate, then the questions raised long ago about poscolonial theory by Robert Young, Arif Dirlik, Benita Parry, and Henry

Louis Gates[7] — to name only a few — would have sufficed to correct conceptual abuses that, on the contrary, have only continued to flourish.) Much postcolonial theory tends to assimilate its psychoanalytic borrowings to, firstly, a Derridean (and very un-Lacanian) domination of the "text," and secondly, to a Foucauldian notion of disciplinary apparatus, thereby only imitating older models of film and gender theory from the 1970s and 1980s. What follows will work with the arguments of Joan Copjec, Tim Dean, and Charles Shepherdson to show that much postcolonial theory, at the very least, *does not make sense in psychoanalytic terms*. Such a diagnosis may then clear the way towards asking what a more careful and properly psychoanalytic reading of (post)colonial writing might be. The critique of postcolonialism means more than merely a (neo-orthodox) "return to Lacan" as well, for what is at stake here is the nature of interdisciplinarity itself. (In chapter 5, we will return to this question of interdisciplinarity in the context of law and literature.) In other words, a psychoanalytic critique of postcolonialism may also help us open up literary studies better to real historical terrain, clearing away predictable moralizing clichés and neat binary oppositions of East and West.[8] In the process, some of the interesting suggestions made by postcolonial theory gain firmer theoretical underpinning.

The conceptual inconsistencies, even the frank incoherence, of postcolonial theory's psychoanalytic borrowings have been pointed out long ago.[9] Eclectic extension of concepts would be of itself no problem, were it not so flatly contrary to the very psychoanalytic context supposedly evoked. Many of postcolonialism's psychoanalytic borrowings are not at all, loud claims to the contrary, Lacanian.[10] It is a great irony that precisely those concepts which Lacan himself most criticized — as having been "deadened by routine use"[11] into a common-sense dime-store Freudianism — are the ones most often deployed by adepts of postcolonial theory. Chief among them would be narcissism, which postcolonial theory derives less from Lacan than Christian Metz. But the term "ambivalence" — "that tired and evasive cliché"[12] — is no less deadened an old-Freudian term; Lacan noted that the term "regression," if not further specified, meant nothing, and this is even more true of "ambivalence." One quote, from Homi Bhabha, should suffice here:

> Although the "authority" of colonial discourse depends crucially on its location in narcissism and the Imaginary, my concept of stereotype-as-suture is a recognition of the *ambivalence* of that authority and those orders of identification. The role of fetishistic identification, in the construction of discriminatory knowledges that depend on the *presence of difference*, is to provide a process of splitting and multiple/contradictory belief at the point of enunciation and subjectification.[13]

"Ambivalence" means, in psychoanalytic terms, very little; the term in fact functions as a kind of pseudo-theoretical performative, in Austin's sense, suggesting an illusory fascination with the mystery of the word itself. (The term is a vehicle for another form of Imaginary identification, namely that with the performativity of the academic shaman: the chief function of the jargon of subversiveness is to define membership in the imagined community of literary-critical wizards. Concepts, instead of having any analytic power, serve here as a "pre-conceptual, mimetic element" (Adorno) to mimic shamanic authority, in an ironic realization of Foucault's knowledge/power nexus. Put otherwise, literary criticism has become a purely closed and recursive system in Luhmann's sense: it refers only to itself, no longer to literature, let alone history.) What is key here is the reduction of psychoanalytic theory to nothing more than a theory of the Imaginary, even a theory which is itself deeply imaginary. Rather than escaping the fascination of the Imaginary — the textual, the rhetorical — by exposing the Real trauma and Symbolic structures that determine it, Bhabha instead invites his readers to another form of Imaginary: namely the endless "gaze" at the clichés of the Derridean textual sublime: the *fort-da* of binary "presence and absence," the play of signifiers, the familiar pseudo-subversive assurances of the "cultural construction of reality." In this, postcolonial theory only repeats the ironic misrecognition of psychoanalysis already effected by film theory and its sempiternal "gaze," or by the perennial and paranoid panoptica of Foucauldians. Joan Copjec has argued forcefully against this misreading of psychoanalysis:

> Why is the representation of the relation of the subject to the social necessarily an imaginary one? This question . . . should have launched a serious critique of film theory. [. . .] With only a slightly different emphasis, the question can be seen to ask how the imaginary came to bear, almost exclusively, the burden of the construction of the subject — despite the fact that we always speak of the "symbolic" construction of the subject.[14]

Postcolonial theory effects such a reduction to the Imaginary most obviously in, for instance, a reading of a famous passage in Fanon's *Black Skin, White Masks,* where the author recalls being named as a child by a hostile viewer ("Look, a Negro . . ."). That this perfectly conscious recollection of Fanon's is called a "primal scene" (Bhabha 1986: 163), although the defining characteristic of Freud's *Urszene* is that it is repressed and must be constructed by the analyst, is symptomatic of postcolonial theory's larger elision of the unconscious. If there is a traumatic dimension to this memory — which Fanon indeed implies — then it must involve more than the Imaginary. When, a few paragraphs later, Bhabha's essay refers to "the aggressive *phase* of the Imaginary" (ibid., 164, my emphasis), it becomes clear that this Imaginary has nothing to do with Lacan's,[15] for Lacan broke early on with any notion of Freudian developmental phases, and would never have called the Imaginary only a phase.

What has been taken over here is only the most superficial aspect of Lacan, namely the mystical resonance of the Other — most often reduced to a merely empirical "other person," not the transcendental instance of speech it is in Lacan — or his punning *linguisterie,* his sporadic claims to speak in the *lalangue* of the Unconscious itself. Like much Foucauldian film theory, postcolonial theory "tends to trap the subject in representation (an idealist failing), to conceive of language as constructing the prison walls of the subject's being."[16]

So too, postcolonial theory takes recourse to the familiar film-theoretical notions of the omnipotence of "apparatus" and "discourse," long after they have been discredited within film studies (and not only there).[17] The tendency of postcolonial theory to rely on straw-man arguments to "construct" that disciplinary apparatus can lead to astonishing imprecisions. One grandiose example is Bhabha's collapsing of "historicism and realism" — these last treated as if they were a pleonasm — with "a predominantly mimetic view of the relation between the text and a *pre-given* empirical reality," which "entails the classic subject/object structure of knowledge, central to empiricist epistemology which further installs the structure of the essential and the inessential."[18]

A great many very distinct strands of thought have been run together into one blur here. Historicism (Ranke?) is conflated with realism (Zola? Lukács?) and then with mimesis (Aristotle?) and empiricism (Hume?) and the Hegelian subject/object — this last hardly a well-known feature of "empiricist epistemology"! In an unashamed straw-man tactic, all of these theoretical Others are conflated for the rhetorical purposes of a purely rhetorical theory. In a telling aside from *A Critique of Post-Colonial Reason,* Gayatri Spivak admits that she is relying on old, outdated nineteenth-century historical sources as straw men in order to make her argument:

> As must be eminently clear, I am no historian. For the literary person interested in colonial discourse . . . and without mature disciplinary judgment, it is the standard rather than the innovative historian who is more important. She [i.e. the "literary person"] has not the scholarship to get into the disciplinary debate.[19]

This is, in effect, a plea for interdisciplinarity without competence: in other words, for dilettantism. Historiography is not allowed to be a serious partner in literary studies' narcissistic strategy of self-aggrandizement, but only forced into the subaltern role of passive other; if ever interdisciplinary colonialism existed, then surely it was here.[20] Imaginary Theory would prefer not to be troubled in its safely rhetorical triumphs.

The same purpose is served by the endless re-hashing of the "now-sterile essentialism-constructivism debate."[21] One senses, above all, that for the English-speaking (and largely American) readers of postcolonial theory — surrounded by a culture of positivism as they are — the sheer heady novelty of any sort of speculative rhetoric is such as to outweigh by far any specific differences between "theories."

More serious than this is the fragility of concepts like "hybridity," "border,"[22] and so on, the hypostatisation of which is anything but psychoanalytic in import. Worst of all is the term mimesis, shared by Butler's brand of gender theory and postcolonial theory. In Butler's influential transposition of Derrida, "gender" comes to occupy the structural place held by writing, iteration, or *différance:* "gender is a kind of imitation for which there is no original,"[23] i.e. no "voice," logos, or presence. In the generalizing of this dictum often found in gender studies, gender becomes nothing more than a kind of free American consumer choice, something worthy of the "lifestyle" sections of the newspapers. As Tim Dean has argued in a powerful critique of Butler-inspired ideas of gender, this is a view closely tied up with "the meritocratic foundation of U.S. society" that "treats almost all identities as achieved." Dean's wry comment on the inflation of drag in gender theory is very applicable to the postcolonial inflation of mimicry:

> What could be more democratic, more essentially American, than a gender that can be "manipulated at will"? Drag turns out to be as American as apple pie. (Dean 74)

As Dean notes, the now-routine poststructuralist reduction to representation is nothing radical in a humanities department:

> There is something quite appropriate, indeed unremarkable, about a bunch of English professors arguing over transsexual phenomena, insofar as the central concept at stake is imitation . . . (71)

Once again, we meet with the disciplinary colonialism of literature departments (English in particular): gender is here reduced to nothing but rhetorical figurality, that familiar province of the literature professor. Could the same not be said of the "textual" reading of "sly civility," or of Fanon? Dean continues:

> The psychoanalytic challenge to this business-as-usual lies in the contention that theories of mimesis or imitation represent the wrong approach to gender altogether, because formulating questions of gender and sexuality in terms of the mimetic or imitative generation of reality effects restricts vital political questions to the arena of ego identifications. In Lacanian terms, the concept of mimicry situates

identification at the level of imaginary representations, excluding the real from consideration. (Dean 71; see also 192–93)

The consequence of this reduction (whether of gender or postcolonial role) to imaginary mimicry is that the deeply disturbing and often frightening aspects of colonial or gender "borders," their relation to an underlying traumatic (i.e. Real) threat to the historical and narrating subject, are aestheticized and thereby rendered harmless. As if in unconscious acknowledgment of this, Imaginary Theory mimics the effects of the very disturbance it is concealing, enjoying them in sublime incomprehension. We have seen this same tactic at work in the sublime omnipotent fantasies of technocracy (chapter 1). In every case, the real cause of trauma, and thus also of history, is elided, in favor of an endlessly manipulable "performativity" or mimicry. So Dean is "struck by the similarity" between gender theory's "repudiation of the real . . . and the transsexual subject's repudiation of the real" (78). Repudiation must here be understood in relation to Freud's *Verwerfung* (Lacan's *forclusion*), the characteristic trait of the psychotic. This is supported by the argument of Catherine Millot that the transsexual subject seeks an identification which is "horsexe," "outsidesex." According to Dean,

> Millot equates an identification "outsidesex" with an identification with the phallus, and hence the transsexual who makes this identification does so in order to escape castration. This identification is with an impossible state, a position no person can actually occupy; and this impossibility points to the function of the unconscious in identification, a function that makes identification much more than a question of imitation or of the imaginary. What does it mean to identify with the phallus? (82)

Postcolonial theory's "borders" and "hybrids" are just as impossible as this transsexual identification "outsidesex," and elude not only the question of the real, but also the unconscious itself, in the same way. Accordingly, in what follows here, these questions of the real and the unconscious will reveal what postcolonial theory has only concealed behind the endless rhetorical tricks of its discourse of the university. For the real of traumatic experience — whether that of sexual difference insisted on by Copjec and Dean, or that of historical trauma — is not reducible to the surface of rhetoric and text. In the recognition of this, psychoanalysis may have something more, and different, to contribute to a theory of history than is commonly assumed.

Chinese Shadows

The direct relation between *Die drei Sprünge des Wang-lun* and then-contemporary colonial Chinese history clearly distinguishes Döblin's novel from the Orientalizing exoticism of the *fin-de-siècle* on which it unquestionably draws. China had, together with Japan, been the object of a renewed wave of interest around 1900, and not only in German-speaking countries. Yet the thoroughly dissimilar uses to which this modern *Chinoiserie* was put by its best-known practitioners should warn away from hasty generalizations.[24] While Ezra Pound followed Fenellosa's reading of Chinese to a poetics of concretion and image ("thinking is thinging"), for Kafka, China meant an allegory of writing at its most abstract and labyrinthine.[25] Döblin shared neither of these writers' fascination with Chinese language (a matter that would turn up again half a century later in the sinophilia of Philippe Sollers). Döblin's China has more in common with that of Karl Kraus, for whom China was an allegory for unleashed female sexuality, "the married prostitute Nature"[26] who must avenge herself on her captors.

In his linkage of China to contemporary revolutionary uprisings, however, Döblin most decisively breaks with Orientalism.[27] In direct contradistinction to Goethe's famous project of fleeing the disorder of the Napoleonic wars to a pure East where one could still breathe "the air of patriarchs" ("Hegire"), Döblin seeks in his China disorder and upheaval, against the deceptive calm of his own late-Wilhelmine environment, and anticipating the carnage of the First World War. Like the more familiar *Wallenstein* (1920), Döblin's novel tells a bloody story of mass destruction and war. Like *Wallenstein*, too, *Die drei Sprünge* is a historical novel, based on a real peasant rebellion in the eighteenth century. The course of the novel traces not only the chronicle of that rebellion and its defeat by the state, but also a philosophical development from a wild millenarian rebellion to pacifism. Central to the book is the Taoist theme of *wu-wei* or non-action.

Döblin's novel relates the story of Wang-lun, a fisherman's son from Shantung province, who goes to the city and first becomes a thief. The murder of his friend Su-koh confronts him with the alternative of accepting injustice or rebellion. After killing Su-koh's murderer, he flees to the mountains, where he meets the escaped monk Ma-noh and discusses Buddhism with him. Wang-lun joins up with a band of robbers and formulates his Taoist doctrine of passive non-resistance, *wu-wei* or non-action. This teaching proves impossible to uphold against the persecution of imperial troops. Part 3 of the novel is devoted to Wang's counterpart the Emperor Khien-lung, who is torn between the ethical imperative of humanity and the responsibilities of a ruler. The Emperor's adviser, the

Lama Paldang Jische, tells him not to persecute Wang's sect, but after the Lama's death from the plague, the Emperor orders an attack on them. Wang realizes that his doctrine of non-resistance leads only to self-destruction. Before his death, he demonstrates to a friend the "three leaps" of the novel's title as a parable of his development. The first leap brought him from the fishing village to meeting Ma-noh; the second brought him back to obscure married life, then to rebellion; the third is the return to his original doctrine of conformity to Nature. At the novel's end, Wang and his followers are besieged and killed in a fortified city.

The aforementioned links between Döblin's novel and German and Chinese history are multiple and more contradictory than in most historical novels. The first is the events from the Boxer Rebellion of 1900, leading to the fall of the last Chinese (Ching, or Manchu) dynasty in 1911, less than a year before the conception of Döblin's novel. Döblin later told Henry Regensteiner that Wang-lun was directly concerned with the "religious movement of the Boxers,"[28] although the novel in fact reworks historical sources dealing with an eighteenth-century peasant revolt.[29] It should be kept in mind that the colonizing power in question in Döblin's novel is not European, but rather the Manchu occupiers who had repeatedly controlled China during both the Yüan Dynasty and the Ching.

Matters are further complicated by the German imperial government's military involvement in China dating from the ceding of the Liaodong Peninsula to Japan in 1895. In 1897, German troops occupied the harbor of Kiaochou, and in 1899 they participated in the struggle against the Boxers and the plundering of Peking. This belated German colonial activity, like the contemporary military intervention in South West Africa, was directly related to the growing tension between working and propertied classes in Wilhelmine society; in 1909, the newspaper *Koloniale Rundschau* wrote openly of a "solution to the workers' problem with a Chinese key."[30] The uprising of eighteenth-century Chinese peasants thus becomes, for Döblin, an allegory anticipating the real German events he describes in *November 1918:* the brief establishment of a workers' state after the violent overthrow of the ruling elite.

China's history, at the *Jahrhundertwende*, was an allegory not only political but also ethnic, namely an allegory for European Jewry. Kafka's Great Wall is only the most well-known instance of this oblique relationship, which Benjamin termed a "force field between Torah and Tao" (1981: 138); Kraus has already been mentioned, but one could also adduce Mahler (*Das Lied von der Erde*), or the unjustly neglected Berlin critic Moritz Heimann,[31] who was responsible for getting *Wang-lun* accepted for publication by Fischer. Less obvious than the Jewish Orientalism of Lasker-Schüler or Werfel,[32] this Jewish China nonetheless accompanied the rediscovery of Hasidism and *Ostjuden* in a manner as close as it was curious. The cliché of Jew-as-Oriental, popularized by Karl Emil Franzos and Jakob Wasserman,[33] could be read as Far and not only Near Eastern. None other than Martin Buber translated Chuang Tzu in 1910, along with Kafka's beloved collection of Chinese love stories and ghost stories a year later; Döblin turned to Buber for historical advice while writing *Die drei Sprünge des Wang-lun,* and Buber would then be the novel's first reader.[34] Given that the "Jewish question" was one which would centrally concern Döblin through his later trip to Poland and his polemical writing on the *Flight and Assembly of the Jewish People,*[35] it is not unreasonable to suspect a Jewish subtext at work in the author's Chinese novel. As Kafka famously took his father's derogatory comment about *Ostjuden* as vermin literally to write *The Metamorphosis,* Döblin may well have done the same with then-current clichés about Jews as Orientals. Döblin thus anticipates what Leslie Adelson, in her recent critical re-working of postcolonial theory in a German-Turkish context, calls "touching tales":[36] for his "tale" of China very much "touches" that of German Jews.

The difficulty is that these multiple allegories pull in different directions: the "Chinese as Jews" brings Döblin's novel right back within that field of exoticist, sensual, and essentialist turn-of-the-century Orientalism which the political and historical dimension of his book would otherwise contradict. A quotation from a contemporary source gives an idea how close Döblin's writing is to German-Jewish *topoi* about *Ost und West:*

> In the East, all is abrupt, wild, bold, markedly individual. Everything is here jumpy, without gradual development, without harmonic rounding-out. There is missing here the normal education by generation, which along brings mere flow into proper channels. Everything in the Eastern European Jew is vibrant life, everything breathes temperament and warmth, everything is also nervous and in an ecstatic condition. It is an ecstasy in which the Russian Jew lives — if he is not sinking into a dull Nirvana.[. . .] Rarely do we find in one soul so many oppositions coexisting as in the Eastern Jews. In the petty, sober merchant we find a childishly soft temper, in the cruel fanatic an incomparable mercy and readiness for sacrifice, in the dry Talmudic pedant, poetic fantasy and flights.[. . .] Under the ice the glowing fire of the Oriental broods, and next to despair there dwells religious resignation. Optimism and pessimism are closely melded to each other, fatalism and light-heartedness go hand in hand.[37]

This unsigned passage, from the German-Jewish periodical *Ost und West* in the year 1903, could serve quite well as a characterization of the style and personages of *Wang-lun,* with their sudden, abrupt shifts from catatonic melancholy to manic violence, their seeming lack of any unitary ego-bound individuality. As Gert Mattenklott has noted, the "Oriental" character here is only an exotic variant of Nietzsche's Dionysius.[38] Yet despite the derivative aspects of this Nietzschean rhetoric, there are new accents to be detected in the fantasy (or perhaps "discourse") of the East and the *Ostjude,* in accordance with their Expressionist setting.

One is a deliberate and polemical inversion of the by-now familiar clichés of Jew as feminine. Of one contemporary Jewish writer it was asserted in *Ost und West* that he "wohnt . . . bei den Quellen, nicht in Jerusalem freilich, sondern 'bei den Müttern.'"[39] The phrase recalls *Faust II* (act 1, 7060–61). Similarly, a reviewer of Yiddish theater finds in the latter a "Muttersprache" and "Mutterboden," a "Volk, zu den Müttern zurückgeführt."[40] These ambiguous mothers, who would come to play a fatal role in German Fascism, have probably as much to do with Germany — Bachofen in particular — as with Judaism; they will play a very strong role in Döblin's *oeuvre,* and not only in *Wang-lun.*

The second new aspect to Jewish Orientalism is the relation to nature, a matter of particular significance for Döblin. Again from the pages of *Ost und West* we may find assertions that "diese Kraft und Energien der Jugend sind denen der elementaren Natur zu vergleichen" (Mattenklott 297). The relation of China to an ideal Nature, which will be central to Döblin's novel, may be found also in the diaries of Count Keyserling's trip to Asia;[41] the same relation is overtly sexualized and maternalized in Hesse's 1913 story "Aus Indien."[42]

For the happy eclecticism of postcolonial theory, it might well be enough to stop here, having found so many multiple (and indeed ambivalent) "identities" at work in this novel, and conclude that it is in his Chinese-German-Jewish images and fantasies — "those orders that figure transgressively on the borders of history and the unconscious" (see note 9 above) — that Döblin "most profoundly evokes the colonial condition." But this is still not yet a reading at all. In particular, we have not yet looked closely at the work in question, which, as a narrative, has to look for some sort of solution and closure for the tensions so far sketched in; nor have we asked what might lie beyond the mere surface of the writing, which cannot, in a psychoanalytic view, ever be entirely sufficient unto itself.

Voyage to the Country of the Real

Döblin's Chinese novel has many structural links to specifically fictional narrative forms, such as the picaresque *Schelmenroman* or even the Gothic horror story[43] (the Chinese parallel would be the famous seventeenth-century bandit-novel *Shui Hu Chuan* or *Water Margin*). It may, however, also be read as an ethnographic narrative, a form which has been internally linked up with literary modernism. With the Surrealist ethnography of modernity of Aragon's *Paysan de Paris* or Breton's *Nadja,* Döblin's half-historical, half-fantasized China shares an impulse to make strange, to thwart normal hermeneutic understanding; with Bataille and the Collège de Sociologie, there is shared a common interest in the primitive, the sacred, and extreme violence.[44] As in the case of Malinowski, Döblin's ethnography "enacts the process of fictional self-fashioning" (Clifford 110) of its own authorial voice, although it does so less through a recourse to the anthropologist's truth than through, again, deliberate self-estrangement. Like Victor Segalen's *Stèles,* written at the same time (1912), Döblin's Chinese novel does "not so much translate a Chinese cultural content as provide their author with an impersonal, official voice, a disguise allowing him a degree of expressive freedom" (Clifford 157) — in other words, Döblin's epic style, his "Tatsachenphantasie," or, in an even more extreme formulation, his "Kino-Stil."[45] As with Mauss's student Marcel Griaule, the "truth . . . recorded" in *Wang-lun* "was a truth provoked by ethnography," or at least by the dispassionate stance of ethnographic "research" (Clifford 77).[46]

Yet this "truth" is not, and indeed cannot be, a truth of anthropological documentary research — which would, at first, seem to invalidate the comparisons just pursued, unless it is recognized that the truth in question is a specifically *subjective* one. The subject in question is not a merely biographical or individual one, but rather the collective subject of anthropology itself, namely humanity. As Nicholas Thomas puts it, "Anthropology, however, is not merely a disciplined expression of a universal human curiosity, but a modern discourse that has subsumed humanity to the grand narratives and analogies of natural history."[47]

Little wonder, then, that this anthropological Grand Narrative which early modernism sought to renew should fit so easily with Aragon's misquotes from Schelling ("Ausschauende Idee," in *Le Paysan de Paris,* probably referring to the *intellektuelle Anschauung* beloved of Idealism), or with Döblin's Expressionist kinship. (Franz Biberkopf himself would exemplify such an anthropological type no less than Wang-lun.) The central role of Nature as actor in *Die drei Sprünge des Wang-lun,* as also in the later *Berge Meere und Giganten,* depends on this larger anthropological claim. The history of peasant revolt is also presented as natural history.

Just as in the case of essentializing Orientalism versus specific history earlier noted, there is a tension here between the totalizing and ontologically founded *grand récit* of natural history, and the absolute decisionistic spontaneity and contingency cultivated by any Expressionist hero, a contingency named directly in the "three leaps" of the novel's title. The tension is not entirely new, dating back at least to the eighteenth century: Döblin has, in a sense, only radicalized an aspect of classical bourgeois ideology, namely the contradiction between individual and subject. The text of Döblin's novel may now be looked at more closely with a view to how the concept of nature articulates this contradiction.

In *Die Drei Sprünge des Wang-lun* the turn-of-the-century revolt against psychology and science (which we have just seen echoed in *Ost und West*'s Nietzschean image of *Ostjuden*) is ostensibly under the aegis of an Expressionist appeal to nature. That appeal renewed the eighteenth century's protest against civilization's discontents newly rebaptized as a *Lebenslüge*; thus one may find in Döblin classical bourgeois elements of nature as legal instances of appeal in a moral lawsuit against culture. Against any priestly or revealed religion, Wang-lun's fellow rebels appeal to what seems to be a classic natural religion with its corresponding idea of natural rights:[48] "Unser, unser Buddha blickt uns aus Himmel, Bergen und Bachen an; die Donnerschläge grüssen ihn besser als Pauken und Gongs; sein Weihrauch sind Wolken und Wind . . ."[49]

The practical consequences of this position are, however, aporetic and unstable: on the one hand, there is the ethics of nonresistance ("nicht handeln; wie das weiße Wasser schwach und folgsam sein; wie das Licht von jedem dünnen Blatt abgleiten") (80); on the other, a rejection of quietism (Wang "kannte von Haus aus nicht die pflanzliche Geduld seiner Landsmänner," 46) and the gradual shift from the *wu-wei* (meaning Taoism's "non-action") sect's peaceful anachoretic begging to the orgy of destruction at the novel's end. The appeal to nature is not only made by both sides of every conflict in the novel, whether Wang versus the Emperor (both claiming political legitimation), Wang versus Ma-noh (over the question of the sect's practice of chastity), or the Emperor versus the Tibetan Lama (on different ways of ruling); it also appears to alter diachronically within the mind and actions of Wang himself. This suggests that there is more than one form of "nature" at work here, that nature has been dissolved or disseminated within the multiple discursive and fantasmatic functions it must support. A lengthy re-exposition of Taoist political metaphysics near the end of the novel suggests that Wang's recourse to military violence was less an internal consequence of the appeal to nature than a pragmatic measure of self-defence against Imperial persecution (471). This flatly contradicts the desire for death and destruction driving Wang's action by the novel's end, which is, moreover, occasionally combined with suggestions of eschatological tension or individual salvation.[50] Nature appears thus to function less as a scientifically referential than a pragmatic-operative notion. But even in legal terms, one could not extract any consistent basis in *Naturrecht* from this novel, as will become clear.

For despite the imagery of silent non-human nature deployed to justify the doctrine of non-action, and the frequent use of natural backgrounds from which human actions seem mysteriously to spring, Döblin's novel is anything but pastoral: the appeal to nature leads rather directly back to a primitive society, one organized by magic and religion and liable to violent outbursts of collective psychosis. Döblin's populist and sectarian China (at the time of the historical eighteenth-century Wang-lun in fact a highly rationalized bureaucracy) is characterized by animism, ancestor cult, ritual, and sympathetic magic and by a corresponding looseness of individual character. The familiar strategies of eighteenth-century *Naturrecht* are dysfunctional when the human "nature" in question tends less to emancipation than to something like Freud's totemic horde. The ambivalent, regressive, and often near-psychotic aspects worn both by the fictive Chinese society and by individual protagonists suggest less a process of emancipatory renewal than one of decay and collapse — a failure which, moreover, suggests a collapse of paternity. The seeming restoration of order at the end of the book cannot dispel the persistent sense of a failure of authority, which is most graphically represented in the Emperor's long interview with the Lama Paldan Jische, but also informs Ma-noh's betrayal of Wang and the ultimate failure of Wang's own military rebellion.

All these contradictions — between nature as passivity and activity, regression and rebellion — are familiar from literature on colonial history. Fanon also noted that "the resistance that forests and swamps present to foreign penetration is the natural ally of the native," yet warned that there could be, for the latter, "no question of a return to nature."[51] More recently, Ranajit Guha has criticized just this reduction of revolutionary history to *Naturgeschichte:*

> Historiography has been content to deal with the peasant rebel merely as an empirical person or member of a class, but not as an entity whose will and reason constituted the praxis called rebellion. The omission is indeed dyed into most narratives by metaphors assimilating peasant revolts to natural phenomena: they break out like thunder storms, heave like earthquakes, spread like wildfires, infect like epidemics. In other words, when the proverbial clod of earth turns, this is a matter to be explained in terms of natural history.[52]

This is, of course, a central aspect of Döblin's fiction of peasant revolt; yet one may question whether Guha's assertion that such an assumed "identity of nature and culture" (1371) necessarily entails a degradation of revolt, or that the latter can only be appropriately grasped through a proper attribution of conscious "agency" to its actors (1397–98). This sort of agency would in fact only restore a familiar strong revolutionary ego psychology, another form of political imaginary to replace the bourgeois form it supplants. On the contrary, Döblin's novel involves a criticism of any such imaginary psychology, as will become clear.[53]

Rebellion against authority must also mean one against the inner authorities of the ego, which Freud termed, not without reason, "institutions." (This need not mean that, like colonialist historiography, Döblin only sees "insurgency ... as pure spontaneity pitted against the will of the State" [1400].)

Döblin's revolt, rather than restoring conscious agency in the manner of Guha's revisionist historiography, has more in common with Fanon's famous "zone of nonbeing, an extraordinarily sterile and arid region, an utterly naked declivity where an authentic upheaval can be born."[54] And as with Fanon, so Döblin's peasant revolt leads ultimately to the death drive, to an outburst of aggressivity leading to "collective autodestruction."[55] Moreover, this destructiveness is not merely a matter of the release of formerly repressed impulses, but is rather bound up with an overall breakdown of the symbolic: as one Lacanian, Richard Boothby, has written of mass gang violence, "in the failure of adequate symbolic mediation, the destructive forces of the death drive are unleashed on the level of the imaginary."[56]

This symbolic breakdown is evident already in the *hors-texte* of the novel's "Dedication," where the author drops his normal epic anonymity to come forth in the first person. The anthropological process of "fictional self-fashioning," as Clifford terms it, is here acutely evident, in accordance with the lyric mode Döblin has adopted. The short text is a prose poem (carefully constructed with parallelisms and refrain-like repetitions) whose descriptive observations tend to hymnic, magical evocation, and virtual address. It is uncertain whether the overwhelming and almost natural, even animist vitality of the city is urging the author to remember or distracting him from his intent:[57]

> That I not forget —
>   A gentle whistle up from the street. Metallic onrushing, whirring, cracking. A blow against my bone pen-holder.
>   That I not forget —
>   What then?
>   I want to close the window.
>   The streets have acquired strange voices in recent years. A rose is tensed under the stones; meter-thick glass shards bob at the end of every rod, grollende iron plates, echo-chewing Mannesmann tubes. A rumbling, rattling around of wood, mammoth maws, pressed air, rubble. An electrical fluting sound along the tracks. Motor-wheezing cars sail along over the asphalt, lain on their sides; my doors tremble. The milk-white streetlights crackle massive beams against the windowpanes, unload cartloads of light into my room. (7)

This passage is very close to Malte Laurids Brigge's famous characterization of the nocturnal city sounds invading his hotel room in Paris.[58] Whereas Malte cannot fall asleep until he hears near dawn the specifically natural, thus organic, sounds of a dog and a rooster, described as a "relief" and an "infinite comfort," Döblin is less threatened by mechanical artifice, and prefers to hear within motors and electricity the vital energy that powers them. "Nature" for Döblin is a large enough category to include the second nature of urban artifice, and this means a potential opening up of modernism's monologic subject as well (a potential, however, not to be realized until the novel's end). The massed adjectives and participial forms of his expressionist prose have the effect of unleashing the dynamic *natura naturans* behind the appearance of artificial *naturata*. Even the near-psychotic, hallucinatory aspect that this modern animism entails — that is, the multiple "strange voices" of the streets, heard in the onomatopoietic muttering of Döblin's German mother tongue (*lalangue*) — are less minatory than simply unfamiliar. Thus at the opposite pole of Döblin's style, the abstract nouns frequently used to designate movement and activity (mostly verbal infinitives, i.e. gerunds) suggest a magical relation of naming and dialogue.[59] In accordance with the expressionist tendency to metonymic exchange between humans and things, this allegorical dimension is extended to the following description of crowds:

> But I know the people on the sidewalk. Their radios (*Telefunken*) are new. The grimaces of greed, the hostile satiety of the blue shaven chin, the thin snuffle-nose of randiness, the roughness, in whose jellied blood the heart diminutively throbs, the watery dog-gaze of ambition, their throats have gaped through the centuries and filled them with — progress.
> O, I know this. I, combed over by the wind.
> That I not forget —
> In the life of the earth two millennia are a year.[60]

Nihil novis sub sole, the narrator sighs with relief: I know this, thus I am a subject, an I. As if in answer to this, the opening imperative sentence, the "original" intent of the narrator, returns like a refrain, Döblin cutting off his groping invocation with an epigrammatic and apodictic sentence: "In the life of this earth, two thousand years are one year." The urban experience of dizzying timelessness, even of a mythic Eternal Recurrence, is here idiosyncratically answered by a gnomic statement first suggesting the tradition of German *Naturphilosophie* and then put into the context of Taoism. From familiarity ("Ich kenne das") the author has arrived at the security of knowledge (*Erkenntnis*). The authority of Döblin's Chinese father arrives in the form of a seemingly unauthored categorial assertion, discursive and abstract after the chaotic flood of concrete images that has preceded. A quotation from the Taoist *Book of Lieh-tzu*[61] follows, then the naming of its father-author whose venerable patronage this modernist novel seeks:

> Gaining, conquering; an old man spoke: "We go and know not where-to. We remain and know not where. That is all the strong life-force of heaven and earth: who could speak here of gain or possession?"
>   I want to sacrifice to him behind my window, the wise old man
>   Lieh-tzu
> with this powerless book.

Lieh-tzu is a father who knows not to resist, not to believe in himself or to attempt mastery, but rather yields to the onslaught of anonymous, causeless natural forces (including those of urban modernity). As a "wise old man" he is more like a grandfather than a father: beyond any possibility of aggressive rivalry with a son. However, Döblin's gesture to him is still one of a sacrifice (*Opfer*) of his "helpless book": authorship is itself here related to the Chinese cult of ancestors. The *Opfer* in question is an identification with the Taoist's deliberate nonaggression. In this way the appearance of the fictional father stabilizes Döblin's narrating I which had, until now, been marked by nervous distraction and anxiety.[62] The closing of the writer's window to the noise of the city represents a turn to the authority of the symbolic: Döblin as author can offer his book in sacrifical exchange to the distant ancient author Lieh-tzu and thereby gains for the first time a will, a definite desire ("Ich will ihm opfern"). It is the father and not the chaotic experience of city as nature which is the object of that desire and the generator of authorial subjectivity. It is difficult to find much "Occidental colonialist hegemony" or appropriation of the other in this self-abnegating, anti-Oedipal gesture of openness to the East. Instead, the non-resisting Father offers here, in his quietistic acceptance of nature, a limit to the violence of human artifice.

This paradoxical pursuit of subjective stability, of fictional self-fashioning, which the poetic "Dedication" already presents in microcosm, will also drive the fictional narrative of *Wang-lun* itself. As also in the case of the near-contemporaneous *Totem and Taboo*, the genesis of the subject is simultaneous with the genesis of a collective political body, that of Wang's peasant rebel movement based on a mythical Taoist version of *Naturrecht*. As in Freud, "a myth of the origin of the subject, the Oedipus complex is consequently also a political myth, a myth with a political function. It is the myth of the Subject Politic . . ."[63]

In Döblin's case, however, the political myth in question is not Oedipal (any more than it could be in the later case of Fanon). Thus, rather than constitute themselves as stable subjects, the novel's individual "characters" tend to break apart into wildly discontinuous, manic extremes of mood and action (like Wang's near the end of the novel, or the Emperor's after his failed interview with the Lama), and their history thus consists of a series of discontinuous "leaps," as the novel's title implies. At most, one could detect along the course of this chronology of revolt the phylogenetic process of a collective move from magic to religion, or, even more modestly, from conjuring (*Zauberei*) to magic (*Magie*), thus a move from metaphoric identification (sympathetic magic) to metonymy (analogy and contiguity).[64] This process would tend then to move from the magical hallucinations of the imaginary towards the sublimated and symbolic structures of religion. There are certainly examples of this in Döblin's text. Magic, characterized by undistanced identification, whether with nonhuman nature or other human subjects, typifies the quasi-totemic tiger-mask used by Wang's father for exorcistic practice, or Wang's stag-mask for his murderous avenging of Su-koh's death (*Drei Sprünge* 41, 67). A more stable form of metaphoric political authority is suggested later on, when, partly in reaction against Ma's betrayal, Wang asserts that "I am the column that must bear all, I am the sky that rests impenetrably over the poor [*der Himmel, der undurchbrechbar über den Armseligen ruht*]" (158–89). Yet even here, the conventional male image of the vertical column is promptly diffused by the more feminine and natural one of a sky "resting" horizontally "over" the poor as if to protect them. This figurative ambiguity would seem to be tied up with the instability of Wang's own authority, depending as it does on the *wu-wei* members' collective identification with him as charismatic leader, more marked more by narcissistic *Verliebtheit* than by identification with a paternal ego-ideal.[65] Wang's betrayal by his erstwhile follower Ma and the members of the "Broken Melon" does eventually teach him at least not to identify magically with masks, as he had earlier: "When they asked him why he, who wanted to bow without resistance to fate as did they, still wore the jacket of a soldier and carried a sword, he answered smiling that many people masked themselves to ward off evil" (161). Key here is Wang's ironic self-distancing from his own mask or role: he no longer believes in it in unreflecting identification, but sees it as merely useful, as a tool.

Wang's shift to a soldierly role thus implies one from a magical identification with nature to a form of socially mediated *Repräsentanz*, but one which is ironic and not fully believed. Yet again, unlike the soldier's uniform of the Imperial troops, his own represents no state instance, only a fictitious function of arbitrarily usurped moral judgment, like the eschatological sword of the Archangel Michael. Thus Wang's own sword, with which he is so centrally associated in the story, is both directed aggressively against others and also finally back against himself. Although it has unquestionably a symbolic function for Wang, the violence by which it helps Wang assume authority, and the magical fashion with which he identifies himself with it, seem to undermine this.

This function of Wang's sword tempts one (almost as a way to test the psychoanalytic claims of postcolonial theory) to a hypothetical comparison with a *grand récit* of Oedipal myth already encountered in these pages, the story of Little Hans.[66] That the subject politic of the charismatic leader is bound up with the confessional lyric subject of the book's dedication implies just this sort of ontogeny-phylogeny relation (beloved of Freud, and still made use of in postcolonial theory). Wang's pursuit of political autonomy would thus become, in such a reading, also a pursuit of subjective and sexual autonomy. Wang's extreme and fetishistic identification with his sword suggests similarity to Hans's deployment of transitional objects. As with Hans, the road to autonomy of the colonial rebel is not a straight one, but one full of detours and *dérives* (Lacan's punning translation of *Trieb*). Just as little Hans must make the circumnavigation of creative and destructive myths (the giraffe drawing and its crumpling, the fantasy of the plumber's *Bohrer*) in order to assume his own subjecthood, so Wang embarks on the circuitous and mathematically combinatory narrative of his "three leaps" which are driven by individual and collective identification, fantasies of imaginary parentage (the *wu-wei* movement as child, like Hans's fantasies of fatherhood; the failed project of imaginary legitimacy, of restoring the Ming dynasty, like Hans's fantasies of marriage), and the representative judging instance of the sword.

Yet a difference from the Freudian model remains. In opposition to Freud's master narrative, there can be no triumphant final assumption of subjectivity for Döblin. Bhabha's intuition of the ultimate instability of colonial rebellion proves thus to be correct, although not for reasons of Derridean "textual slippage" (e.g. the predictable instability of rhetorical tropes), but rather for much more real psychoanalytical ones. As with Hamlet's mother, the desire of Mother Nature will not allow for the formation of a stable subject. The mother of late-nineteenth-century Germany, of Bachofen, or the mother of Jewish Expressionism, mentioned earlier on here, must interfere with such a closure.

Thus Wang's political trajectory ends not with successful sublimation and acceptance of the father, but rather — as Fanon later predicted in the case of Algerian mass uprisings[67] — with the triumph of the death drive. The various subnarratives of the novel (which do not so much causally motivate the final failure of Wang's rebellion as provide analogous models) thus tend to retell one central story of the failure of the father (as giver of the symbolic law) and the consequent desire for aggressive self-destruction.

The most important of these paternal collapses is the long interview between Emperor and Lama, representatives of secular and sacred power, whose confrontation in *Die drei Sprünge* allegorizes that between the

Pope and the Holy Roman Emperor at Canossa in 1077, or even Hapsburg traditions of imperial humility; this Christian subtext is strengthened by the un-Chinese idea that Wang's rebellion is the punishment for the Emperor's sins (305). (The properly Confucian position would be that rebellion follows when the natural order of things, *li,* is disturbed and needs to be set right, *zheng.* Thus the Emperor's sense of *personal* guilt is not Chinese).

Just as in the medieval Latin church, the Emperor is here subject and son to the Lama as father, desperately and abjectly pleading for the latter's power and grant of religious legitimation, with a simultaneous undertone of hostility and rage finally bursting out in an accusation of murder which is at once a reproach and expression of desire to be killed by the father: "Are you not a murderer in your pity for me, your desire to save me?" (309). But like little Hans's reasonable and enlightened father, the Lama will not grant the Emperor the punitive authority the latter seeks, offering instead a political ethics of quietism not far from that of the rebels' *wu-wei* movement itself. Relative to the superior power of religion, the Emperor is here paradoxically in the position of the colonized, attempting to provoke a reaction from the Master, much as in Fanon:

> When it does happen that the Negro looks fiercely at the white man, the white man tells him, "Brother, there is no difference between us." And yet the Negro knows that there is a difference. He *wants* it. He wants the white man to turn on him and shout: "Damn nigger." Then he would have that unique chance — to "show them" . . .
> But most often there is nothing — nothing but indifference, or a paternalistic curiosity.[68]

Unlike the author Döblin in his dedicatory preface, the Emperor cannot accept the wise passivity of the Lama. Instead, helplessly raging, he understands this withdrawal into quietism only as an even more effective means of domination. The long interview between Emperor and Lama has analogies with a psychoanalytic session, with the Lama as an analyst who cannily adopts the stance of silence and playing dead.[69] Deprived both of the Lama-father's blessing of his action and of any chance to rebel or disobey, to break the imaginary identification with the father evident in his helpless demand for love, the Emperor can only watch the Lama beat him in the race to death, a death at once gloriously transfigured and nauseatingly repulsive.[70] With the object of his ambivalent and aggressive love gone, the Emperor turns his rage against himself in a (failed) attempt at suicide, which is both an identification with the dead Lama-father and also a desire to punish him.

At this point, Döblin's text is at its most figuratively dense and complex. Its multiple subnarratives are linked to each other by a series of oblique analogies such as that between the Emperor's voodoo puppet, or homunculus (which a clique of conspirators had tormented and proleptically buried in the palace gardens just prior to the Lama's death, 349–51), and the Lama's own relic-like doll-corpse, or the punning resemblance between the Emperor's lost necklace and his attempted hanging, or his delirious accusing of his son of murder, as he had the Lama. The entire concluding section of part 3 of the novel, centered on the interview between Lama and Emperor, the failed voodoo plot against the latter, and his equally failed suicide, is poetically condensed into the motifs surrounding the poet Tu Fu's elegiac song, performed "on violin and lute" at the Lama's funeral:

> As it says in the old song: in muted tones, veiled by sadness, the deep strings rustling like a flood, the higher ones whispering, — and as the tones became more lively, one thought one heard a rain of pearls falling onto a marble slab . . . And as it says in the old poem: the end of the performance was like a broken vase, from which water streams; and at the close, the bow ran over the violin strings, which trembled under a single stroke, as when one tears a piece of material. (345)

In this passage, a great many motifs from the narrative are condensed, such as the pearls that will shortly fall from the Emperor's necklace before his suicide attempt, and the tearing of the noose. There is indeed no want of "textual" complexity here at the close of part 3 — of punning "ambivalence," or of evidence of anxiety on the part of rulers as well as of ruled. Yet mere rhetorical surface on its own cannot play any determining role: it can neither be a cause nor can it offer any conclusion to the narrative. To isolate rhetorical effects for their own sake is to freeze reading and interpretation within mere Imaginary fascination (like Bhabha's endless "borders" and "hybrids" and mimicry). Much less would it be possible to find any political *desideratum* in the paranoid intricacies of Döblin's writing here, which suggests instead (if one were to read it literally) a frightening regression into collective psychosis, into the same violently primitivist totemism Freud was analyzing in *Totem and Taboo* at the time this novel was written. Döblin's investigation of mass psychosis leads him, still on the eve of the First World War, to an anticipation of the masses of Fascism.

Rather than focus only on rhetorical surface, however, one should attend to what this surface is signifying. Like the magic and conjuring earlier mentioned, Döblin's metonymic figuration is as interminable as the narrative in which it is embedded, and cannot arrive at any stable sense (any secure *point de capiton,* any subject of the statement). In terms of meaning, it thus breaks down; and as such a breakdown, it points to something real beyond. "There is cause only in something that doesn't work."[71]

What this rhetorical instability is pointing to is (somewhat as in *Totem and Taboo*) a fascination with and a desire for death. And since "there is no example of the death drive,"[72] the latter cannot be represented except obliquely, through "that which does not work." The insistent presence of the death drive has a tendency not only to undermine metaphor, but also to convert ostensible intent into the opposite of what it means. Thus both the Lama's attempt at metaphysical salvation of the Emperor and the latter's son's saving him from suicide are paradoxically seen as murder by the Emperor, who wants neither ethical goodness, nor biological existence, but only his frustrated desire for the father, that is, for death. As he says to his son, the prince Kia-king: "If it were not for the dead, we would be completely forsaken. They are my only friends; in them I still hope. The shadows are my only friends" (349). Earlier, during the long meetings with the Lama, during which the Emperor is tormented by guilty fears of his ancestors' displeasure, it is stated of the Emperor that "He fought for his position among his fathers as he never had for a country" (332).

The same desire for death informs Ma-noh's action after he has fallen out of his homosexual identification with Wang-lun as narcissistic ideal ego (in the sense of *Group Psychology and the Analysis of the Ego*). Deprived of this by Wang's prolonged absence, Ma falls into sullen and rebellious despair; it is only a question of when and how to die, of the right *kairos* and preparation for death. "It would be good to die. Why not? It was not a question of living, but rather of arriving at the gates of that quiet, beautiful Paradise well-armed, with arms full . . . Was one prepared?" (190).

Thus Wang himself, who first experiences an erotic temptation to allow his body to be dismembered by the authorities, arrives at the "doctrinal" conclusion that "a Truly Weak can only be a suicide" and then at the ecstatic sense of liberation in destruction at the end (163; also 403, 460). Yet like the Emperor's failed suicide, Wang's final self-annihilation remains only within the domain of imaginary aggression, of acting out and not taking conscience. The mass panic ensuing at the end "liberates nothing at all, and especially not autonomous subjects (individuals),"[73] since the (Mother) Nature it has liberated is also in a sense nothing at all, that is, it does not exist.

Thus at the end of the narrative, the mother triumphs, albeit ambiguously, in the *person of* Kuan-yin on the novel's last page, and also in Wang's dream of being absorbed into the body of a tree (367), whose multiple branches suggest analogies with Kuan-yin's many arms — the same Kuan-yin whose fetishistic doll had presided over the wild sexual orgy which transformed the *wu-wei* into the heretical Broken Melon (130–31). Döblin's Kuan-yin is very similar to the murderous and mourning Niobe who presided over history in Benn's "Der spate Mensch." The matriarchal fantasy of being absorbed into a tree recurs in Döblin's work from *Die*

Ermordung einer Butterblume to *Berge Meere und Giganten* and onward, and is something of an Expressionist topos, found also in early Brecht (in the latter's 1920 poem "Der Geburt im Baum").[74] The visual equivalent to this uncanny nature would be the series of eerily petrified *Forests* painted by Max Ernst in the same decade of the 1920s.

The fantastic body of Kuan-yin moreover suggests the collective and femininized mass identity of the *wu-wei* movement, which is repeatedly described as one monstrous total body (140–41).[75] At the end there is only a strange theophany of the Mother-Goddess Kuan-yin, like Benn's Niobe left in mourning for her children. The message of non-resistance which the book's dedication had assigned to the wise father Lieh-tzu has now passed to a Buddhist matriarch. It is thus not surprising that the last sentence of the book should be a question. Bathed in moonlight, Kuan-yin walks "past" the woman Hai-tang, who is tearing at her own breast in a gesture of ritual mourning, and gives her a concluding message:

> She smiled, looked at Hai-tang, said: "Hai-tang, leave your breast alone. Your children are asleep with me. Be quiet, do not resist, oh, do not resist.
>
> Hai-tang looked further into the green-trailing moonlight. She sat up, pushed the shovels of her hands over her cold face: "To be quiet, not to resist, can I do it then?" (480)

This echo-like concluding question reminds one of the conclusion of *Black Skin, White Masks:*

> My final prayer:
> O my body, make of me a man who always asks questions![76]

Or of an earlier passage from the same book:

> I say that he who looks into my eyes for anything but a perpetual question will have to lose his sight; neither recognition nor hate.[77]

Such a concluding question means that the narrative has not ended with any definitive assertion of identities. Yet it is not merely "ambivalent" either, nor does it simply expose all subjectivity as imaginary "mimicry" or role playing.

In light of the preceding discussion of death-driven destruction and the novel's final apotheosis of the mother, we may return to the larger question of "nation and narration" (Bhabha) in Döblin. The presentation of colonial history here, as in the more famous *Berlin Alexanderplatz,* is indeed marked by discontinuity, contingency, and a dissolution of any unitary subject to direct or authorize its course. But merely to abolish the supposedly "metaphysical" subject in favor of the presumed "functioning" of "discourses," however (as so many literary readings of the 1980s were fond of doing), seems as incomplete as to indulge in encomia of "ambivalence" for its own sake — and perhaps for the same reasons. A look at a representative analysis of *Berlin Alexanderplatz* shows why. Instead of the older "contemplative gesture of the Parisian flaneur" exemplified in Benjamin's reading of Baudelaire, *Berlin Alexanderplatz* uses, in Klaus Scherpe's theoretically ambitious reading, "a type of aesthetic representation of the city . . . that takes pure functionality, the pure abstraction of metropolitan complexity, as its non-objective object." Thus "the representationality of the city . . . is replaced in Döblin's novel by a structural and discursive method of city narration (city as narrator)."[78] The similarity to *Wang-lun,* where the chief agent of history is the mass or the collective, is clear.

Unsurprisingly, though, Scherpe has difficulty with the novel's transfigurative and religiose ending, which is an embarrassment to his conception of collective discourse instead of individual authorship as agent of literature. Instead of trying to puzzle out Döblin's odd conclusion (which need not entail old-hermeneutical assumptions of a total *Sinn*), Scherpe tries to suggest that the reader find meaning in the meaningless, in "the logic of ever-increasing differentiation in the modern capitalist exchange society that, preeminently in the city, incessantly produces this *specific* anonymity, this *remarkable* emptiness" (172) In a word, Deleuzian difference (or perhaps a Foucauldian "discursive inscription"). Yet Scherpe senses that even this is not enough, and has to go on to posit some form of resistance to the very "discourse" he has been putting in place of subjectivity:

> But again, if we do not simply follow the author's intention, if instead we doubt his metaphysical prescriptions, we can recognize in the functional, systematically structured narrative text of the city a liberated potential for meaning that is not necessarily synonymous with the forced symbolic order of the text. Here the text touches upon an imaginary surplus of meanings that calls for closer reading. Not in the progressive transfiguration and sublation of the self, but rather in Biberkopf's linguistic regression — in his babbling, groaning, panting and screaming, and in his hallucinations — here in the reservoir of prelinguistic utterances, a residue of resistance manifests itself against the symbolic power of the discourses. (175)

Biberkopf as *flaneur* becomes here an ancestor of Deleuze and Guattari's "schizophrenic out for a walk" (*Anti-Oedipus*). Scherpe's reading does indeed do justice to this pre-Oedipal aspect of Döblin's heroes. Yet there are also problems left unsolved by his reading. How can "functional, systematically structured narrative" provide "resistance" to "the forced symbolic order"? Scherpe does not mean that "functional" modernity has the rational potential ascribed to it by Habermas, but rather that the "text of the city" is a capitalist machine in Deleuze and Guattari's sense. But as we have seen at the beginning of this chapter, the Imaginary is anything but subversive. As in Tim Dean's discussion of transsexualism, quoted earlier, and as in Bhabha's fetishizing of "borders" and "mimicry," an Imaginary Theory opposes a supposedly pre-linguistic, pre-symbolic bliss to the oppressive Symbolic. As in our extension of Huyssen's reading of *Metropolis* in chapter 1, we may here bring out the strength of Scherpe's analysis by further differentiation. The source of Biberkopf's "prelinguistic utterances" as "residue of resistance" is nothing other than his creaturely Nature, as radically powerless as in *Wang-lun*. This is why the end of *Berlin Alexanderplatz* juxtaposes Biberkopf's death with insistent imagery of trees, wind, and storm. The "babbling, groaning, panting and screaming" is in some ways a more uncanny, modernized version of Nature's *Rauschen* familiar from German Romantics (Eichendorff). Thus one must agree with Scherpe in feeling uncomfortable with this ending, which is far less open and more laden with traditional metaphysical, metaphorical significance than the end of *Wang-lun*.

Unlike Scherpe, we must recognize that the city — as a totality, itself also an imaginary fantasy — cannot be a narrator, any more than can nature. Just as the city was, in Benjamin's famous reading of Baudelaire, always "offstage" and implied in the latter's poetry, creaturely nature is an absent source here.[79] Like *Totem and Taboo*, written at nearly the same time, Döblin's historiography — in *Wang-lun* and elsewhere as well — is one of collective trauma, not only of the function of discourses; and again like *Totem and Taboo*, it is an allegorical historiography, as *Moses and Monotheism* would later be. In *Totem and Taboo* as in *Moses,* the motor of history is a combination of psychotic *Wahn* and bloody sacrifice with the structural repetition of a repressed historic truth, which process nonetheless results in an ultimate triumph of sublimated spirituality.[80] So Lacan insisted on this essentially father-driven model of history, centered on the absolutely causeless *creatio ex nihilo* of the metaphoric Name of the Father.[81] At one point in the third *Seminar* he discussed in detail the catastrophic and contingent quality of historical change:

> The emergence of a new signifier, with all the consequences, down to one's most personal conduct and thoughts, that this may entail, the appearance of a register such as that of a new religion, for example, isn't something that is easily manipulated — experience proves it. Meanings shift, common sentiments and socially conditioned relations change, but there are also all sorts of so-called revelatory phenomena that can appear in a sufficiently disturbing mode for the terms we use in the psychoses not to be entirely inappropriate for them. The appearance of a new structure in the relations between basic signifiers

and the creation of a new term in the order of the signifier are devastating in character.[82]

Here a central problem for so many critics of poststructuralism (under which rubric Lacan is too often hastily subsumed) — namely the question of diachronic change in linguistically modeled systems of signification — is addressed head on with exceptional tact and modesty (note that Lacan does not, like Freud, simply equate phylogenic and ontogenic levels, but only suggests an analogous appropriacy). Like Freud's *Moses*, another "historical novel," *Die drei Sprünge des Wang-lun* is the history of precisely such a ravaging outbreak of a new religion. Yet the paradox is that its "new signifier" is not merely a new Name of the Father, but rather something that eludes and elides the metaphorical stability of such master signifiers. Thus in a sense the new religion in question cannot do other than fail. It is the great paradox of Döblin that what bursts out with such novel and ravaging consequences appears to be nothing other than the, for German tradition, so familiar signifier of Nature, now become uncanny in the extreme. We will need, in closing, to look briefly at one other novel of Döblin to bring out the full implications of this rewriting of Nature.

The Latency of Natural History

The catastrophic historical contingency of *Wang-lun* is staged even more hyperbolically in *Berge Meere und Giganten*, a science-fiction phantasmagory related not only to the work of Döblin's acknowleged model, F. T. Marinetti's 1910 novel *Mafarka le Futuriste*, but also to H. G. Wells, and perhaps even more to the Soviet technological fantasies of Boris Pil'nyak (*The Hungry Year, Machines and Wolves*). With them it shares a rhetoric of violence extreme unto cartoon-like caricature.[83] But unlike Marinetti or Pil'nyak, Döblin ends his novel with elegiac reflection on the limits of violence and of technological mastery.[84] In this, he could be compared to Andrei Platonov, who after an initial infatuation with Lenin's famous project of "electrification" turned to a work of mourning for the victims of collective technocratic fantasies (in *Chevengur* and *The Foundation Pit*). For Platonov as for Döblin, the first victim of these violent fantasies of total technological control is nature in its largest sense; but Platonov returns as little as Döblin to any restorative, compensatory Imaginary visions of nature in his critique of technocracy.

As with *Wang-lun, Berge Meere und Giganten* begins with a dedication, in which the addressee has shifted: the ancient father-as-writer (Lieh-tzu) has been replaced by nature itself, an interlocutor whose name is legion as only the devil's, so that its pronominal form of address slips almost continuously (from *Du* to *ihr* to *er*) until it seems to stabilize in the neutral it (*es*):

> What am I doing if I write about you [dir]. I have the feeling I ought not to write a word about you, indeed, not to think too clearly about you. I name you "you" as if you were already an essence, animal plant stone like me. There I see already my helplessness and that every word is futile. I don't dare to approach you [euch] too closely, you monstrous ones, monsters who have borne me into this world, there where I am and how I am . . .
>
> Now I speak — I won't write thou [Du] or you [ihr] — of him, the thousand-foot-thousand-arm thousand-head. Of that which is a whirring wind . . . Always new crackling melting disappearance . . .
>
> Every minute a change . . . On every leaf stem root happens something each second.
>
> There works the Thousand-Named One. There it is.[85]

There is no Buber-like I and Thou with Mother Nature, as there can be with Father God. This millennial, millicephal millipede is not even the Hero With a Thousand Faces, the "monsters who have borne me into this world" suggest once more Goethe's Mothers at work — or at very least the existence of mass psychology within nature. The primitive expression of triumph in naming — "There it is!" — recalls the child's acquisition of language, although the text still does not manage to stabilize even at this point. The "there it is" ("da ist es") suggests an appellative, demonstrative moment, as if Döblin were pointing to something which the reader had to see off the page. The forms of address for nature thus continue to shift ("wer ist das," then *sie,* then *ihr* again) — until the entire dedication ends with an allusion to Goethe: "I do not want to have left this life without having opened my throat for that which I often feel with terror, and now listening in silent inkling [*das, was ich oft mit Schrecken, jetzt stille lauschend, ahnend empfinde*]." Once more we have the stylized and archaic language not only of *Naturphilosophie*, but also of lyric poetry. Goethe, it should be noted, is a father decidedly nearer to hand than Lieh-tzu.

The narrative which follows is again an anthropological one, one of natural history, of the human species itself. The first sentence is: "No one was living any longer of those who had survived the war they called the world war" (13). Döblin's history thus starts with an absence of historical or biological continuity, and thus of collective memory: the beginning of history is a trauma, a shock. The massive death of the war, depicted in broad, *al fresco* manner, is continued, apparently without cause, in peacetime: "The young men who had returned from the battles had fallen into their graves," and then acquires Biblical paratactic sonority: "Generation after generation [*Geschlecht um Geschlecht*] was requartered by a slowly slipping wall. They went into the dark apartments prepared by the elements. Behind them there were raised already the new races [*Geschlechter*] ...." History is here presented as a discontinuous series of unrelated events, more like a chronicle or annal than *Geschichtsschreibung*.

What results from this discontinuity is the amnesia of 1920s *Sachlichkeit*, a slick cosmetic consumerism which appears as a mutation of the human animal itself, become inherently irreal: "Young men with gleaming combed-back hair, lively eyes, fresh mouths and cheeks, who liked to laugh." The grotesque metonymies of Expressionism have continued into New Objectivity, depicted as a parody of the pseudo-biological myth of Youth traceable from the turn of the century to the heroic mass identity of Fascism.[86] The "bright young boys and girls" are already a fatherless, parentless generation, their succession a meaningless discontinuity ironically underlined by the omnipresence of death. No further history can be written other than that of the human species as pure blind nature with no paternal telology inscribed into it. The novel may be read as a search for a subject of history in the wake of a collective trauma, and thus as an attempt at the anthropological reconstitution of Man, after mass decimation and fragmentation.

This process is pursued through an anthropological conflict and ostensible reconciliation with nature, moving from national or geopolitical struggle (the Uralic war) to internal social tensions (the international senate's establishment of hegemony) and a quasi-Luddite revolt against technology, to a colossal hubristic unleashing of nature's productive forces (Iceland/Greenland), which then disastrously backfires. The outbreak of fiery volcanic destruction and monstrous genetic mutation that follows the unleashing of the Icelandic volcanoes is the point where nature itself becomes a narrative and historical subject, in a sublime spectacle outbidding even the grandiose Enlightenment *Naturtheater* that Lisbon and the Bastille, analogously, were for Kant. As the "Dedication" makes clear, the subject of this history is nature as actor, as in the marginal tradition of Romantic *Naturphilosophie* (Schelling, Bloch). In the imagination of the Romantics, stones could speak, and the boundaries between organic and inorganic would be lifted; Schelling in particular opposed the dynamic power and becoming (*das Werden*) of *natura naturans* to the dead empirical facts of *natura naturata*.[87]

Stripped of his cryptic theological underpinning, "man" in Döblin's "Dedication" is subject to evolutionary, experimental, and mutant vagaries that distort him often beyond recognition. The anthropological thematics familiar from Benn's poetry of the 1920s, with its echoes of Spengler's monumental pessimism, occasionally resonate here as well:

wild animals return, the earth calms down, the perverted species of man has been disposed of. The whole earth needs to recover from man ... Man is an evolutionary mistake [*eine Fehlart*] ... There is no doubt, the human species has no perdurability. It destroys itself, devours itself ... (109)

Before assigning this anti-humanism any hasty political index, or leaping to facile analogies to current environmentalism, however, one should remember that Karl Kraus made similar statements ("Being human is a mistake").[88] Shortly before this anthropological jeremiad, a form of social engineering is discussed in the novel, which would tend to the extinction of the individual in favor of the anonymous totality of the species (recalling Jünger's right-wing utopian model of the Worker), an idea framed in paradoxically *Wang-lun*-like terms of approximating man to a deindividualized element such as water (61). Marx's famous idea of a *Stoffwechsel* between humanity and nature here acquires grotesquely literal realization. Like Platonov's "secret men," Döblin's heroes have a deep desire to extinguish their individuality in larger anonymous forces, as if their self-sacrifice might further the impersonal course of natural history; and in Döblin's case, this depersonalization, this disappearance into the natural already has a gendered and racial coding comparable to the feminizing fantasies of Dr. Schreber,[89] who imagined himself transformed into a woman for the salvation of humanity. "Redemption" must depend here on the sacrifice of the *principium individuationis,* and thus also of manhood.

Berge Meere und Giganten does not sputter out in the futile orgy of raging self-destructiveness of *Die drei Sprünge des Wang-lun,* but appears to reconstitute a narrative subject, precisely when Delvil, and then Kylin, stranded like Deukalion or Noah in the catastrophic aftermath of a technocratic historical disaster, tautologically affirm their human identity: "I am a human [ein Mensch] You will not convince me of the contrary" (409). Yet the anthropological self-constitution of species-being does not yet take place here. For the immediate denegation (*Verneinung*) called up by this affirmation of species-being is almost comical, exposing the paranoid aggression inhering in any such collective identification. (As Lacan had it in his parable of the prisoners; "I affirm myself to be a man, out of fear the others might convince me I am not one.")[90] The reconstitution of a human subject and the subduing of the violent death drive which have determined the narrative until now — which is the point where this novel goes "beyond" the destructive end of *Wang-lun* — is sealed rather in Kylin's primitive, quasi-Zoroastrian fire religion. The moment of magical identificatory fascination with fire both defines a social order (a clan identity distinguished by tattoos) and ritually constitutes a historic memory, that of the fiery destruction of Iceland, which is here first assumed and consciously acknowledged by man. Fire thus represents both the anarchic, illimited productive power of nature as *natura naturans,* and man as its reflective instrument, its tendency toward metaphor checked by its inherent ambiguity. Unlike the totemic identificatory animal masks of *Wang-lun,* fire is a spiritualized form of magic, perhaps the latter's earliest form.

A closer look at this moment in the narrative shows that Kylin's reaffirmation of the "human" is in fact profiled against the traditional idea of *Gattungswesen,* of species as totality. The ethical responsibility of humanity is inseparable from its particularity.[91] The key passage occurs late in the last of the novel's nine books, as Kylin and his nomadic followers view the panorama of natural destruction of which they must recognize themselves as authors:

> "Just let one say," Kylin lamented, "that a man is like a tree, a stick, a heap of sand. He is not the same as air or stone. The stones are smashed. The Giants crushed the rocks; the trees they have trampled make me sorry for them. But to see this: humans [*die Menschen*]. Look at them: they are humans. It is more than muscles and bones and skin. The Giants did not see it. Even I myself didn't see it. They lived. They're gone." They cried around him. (496)

De singularibus est scientia, says Kylin: it is the birth of history from the failure of technocracy. Kylin's statement is a direct rejoinder to the earlier experimental attempt to convert the species into an anonymous element, a form of mimesis nature unto death. His rejection of the classic Idealist notion of the *Gattungswesen* — the subject of all anthropological philosophies of history from Marx to Adorno — is, within Döblin's narrative, tied up with a rejection of the giants who appear in the third part of the novel's anti-metaphoric title. These giants, huge and obscenely totemic towers of flesh more impotent than omnipotent,[92] are the logical outcome of the narcissistic fantasm of the species as such, a parodic miscarriage of the species-being, which unmasks itself as being death driven, a mimesis of the inorganic and unconscious.[93]

The mimesis of the inorganic leads, however, not only to destructiveness, but also to a resurrection of the inorganic mineral world, a favorite idea of Romantic *Naturphilosophie,* and tied to a magical, incantatory power of naming: "It then seemed to the stones as if each one were being called by name" (317). As a consequence, the boundaries between organic and inorganic, and living and dead, are annulled, and an apocatastasis (or general resurrection) of all of nature and of prehistory, one of the oldest heretical margins of orthodox Christianity, ensues.

As in *Wang-lun,* the multiple subnarratives of the novel, such as the three fairy tales which occupy much of Book 5 (a caesura in the course of the narrative), are largely concerned with the collapse of paternal authority. Döblin uses African fairy tales not to reassert an exotic primitive virility against feminized European decadence, but rather to show the global universality of the decline of the Oedipus Complex. The African King Mansu collapses under the narcissistic immobility of his own authority as if in a paroxysm of autoerotic pleasure, drowned in "the soft seedy mealpap" of bananas (253); a lion is gradually deceived, rendered helpless, and treacherously murdered by a cunning dog, a narrative of the dialectics of reason not unlike Odysseus's outwitting of Polyphemus (264). Most apposite here is the fable of the Eulenspiegel-like, psychotic wild-child Hubeane, who ritually murders his father in a moon-mask and then denies the deed outright (258–59).[94] The triumph of the mother runs through the entire novel, from the *Venus barbata* Melise to the invention of "Männinnen" ("she-men") to replace women (432), to the final redemptive appearance of Venaska (a modern variant of Diana the huntress).

In this novel, Döblin has pushed the circumvention of normalizing Oedipal structures, the exposure of trauma, and the proximity to psychosis (a modernist topos), further than in any of the literary works previously discussed here. But as at the end of *Berlin Alexanderplatz,* he is not content to leave things there, adding, as a surprising natural-historical conclusion to the narrative, what might be called an anthropological *Urszene.* In place of any contemplative symbols of the Eternal Feminine — as implied by *Wang-lun*'s final theophany of the Goddess — the book concludes with a radical anthropological renewal, a literal illumination of "human nature," after a long hymnic peroration on nature faintly recalling the "Dedication":

> Black the aether above them [= the human race], with little sun-balls, sparkling scorified heaps of stars. Breast on breast lay the blackness with people, light gleamed from them. (511)

This scene contrasts with the conception of Mafarka's son, where Mafarka goes out into a wheat field to lie on his back and be impregnated by the sun, "a colossal solid copper hen, spreading its wings of light over the horizon."[95] (The unwittingly comical aspect is, in Marinetti's feverish hyperboles, even more evident than in Döblin's.) In Döblin's variant, the human collective subject is less feminized than Marinetti's hero. As an almost Paracelsan cosmic macro-body of a human collective, become itself a new star, humanity couples with a black maternal sky:[96] Döblin's religion of light evokes Zoroastrianism and its aesthetic expression in Hegel's symbolic artwork. Light is "the first ideality, the first self of nature," or in terms very close to Döblin's essay *Das Ich über die Natur,* "the general physical ego [Ich]." "In light, nature begins for the first time to become subjective."[97] That is, nature almost approximates here a language, and the acquisition of language is tied up with a specifically natural sexuation. Light is one of the places where language (the symbolic) anaclitically "leans" on the real, as it does in all natural imagery, or in mythic actions which mimic a bridge over the chasm between nature and culture. If the real is that which is always in the same place, then that place had historically to be discovered. This happens via the favorite modernist trope of the constellation.[98]

> The perfectly regular movement of the sidereal day is clearly what gave men their first opportunity of sensing the stability of the changing world around them, and of starting to found the dialectic of the symbolic and the real, in which the symbolic apparently springs from the real, which naturally isn't any more well-founded than thinking that the so-called fixed stars revolve around the Earth. Similarly, one shouldn't think that symbols actually have come from the real. But it is nonetheless striking seeing how captivating these singular forms have been, whose grouping, after all, is not founded on anything. Why did human beings see the Great Bear that way?[99]

The wound of the Kantian sublime is also the seam of the origins of language; and the gigantic history of Döblin's novel closes on this open seam, the trace and memory of a collective historical and technological trauma which the book has attempted to narrate.

Trauma as Limit

In these novels of Döblin, "nature" has radically changed its anthropological (and thus narrative) function. No longer the traditional Imaginary maternal complement and ground to the Law of the Father, it appears first as a violent and even inherently self-destructive opponent of an unstable human subject, and then as an unpresentable limit. In contradistinction to Lacan's idea of paternally (symbolically) driven history, Döblin's aesthetic modernity depends on a traumatic decoupling from the father's name, similar perhaps to Freud's *Moses*-narrative of repetitive identifications no longer resulting in an irreversible "Schritt in die Geistigkeit" (step into spirituality). If Döblin could assert, in a formula reminiscent of Ernst Bloch, that "the physical world is incomplete and therefore not real"[100] — thereby cutting through every fantasm of total Nature, which can exist as little as Woman — then this must apply to *Naturgeschichte* as well, a philosophical totalization of history which has not yet begun. The traditional constructions of *Naturgeschichte* familiar from the German Idealist inheritance, with their telos of ultimate reconciliation, have thus been rewritten through the experience of trauma.

Rather than a totality, nature becomes, for Döblin, a remainder, the literal fallout in the wake of human catastrophe as it was sketched out in chapter 1 here. This aspect is evident in the anecdote he later wrote of

Berge Meere und Giganten's origin, as of his larger turn to *Naturphilosophie*.[101] After the completion of *Wallenstein*, there followed a period of intensive political pamphleteering (under the name Linke Poot), then the medieval play "The Nuns of Kemnade."

> In the meantime I had seen on the Baltic coast a few stones, ordinary pebbles [*Geröll*], which affected me. I brought the stones and sand home with me. Something moved within me, around me. [. . .] Then I was deeply affected, early in 1919 in Berlin, by the sight of a few black treetrunks on the street. He's got to go, I thought, the Emperor Ferdinand. That which affected me, the current of emotion, the new spiritual thing, grabbed immediately onto what it encountered.[102]

The weakness and obscurity, even the abjection of these random scraps of nature, moved Döblin: they were the opposite of the technological sublime. One could imagine these natural leftovers strewn over the sand as part of a sculpture of Josef Beuys, or glued onto one of Anselm Kiefer's monumental landscapes of catastrophe. So the Knight Templar says to Judith in the play Döblin had just written: "Worship when I uncover the stone. It is youth with the soul of a man and of a woman, the low God. He is in you. When he leaves you, you will be dead. He is in all of us, in the animals, the trees, the air."[103]

The Low God of nature is the Abject, the object a. As Real, it "has no predetermined content because it is always in some sense contingent: it comes as a surprise."[104] It is a limit, yet not a prohibitive one. Through the multiple allegories of technocratic disaster and a colonial struggle masking the gendered ambiguities of Jewishness in early-twentieth-century Germany, Döblin has also confronted a further trauma still, namely that of Real sexual difference. This last, as inherently resistant to representation, can only appear through the allegorical mediation of Imaginary formations such as nation, race, and gender.[105] Thus also "nature" as such cannot be figured as anything positive here, that is, neither as fantasy nor as narrative conclusion (*point de capiton*, master signifier). Nature as Real difference, remnant and limit, must remain offstage, "hors-texte," implicit. As Tim Dean puts it,

> . . . the real can be defined only negatively, as a zone of impossibility. Yet far from its negativity rendering it conceptually redundant, the real's impossibility is what renders it constitutive. That is, the real represents the condition of possibility for both the subject and the discourse, insofar as the real is what must be excluded for the subject as a speaking being to constitute itself. The real is not an effect of symbolic or imaginary orders; at most it is a theoretical construct that explains negatively the function and limits of these other two orders.[106]

Döblin's writing repeatedly and traumatically encounters this real limit, right from the "Dedications" of the two novels here discussed through their violent and aporetical "conclusions"; and in Döblin, the real is historically figured as a limit to technocracy and its violence. Thus the earlier-quoted end of *Berge Meere und Giganten* rewrites the gendered primal scene of scientific reason, Sir Francis Bacon's "chaste and lawful marriage" between mind and nature,[107] and it does so in such a way as to expose the real which is excluded by the scientific subject's entry into the symbolic. "Nature" thus becomes, for Döblin, the real limit to technocratic fantasies of total domination, and that limit rests ultimately on the bedrock of sexual difference figured in his science-fiction novel's final coupling. With this, we may return to the motto from Irigaray which preceded this chapter:

> A machine has no sex. Nature, on the other hand, always has a sex. Obviously, there are times when a machine mimics sex . . . But it never creates or engenders life.
>
> The human spirit already seems subjugated to the imperatives of technology to the point of believing it possible to deny the difference of the sexes. Anyone who stresses the importance of sexual difference is accused of living in the past . . . But as long as we are still living, we are sexually differentiated. Otherwise we are dead. The question of whether language has a sex could be subtitled: *Are we still alive?*[108]

In order to answer this question (related to Hai-tang's closing question in *Die drei Sprünge des Wang-lun*) in the affirmative, Döblin must first pass through the narrative and historical trauma of delirious technocratic omnipotence. That trauma becomes paradoxically redemptive in a way similar to Dr. Schreber's. Eric Santner has, in an extended reading of Schreber's memoirs, suggested that Schreber's writing produces a "residue or waste product, a kind of surplus enjoyment"[109] outside the limits of the strict and disciplinary version of Kantian *Aufklärung* he had received from his father. The present reading of Döblin has attempted to work out a cognate logic of the remnant or residue as well, a residue multiply overdetermined by Döblin's Jewishness, his fatherlessness, and his modernism, and yet ultimately represented by Nature. If Santner's Schreber is the author of a "secret history of modernity" centered on what the logic of modernization has left out or traumatically excluded, on "the negative space hollowed out by the will to autonomy and self-reflexivity" (145), this is a secret history clearly related to Freud's own historical novel about religion and rationality, *Moses and Monotheism,* and to Döblin as well.

Irigaray goes on (following the passage just quoted) to suggest that "in our becoming there has been no sexual difference established on the level of the *subject*." Given the impossibility of representing the real of sexual difference, such an establishment could only be negative: namely as a limit and a distinction. For Döblin, nature must hold open this empty place.

The preceding discussion of trauma and history cannot help evoking a considerable scholarly literature around those terms, as they pertained to the historiography of the German-Jewish trauma of the twentieth century and the possibilities of its representation. In fact, the thematics of trauma may offer a trap to the interpreter complementary to those of fantasy and text. If postcolonialism's fixation on "textual effects" threatens to dissolve history into the crossword puzzles of the literary scholar, then a great deal of writing on "unrepresentable trauma" threatens to become stuck on by now predictable Derridean sacralized sublime aporias of unknowability. To generalize that "all history is traumatic" is to subsume historical specificity and contingency in a structural invariance that is interpretatively unhelpful and politically pernicious.[110] For the present argument to result only in the huge generalization that "nature is equal to trauma" would be similarly vague — little more, in fact, than a psychoanalytically updated version of a familiar Adornian metaphysics of history. The "ambivalent" fascination and pathos of trauma should be resisted as much as those of "textual" ambivalence. As La Capra has noted, much literary scholarship on "writing trauma" falls into bathetic and even voyeuristic identification with its subject, as if there might be something perversely desirable about traumatic experience.[111] Predictably, too, the discussion of "writing trauma" has rehearsed its own form of straw-man rhetoric, attacking in this case the old enemy historicism, or "narrative history," and thereby often repeating a gesture made long ago in Benjamin's *Theses*.[112]

To bring this point back to Döblin: the author has not simply put forth some sort of positive model of the "writing of trauma" for the sublime enjoyment of latter-day exegetes. The extreme violence and hyperbole of Döblin's writing do indeed suggest an acting out as much as a reflective working through of trauma (to borrow La Capra's alternative for responses to traumatic experience). Yet at the same time the very destructiveness in which this repetitive acting out results suggests the need for a limit, a frame, and thus an end to historical trauma. If we return to the passage quoted earlier from Lacan on the ravaging outbreak of a new signifier, we need nonetheless to keep in mind that the latter must still signify, and it can only do so relative to a frame — to, that is, precisely that larger historical and narrative continuity against and within which it defines itself. Döblin's testing of the frame of history recalls his contemporary Durkheim's pursuit of social limits in a book written at the same time as *Wang-lun,* namely *The Elementary Forms of Religious Life* (1912). Like Durkheim and Freud in *Totem and Taboo,* Döblin "postulated a hypothetical horde"[113] as prior to social differentiation.

La Capra has described the tension between immediate experience and narrative in specific rhetorical terms:

> history is a field of framed hyperbole — a field in which continually challenged and renewed limits play an important role and in which hyperbole may be required to make a challenge register. In other words, hyperbole or going against the grain also requires the resistance of a grain . . .[114]

To be sure, many historians might raise an eyebrow at the idea of hyperbole's centrality — hardly something characteristic of the understated decorum and irony of so much historiographical prose from Burckhardt down to Momigliano and Peter Brown. For the historical novelist Döblin, however, for whom history was, as it was for Freud, a pretext for exploring persistent underlying tensions of community and continuity, the use of hyperbole has a distinct historical signature, and not just that of Expressionism. The moments of traumatic shock and discontinuity in Döblin have the function of breaking apart the traditional collective subject of anthropological history, thus of the philosophy of history: of undoing humanity's natural species-being (*Gattungswesen*). Paradoxically, nature itself in a specifically modernist form effects this.[115] Yet to hypostasize nature as inherently unspeakable trauma would only replace one old essentialism with another. The tension between nature and history, or trauma and narration, constitutive for both, cannot be split apart.

Notes

[1] Cf. Friedrichsmeyer, Lennox, and Zantop, *The Imperialist Imagination* (Ann Arbor: U of Michigan P, 1998).

[2] Homi Bhabha, "The Commitment to Theory," in *Questions of Third Cinema*, ed. Jim Pines and Paul Wellemer (London: BFI, 1989), 111–32.

[3] For the latter, cf. David Bordwell and Noel Carroll, eds., *Post-Theory* (Madison: U of Wisconsin P, 1996); the present writer is most indebted to Joan Copjec, *Read My Desire: Lacan against the Historicists* and Tim Dean, *Beyond Sexuality*. Nonetheless Bordwell's warnings against the monolithic syncretism of what is often sloppily called "Theory" with a capital T are well taken; one can only agree with him that there are only specific theories, as also with his dethroning of rhetoric, which has reigned now for too long in literary studies. The aspect of Lacan to be developed here is thus emphatically not the rhetorical one favored by film and literary studies (metaphor/metonymy, "unconscious structured like a language," etc.).

[4] See Willi Goetschel's article in Friedrichsmeyer, Zantop, and Lennox, *The Imperialist Imagination*. ("'Land of Truth — Enchanting Name!' Kant's Journey at Home," 321–36).

[5] Slavoj Žižek, *The Fright of Real Tears* (London: BFI, 2001), 5.

[6] Adorno, *Jargon der Eigentlichkeit, Gesammelte Schriften* 6, 416, 418.

[7] Benita Parry, "Problems in Current Theories of Colonial Discourse," *Oxford Literary Review* 9 (1987): 27–59; Henry Louis Gates, Jr., "Critical Fanonism," *Critical Inquiry* 17 (1991): 457–70; Arif Dirlik, "The Post-Colonial Aura," 5.

[8] In this, the present work has precedents in recent comparativist work such as Pamela Cheek's *Sexual Antipodes: Enlightenment Globalization and the Placing of Sex* (Stanford: Stanford UP, 2003), which "challenges the perception" that European representation "of non-Western societies was always an exercise in producing the latter as distorted and denigrated mirror images" (review by Betty Joseph, *Comparative Literature Studies* 42.2 [2005]: 313–16).

[9] Cf. Young, *White Mythologies: Writing History and the West* (London and New York: Routledge, 1990). According to Young, Homi Bhabha "speaks of the need to examine colonial discourse in terms of psychoanalytic as well as historical terms but does not risk any account of how they might be articulated" (144). "[I]n [Bhabha's] essays we see him move from the model of fetishism to those of 'mimicry,' 'hybridisation,' and 'paranoia' . . . On each occasion Bhabha seems to imply [. . .] that the concept in question constitutes the condition of colonial discourse itself and would hold good for all periods and contexts — so that it comes as something of a surprise when it is subsequently replaced by the next one . . . Inevitably, of course, different conceptualizations produce different emphases — but the absence of any articulation of the relation between them remains troubling" (146).

[10] Some aspects of the current jargon of subversion could be traced to Deleuze and Guattari, whose weaknesses the jargon thus inherits. Here one would have to distinguish between *Anti-Oedipus* on the one hand, and Deleuze's earlier, more careful work on the other, as do Žižek (*Organs Without Bodies: Deleuze and Consequences* (New York: Routledge, 2004) and Dean. In the German context, one transmitter of the influence of Deleuze and Guattari was Klaus Theweleit.

[11] Lacan, *Écrits*, 33; see also Dean, *Beyond Sexuality*, 23.

[12] Yosif Hayim Jerushalmi, *Freud's Moses: Judaism Terminable and Interminable* (New Haven, CT: Yale UP, 1991), 6.

[13] Homi Bhabha, "The Other Question: Difference, Discrimination and the Discourse of Colonialism," in *Literature, Politics and Theory: Papers from the Essex Conference, 1976–1984*, ed. Francis Barker, Peter Hulme, Margaret Iversen, and Diana Loxley (London: Methuen, 1986), 167.

[14] Joan Copjec, *Read My Desire: Lacan Against the Historicists* (Cambridge: MIT, 1994), 23.

[15] It is certainly symptomatic that, like Judith Butler, Bhabha prefers quoting Christian Metz or Jacqueline Rose to quoting Lacan himself (cf. Bhabha, "Other Question," 163, note 2). The same methodological problem occasionally dogs the more careful work of Susanne Zantop, who admits early on in her *Colonial Fantasies* (Durham, NC: Duke UP, 1997) that she uses "the terms 'desire' and 'unconscious' metaphorically, not in their strictly psychoanalytical context" (4) — thereby, as Zantop admits in the footnote (212), reducing them to no more than

the historian's quite conscious "mentalities." Like Young and McClintock, she wants to "use psychoanalytic terminology to analyze the sociopolitical imaginary" (212), seeing "fantasies" as "the driving force behind colonialist ideology" (4). But from a psychoanalytic perspective, *fantasy cannot be an ultimate cause* — without eliding fantasy's Real cause itself. Making fantasy into a cause is ultimately a return to the old hermeneutical circle.

[16] Copjec, *Read My Desire*, 34.

[17] See now the sharp critique of Said by Robert Irwin, *Dangerous Knowledge: Orientalism and Its Discontents* (Woodstock: Overlook, 2006).

[18] Bhabha, "Representation and the Colonial Text: A Critical Exploration of Some Forms of Mimetism," in *The Theory of Reading*, ed. Frank Gloversmith (Sussex: Harvester, 1984), 93–122; here 96 and 99.

[19] Spivak, *A Critique of Post-Colonial Reason* (Cambridge, MA: Harvard UP, 1999), 222.

[20] "Contrary to the promise of a 'new historicism,' that wished to historicize literature, historical thinking over the last decade has been converted into a subfield of literature" (Arif Dirlik, *The Postcolonial Aura* [Boulder, CO: Westview, 1997], 5). Keya Ganguly's Marxist critique of postcolonial theory's "textualism" makes a similar point to Dirlik's (Ganguly, *States of Exception: Everyday Life and Postcolonial Identity* [Minneapolis: U of Minnesota P, 1991]). The archival research model of the Subaltern Studies group can lead to very different couplings of literature and history than this, though (see Betty Joseph, *Reading the East India Company, 1720–1840: Colonial Currencies of Gender* (Chicago: U of Chicago P, 2004).

[21] Dean, *Beyond Sexuality*, 87.

[22] To cite one instance: "It is through image and fantasy — those orders that figure transgressively on the borders of history and the unconscious — that Fanon most profoundly evokes the colonial condition" (Bhabha 1994, 43). Neither image nor fantasy are "orders." Fantasy is, by definition, unconscious, and thus cannot "figure" on the latter's supposed "border." Nor is the unconscious necessarily "transgressive," as any reader of Freud or Lacan should know.

[23] Butler, "Imitation and Gender Insubordination," in *Inside/Out: Lesbian Theories, Gay Theories*, ed. Diana Fuss (New York: Routledge 1991), 21.

[24] As Peter Mason (*Infelicities: Representations of the Exotic* [Baltimore: Johns Hopkins UP, 1998], 3) has it, "exoticist representation can be seen as the opposite of Edward Said's 'Orientalism.'"

[25] For some cognate variants of Orientalism in other literatures, see Robert Kern, *Orientalism, Modernism, and the American Poem* (Cambridge: Cambridge UP, 1996). David Lattimore, "Discovering Cathay," *Parnassus* 1 (1973): 5–26, Rolf Goebel, *Constructing China: Kafka's Orientalist Discourse* (Rochester, NY: Camden House, 1997).

[26] Kraus, "Die chinesiche Mauer," *Die chinesiche Mauer*, in *Schriften*, ed. Christian Wagenknecht (Frankfurt: Suhrkamp, 1987), 2:281.

[27] Said's familiar model, designed to explain the Levant, has never gained much acceptance among Sinologists, who rejected it from the start — as for instance

Jonathan Spence in *Chinese Roundabout* (New York: Norton, 1992), Simon Leys in *The Burning Forest: Essays on Chinese Culture and Politics* (New York: Holt, Rinehart and Winston, 1986), and Nicholas Thomas in *Colonialism's Culture* (Oxford: Blackwell, 1994) among others; German Orientalism is one of the most egregious *lacunae* in Said's work. The present chapter must therefore differ from Nina Berman's attempt, in her *Orientalismus, Kolonialismus und Moderne: zum Bild des Orients in der deutschsprachigen Kultur um 1900* (Stuttgart: M&P, 1997), at subsuming German literature under the Orientalist model, based largely on an examination of obscure and minor writers. For a more nuanced view of the problem, see Todd Kontje, *German Orientalisms* (Ann Arbor: U of Michigan P, 2004). Susanne Zantop, too, was careful to distinguish between the complexity of Kleist and Heine and the crude xenophobia of popular fiction.

[28] Regensteiner, "Die Bedeutung der Romane Alfred Döblins von *Die drei Sprünge des Wang-lun* bis *Berlin Alexanderplatz*" (Thesis, NYU, 1952), 52.

[29] For a look at how Döblin reworked his original sources, see Zhonghua Luo, *Alfred Döblins "Die drei Sprünge des Wang-lun": Ein chinesischer Roman?* (Frankfurt: Peter Lang, 1991), chapter 4, 126–39.

[30] Cited in Ulrich von Felbert, *China und Japan als Impuls und Exempel* (Frankfurt: Peter Lang, 1986), 14.

[31] Cf. Heimann's "Tao," posthumously reprinted in *Die Spindel* (Vienna: Bermann-Fischer, 1937), 155–59.

[32] Donna Heizer, *Jewish-German Identity in the Orientalist Literature of Else Lasker-Schüler, Friedrich Wolf, and Franz Werfel* (Columbia SC: Camden House, 1996).

[33] On Franzos, see George Mosse, *Germans and Jews* (New York: Fertig, 1970); for Wasserman, see *Juden in der deutschen Literatur* Berlin, ed. Gustav Krojanker (Berlin: Welt, 1922) and discussion of both figures in Heizer, *Jewish-German Identity*, 14–27).

[34] On this, cf. the first volume of Buber's correspondence, 1972: 412 (letter 288), and Döblin's letters (*Briefe* [Olten: Walter-Verlag, 1970], 57–60). Other translations important for Döblin were those of Richard Wilhelm, of Confucius (1910), Lao-tzu (1911), and most especially Lieh-tzu (1912).

[35] The *Journey to Poland* (originally published in 1925) is available in English (trans. Joachim Neugroschel, ed. H. Graber [London and New York: Tauris, 1991]); *Flucht und Sammlung des Judenvolks* (originally Amsterdam 1935, repr. Hildesheim: Gerstenberg, 1977) is not.

[36] Leslie A. Adelson, *The Turkish Turn in Contemporary German Literature: Toward a New Critical Grammar of Migration* (New York: Palgrave, 2005).

[37] Cited in Gert Mattenklott, "Ostjudentum und Exotismus," in *Die andere Welt: Studien zum Exotismus*, ed. Thomas Koebner and Gerhart Pickerodt (Frankfurt: Athenäum, 1987), 295–96.

[38] Mattenklott, "Ostjudentum," 296.

[39] Cited in Mattenklott, "Ostjudentum," 299.

[40] Cited in Mattenklott, "Ostjudentum," 303.

[41] Count Hermann von Keyserling, *Das Reisetagebuch eines Philosophen* (Munich: Duncker and Humblot, 1919), 2:481–82.

[42] Hesse, *Gesammelte Erzählungen,* ed. Volker Michels (Frankfurt: Suhrkamp 1982), 102.

[43] On this, see von Felbert, *China und Japan,* 42.

[44] On the relation of these writers to ethnography, see James Clifford, *The Predicament of Culture* (Cambridge: Harvard UP, 1988), esp. 118–22; it is, however, very misleading to subsume (as Clifford unfortunately does) the very different aims of Bataille and the Collège under the vague moniker of "Surrealism," as Jean Jamin has rightly pointed out ("L'ethnographie mode d'inemploi," in *Le Mal et la douleur,* ed. Jacques Hainard and Roland Kaehr [Neuchâtel: Musée d'Ethnographie, 1986], 45–70).

[45] Anton Kaes, ed., *Kino-Debatte: Texte zum Verhältnis von Literatur und Film, 1909–1929* (Munich: DTV, 1978), 29.

[46] Clifford continues: "One is tempted to speak of an *ethnographie vérité* analogous to the *cinéma vérité* pioneered by Griaule's later associate Jean Rouch" — a technique one would have to relate rather to *Berlin Alexanderplatz,* a work which, in its own way, is as much an "ethnography" of modern Berlin as *Nadja* was of Paris.

[47] Nicholas Thomas, *Colonialism's Culture* (Oxford: Blackwell 1994), 6.

[48] On this, see the next chapter on Brecht and *Naturrecht:* it is arguable that *Wanglun* influenced Brecht precisely in this question of natural law.

[49] Döblin, *Die Drei Sprünge des Wang-lun* (Olten: Walter Verlag, 1960), 389.

[50] Cf. the suggestion of various "Weltalter" on 297; also Georg Klymiuk's comments on eschatological elements in *Kausalität und moderne Literatur: Eine Studie zum Werk Alfred Döblins* (Frankfurt: Peter Lang, 1984), 202–6.

[51] Frantz Fanon, *The Wretched of the Earth,* trans. Constance Farrington (New York: Grove Press, 1991), 294 and 314.

[52] Ranajit Guha, "The Prose of Counter-Insurgency," in *Postcolonialism: Critical Concepts,* ed. D. Brydon (London and New York: Routledge, 2000), 4:1371.

[53] "Psychoanalysis as the alternative to the colonialist vocabulary of psychology provides an at least partial critique of colonialism as the psychology of the colonizers. Psychoanalysis undermines colonial discourse precisely at its most gendered point" (Russell Berman, *Enlightenment or Empire* [Lincoln: U of Nebraska P, 1998], 153). We will return to the question of gender.

[54] Frantz Fanon, *Black Skin, White Masks,* trans. C. L. Markmann (New York: Grove, 1967), 8.

[55] Fanon, *The Wretched of the Earth,* 54; also 298–300.

[56] Boothby, *Death and Desire,* 181.

[57] Important here is the evoked negation ("that I *not* forget"), cf. Lacan, *Les quatre concepts,* 67, *Ecrits,* 800, and *Sém. VII,* 79, on expletives and negations as the discursive place of the subject — following Freud, "Das Unheimliche," *Studienausgabe* (Frankfurt: Fischer, 1970), 4:267.

[58] Rilke, *Die Aufzeichnungen des Malte Laurids Brigge* (Frankfurt: Suhrkamp, 1978), 8.

[59] The caricatures of the human animal that follow answer the abstract nouns of nature with an allegorical catalogue of vices or sins: *Habgier, Sattheit, Geilheit, Roheit, Ehrsucht*. (Compare the comments on this passage in David Dollenmayer, "The Advent of Döblinism: *Die drei Sprünge des Wang-lun* and *Wadzeks Kampf mit der Dampfturbine*," in *A Companion to the Works of Alfred Döblin*, ed. Roland Dollinger, Wolf Koepke, and Heidi Tewarson [Rochester, NY: Camden House, 2004], 55–74; here 58.)

[60] These metonymic grotesques may remind one of Benn's Ensor-like "Nachtcafé," where Green Teeth, Pimples-in-the-Face gestures to an inflamed eyelid (Benn, *Gedichte*, ed. Hillebrand, 29).

[61] The current English translation is by A. C. Graham, *The Book of Lieh-tzu* (New York: Columbia UP, 1990). In the context of Döblin's urban evocations of Taoism, one should recall that the latter had an oblique relation both to scientific rationality and political anarchism (most famously discussed by Sir Joseph Needham in *Science and Civilization in China*).

[62] On the stabilizing function of the grammatical third person, cf. Lacan, *Sém III*, 116: "The notion of the subject is correlative to the existence of someone of whom I think — *it's he who did that* . . . without this *he* my being might not even be able to be an *I*." The relation of this *he* to the addressing *you* will need to be further developed later on here.

[63] Mikkel Borch-Jakobsen, *The Freudian Subject*, trans. C. Porter (Stanford: Stanford UP, 1988), 194.

[64] Cf. Freud, *Totem und Tabu, Studienausgabe*, 9:367.

[65] Freud, *Massenpsychologie, Studienausgabe*, 9:88.

[66] Cf. Lacan, *Sem. IV*, 360–7. See the discussion of Rilke in chapter 1.

[67] See Fanon, *The Wretched of the Earth*, 54–55, 300–301.

[68] Fanon, *Black Skin, White Masks*, 221; compare Little Hans's demand to his father: "Du musst eifern!" (You must get mad at me!) In Lacan's terms, this is the neurotic's confusing the Other's desire with its demand, meaning that the neurotic is still in the dual imaginary relation of mother and child (cf. Lacan, *Écrits*, 823): the Emperor and Fanon's Negro corresponding to child, Lama and White Man to mother.

[69] Cf. Lacan, *Sém. III*, 182.

[70] This too is an Expressionist topos: think of the rat-infested girl's body of Benn's *Morgue*.

[71] Lacan, *Sém. XI*, 22 ("il n'y a de cause que de ce qui cloche" [there's no cause but something that doesn't function], 30).

[72] Borch-Jakobsen, *The Freudian Subject*, 172.

[73] Borch-Jakobsen, *The Freudian Subject*, 166.

[74] Brecht, *Werke* (Frankfurt/Berlin: Suhrkamp/Aufbau, 1993), 13:160–61); compare also the singing and preaching trees when Mieze and then Biberkopf himself die in *Berlin Alexanderplatz* (Olten: Walter Verlag, 1994), 311, 318, 378.

[75] Here, in a collective sexual orgy, the mass has only one mouth; compare to page 220: "the body of the covenant"; and page 449: "finally the mass itself stood there, simultaneously growing from all the surrounding streets, a thousand-armed Buddha with a black face": here the collective body becomes vegetal. In Borch-Jakobsen's words, it is "a matricial mass: the group as womb" (*The Freudian Subject*, 139).

[76] Fanon, *Black Skin, White Masks*, 232.

[77] Fanon, *Black Skin, White Masks*, 29.

[78] Klaus Scherpe, "The City as Narrator: The Modern Text in Döblin's *Berlin Alexanderplatz*," in *Modernity and the Text*, ed. Andreas Huyssen and David Bathrick (New York: Columbia UP, 1989), 162–79; here 166–68.

[79] It is indeed the weakness of the end of *Berlin Alexanderplatz* — as opposed to the earlier *Wang-lun* — that it makes this natural reference too explicit. One would need to contrast the end of *Berlin Alexanderplatz* (nature as *telos*) with the dedicatory opening of *Wang-lun* (nature as contingency).

[80] Freud, *Der Mann Moses und die monotheistische Religion*, Studienausgabe 9:580.

[81] Lacan, *Sém. VII*, 171, 253.

[82] Lacan, *Sém. III*, 226; English translation by Russell Grigg, *The Seminar of Jacques Lacan, Book III* (New York: Norton, 1993), 201.

[83] On this, see Cinzia Sartini Blum's book on Marinetti, *The Other Modernism: F. T. Marinetti's Futurist Fiction of Power* (Berkeley: U of California P, 1996), especially chapter 3, where Blum notes that "the delirious tone of Marinetti's fantasy invites a comparison with psychotic delusions," specifically that of a total technological mastery of and rupture with nature: "Marinetti envisages his utopian solution in terms of rejection and transcendence of the natural order" (75).

[84] So Ingrid Schuster (*China und Japan in der deutschen Literatur, 1900–1925* [Bern Francke, 1977], 168) already saw *Wang-lun* as a correction of Marinetti through nature.

[85] Döblin, *Berge Meere und Giganten* (Olte: Walter-Verlag, 1977), 10.

[86] Cf. the pathos of tautological "objectivity" of Ernst Glaeser's 1928 *Jahrgang 1902*: "Zum erstenmal war mir das Leben hell, eindeutig ... Gras war Gras, Erde war Erde, Vieh war Vieh, das Leben eine Tatsache" (cited in K. Prumm, "Jugend ohne Vater," in *Mit uns zieht die neue Zeit: Der Mythos Jugend*, ed. T. Koebner, R. P. Janz and F. Trommler [Frankfurt: Suhrkamp, 1985], 578).

[87] See esp. Schelling's *Einleitung zu seinem Entwurf eines Systems der Naturphilosophie* (1799) (Stuttgart: Reclam, 1988).

[88] Karl Kraus, *Aphorismen*, in *Schriften* 8 (Frankfurt: Suhrkamp, 1986), 300.

[89] On the paranoid aspects common to Döblin's and Schreber's writing, see Wolfgang Schäffner, *Die Ordnung des Wahns: Zur Poetologie psychiatrischen Wissens bei Alfred Döblin* (Munich: Fink, 1995). See also Veronika Fuechtner, "Alfred Doeblin and the Berlin Psychoanalytic Institute" (PhD Dissertation, University of Chicago, 2002).

[90] Lacan, "Le temps logique . . ." (*Ecrits*, 213).

[91] This is, again, Alain Badiou's polemical point already referred to in chapter 1 (*Ethics*, trans. Peter Hallward [London: Verso, 2001]).

[92] Compare Blum's *The Other Modernism*, 64–65, on Marinetti's "confrontation with an abject authority figure: a grotesque surrogate father . . . who embodies the recurrent theme of gender confusion."

[93] This perverse naturalization of man is obliquely anticipated early on in the book by the neologism *Stadtlandschaft*, which reveals itself as composed of humans: species-being as Freud's mass-psychological *Urhorde:* "Die Stadtlandschaften bewegten sich. Scharen uber Scharen von Mannern Frauen" or "Die märkische Landschaft warf sich dann auf das anlagernde Strassen- und Fabrikungetüm Hannover" (23, 87, 174). The precedent for this would be the scenes in *Wang-lun* where the mass is attributed one mouth and one body.

[94] Döblin seems to have used real African folk tales as a basis here: a variant of his Hubeane story can be found in a current English translation in *African Folktales*, ed. R. D. Abrahams (New York: Pantheon, 1983), 166–76.

[95] F. T. Marinetti, *Mafarka le futuriste* (Paris: Christian Bourgois, 1984), 153.

[96] The blackness of the sky, a Biblical darkness at noon, recalls the decisive earlier moment in the novel when the skies blackened over Iceland (318–19). The implication is that the memory of this apocalyptic event has not vanished — or even that it might recur.

[97] Hegel, *Asthetik* III (Frankfurt: Suhrkamp, 1970), 31.

[98] Compare also Mary Douglas's discussion of bodily symbolism in *Natural Symbols* (Harmondsworth: Penguin, 1970).

[99] Lacan, *Séminaire II: Le moi dans la théorie de Freud et dans la technique de la psychanalyse* (Paris: Seuil, 1978), 278–79. English translation by Sylvana Tomaselli (New York: Norton, 1988), 238.

[100] Döblin, *Das Ich über der Natur*, 243.

[101] On this period of Döblin's work, see Roland Dollinger, "Technology and Nature: From *Berge Meere und Giganten* to a Philosophy of Nature," in *A Companion to the Works of Alfred Döblin*, ed. Dollinger, Koepke, Tewarson, 93–109.

[102] Döblin, *Aufsätze zur Literatur* (Olten: Walter Verlag 1963), 345.

[103] Döblin, *Die Nonnen von Kemnade* (Berlin: S. Fischer, 1923), 80. Translation in Wolfgang Kort, *Alfred Döblin* (New York: Twayne, 1974), 78.

[104] Dean, *Beyond Sexuality*, 92.

[105] On the difference between gender and sexual difference, see Charles Shepherdson, "The Role of Gender and the Imperative of Sex," in *Supposing the Subject*, ed. Joan Copjec (London: Verso, 1994), 158–84.

[106] Dean, *Beyond Sexuality*, 88.

[107] See the discussion of this in Evelyn Fox Keller, *Reflections on Gender and Science* (New Haven: Yale UP, 1985), 95.

[108] Irigaray, *Sexes and Genealogies*, trans. G. Gill (New York: Columbia UP, 1993), 107. (One might replace "the human spirit" with "the subject.") For a look at

feminist reception of Irigaray's work on nature, see Alison Stone, "Irigaray and Hölderlin on the relation between nature and culture," *Continental Philosophy Review* 36 no. 4 (December 2003): 415–32. Irigaray tends to follow the Heideggerian strain of philosophy of nature more than the Critical Theory-inspired variant pursued by this book. Yet her central insight that culture arises from a tension within nature is related to Lacan's idea of nature's soliciting culture discussed in chapter 1.

[109] Eric Santner, *My Own Private Germany* (Princeton, NJ: Princeton UP, 1996), 32.

[110] Dominick La Capra has argued repeatedly against this sort of generalization: see his *Representing the Holocaust* (Ithaca, NY: Cornell UP, 1994), 223, and *Writing Trauma, Writing History* (Baltimore: Johns Hopkins UP, 2001), esp. 49 and 64. See also the criticism of Michael Roth ("Trauma, Repräsentation und historisches Bewusstsein," in *Die dunkle Spur der Vergangenheit*, ed. Jörn Rüsen and Jürgen Straub [Frankfurt: Suhrkamp 1998], 153–73).

[111] La Capra, *Writing Trauma, Writing History*, 183–87.

[112] Eric Santner's notion of "narrative fetishism" bears some similarities to film theory's global "disavowal" (popularized by Christian Metz), and thus occasionally comes close to the same rhetorical straw-man tricks as Bhabha: "narrative fetishism" is "a strategy of undoing, in fantasy, the need for mourning by simulating a condition of intactness, typically by situating the site and origin of loss elsewhere" ("History Beyond the Pleasure Principle: Some Thoughts on the Representation of Trauma," in *Probing the Limits of Representation: Nazism and the 'Final Solution,'* ed. Saul Friedlaender [Cambridge, MA: Harvard UP, 1992], 143–54; here 144). Yet Santner's powerful later reading of Schreber, mentioned earlier, works out his model more subtly by finding a more convincing alternative to normative, ego-bound historical narration in the death drive and the Real.

[113] Dominic LaCapra, *Emile Durkheim* (Ithaca, NY: Cornell UP, 1992), 86.

[114] La Capra, *Writing Trauma, Writing History*, 194.

[115] In the terms of Luhmann, "nature" thus performs a differential re-entry into itself; the following chapter will show how this works in a legal, and not historiographical, context.

5: Nature as Paradox: Brecht's Exile Lyric

Law and Literature

WORKING BETWEEN DISCIPLINES ought not to mean simply blurring their boundaries, or worse, colonizing one discipline by means of another. Yet this is what a great deal of recent literary studies has done, indulging in deluded assertions of juridical omnipotence over other fields, which grow all the louder the more quixotically isolated and jargon-ridden literary scholarship becomes. Against this tendency, interdisciplinarity ought to serve as a healthy curb to those sorts of totalizing fantasies, as a gentle reminder of the limits of purely rhetorical analysis. History and society are not, after all, just texts.

The by now considerable field of law and literature is a case in point. Through all the volume of work produced, one detects a common strand of argument best summed up by the initiator of the field:

> To attend wholeheartedly to the central rhetorical and ethical questions — who we make ourselves in our speech and writing, what relations we establish with our language and with other people — is, I believe, to attend to the first questions of justice. If we address these questions well, good answers will emerge to the secondary questions too, for implicit in any tolerable response to them are standards of justice — attitudes toward ourselves and others — that will inform what we say and do far better than any a priori theory or empirical science could do. If we can get our voice and sense of audience right, everything else we care about, or should care about, will follow.[1]

The need to link law with morals has been argued by figures as different as Ronald Dworkin and Jürgen Habermas. Yet neither would assert that legal procedurality simply follows from ethics. One can only imagine the results of putting such moral reductivism into concrete practice. Does the author seriously believe that mere generalized "rhetorical and ethical attitudes" could be a sufficient replacement for technical competence in law or literature? It is hard to overhear in this a very American spirit of moral exhortation (everything else we care about, *or should care* about").[2] One would want to see the phenomenon as harmless, were it not so frequent in academic writing, and thus diluting of argumentative rigor (without thereby being any the more politically effective).

Simply to focus on the surface of rhetoric and figuration when writing of the relations between literature and other fields is, for professors of literature, a temptation so obvious that at least a little resistance is in order. To counteract that reductive tendency, the present discussion will need to have recourse to a strong antidote — namely Niklas Luhmann's systems-theoretical sociology.[3] For only an awareness of the functional distinction between literature and law can prevent one from falling into the trap of rhetorical reductivism. Law and literature are indeed bound up in a relationship that goes much farther than rhetoric and ethics, as will be shown here. It is a paradox that the twentieth century's linguistic turn has often resulted in an extremely undifferentiated concept of language, one reduced almost entirely to all-encompassing rhetoric. In this, we meet again another form of what has earlier been termed Imaginary Theory. To answer this with a robust return to empirical common sense is inadequate (as is evident in the endless aporetical face-off of Derrida and Searle).[4] Instead, one should try to replace language in its larger matrix of social complexity, wherein it functions as only one of many symbolic media of communication. Thus in the present case of law and literature, the validity of law is not functionally reducible to its rhetoric. For with the differentiation of the modern legal system,

> The immediacy of the experience of law, the forms of self-representation and assertion of expectation, the use of physical violence, indeed even the practices and conceptual appratuses of the jurist — interpretation, rhetoric and argumentation, principles, concepts of law, dogmatic figures and the like — are all distinguished from law in its strict sence, since one can no longer say of them that they are valid.[5]

A law constitutionally dependent on rhetoric would be a premodern law, one as bound up with forms of representation, as was Baroque sovereignty with its court rituals.

We can be grateful for the field of law and literature studies for calling attention to the connection between these fields at all. For law has been in fact rather marginalized by many influential late-modern thinkers, among them Foucault and Geertz, in whose work the social function of legal structures becomes swallowed up either in "power" or "social energy" (in Steven Greenblatt's influential formulation).

Such a marginalization is impossible from a sociological perspective. Law has always been central to sociology, whether in Émile Durkheim, Max Weber, Talcott Parsons or Niklas Luhmann. Luhmann was himself trained as a lawyer, worked for years as an administrator in Lower Saxony, and set the evolution of law at the very center of his theory of modernity. The modern functional differentiation of society into distinct subsystems such as the economy, politics, law, art, and religion — a phenomenon described also by Kant and Weber in different terms — is in fact driven largely by law, which was one of the first subsystems to emerge historically (in the Middle Ages) from the older, religiously unified hierarchical social order. Law's autonomy is thus a cornerstone of social modernity for Luhmann, just as it is for Habermas, even if the two interpret this centrality very differently. It is also this crucial function of law that distinguishes Luhmann, despite the attacks on him from the left, as a liberal from older political thinkers on the right like Arnold Gehlen, Helmut Schelsky or Carl Schmitt. As we will see, though, Luhmann's theory will need extension in order to make sense of human rights, which have an inherently paradoxical status in his thought on law.[6]

Despite the differentiation of society into distinct subsystems, these last cannot function completely independently of each other, but must be "structurally coupled." Thus, in place of the blurring of law and literature into a mere common rhetorical figurality, it is more precise to see their relation as defined by structural coupling, which is a concept less familiar than that of functional differentiation, and one which Luhmann only developed subsequent to *Social Systems*. (We have already encountered the idea of technology as structural coupling in chapter 1.) Yet without it the notion of differentiation is incomplete, as Luhmann himself acknowledged: system differentiation is in fact not possible without structural couplings between systems,[7] which (as paradoxically as communication itself both increases and reduces complexity) both heighten and limit their interdependence. In structural couplings, two distinct function systems make use of the same elements for different systemic purposes. Law and politics, for example, are coupled by the constitution; law and economics by the institutions of contract and private property; politics and economics by taxation[8]

Significantly, Luhmann omits the art system from his examples of structural coupling in *Die Gesellschaft der Gesellschaft*. In *Die Kunst der Gesellschaft* he argues that the art system, relative to other subsystems, is characterized more by de-coupling than coupling with them.[9] This assertion is, however, borne out neither by Luhmann's own systemic logic, according to which increased differentiation actually heightens the "irritability" or sensitivity of systems to each other (while nonetheless according a clear hierarchical priority to the economic system), nor by the evidence of historical semantics he marshals in the essays of *Gesellschaftsstruktur und Semantik*. In fact, modern art as such is inseparable from the institution of private property, which means not only the art market, but also legal authorship, as Gerhard Plumpe and others have shown;[10] it has also been involved in various structural couplings with the political, from its deployment in Baroque court masques to twentieth-century Socialist Realism and *littérature engagée;* and finally, aesthetic modernity as such is hardly conceivable without a specific coupling between the art system and the scientific system dating back to the Renaissance and becoming acute in the nineteenth and twentieth centuries. This chapter will thus need to differ somewhat from Luhmann's own too-stable assumption of the autonomy of the art system — as it will also give greater weight to the historical variability and fragility of structural couplings. Systems theory, like Parsonian functionalism before it, has at times given the impression that modern social differentiation might be a process as unstoppable as it is irreversible, resulting in a tidily compartmentalized society whose various subsystems run on in neat isolation, completely oblivious to each other. Nothing could be further from the truth. For the structural relations between the various social systems, including art, are highly labile and subject to drastic and dramatic fluctuations. Parsons himself analyzed the phenomenon of "deflation" of political confidence during the crisis of McCarthyism,[11] and it is with such a crisis that the present chapter is concerned.

In arguing for a contextualized opening up of the "prison-house of language," Luhmann gives an unusually concrete and intuitive example of language's limits:

> Language converts social into psychic complexity. But consciousness is never identical with linguistic form, not even with the "application" of linguistic "rules." . . . One needs only to observe oneself while experimenting with thought, looking for clarifying words, or during the experience of lacking a specific turn of phrase, or the delay of fixing an expression, listening to noise, being tempted to distract oneself or becoming resigned when one can't find the right term, and one sees immediately that much more is present than the sequence of words and its meaning which may be separated out for communication.[12]

The kind of subjective difficulties with language Luhmann here describes may also occur on a larger, collective scale, namely at moments of historical crisis, when the force of events appears to exceed any verbal form. Long before Adorno's pronouncement on poetry after Auschwitz, Hitler's seizure of power was felt at the time to be just such an unspeakable crisis. Thus Karl Kraus described his own desperate inability to write in *Dritte Walpurgisnacht:*

> and when language is found for this, it gets lost again in a maze of multiple antitheses, where motives bump into each other and one word suggests another: it must bear the shame of losing itself and and the fortune of coming to itself again, always in pursuit of a reality from which nothing but chaos separates it.[13]

Brecht's severely reduced and pared-down lyric of exile is a response to this threat, and that severity and reduction may themselves best be understood through reference to the law.

From Politics to Law

To read Brecht's poetry in relation to the legal system may seem at first to fly directly in the face of considerable evidence. Brecht was, after all, the exemplary practitioner of politically engaged literature, and that engagement has been largely followed by most of his exegetes, whether enthusiastic or critical. Adorno, one of the most ambivalent of his critics, could not deny the fineness of Brecht's intelligence and ear, yet insisted that his work was finally compromised by a Stalinist politics from which it could not be separated.

> His work, for all its evident weaknesses, would not have such force if it were not imbued with the political . . . It is futile to try to separate the real or imagined beauty of his work from its political intention.[14]

Yet the relation of Brecht's work to the political was a variable one, and not only in the years preceding the conversion to Marxism circa 1930. In particular, the work from the early years of exile in Svendborg and Finland differs markedly from the direct engagement of what had preceded. This is most evident if one confronts the *Svendborger Gedichte* or the *Steffinsche Sammlung* with the previous volume of poetry, the *Lieder Gedichte Chöre* of 1933. The metropolitan poet of the *Hauspostille*, the author of "Lob der Partei," is now writing *Naturlyrik*, albeit of a very particular kind. We will have to listen carefully to the tone of these poems, for nuance means everything here. What is clear from certain of Brecht's work immediately following Hitler's seizure of power is a sense of defeat and powerlessness which makes simply irrelevant the usual clarion calls for direct action. Instead, there is a reliance on paradox, as in the angry address to the "Objective Ones," whose supposed "objectivity" is only that of *Realpolitik:*

> GEGEN DIE OBJEKTIVEN
>
> 1.
> Wenn die Bekämpfer des Unrechts
> Ihre verwundeten Gesichter zeigen
> Ist die Ungeduld derer, die in Sicherheit waren
> Groß.
>
> 2.
> Warum beschwert ihr euch, fragen sie
> Ihr habt das Unrecht bekämpft: jetzt
> Hat es euch besiegt: schweigt also![15]

[AGAINST THE OBJECTIVE ONES
1.
When the opponents of injustice
Show their wounded faces
The impatience of those, who were safe
Is great.
2.
Why do you complain, they ask
You have fought injustice, now
It has beaten you, be silent then!]

To this Brecht can answer only:

> Wenn die Kämpfer gegen das Unrecht besiegt sind
> Hat das Unrecht doch nicht recht!!
>
> [When the fighters against injustice are defeated
> Injustice is still not just!]

In other words: the only means not to stay silent, as an "objective" grasp of real power relations would require, is to shift the reference of literature from politics to law. This shift is similarly evident in Brecht's commentary on Karl Kraus's famous poem of October 1933 (*Fackel* No. 888), "Man frage nicht":

> Als der Beredte sich entschuldigte
> Daß seine Stimme versage
> Trat das Schweigen vor den Richtertisch
> Nahm das Tuch vom Antlitz und
> Gab sich zu erkennen als Zeuge.[16]
>
> [When the eloquent one excused himself
> That his voice failed him
> Silence came up to the judge's desk
> Took the cloth from its face and
> Acknowledged itself as witness.]

The role of silence as testimony, as stylistic principle, will be key to a great deal of Brecht's exile lyric. It is a corrective to the one of the dangers of writing in exile, namely of speaking too loud, too rhetorically, in order to drown out the reality of isolation and powerlessness.

ÜBER DAS LEHREN OHNE SCHÜLER
Lehren ohne Schüler
Schreiben ohne Ruhm

Ist schwer. [. . .]
Dort spricht der, dem niemand zuhört:
Er spricht zu laut
Er wiederholt sich
Er sagt Falsches:
Er wird nicht verbessert.[17]

[ON TEACHING WITHOUT STUDENTS
Teaching without students
Writing with no praise
Is hard.[. . .]
There one is speaking to whom no one listens.
He talks too loudly
He repeats himself
He says wrong things
He is not corrected.]

Thus Brecht may write of those who are in exile that

Sie werden nicht angerufen. Sie werden nicht angehalten.
Niemand schilt sie und niemand lobt sie.[18]

[They are not called upon. They are not stopped.
No one criticizes them and no one praises them.]

In exile, any assertion of one's rights becomes impossible.

Früher,
Lebend in dem Land, wo ich geboren war
Gebrauchte ich meine Ellbogen in dem Gewühl
Wünschte abgefertigt zu werden nach der Reihe
Setze mich, wenn die andern saßen und verlangte
Daß mir gehalten wurde, was mir unterschrieben war.

2.
Wer auf seiner gerechten Forderung nicht besteht, handelt
   unsittlich.
Wer sein Recht wegwirft, läßt das Recht verfaulen.[. . .]

3.
Jetzt
Lebe ich in fremdem Land, verjagt aus meiner Heimat [. . .]
Und schweige, wenn ich angeschrieen werde.[19]

[Earlier, living in the land where I was born
I used my elbows in the crowd
Wanted to receive my due when my turn came
Sat down when the others did and demanded
That what had been promised to me was delivered.

2.
Whoever doesn't insist on his legitimate claim, acts immorally.
Whoever throws his rights away, lets law go bad.

3.
Now
I live in a foreign country, driven out of my homeland.
And am silent, when I am screamed at.]

That the poetry of exile should, in its political powerlessness, turn to ideas of Justice and thus to the law is an old motif, which can be followed from the bitter invectives of the exiled Theognis through Dante, the Minnesänger and beyond.[20] (See Brecht's comments on this tradition of exile in "Besuch bei den verbannten Dichtern.")[21] For law, to one who is unjustly exiled, serves to oppose the "objective" reality of powerlessness with contrafactually stabilized expectations of behavior:[22] even if it may have won the day, "das Unrecht hat doch nicht recht." The social norms thereby established help de-pathologize situations of crisis.[23] Moreover, the situation of conflict created by legal claims against an injust political reality create, within the contingency of crisis, a paradoxical stability. A well-defined conflict, such as one which refers to law, has thus the paradoxical function of creating "a stable relation to one's own instability."[24]

This shift from a primarily political to a legal programming of art may be linked back to the "deflation" of political confidence mentioned earlier, to the corresponding loss of trust in the political system. Its resonance within poetry is expressed in terms of a *deflation of rhetoric*, of rhetorical figurality (tropes, especially metaphors) in favor of a reduction to semantics and grammar.[25] In rhetorical terms, Brecht's exile poetry gives prevalence to ethos and logos[26] over pathos, an attention to *kairos* and decorum, a careful reliance on grammatical figures of position (such as parallelism or chiasmus), and a general tone of understatement (litotes) which does not, however, exclude the use of *epitheton ornans* or exclamation.[27] An aesthetic once developed in relation to New Objectivity (*Neue Sachlichkeit*) thereby takes on a newly heightened urgency.

Truth as Process

Merely to acknowledge the reference to law and justice in Brecht's exile poetry is still, however, only a loose generality. One cannot forget the deep skepsis about the law datable back to earlier satirical poems such as "Drei Paragraphen der Weimarer Verfassung"[28] and then staged in the corrupt court scenes of *Arturo Ui* and, finally, in Azdak's ironic higher justice of overt bribery in the *Caucasian Chalk Circle*. And Me-ti warns against the fetishization of the legal order for its own sake:

> Me-ti sagte: Früher dachte man sich Gesetze als die Grundzüge eines Plans höherer Wesen für die Menschen. Jetzt werden sie nur als Fingerzeige betrachtet, welche Menschen anderen Menschen geben, sehr unvollkommene Richtlinien. Über ihren Nutzen entscheidet allein, ob sie in dem Fall, für den sie angewendet werden sollen, nützlich sind. (*GW* 12: 541)

Legality is here subordinate to usefulness. To be sure, such a subordination might be attributed to Brecht's Nazi opponents, as in Carl Schmitt's "konkretes Ordnungsdenken" which subordinated legal validity to matters of sovereignty — or, worse still, Papen's use of Article 48 of the Weimar Constitution against the idea of constitutionality itself.[29] This sort of instrumentalizing of law led to the perversities of the Nazi *Unrechtsstaat*, the pseudo-legal language which Brecht himself dissected at painstaking length.[30]

> Nachblätternd in dem alten Buch, erkannte der Ankläger
> Die alten Wörter auf den gewohnten Seiten, nur bezeichneten sie
> Jetzt andere Dinge: Mörder hieß
> Jetzt der Erschlagene. Verwüstete Wohnstätten
> Hießen im Aufbau begriffene. Raub hieß
> Entgegennahme von Opfern. Zwangsmäßig hieß freiwillig.[31]

The same attention to semantics is mentioned as a key tactic in "Fünf Schwierigkeiten beim Schreiben der Wahrheit," with Confucius adduced as witness.[32] Like law, semantics is, however, implicitly subordinate to *Nutzlichkeit,* for Brecht himself frequently violated in his own writing praxis the injunction in "Fünf Schwierigkeiten" *not* to use the deceptively universalizing term *Volk*.

The key to Brecht's complex functionalist understanding of law lies in the still-under-analyzed *Threepenny Trial*. This "sociological experiment" is usually taken to be no more than the in itself unremarkable demonstration that law under capitalism is no more than the servant of production, thus of capital. As a recent commentator notes, "as a Marxist intellectual, Brecht would have been naïve to suppose that any other state of affairs might prevail in a capitalist society."[33] Yet Brecht himself (following his mentor Korsch) warned about the "dangerous passivity"[34] resulting from an overly totalizing or functionally positivist use of Marxism: to reduce law to nothing more than an instrument of capital would fall victim to precisely this. As Brecht noted, "it was not necessarily foreseeable that the courts would decide against us, and it would only have been cynical to have assumed this from the start."[35]

Instead of assuming *ab initio* what the outcome would be — according to a model of pure economic determinism, that of Benjamin's famous mechanical chess player — Brecht insisted that "Die Wirklichkeit war im Prozess zu konstitutieren" (152). One of the most important aspects of the *Threepenny Trial* is its repeated insistence on the distinction between law and morality, or even law and justice.

> When the question arises whether justice exists or legal practice [Rechtspflege] (for the two do not entirely coincide), then the answer must be: legal practice. And if one has the choice — legal practice or justice? (in that both can't be preserved at once), we would have to choose legal practice. (140)

In other words: *fiat lex pereat iustitia*. Brecht goes on:

> We had to rid ourselves entirely of the wish to be right, which is something completely different from the desire to receive justice. We had to determine what existing law was, the law that was being handed down at that moment (i.e. pay for it) and to claim it for precisely long enough for it either to justify or compromise itself. The trial had to become an image of reality and say something about the latter. (152)

This is the complete opposite of James Boyd White's notion that one must begin with "central ethical and rhetorical questions" or attitudes, and all the rest will follow. Reality, for Brecht, thus emerges as a *difference from the claims of law:* it is not given as a moral certainty or ideal of justice in advance. Without the procedural instance of the law, reality is unknowable.

> For the court, to whom it was at first permitted to give judgments, is soon forced to say something about law. [Denn das Gericht, dem anfänglich erlaubt wurde, Recht zu sprechen, wird bald gezwungen, etwas über das Recht auszusagen]. The legal case is unimportant, but the case of justice becomes acute. [Der Rechtsfall wird unwichtig, der Fall Recht wird akut] . . . Since law is corrected by reality, one will be able to perceive the latter, once one corrects the former. (155)

As Luhmann might later have put it: *Wirklichkeit als Verfahren*. For this procedural, experimental aspect of Brecht's method here is due to the fact that law is not merely subordinate to the economic system, but rather also bound up with the scientific system, or in Brecht's terms, technology. For the destruction of traditional notions of authorial copyright and property, thus of originality, which Brecht sees proven by the object lesson of the Threepenny Trial, are themselves bound up to changes in the means of production (and distribution), namely in the shift to the mass production of film. The medium of law must change in accordance with the media of aesthetic production. Speaking of the "apparatus" of filmic production (which he understands not in the manner of Baudry as producer of a Lacanian Imaginary, but rather as the entire corpus of organized social behavior — *Verhalten* — necessary for film production), Brecht notes that all artists will be increasingly dependent upon it.

> For this type of production will ever continue to replace its predecessor, and we will have to speak through ever denser media and express that which we want to say with ever less adequate means. The old forms of communication do not remain unchanged by the new ones, and cannot simply go on existing beside them . . . The technification of literary production can no longer be reversed. (156)

Although Brecht does not mention poetry here, it follows from his logic that poetry, too, could not remain unaffected by this development; moreover, these effects might well be even more drastic in poetry than in other genres such as novel or drama, given poetry's long association with inner experience: "For whoever presents that which is experienceable of reality, does not present it. Reality has long ceased to be experienceable as a totality" (162).

Such a loss of *Erlebnis* was hardly new to Brecht; it is a familiar topos of modernity best known from Benjamin's reading of Baudelaire. But Brecht's answer to this loss of experience would be different from Baudelaire's: it lay in a particular deployment of paradox, as at the end of the *Threepenny Trial*: "The sociological experiment shows the social antagonisms *without resolving them*" (208).

The same unresolved antagonisms will figure in the poetry of exile.

Code, Program, Technique

In light of the sophisticated treatment Brecht gave to questions of law in the *Threepenny Trial*, it is almost incredible to discover him having recourse to natural-law references in his exile poetry. Within the larger Marxian tradition, natural law had been thoroughly discredited,[36] and it had played no role in the debates over the Weimar constitution, neither for Schmitt nor Kelsen, who were both thus heirs rather to the positivism of Paul Laband than to Otto von Gierke's conservative "organic" state theory.[37] To be sure, Marxism had in a sense smuggled natural-law traditions in the back door of the labor theory of value, as Weber pointed out,[38] and this is a matter not irrelevant to Brecht, for whom nature as productive force was a central concept, right down to his poetic reworking of Lucretius's *de rerum naturae*. The link between traditions of natural law and the forms of German lyric was too perdurable to be shattered all at once. Brecht's own earlier work had in fact whole-heartedly participated in what was arguably the last avatar of classical poetic natural law, namely Expressionism: we need think only of Baal's vitalism, or of poems such as "Vom Klettern in Bäumen" or "Vom Schwimmen in Seen und Flüssen" (both from the *Hauspostille*).[39] This materialist inheritance would of course not vanish from Brecht's later work either, and yet it is not central to the present argument, which seeks to find a *differential concept of nature* in Brecht's exile work (and not merely the old theological concept of *hyle* or quintessence underlying much materialism).[40] For the key to Brecht's deployment of natural law is its inseparability from crisis; his reference to natural law distinguishes Brecht's response to that crisis from Benjamin's theological turn, or equally from the paradoxes of Kafka, about which Benjamin and Brecht were arguing at the time many of the latter's most important exile poems were written.

Thus we must here again insist, against the letter of systems theory, on the historical particularities of legal history: as Luhmann himself acknowledged, natural law came very late to Germany,[41] which gave it, in the German context, different connotations. Not by chance did the postwar founders of the Federal Republic take recourse to natural-law traditions, in an attempt to bolster law better against political risk than positive law had done,[42] and in a sense one could read Brecht's turn to natural law in the 1930s as a predecessor of that. (To argue this more closely would require a careful look at Brecht's — and possibly Bloch's — relations with the *Liga für Menschenrechte* during the emigration.) However, unlike the short-lived post-1945 renaissance of natural law, Brecht *did not in fact use natural law as a foundational discourse*. Instead his reference to it is inseparable from a specific moment of crisis. Once more, even Luhmann, for all his mistrust of natural law, and his insistence on its outmodedness for functionally differentiated society, must admit that positive law depends upon conditions of peace for its maintenance,[43] and notes that reference to natural law was most often made in times of historical crisis and instability, as by Hobbes:

> Viewed through the history of legal doctrine, this idiom of natural rights is only a transitional semantics conditioned by the spirit of the age [eine zeitgeistbedingte Überleitungssemantik], only a symbol for *politically uncontrolled production of law,* which becomes dispensable as soon as forms of positive law are developed that are sufficient for this state of affairs.[44]

Yet such forms of positive law are, according to systems theory itself, historically dependent on structural couplings with the political system which are extremely variable; at moments of crisis and breakdown such as that of 1933, recourse might again be had to such "zeitgeistbedingte Überleitungssemantik" — which had, after all, in the revolutionary eighteenth century offered a justification for resistance to tyranny.[45] Nature functions in Brecht's exile work as just such a "transitional semantics": namely as a contingency formula linking the art system and the legal system.

We will return to this notion of contingency formula again. Before doing so, however, it is necessary to differentiate Brecht's poetic use of natural imagery from that of traditional *Naturlyrik* — a tradition that was in fact still in use among the so-called "inner emigrants" in Brecht's own day. Even among these latter, there were important distinctions as to the manner in which natural symbolism was used. One of the most traditional practitioners was Wilhelm Lehmann, whose "Signale" was written in 1941 in North Germany, distant neither in time nor space from Brecht's Svendborg and Finland:

> Seewärts hör ich Signale tuten:
> Sie schießen die Torpedos ein.
> Auf fernen Meeren, nah dem Ohre,
> Gesprengter Leiber letztes Schrein.
>
> Der Märzwind greift den Wandernden,
> Ich gleite wie auf Flügelschuhn;
> Dann bin ich selbst ihm aufgestiegen
> Und kann auf seinem Rücken ruhn.[. . .]
>
> Hör ich noch die Signale rufen?
> Sie wurden Klang von Roncevalles;
> Woran die Herzen einst zersprangen,
> Schwebt echoleicht als Hörnerschall.[. . .]
>
> Tief innen übte sich inzwischen
> Gesang, der Thebens Mauer baute.
> Fang an mit zwiegespaltnem Laute:
> Und "heile, heile, heile!" tönt es,
> Kuckuck! Kein Fluch der Erde höhnt es.
>
> Granaten und Schrapnell verzischen.[46]
>
> [From the ocean I hear signals toot:
> They are firing torpedoes.
> On distant seas, yet close to the ear,
> The last scream of exploded bodies.

> The March wind takes hold of the wanderer,
> I glide as if on winged shoes;
> Then I climb up upon him
> And rest upon his back.[. . .]
>
> Do I still hear the signals calling?
> They become the sound of Roncevalles;
> Wherein hearts also once burst open,
> Floating light as an echo, as sound of horns.[. . .]
>
> Deep inwards in the meantime is rehearsed
> The song that built the walls of Thebes.
> Begin with a divided lute:
> And "hale, hale, hale" it sounds,
> Cuckoo! No curse of earth may mock it.
>
> Grenades and shrapnel hiss away.

On the surface, this is an extreme example of "inner emigration" aesthetics, and perhaps too easy a target; yet given the neo-conservative attacks after 1989 on the "Gesinnungsliteratur" of post-1945 political consciousness, it is worthwhile to keep work like this in mind. For although Lehmann's therapeutic evocation of natural harmony in answer to wartime violence is cast in the form of conventional strophic form and imagery ("the wanderer," "winged shoes," the Eichendorff-like horns), his mythification of war is actually not so far from Benn's "ein Flammenwurf — ein Sternenstreich" praised by Kittler in chapter 3. Benn may prefer a more austere sublime to Lehmann's cozy beauty, but in both cases historical specificity is being elided and anesthetized as mythic spectacle. No less than Benn, Lehmann must actively imagine the spectacle of violent death here: "auf fernen Meeren, nah dem Ohre" means that the poet is hearing something in the inner ear, beyond the range of physical hearing. The difference between the two poets is one between distanced visual externalization and the nearness of aural inwardness. Even Benn, though, reverts to rhyme and Knittelvers as the preferred form of mythic timelessness. Little wonder Brecht had such mistrust of euphony and musicality.

The range of possible approaches to nature in wartime is still a large one. In contrast to the theodicy of "Signale," Lehmann's friend Oskar Loerke used natural imagery to evoke apocalyptic catastrophe, much as Karl Kraus had on the eve of the previous world war and again in 1933.[47] Although his earlier works (such as *Baal* and the early poetry) had referred to nature as immoral and apocalyptic, Brecht in exile rejected such tactics. The exile poetry also refused to view nature as counterweight to the political, not only in the famous line from "An die Nachgeborenen" regarding a "Gespräch über Bäume," but also in "Lektüre ohne Unschuld":

> In seinen Tagebüchern der Kriegszeit
> Erwähnt der Dichter Gide einen riesigen Platanenbaum
> Den er bewundert — lange — wegen seines enormen Rumpfes
> Seiner mächtigen Verzweigung und seines Gleichgewichtes
> Bewirkt durch die Schwere seiner wichtigsten Äste.
>
> In fernen Kalifornien
> Lese ich kopfschüttelnd diese Notiz.
> Die Völker verbluten. Kein natürlicher Plan
> Sieht ein glückliches GLeichgewicht vor.[48]
>
> [In his war diaries
> The poet Gide mentions a huge chestnut tree
> Which he admires — for a long time —for its enormous rump
> Its powerful branches and its balance
> Effected by the weight of its strongest limbs.
>
> In distant California
> I read this note, shaking my head.
> The peoples bleed to death. No natural order
> Offers a happy equilibrium.]

Like Lehmann, Gide is making use of natural beauty as a transcendental vanishing point: as an ideal at once moral and aesthetic which hides the paradox of art, namely its difference of function and coding. As an aesthetic program, natural beauty recouples art and its human technique (a form of second-order observation) back onto the seeming naïvete and directness of immediate intuition (*Anschaulichkeit*, which pretends to be first-order observation).[49] Nature becomes, as was once God, a figure for the "Letztmedium Sinn,"[50] the inevitability of meaning for human communication. Brecht cannot accept this metaphysical flight into natural beauty, knowing as he does that "die Natur selbst ist in keinem verständlichen Sinne gerecht."[51] The little four-line "Kriegsfibel" on the olive trees shading German bombs[52] particularly demythifies traditional feminine imagery of natural innocence:

> Olivenbaum, der du mit sanftem Laub
> Die Mörder meiner Brüder birgst, zumeist
> Gleichst du der Frauenschar mit weißer Haub
> Die für den kleinen Mann die Bomben schweißt.
>
> [Olive tree, who with gentle foliage
> Protect the murderers of my brothers, most of all
> You resemble the horde of women in white bonnets
> Who for the Little Man assemble bombs.]

The olive trees shading the bombs resemble German women working in military factories, thus participating in their feminized war technology; Hitler, as the "kleiner Mann" for whom they work, seems to be little specifically relative to the maternal collective of bomb producers. The enemy of Fascist women is a fraternal male group of the poet and his "Brüder."[53] Brecht's conversion of the familiar *Vaterland* into a "bleiche Mutter" was not without deeper motivation: a near-allegorical hostility to Mother Nature (already found in his friend Benjamin's discussion of Baudelaire) is evident here. Readers of Brecht's poem should keep in mind, however, that the women on the bomb assembly line were themselves as much objects as subjects of a gender-coded war technology policy. This last had deemed them more suited to mindless assembly-line work than men, because of their family loyalties (suggested by the nurse-like "white bonnet" they wear in the photograph to which Brecht's poem is the ironic commentary) and the notion promoted by the Nazi war labor bureau that "the internal laws of machines and tools are in principle alien to a woman."[54] Brecht's implicitly misogynist rhetoric here has more to do with attacking an outdated *topos* of Mother Nature than with historical accuracy.

If Brecht refuses the traditional *topoi* of nature as innocent refuge from the corruption of civilization, he does still make reference to natural right in several of the Svendborg poems. One is the dialogical, question-and-answer poem "Gedanken über die Dauer des Exils":

> Schlage keinen Nagel in die Wand.
> Wirf den Rock auf den Stuhl.
> Warum vorsorgen für vier Tage?
> Du kehrst morgen zurück.
>
> Laß den kleinen Baum ohne Wasser.
> Wozu noch einen Baum pflanzen?
> Bevor er so hoch wie eine Stufe ist
> Gehst du froh weg von hier.[. . .]
>
> Sieh den Nagel in der Wand, den du eingeschlagen hast:
> Wann, glaubst du, wirst du zurückkehren?
> Willst du wissen, was du von deiner Befreiung hältst?
>
> Tag um Tag
> Arbeitest du an der Befreiung
> Sitzend in der Kammer schreibst du.
> Willst du wissen, was du von deiner Arbeit hältst?
> Sieh den kleinen Kastanienbaum im Eck des Hofes
> Zu dem du die Kanne voll Wasser schlepptest![55]

[Drive no nail into the wall!
Throw your coat on the chair.
Why get supplies for four days?
You'll go home tomorrow.

Leave the little tree without water.
Why plant a tree?
Before it's as high as a step
You will happily leave.[. . .]

Look at the nail you've driven into the wall:
When, do you think, will you return?
Do you want to know what you think of your liberation?

Day after day
You work for liberation
Sitting in your room you work.
Do you want to know what you think of your work?
Look at the little chestnut tree in the corner of the courtyard
To which you carried the pail full of water!]

The watering of the little chestnut tree, which has none of the sublime grandeur and harmony of Gide's immense "platane," comes here to stand for Brecht's "schwieriges Geschäft: das Hoffen." The same imagery recurs in "Frühling 1938":

Heute, Ostersonntag früh
Ging ein plötzlicher Schneesturm über die Insel.
Zwischen den grünenden Hecken lag Schnee. Mein junger Sohn
Holte mich zu einem Aprikosenbäumchen an der Hausmauer
Von einem Werk weg, in dem ich auf diejenigen mit dem Finger
    deutete
Die einen Krieg vorbereiten, der
Den Kontinent, diese Insel, mein Volk, meine Familie und mich
Vertilgen muß. Schweigend
Legten wir einen Sack
Über den frierenden Baum.[56]

[Today, early on Easter Sunday
A sudden snowstorm came over the island.
Between the green hedges lay snow. My young son
Led me to a little apricot tree against the wall
From a work wherein I pointed to those
Who are preparing a war that

Must annihilate
The continent, this island, my people, my family and me. Silently
We laid a bag
Over the freezing tree.]

Here Brecht even makes oblique reference to the religious hope of Easter Sunday. The reference to his own son places the argument of this poem in the context of the right to reproduction (Fortpflanzungsrecht), which was a crucial point of differentiation between *ius gentium* and *ius naturale,* humankind and animals. Interestingly, the discussion of this took its point of departure in the status of traveling foreigners, a matter directly pertinent to Brecht's exile status. Luhmann discusses the historical origin of this in the medieval discrepancy between territorial state and inter-territorial trade.

> Viewed in social-structural terms, natural law had an important point of departure in the discrepancy bewteen legal and political unities, especially city states or small territorial states. and a trade that ranged far beyond these latters' boundaries. From this there arose constant questions about the legal status of foreigners in one's own city, to whom the law reserved for citizens could not simply be applied — that is, in Roman terms, questions of ius gentium.

This is the figure that Agamben has seen as embodying "bare life," mere natural existence outside of normal political rights. Yet rather than hypostasizing this state of the deterritorialized individual as "exceptional," legal thought here draws a distinction between natural law and the *ius gentium.*

> From this there proceeeds a passage in the Digests that would be important for the Middle Ages, and which includes animals and thereby can distinguish natural law from the law of the peoples (law of all humans). This detour via the animal is significant in terms of argumentational practice, for it enables a tradition that has endured into modern times to ground departures from a virtually animal natural law: marriage as a deviation from natural drive to procreation, slavery as deviation from natural freedom, property as deviation from natural commonality of goods, in short, culture as a deviation from natural law.[57]

Natural law is, other words, here bound up with an individual state of emergency. Luhmann goes on in a footnote to add that this right to propagation "*may be limited relative to natural law* via ius gentium and above all through civil law," referring to a passage from a standard work of Weigand on natural right. (A contemporary example would be the Chinese state's limitation on the number of children permitted its citizens.) But other important passages from canon and Roman law undermine this assertion of Luhmann's, namely:

> Civilis ratio civilia quidem iura corrumpere potest, naturalia vero non potest.[58]
>
> [Civil/civic reason may certainly corrupt civil law, but not in truth natural law.]

For trumping any potential limits from civil law was the injunction of Genesis 1:28 to be fruitful and multiply:

> Fuit etiam coniunctio in primis parentibus de iure naturale quod dicitur preceptum; nam eis preceptive dictum est: "Crescite et multiplicamini" etc. quod preceptum fuit iteratum post diluvium.[59]
>
> [There was a union of our primeval parents which is said to be a precept from natural law; now of them it is said [as a precept], "Be fruitful and multiply." This precept was repeated after the flood.]

The religious background is also present in Brecht's poem, which begins in the manner of a chronicle: "Heute, Ostersonntag früh." Luhmann's main point, however, is well taken: that natural law here functions less as a foundational discourse (or "höherwertiges Recht") than as a specific difference for the purposes of argumentative distinction. Brecht makes use of the reference to nature as just such a difference.

The central reference of Brecht's poetry to natural law is not only a thematic question. One cannot avoid a discussion of the form and tone of these works, many of which are written according to the declared program of "rhymeless lyric with irregular rhythms." That program is, like the rhetorical reduction earlier mentioned and the lapidary brevity of many poems, paradoxical. (Not to see the paradox inhering in this minimal program would be to fall victim to the illusion of classicism that Benjamin could only helplessly confirm in his disappointing "Commentary on Poems of Brecht" — "plumpes Denken" at its self-denying worst.)[60]

Brecht's justification for rhymeless lyric was a distaste for the "trance-like state" into which regular rhymes and meters lulled one[61] — that is, for the hermeneutical illusion of infinitude that the Romantics, above all, had favored, and that Rilke and Benn had used for their own Cratylic practices. Regular meter and rhyme stress the self-referential element of poetic technique, and Brecht's aesthetic program here prefers heteroreferentiality, although his central concept of *Gestus* must, as a form, nonetheless designate the unity of a distinction[62] between self-reference (style) and hetero-reference (the signified).

Programs have, within the art system, themselves an ambiguous status. In fact, the very separation itself between code value and program made by systems theory touches on one of that theory's most contested aspects, namely its supposed tendency to absolutize system differentiation and deny the reality of mediation between systems.[63] This chapter has attempted to counter this problem with an accent on structural coupling, but the question must be dealt with on a micro-systemic level as well, with regard to the distinction between code and program. Programs may seem derivative, since they are both less fundamental than the code in the system hierarchy, and also appear more historically variable; yet they are not any the less structurally necessary for being so. In fact, codes cannot function without supplementary programs to allow them to express preference for one of the code values. The mere abstract distinction of "beautiful/ugly," most often referred to by systems theorists of art, means very little without an aesthetic program to specify what constitutes the code value of beauty. As Luhmann puts it with regard to the legal system: "Codes allein sind mithin nicht existenzfähig."[64]

Given the extreme abstraction of the binary codes (beautiful/ugly, or valid/invalid for law), which is itself an expression of contingency and thus risk, there is a need for this code to be reintegrated into society through a specifying program. Luhmann describes this at one point with specific reference to natural law:

> The risk of coding via just/injust is accepted, but the level of programming is used in order to integrate law into society. The level of programming is then a level of equilibrium for possible discrepancies [etwaige [!] Diskrepanzen] that may occur between law and society. The result is then called "natural law." Via the concept of nature, which itself takes on a normative form (namely to distinguish between perfection and corruption), social self-evidences are converted into law, above all those of social differentiation . . .[65]

The irony of Luhmann's "possible discrepancies between law and society" is that it is precisely such discrepancies which are the stuff of actual praxis — including, as shall become clear, poetic and not only political praxis. Natural law is, of course, not the only conceivable program for this re-coupling of law back into society; Habermas would argue for a deployment of moral normativity,[66] and Luhmann himself proposed the idea of justice as contingency formula.

To return, however, to Brecht: the difficulty one has with applications of systems theory to specifically modern art is that aesthetic modernity has so often consisted in an attempt to subvert or reject the autonomy of the art system, which means to subvert the distinction of code and program. Does a reference to systems theory not inevitably mean a denial and betrayal of what is specifically modern in the work of an artist like Brecht? A great many systems-theoretical discussions of art have failed to do justice to the historical specificity of either artistic periods or, worse still, of specific artworks themselves, submerging these latter in overly abstract generalizations (especially the ever-present telos of "Ausdifferenzierung," which becomes as mechanically inevitable as the "laws of history" of *Diamat,* or official "dialectical materialism") that often say very little that is illuminating about art.[67] The differentiation of the art system is, like any other form of differentiation, historically fragile and fluctuating, and not simply a given once a certain historical threshold has been passed.[68] Art in particular has not always been comfortable with the consequences of differentiation. On this, Luhmann is himself as sanguine as only Hegel or Adorno with their warnings of a "dying off of interest in art," even though he may formulate this predicament differently.

The question, then, for Brecht's exile poetry, tense with the pressure of kairos and catastrophe[69] as it is, is whether one does justice to its aesthetic coupling with law and justice merely by terming it a program in Luhmann's sense. The answer must be no.[70] For even beyond the level of program, of style, the modernity of these poems lies in the challenge they offer not merely to traditional aesthetics of beauty and nature, but also to the structural couplings between the art system and the legal system that lie at the basis of modern functional differentiation. As we have seen, Brecht's rethinking of those structural couplings — such as intellectual property and copyright, even the authority of authorship itself — took place, in the *Threepenny Trial,* with the help of technological media, that is film. For modern communications media, as both Brecht and Benjamin argued, cannot help affecting the relations between art and other social systems.

The temptation to fall back on White's fatal pair of "rhetoric and ethics" is, in the case of Brecht, a considerable one. One could, for instance, borrow the moral categories of Adorno's musical modernity and transpose them onto Brecht's exile lyric. So Adorno wrote of Schönberg's aesthetic program of twelve-tone composition as a paradigm of modernity: "It has all its happiness in the knowledge of unhappiness, all its beauty in denying itself the appearance of beauty."[71]

That Adorno's formulation had to be paradoxical is itself no surprise, and one could argue with Brecht that the program of "rhymeless lyric with irregular meters" was just such a technique of renouncing beautiful appearance (*Schein*) for the sake of stark truthfulness. Yet this would not quite do full justice (in any sense of the term) to Brecht's poetic practice here. As Brecht himself admitted in conversation to Benjamin — and this in 1934! — "I think too much of artistic questions . . . to be entirely serious about it."[72] The artist in Brecht knew he could not, *pace* Adorno, do without a bare minimum of the "Schein des Schönen" (one suspects Schönberg's irritation with Adorno may have been due to his own recognition of the same need). Even the exile work of Brecht, most especially the Finnish poems and *Puntila,* could not be entirely free of pleasure in the most sensual meaning of the word (*Glück, hedone*). That this is so is indeed paradoxical, but it is not only the moral-epistemological paradox of Adorno's modern sublime (pleasure=displeasure, beauty=ugliness).

Brecht himself was untiring in his warning against hollow rhetorical moralizing *in tempore belli:*

> It does not take much courage to complain about the badness of the world and the triumph of vulgarity in general, and threaten with the triumph of the mind, in a part of the world where this is still permitted. Many act as if cannon were aimed at them, when only opera glasses are.[73]

That is: the opera glasses of the art system, which cannot be subverted by mere moral exhortation.

> They yell their general appeals to a world full of friends and harmless people. They demand justice in general, without ever having done anything for it, and a freedom in general, to receive part of the booty that was always shared with them. *They only take for truth what sounds pretty* (emphasis added)

Against these sorts of generalizing moral platitudes, Brecht insisted on the *technical* aspect of knowing, writing and disseminating truth:

> Since it is hard to write the truth, because it is everywhere suppressed, it seems to many to be a question of mentality, whether truth is written or not. They think one only needs courage for this. They forget the second difficulty, that of *finding* the truth. There can be no talk of its being easy to find the truth.

Brecht is not denying the moral component altogether, which Adorno reconceived as the moral testimony of aesthetic modernity; he is, however, insisting that "the central rhetorical and ethical questions" are not "all we should care about": that they are in themselves, without technique, not sufficient for art.

Nature as *Kairos*

This consciousness of technique was, as has been shown in the case of the *Threepenny Trial,* bound up with an awareness of communications media and their inevitable resonance within literature. In Brecht's exile poetry, this is staged via the frequent presence of the radio within an otherwise silent landscape. These poems could almost be titled "still life with loudspeaker."

WENN DER ANSTREICHER DURCH DIE LAUTSPRECHER ÜBER DEN FRIEDEN REDET

Schauen die Straßenarbeiter auf die Autostraßen
Und sehen
Knietiefen Beton, bestimmt für
Schwere Tanks.

Der Anstreicher redet vom Frieden.
Aufrichtend die schmerzenden Rücken
Die großen Hände auf Kanonenrohren
Hören die Gießer ihm zu.

Die Bombenflieger drosseln die Motore
Und hören
Den Anstreicher vom Frieden reden.

Die Baumfäller stehen horchend in den stillen Wäldern
Die Bauern lassen die Pflüge und haben die Hand hinters Ohr
Die Frauen bleiben stehn, die das Essen aufs Feld schleppen:
Auf dem ungebrochenen Acker steht ein Wagen mit Schalltrichtern.
    Von dort
Hört man den Anstreicher Frieden fordern.[74]

[WHEN THE HOUSEPAINTER SPEAKS OF PEACE ON THE LOUDSPEAKERS

The streetworkers look onto the highways
And see
Knee-deep concrete, meant for
Heavy tanks.

The housepainter speaks of peace.
Raising their aching backs
With their big hands on the cannon barrels
The ironcasters listen to him.

The bomber pilots turn down their motors
And hear
The housepainter speak of peace.

The loggers stand listening in the silent woods
The peasants leave their plows and have their hand behind their ears
The women stop who bring food to the fields
On the unplowed field stands a car with megaphones. From there
One hears the housepainter demand peace.]

The ironic contrast of image and voice is an extension of the semantic irony earlier noted in the context of Nazi legal language. The effect of the split between sound and image, which might almost suggest allegory,[75] is to freeze the image with photographic precision, as if the human actors had been abruptly caught in mid-gesture. Brecht's little gallery of arrested-motion figurines has something of the documentary effect of Agee and Percy's *Let Us Now Praise Famous Men*. But it is the Master's Voice here, more than the images, which has ultimate jurisdiction over reality. The images are as if held within the sonorous envelope of the radio's speaking voice.[76]

DER LAUTSPRECHER

Mehrmals am Tage
Höre ich den Lautsprecher mit den Kriegsnachrichten
Um mich zu vergewissern, daß ich noch in der Welt bin
So
Bittet der heimgekehrte Seemann seine alte Mutter
Aus einem alten Kübel Wasser auszuschütten
Bis er einschläft.[77]

[THE LOUDSPEAKER

Several times a day
I hear the loudspeaker with war news
In order to reassure myself I am still in the world
Thus
The returned sailor asks his old mother
To pour water out of a bucket
Until he falls asleep.]

War news has become here a paradoxical form of lullaby, sung at the poet's bedside by Mater Techne. Brecht mistrusts the silent image and consistently awards authority and preference to the spoken word: one is reminded of the primacy of voice-over over image often remarked in German film history. With the radio as much as with silent nature, the exile poet seeks to maintain his dialogue (so many of these poems were themselves written to be broadcast over radio); without the radio he fears near-madness.

AN MEINEN RADIOAPPARAT

Du kleiner Kasten, den ich flüchtend trug
Daß seine Lampe mir auch nicht zerbrächen
Besorgt von Haus zum Schiff, vom Schiff zum Zug
Daß meine Feinde weiter zu mir sprächen

An meinem Lager und zu meiner Pein
Der letzten nachts, der ersten in der Früh
Von ihren Siegen und von meiner Müh
Versprich mir, nicht auf einmal stumm zu sein![78]

[TO MY RADIO RECEIVER

You little box I took with me in flight
That its little lamp would not break
Carried from house to ship, from ship to train
That my enemies continue to speak to me

On my cot and to my pain
The last thing at night, the first in the morning
Of their victories and my labors
Promise me never to go silent!]

The full irony of this little poem is only appreciated if one sees it as a variant on the famous tradition of the *Dinggedicht*. This latter had given priority to visual intuition while nonetheless ordering the image around a central inwardness (*Innerlichkeit*): as the last line of Mörike's "Auf eine Lampe" has it, "Was aber schön ist, selig scheint es in ihm selbst."[79] Brecht's radio, by contrast, offers no such semblance of self-sufficient harmony, and its very presence is the negation of any protected domestic privacy.

Brecht's radio poems are in fact staging precisely this split between voice and image as index of historical crisis. We may link this divergence to a larger one of consciousness and communication, which both necessitates the structural coupling of these latter by communications media and varies with those media as well:

> The general coupling of consciousness and communication with all its consequences, regarding socialization, expectation of individuals, depth and precision of irritability etc., relates to the social system in all its domains; for without communication and without participation of consciousness in it, nothing happens. Thus transformations of this relation [of consciousness and communication, LP] in the direction of modern individualism lie on a more basal level than that of the institutions that control and limit the mutual inputs of individual social systems to each other.[80]

One would only need to add that this split of communication and consciousness, this "seam of psychic and social systems"[81] at which the artwork is situated, is itself historically produced and variable. This split not only "dissolves the subject" (*Kunst* 80) in its traditional inwardness: it must mean also the end of a certain kind of "nature." What Benjamin noted regarding photographic landscapes is pertinent to Brecht's snapshots of nature in exile as well: "Evidently a different nature opens itself to the camera than opens to the naked eye — if only because an unconsciously penetrated space is substituted for a space consciously explored by man."[82]

What Benjamin omits from his opposition of conscious and unconscious is the heightened role of anxiety (*Angst*) in technologized perception: its "ruhende Besetzung"[83] is omnipresent in these images. Nature is thus theatralized, denaturalized here. Brecht wrote about his 1940 epigrams:

> And it isn't a question of Hitler's momentary victories, but exclusively of my isolation regarding production. When I hear the radio news in the morning, reading Boswell's *Life of Johnson* in the meantime and looking out into the birch landscape with fog from the river, the unnatural day does not begin with a disharmony [Mißklang], but with no sound [Klang] at all.[84]

In answer to an entire tradition of Baroque and Romantic nature poetry, Brecht asserts here: *natura non loquitur*. The visible scenery of nature is thus paradoxically unnatural; real nature would be "die Produktion." Landscape becomes less a panoramic opening of promise, of release from the evils of civilization, than a limiting frame or stage.[85] This is even clearer in one of the "Kriegsfibel":

> Der Anstreicher spricht von kommenden großen Zeiten.
> Die Wälder wachsen noch.
> Die Acker tragen noch.
> Die Städte stehen noch.
> Die Menschen atmen noch.[86]
>
> [The housepainter speaks of great times to come.
> The woods are still growing.
> The fields still bear.
> The cities are still standing.
> People are still breathing.]

The very existence of nature is here reduced to a state of absolute contingency: it is the polar opposite of the ontology of language Heidegger read into Trakl's repeated listing of "Es ist" (in "Psalm" or "De Profundis") or Rimbaud's "il y a" (in the third poem of "L'Enfance," from *Les Illuminations*).[87] Adorno already disputed the notion that Trakl's copula expressed a predication of existence, instead viewing that "ist" as "the pale image" of such a predication: "dass etwas sei, ist darin weniger und mehr, führt mit sich, dass es nicht sei."[88] In Brecht's poem, the fragility of Trakl's blankly repeated "there is," linked to a structure of individual traumatic depersonalization, has acquired a specific historical and political index. The same serial, metonymic technique is evident in another short poem from "1940":

> Nebel verhüllt
> Die Straße
> Die Pappeln
> Die Gehöfte und
> Die Artillerie.[89]

> [Fog envelops
> The street
> The poplars
> The farmyards and
> The artillery.]

Everything is a matter of timing. The entire second poem of "Fruhling 1938" depends upon saving the mention of human history for the end:

> Über dem Sund hängt Regengewölke, aber den Garten
> Vergoldet noch die Sonne. Die Birnbäume
> Haben grüne Blätter und noch keine Blüten, die
>   Kirschbäume dagegen
> Blüten und noch keine Blätter. Die weißen Dolden
> Scheinen aus dürren Asten zu sprießen.
> Uber das gekräuselte Sundwasser
> Läuft ein kleines Boot mit geflicktem Segel.
> In das Gezwischer der Stare
> Mischt sich der ferne Donner
> Der manövrierenden Schiffsgeschütze
> Des Dritten Reiches.[90]

> [Above the bay rain clouds hang, but the garden
> Is still gilded by the sun. The pear trees
> Have green leaves and no blossoms yet, the cherry trees
>   however
> Blossom and still no leaves. The white umbels
> Seem to sprout from dry twigs.
> Above the rippling waters of the bay
> Runs a little boat with a patched sail.
> Into the twittering of the starlings
> Is blended the distant thunder
> Of the maneuvering warships
> Of the Third Reich.]

The force of the historical-political proper name breaks the timeless symbolic generality of natural objects. This poem mirrors Lehmann's "Signale," which proceeds in reverse order, beginning with military sounds at sea, and then seeking the consolation of a "heile Welt" in a cuckoo's call. Time is here literally of the essence: for the death awaiting the poet in an ironic *pointe* at the end of these poems has nothing of the reconciliation of traditional *Naturlyrik* ("Warte nur, balde"), nor is it possible, at this point in history, to unfold the paradoxes of modernity by reference to a hoped-for utopian future. The cosmic promise of nature is now inseparable from deadly and collective menace.

> Das Frühjahr kommt. Die linden Winde
> Befreien die Schären vom Wintereis.
> Die Völker der Nordens erwarten zitternd
> Die Schlachtflotten des Anstreichers.[91]
>
> [Spring comes. The mild winds
> Free up the flocks from winter ice.
> The people of the North await trembling
> The battle fleets of the housepainter.]

In a few years, viewing the progress of the war from his own and Charles Laughton's California gardens,[92] Brecht will be able to regain this lost perspective on the future, and with it a goal program (*Zweckprogramm*): the "labors of the plains" (*Mühen der Ebene*) of building socialism in the GDR, the cunning of Azdak's postwar justice. For now, the only future available is the plea to be remembered with "consideration" (*Nachsicht*) made to those born later ("An die Nachgeboren"). Even with posterity, Brecht must now be as self-effacing as he is with his hosts in exile.

Emergency Formulae

The form of these poems is the paradox, a form that brings into sharp definition the grammatical and semantic dimensions of poetic language. Cleanth Brooks once claimed (in a book itself written during the Second World War) that "paradoxes spring from the very nature of the poet's language: it is a language in which the connotations play as great a part as the denotations."[93]

In many of these exile poems of Brecht's, connotation (semantic variability, tone of voice) is indeed everything. One need only add that the "nature" of language in question is, as this chapter argues, historical through and through; Brecht's deployment of natural imagery acts as index of this historicity.

The paradoxes deployed in these poems are multiple: law is injust, language does not mean what it claims to; nature is at once beautiful and unjust (the olive trees shading the bomb-making women); the poet's own survival is at once injust and necessary:

> Man sagt mir: iß und trink du! Sei froh, daß du hast!
> Aber wie kann ich essen und trinken, wenn
> Ich dem Hungernden entreiße, was ich esse, und
> Mein Glas Wasser einem Verdurstenden fehlt?
> Und doch esse und trinke ich.[94]

> [They tell me: eat and drink! Be glad you have something!
> But how can I eat and drink when
> I take from the hungry what I eat, and
> My glass of water is needed by a thirsting person?
> And yet I eat and drink.]

This becomes even more acute in Finland, as will become clear:

> Bier, Ziegenkäse, frisches Brot und Beere
> Gepflückt im grauen Strauch, wenn Frühtau fällt!
> Oh, könnt ich laden euch, die überm Meere
> Der Krieg der leeren Mägen hält![95]

> [Beer, goat's cheese, fresh bread and berries
> Plucked in the grey bushes, when early dew falls!
> O could I invite you who beyond the seas
> Have your stomachs kept empty by war!]

Form becomes here identical with paradox, with silence and arrested movement. The paradox is at once an ethical one — I have no more right to eat than others who are hungry — and also exposed through a seemingly natural timelessness or indifference. That timelessness is however a specific effect of language. As Luhmann put it:

> Paradox arrests in the form of a short-term oscillation that observation that refers to it and would refer to it, designate it. It allows for no continuation, but turns upon itself.[96]

The oscillation in question is between "abundance of nature" and "scarcity of society," or between the ethics of individual self-preservation and a more communitarian one. Elsewhere Luhmann elaborated:

> Paradoxes are nothing other than representations of the world in the form of self-blocking of observation. One can stage art works, as noted, as paradoxes — but only to show that it won't work that way, only to symbolize the inobservability of the world. (*Kunst* 191–92)

Luhmann is, in other words, viewing art as an interruption of communication (which is, in itself, always potentially infinite, permitting of no "final word") — as, therefore, a paradoxical form of the latter. The resonances of this with the famous Brechtian *Gestus* are certainly suggestive. Jameson has recently claimed that

> what seems to characterize the *Grundgestus*, as opposed to the *gestus* itself, is its paradoxicality. Something in the situation seems to designate or to call for the Salomonic solution, the cutting of the Gordian knot, the unexpected necessity of opposites; whereas the gestus simply identified the nature of the act itself . . .

Thus Jameson could also note that "one needs a word for this specific gestus, on the analogy of deixis in linguistics for the act of pointing";[97] as we have seen, the poetic equivalent for the *gestus* is what Jakobson called the grammatical nature of Brecht's poetry, with its deictic aspect. The "solution" called for by Brecht's poetic paradox is, however, not necessarily dialectical, so that these paradoxes are indeed distinct from classical Marxian contradiction.

At this point we may return to the earlier-made suggestion that nature may, in times of political instability, function as a contingency formula. To view nature in this way appears to run directly counter to Luhmann's own definition of the term, which he conceived as a replacement for an outmoded classical natural right, and even more specifically for natural right's claim to be "the only possibility for a critique of valid positive law" (*Das Recht* 220). Yet the definition of contingency formula which follows this assertion is not self-evident.

> In place of assumptions about nature, there are assumptions about the self-specificiation of the formula. Contingency formulae have the form of a circular conclusion — and precisely therein lies their self-stating, not further soluble originality.

Contingency formulae would thus seem to be tautological, a form of basal and irreducible self-reference. They might remind us, in structural terms, of the familiar hermeneutical circle transposed into a sociological context. Another, more specifically sociological analogy might be Bentham's idea of necessary social relations. (Thus Luhmann can assert later in this same chapter that "the foundation of law is not an idea functioning as principle" — i.e. a normative idea of justice or ethics — "but a paradox"; *Das Recht*, 235.) These formulae must therefore, almost like what was once called "ideology," be concealed.

> Their function must be, to put it otherwise, latently fulfilled. The exposure of them would point to the paradox at the point of departure . . . The function of invisibilization [Invisibilisierung] of

such foundational paradoxes must in turn be invisibilized, and this happens through the self-setting of contingency formulae that demonstrate their own systemic adequacy.
Thus too with justice. (*Das Recht*, 221).

This is the sort of "latency" to which Habermas has so strenuously objected since the beginning of the Bielefeld-Frankfurt controversy. It would seem here that justice as contingency formula functions as a working hypothesis or quasi-transcendental assumption to conceal the legal system's ultimate lack of any (natural or ontological) foundation.

Against this assumption of an inescapable basal system self-reference, however, one might cite just as easily a great many other passages in Luhmann's work where he stresses the crucial need for that self-reference to be interrupted or "asymmetrized" by conditioning, programming — or, even more interestingly, by structural coupling with other systems. The clearest formulation of this may be in *Social Systems:*

> For any kind of self-reference there arises the problem of the interruption of a tautological circle, as we have noted in passing before. Mere self-indication must be enriched with further meaning [Zusatzsinn].[98]

Luhmann's logic here resembles that of a sociological Gödel; yet self-reference means as little mere "free play" as does Gödel's much-misunderstood incompleteness theorem.[99] In fact, Luhmann is decidedly uncomfortable here with mere self-reference. There is no reason not to be as attentive to questions of nuance and tone when reading a theoretical text as when reading poetry (which need not mean reducing the claims of theory to rhetoric). Note the phrases: "eines *nur* tautologischen Zirkels" and "das *bloße* Hinweisen des Selbst auf sich selbst." Words like *nur* and *bloss* seem to want to minimize the circularity of Luhmann's reasoning here, as if he were slightly embarrassed to have to admit it.

A later passage details this problem of de-tautologizing in finer detail. Luhmann is discussing the self-legitimation of a modern democratic constitution, which must abandon older notions of sovereignty in favor of a division of powers and the differentiation of the legal and political systems.

> The set form of a hierarchical differentiation of levels must (here as in logic) be given up. It can only be replaced by making-abignous of the difference of inner and outer. The constitution culminates in points where it is unformulable whether their validity is due to the system or its environment ... Seen from a sociological distance, a mechanism of structural coupling is thereby established that is only accessible to the participating systems in respective system-internal interpretation (*Das Recht* 477)

In other words — as the beginning of this chapter asserted — systems cannot close without structural couplings with other systems. In this way Brecht's exile work uses a reference to natural law to unfold an aesthetic paradox. Nature is beautiful and yet complicitous with injustice. Art cannot represent this without referring outside of its own code (of beautiful/ugly or interesting/dull). In the same way, the reference to nature unfolds a legal paradox: Unrecht ist nicht Recht. "The nature in the poem makes for the first time the unnaturalness of contemporary politics visible and transparent,"[100] much as it did in the right of resistance of the seventeenth and eighteenth centuries, and it does so as a specific difference, not necessarily as a foundational discourse. If Luhmann could speak of an "Umweg über das Tier" in the differentiation of ius gentium and ius naturale, we can extrapolate from this an "Umweg über die Natur."

The key is that "nature" here in Brecht must function allegorically, that is, as an overdetermined linchpin between systems. It cannot function as a traditional symbol for the unity of one of those systems, either the legal system or that of art.[101] A symbol, in the traditional sense, represents "a re-entry of form into form,"[102] and thereby also the unity of the system in which it happens. The traditional symbol of natural harmony (evoked by Gide and Lehmann) is inadequate for the historical *kairos* of these poems. So is the traditional symbol of the legal system's operative unity, namely validity (*Geltung*) (*Das Recht*, 98).

> It is a question here, with legal norms, of a network of symbolically generalized expectations. With this are given not only generalized, situation-independent indications, for symbols also stand for something which is as such invisible and cannot become visible — meaning here the future. With symbolizations, society produces, as we know from religion, specific stabilities and specific sensitivities. One relies on the symbol because one can't see what is intended by it. The sign becomes — as the symbol concept defines it for us — reflexive as sign, it is designated as sign. (*Das Recht*, 129–30)

Brecht's exile poetic must resist this symbolic reflexivity, and its underlying latency, with the help of paradox; and thus (with all due mistrust of facile neologisms) one is tempted to suggest a new term to add to Luhmann's descriptions of structural couplings. If contingency formulae (such as justice for the legal system, limitationality for the scientific system, etc.) (*Das Recht* 218)[103] still function to conceal ("invisibilize") paradox, then what might be called *emergency formulae* must expose them. The meaning of "emergency" is here double, referring both to the state of historical emergency in which these poems were written and also to an interesting idea from modern science, that of "emergent order." "Emergent order" is one that cannot be (mechanically) derived from any preceding state of affairs: it is sudden, almost as if *ex nihilo*.[104] Luhmann refers to this in a discussion of art and its relation to nature. In both of these domains, he notes, a change in relation between the various elements cannot help altering the latter in themselves. This quality defines "emergent order":

> Everything which can be described as emergent order lies at the basis of this state of affairs: that the qualities of the components can't come about without their composition, and the composition cannot do so without changing those qualities. The same is true for semantic concepts.[105]

Such an interdependence is, of course, a quality Luhmann claims for all social systems; what is specifically relevant here is the way in which (to extrapolate Luhmann's argument) a structural coupling would also have to affect the systems it couples. In this sense, "emergency" becomes a term to designate historical variability and discontinuous evolution. But, says Luhmann, "'emergence' is rather the component of a narrative than a concept which can itself be used to explain itself."[106]

The component of a narrative! Could one imagine a better way to keep systems theory free from the danger of ahistorical stasis of which its opponents have so often accused it? Luhmann himself always insisted on the importance of temporalization (for instance, to unfold paradoxes), but here it is built into the concepts themselves. Better yet, Luhmann describes "emergency" at one point quite candidly as a metaphor: "Society is the result of evolution. One also speaks of 'emergence.' This is however only a metaphor that explains nothing, but leads back to a logical paradox" (*Die Gesellschaft* 413).

Luhmann is here emphatically not simply reducing all of his thought to nothing more than metaphor.[107] But he is designating the culmen of a constitution (*Verfassung*)[108] where the difference between inner and outer, system and environment, must necessarily be blurred. If contingency formulae have the form of a self-referential, circular argument (*Zirkelschluß*), which functions to conceal the basal tautology of system self-reference, emergency formulae expose this last via a paradox which sets up an inevitable mutual interference between systems.

Nature as Distinction

To illustrate this extremely abstract notion, we might now return to Brecht, to one of the exile plays, *Herr Puntila und sein Knecht Matti*. As no other of the plays written in exile, this one stages the paradoxical relation of nature and justice, and as a play, it can unfold this paradox at greater length than the poems, which are, as noted, paradoxes arrested rather than unfolded (cf. p. 37 on "Kurzzeitoszillation"). In *Puntila*, emergency formulae work rather as narrative (*Erzählung*) than concept (*Begriff*).

Right from the opening prologue addressed to the "honored public," the play sets itself in the context of a sociological natural history:

> Wir zeigen nämlich heute abend hier
> Euch ein gewisses vorzeitliches Tier
> *Estatium possessor,* auf deutsch Gutsbesitzer genannt
> Welches Tier, als sehr verfressen und ganz unnützlich bekannt
> Wo es noch existiert und sich hartnäckig hält
> Eine arge Landplage darstellt.
> Sie sehn dies Tier, sich ungeniert bewegend
> In einer würdigen und schönen Gegend.
> Wenn sie aus den Kulissen nicht erwächst
> Erfühlt ihr sie vielleicht aus unserem Text:
> Milchkesselklirrn im finnischen Birkendom
> Nachtloser Sommer über mildem Strom
> Rötliche Dörfer, mit den Hähnen wach
> Und früher Rauch steigt grau vom Schinideldach.
> Dies alles, hoffen wir, ist bei uns da
> In unserem Spiel vom Herrn auf Puntila.[109]

> [We show you tonight here
> A certain prehistoric animal
> *Estatium possessor,* in German called *Gutsbesitzer* [owner of lands]
> Which beast, known to be overfed and useless
> Where it still exists and stubbornly survives
> Represents a baneful plague to the land.
> You see this animal, moving quite naturally
> In a worthy and beautiful region.
> If this latter doesn't grow out of our pasteboard props
> Perhaps you'll imagine it from our text:
> Milk-pails clattering in the cathedral of Finnish birches
> Nightless summer above the mild stream
> Reddish villages awakening with the cock's crow
> And early smoke rising from the shingled roof.
> This all, we hope, is there in our
> Play about the Lord of Puntila.]

The reference to the "prehistoric animal" reminds one irresistibly of the prologue to Wedekind's *Erdgeist,* where the animal trainer brags to the audience that only here will they be able to see "the real animal, the wild and beautiful beast"[110] who will be Lulu. But whereas Wedekind's turn-of-the-century *Zivilisationskritik* could still optimistically put its faith in a liberation from social confines through unleashed feminine nature, Brecht is, by the time of *Puntila,* no longer so sure. The "animal" of the landowner is, to those who would make use of that land productively, now only a scourge or calamity (*Landplage*).

As the prologue tells us, nature is in many ways not merely the backdrop, but also the real theme of Puntila.[111] In many ways, the figure of Puntila himself is the revision of Baal Brecht long imagined without ever being able to execute it; in Puntila's anarchic and aggressive vitalism, that of Baal is held up in a court of law and found wanting. Mere blind *Naturtriebe* are again and again found to be inadequate for the realization of justice. At one point, Matti sarcastically characterizes the trees struggling to live on barren rocks on Puntila's property as "ideal servants" (*ideale Bedienstete: Puntila* 1705). At another, his parodic encomium of herring, the poor man's food, shows how nature serves to maintain the status quo of inequality: "O Herring, you dog, if it weren't for you, we'd start asking for pork from the landlords, and what would happen to Finland then?" (*Puntila* 1687).

In the conversation between the Lawyer and the Judge, the connection between nature and the law is made explicit:

> LAWYER: The Finnish summer night!
>
> THE JUDGE: I have a lot to do with it. The paternity suits are a Song of Songs about the Finnish summer night. In a courtroom you can see what a pretty place a birch forest can be. They ought to put a barbed wire fence around every bush by the road. (1657)

"From a courtroom one can see what a pretty place a birch forest is": this is the sort of paradoxical emergency formulation we have seen in poems like "1940" ("Nebel verhüllt . . . die Artillerie"). The Judge means that nature has, beyond all mere aesthetic contemplation, real legal consequences: it functions here as the most irresistible of all procuresses, the instigator of an almost sacred prostitution. The implication is that the charms of nature should be handled with care, and not blindly trusted. The same conceit informs the folk song sung by Red Surkkala at the end of scene 9, where nature becomes a folkloristic femme fatale:

> There was once a love between vixen and cock,
> "Oh Golden One, lov'st thou me too?"
> And fine was the evening, but then came the dawn
> Came the dawn, came the dawn:
> All of her feathers are hanging in the bush. (1694)

As in the case of the girl from Kausala who loves her ex-lover so much that she cannot bear to have his letters read in court and thereby loses her paternity suit (1674), uncontrolled Eros is unwise. The Judge notes drily about Romeo and Juliet that "Such a love that is capable of such sacrifice could easily become uncomfortable, for it is by nature too fiery and thus proper to occupy the court" (1688).

Most important, however, is the final scene where the drunken Puntila has Matti smash up his library furniture to construct a parody of the sublime landscape. It is as if Brecht were staging his observation (from the *Keuner-Geschichten*) that an untempered use of pure nature leads to "diseased states of mind." When Puntila suggests to Matti that they might climb the Hatelmaberg "in spirit," the erstwhile purity of German Spirit (*Geist*) is reduced to the effect of alcoholic spirits. God's Creation is made to depend on the help of slave labor, parodying somewhat in the manner of *Candide* the old ideas of eighteenth-century theodicy.

MATTI: So, the mountain's ready, now y'can climb it. It's a mountain with a path, not in such an unready condition as the one the dear Lord created in his haste, since he had only six days for it, and had to create a mass of servants so that you could do something with it, Mr. Puntila. (1704–5)

Ironically referring to his dispossessed economic condition, Matti agrees to "take only the view (*Anblick*)" (1706) of nature to contemplate, and not its productive use-value. His last words to Puntila are the most ironic of all:

PUNTILA: O Tavastland, blessed land! With its skies, its lakes, its people and forests! (*To Matti:*) Say that your heart leaps when you see it!

MATTI: My heart leaps for joy, when I see your forests, Mr. Puntila! (1707)

Here, as in the exile poetry of nature, the traditional natural sublime is being ironically contextualized, by the same individual property rights and law that undermined sublime natural artistic genius in the *Threepenny Trial*. Jameson has suggested that such a rewriting of the sublime is a central aspect of Brecht's work. In Jameson's reading, Brecht's parodic or ironic sublime would be not elevation, but "the simultaneous possibility of a satiric dimension or lowering so dramatic and prodigious as to evoke sublimity in its own right in turn."[112] In this scene, Puntila's grandiloquent visions of natural sublimity are multiply ironically undercut: by the artificial elation of drunkenness, by the particularism of private-property ownership, and by the vulnerable creaturely Nature (in the theological sense of "created being") of both Puntila the master and Matti the servant. Yet it is precisely this lowly animal *Kreatürlichkeit,* which we have seen evident in the legal "Umweg über das Tier," that holds out hope in this passage. Nature has been ironically liberated from the sublime here. Throughout the play, Brecht is using natural right as a differential tool to re-enter into itself for the purpose of drawing distinctions: like Puntila's and Matti's drunken trip up the Hatelmaberg, nature is here a paradoxical but necessary detour (*Umweg*)[113] in order to generate implicit ideas of justice.

Luhmann describes this differential use of natural right with regard to medieval law as follows:

> Borrowing from Aristotle, above all since the high Middle Ages, natural law presupposes that there are in nature natures (beings) (Wesen), that have self-knowledge. Reason (ratio) finds its place and unfolds itself as nature within nature. [...] In addition, knowledge of nature gives no answer to many questions. These "adiaphora" need regulation. That things are so, may again be seen from nature, to which belongs also the fact that action orients itself to goals and and must work with very different natural and social conditions. The need for positive law and authoritative legislation thus far results from nature itself. *Natural law itself produces the difference of natural law and positive law.* The problem of the distinction of natural law and positive law is copied back into natural law, *and only under these conditions can one seriously speak of a foundation of law via natural law.* (*Das Recht* 508–10, emphasis Luhmann's)

We return here to the idea put forth in chapter 1 that nature "solicits" the symbolic.[114] It is just this deployment of nature as difference and distinction, as paradoxical, which *Puntila* unfolds. The sensual seductions of the birch forest create offspring who are in need of the protection of the court (the alimony trials as "need for positive law"). Mere natural drives (Triebe) are in themselves inadequate and need the supplement of rights and laws to protect them. Paradoxically, the pressure of Puntila's unbearable *Natürlichkeit* (ironically released by alcohol) forces Matti to assert his rights by leaving. Only Puntila himself denies nature as difference, insisting on the old idea of a unitary whole of character against any need for contractual regulation or calculating *ratio* (cf. pp. 1646, 1700). When Matti protests to Puntila in the penultimate scene that he had only been literally carrying out the latter's orders, Puntila argues that "you should have seen that my orders were without sense or reason (*Sinn und Vernunft*)," and thus known not to carry them out, according to a higher hermeneutics of *Herr und Knecht;* in a sense, Puntila is arguing from Carl Schmitt's notion of sovereignty above the letter of the law.

The Modernity of Nature Poetry

Nature in *Puntila* and the exile poetry functions as a conditional program, and not a goal program: Matti's last words to Puntila are: "Mein Herz geht auf, *wenn* ich Ihre Wälder' seh, Herr Puntila!" — implying also that it is the sight of these forests, at once beautiful in themselves as object of contemplation and pleasure and also, paradoxically, an emblem of Matti's own unfreedom, which inspires him to depart. A great number of the exile poems similarly use this *Wenn/Dann* structure (which one may recall from a song in the Threepenny Opera as well):

> Wenn der Anstreicher durch die Lautsprecher vom Frieden redet . . .
> Wenn der Propagandaminister von der Not des Volkes spricht . . .
> Wenn der Trommler seinen Krieg beginnt . . .
> Wenn die Oberen vom Frieden reden . . .
>
> [When the Housepainter speaks of peace through the loudspeakers . . .
> When the propaganda minister speaks of the people's need . . .
> When the drummer boy begins his war . . .
> When the superiors talk about peace . . .]

By contrast, the *Caucasian Chalk Circle* has reverted to a goal program, the aesthetics of production, and *Nutzlichkeit:*

> Ihr aber, ihr Zuhörer der Geschichte vom Kreidekreis
> Nehmt zur Kenntnis die Meinung der Alten:
> Daß da gehören soll, was da ist, denen, die für es gut sind, also
> Die Kinder der Mütterlichen, damit sie gedeihen
> Die Wagen den guten Fahrern, damit gut gefahren wird
> Und das Tal den Bewässerern, damit es Frucht bringt.
>
> [You, however, you listeners to the story of the Chalk Circle
> Take heed of the opinion of your elders:
> That that which is there should belong to those it is good for, thus
> Children to the maternal ones, that they prosper
> The wagons to good drivers, that they be well driven
> And the valley to the waterers, that it bear fruit.]

The problem with this goal programming is, of course, that art itself becomes a means to the goal (*um . . . zu . . .*), and that once again the old Weimar pedagogical ideal of anticipatory *schöner Schein* must be deployed "in order to" inculcate right ideas. This is the rhetorical trick of Brechtian "wisdom." Luhmann describes wisdom as a form of knowledge which, although self-referential, "remains on the level of first-order observation in immediate vision of the world." This assertion of (first-order) immediacy is the problem here, since it contradicts the modernity Brecht elsewhere claims for his work.

Luhmann goes on to note that wisdom "presents knowledge against the background of ignorance," and one must add in this case that this ignorance, in Brecht's case, was a specifically political one: namely the tactical refusal to observe, except in private conversation, the problems with real existing Stalinism.[115] "Wisdom" thus begins to resemble Weberian authoritarian charisma at its most dubious:

> Inconsistencies in the use of wisdom are either not noticed or not felt to be disturbing, since one knows anyway that one doesn't know ... Precisely this admitted insufficiency is compensated by the fact that one lives wisdom, guarantees it by purity ... With this withdrawal to conduct is also ensured that the wise person lives in a certain distance from the normal behavior of the upper classes, indeed, in a certain way outside class order at all, in the manner of prophet or monk, as warner and admonisher; *and naturally it must also be presumed that the authenticity of his statements cannot be questioned*, but rather results from his wisdom. Any second-order observation [i.e. asking: *Who is observing? Who is making these statements?*] is excluded, and so is any concordance with other opinions or any anticipatory control with regard to possible other opinions. *Wisdom is a cult form of naivete.*[116]

This is the problem with the goal-programmed work of plays like the *Caucasian Chalk Circle*, or even with the *Legende der Entstehung des Buches Tao-Te-King*: the self-celebration of arbitrary authority (one is tempted to say, in Schmittian fashion, of "authorial sovereignty") styled as "wisdom." This is not a blanket condemnation of the *Caucasian Chalk Circle*, which still contains many subtle and fine passages. Jameson, in his recent defense of Brecht, specifically cites the line, "Fearful is the seduction to goodness!" (at the end of scene 2) as such a moment, calling this "luminous verse" "well-nigh sublime" in its drastic revision of our normal conceptions of sinful human nature (Jameson, Brecht 174). Brecht is, in other words, revising the natural sublime not only of non-human nature, but of human nature as well: in the familiar Kantian image, not only "the starry sky above me," but also "the moral law within me." It is here no longer the familiar Sadeian sublime of mastery that is "schrecklich." Jameson goes on to add that "This is Brecht at his most utopian and salvational, and it is significant that it should take place precisely in the context of a protophilosophical grappling with the issue of nature itself" (174).

Indeed, this play still works with some of the nature thematics we have seen in Brecht's exile poetry. As the same Singer comments later in the play (scene 4), "For the little tree needs its water." Brecht deploys here the same imagery for Gruscha and her foundling child that we earlier saw him use to describe his relation to his own son in Danish exile. So too the "Sachverständiger" in the first scene notes about nature: "It is correct, we must see a piece of land like a tool with which one produces useful things, but it is also correct that we must recognize the love to a particular piece of land."

This returns us to our opening problem of law, literature and ethics. Nature is here bound up to a localized ethics, but it is not merely an ethics of the suffering creature: it is that of an individual natural creature in a specific historical situation.[117] Within the *Caucasian Chalk Circle*, we would have to see how the survival ethics of Grusha relates to the tactical ethics of Azdak, whose "wisdom" occasionally takes the form of wisecracks. The problem with Azdak is that his carnivalesque inversion of law can implicitly justify law's political instrumentalization under dictatorship. This rational goal program is then disguised in the form of earthy peasant "wisdom." To return to Adorno: the problem with Stravinsky's neoclassical work is its false claim to authenticity (what Benjamin called the "classical" in Brecht). All art, even modern art, seeks authenticity.

> But everything depends on whether it [here: music, or for our purposes: modern art in general] claims authenticy through attitude as if it were already won, or whether it, as if with closed eyes, follows the objective demands of the artwork, in order to gain them first in this way.[118]

Although Brecht may not have done it with the "closed eyes" of Adorno's composer (who may remind one of the Surrealists' closed eyes), he did, in cases like the *Threepenny Trial* and the poems discussed in this chapter, very much "abandon himself to the demands of the matter." In system-theoretical terms, one could formulate this tactic as follows: "Like religion, art is fascinated by what escapes it, and its effort might culminate precisely in not letting this fascination escape it."[119]

Art observes latency, observes precisely that which first-order observation cannot observe, its blind spot. (This might even be, although Luhmann would not describe it thus, art's paradoxical *moral function*.) Contingency formulae are already described as "Making observable of the unobservable through substitution of a distinction for a unity, which may only be described in paradoxical or tautological fashion."[120]

So Brecht's exile poetry uses a differential reference to nature to expose a political reality that would otherwise have remained latent. (His plea to his little radio box not to fall silent is a plea not to be abandoned to precisely this latency.) Most crucially, Brecht's reference to nature distinguishes his response to *kairos* and crisis from that of his friend Benjamin, who took recourse to theology in his ideas of "divine force" (*göttliche Gewalt*) and Messianism.[121] And finally, the reference to nature and natural right differentiates Brecht's paradoxes and parables from those of Kafka, about whose work Brecht and Benjamin argued in Svendborg at the time many of these poems were written. If Kafka's central reference to theology functioned as a modernist contingency formula, taking the form of endless, timeless self-reference and circular argument — thereby referring to the older, archaic, social-integrative function of law[122] precisely through its ironic negation — then Brecht's emergency formulae insist on precisely the temporal, "kairotic" element which the infinite re-entry of Kafka's religious paradoxes elide. And although Brecht's poetry of exile has not seemed as central to literary modernity as Kafka's religious paradox, these poems are, for all their seeming simplicity, nonetheless still very modern.[123] That they are so must be due to the uncompromising rigor with which they observe their own self-imposed technical constraints.

Notes

[1] James Boyd White, *Heracles' Bow: Essays on the Rhetoric and Poetics of the Law* (Madison, WI: U of Wisconsin P, 1985), 107–8.

[2] One response from a practicing judge may be found in Richard Posner, *Law and Literature*, 2nd ed. (Cambridge, MA: Harvard UP, 1998), esp. 299–301; Posner has, however, since September 2001 adopted a position of politically driven pragmatism that instrumentalizes the law no less than his opponents on the left. It should be made clear here that this chapter's critique of moralization is not simply identical to current attacks from the right on "politicized scholarship." What is criticized here is the use of moral *rhetoric* to hide conceptual weakness. This critique of rhetoric has already been undertaken in the discussions in chapters 1 and 4 of Imaginary Theory. For a very different view of the function of rhetoric in law and literature, indebted rather to New Historicism, see Stefan Andriopoulos, "Die Zirkulation von Figuren und Begriffen in kriminologischen, juristischen und literarischen Darstellungen von 'Unfall' und 'Verbrechen,'" *Internationales Archiv für Sozialgeschichte der deutschen Literatur* 21/2 (1996): 113–142.

[3] As noted previously, readers unfamiliar with Luhmann's work may consult the appendix of this book for a brief outline of his theory and its reception.

[4] White's coupling of "rhetoric and ethics" is less surprising than one would think. Like language, morality, in modern differentiated societies, "is a mode of communication that circulates throughout all of society" rather than being a functional "subsystem" of its own (Luhmann, "Ethik als Reflexionstheorie der Moral," in *Gesellschaftsstruktur und Semantik* [Frankfurt: Suhrkamp, 1989], 3:432). And whenever the functional codes of separate systems, such as law or politics, are weakened or undermined, as in times of crisis, they tend to fall back onto moral or rhetorical grounding (ibid., 432). The opposition of rhetoric and ethics is thus only one of appearance.

[5] Luhmann, *Ausdifferenzierung des Rechts* (Frankfurt: Suhrkamp, 1981), 20. Luhmann's unusual (and difficult to translate) verb for the severing of law from these practices is *ausscheren*.

[6] For an overview of critical readings of Luhmann and law in English, see *Luhmann on Law and Politics: Critical Appraisals and Applications*, ed. Michael King and Chris Thornhill (Portland, OR: Hart, 2006), especially the essay by Gert Verschraegen, "Systems Theory and the Paradox of Human Rights," 101–26.

[7] Luhmann, *Die Gesellschaft der Gesellschaft* (Frankfurt: Suhrkamp, 1997), 695. This idea of coupling has been further developed by Richard Münch, who remains closer to Parsons than Luhmann (see his *Die Struktur der Moderne* [Frankfurt: Suhrkamp, 1984], and *Die Struktur der Moderne*, 2 vols. [Frankfurt: Suhrkamp, 1986]).

[8] Luhmann, *Die Gesellschaft der Gesellschaft*, 778–79. Habermas and others have argued that science and economics are coupled in the form of "technology" (cf. *Technik und Wissenschaft als Ideologie* [Frankfurt: Suhrkamp, 1968]).

[9] Luhmann, *Die Kunst der Gesellschaft* (Frankfurt: Suhrkamp, 1995), 391.

[10] See Gerhard Plumpe, "Der Autor als Rechtssubjekt," in *Literaturwissenschaft. Grundkurs 2*, ed. Helmut Brackert and Jörn Stückrath (Reinbek: Rowohlt, 1981), 179–93; Heinrich Bosse, *Autorschaft ist Werkherrschaft: über die Entstehung des Urheberrechts aus dem Geist der Goethezeit* (Paderborn: Schöningh, 1981).

[11] "On the Concept of Political Power," *Sociological Theory and Modern Society* (Glencoe, IL: The Free Press, 1967), 342–44; "On the Concept of Value-Commitments," *Sociological Inquiry* 38 (1968): 153–59.

[12] Luhmann, *Soziale Systeme* (Frankfurt: Suhrkamp, 1984), 368–69.

[13] Kraus, *Dritte Walpurgisnacht* (Frankfurt: Suhrkamp, 1989), 24.

[14] Adorno, "Engagement," in *Noten zur Literatur, Gesammelte Schriften* 11:419–20.

[15] Brecht, *Werke. Grosse Berliner und Frankfurter Ausgabe*, ed. Werner Hecht et al. (Berlin: Aufbau; Frankfurt: Suhrkamp, 1988–2000), vol. 9 (*Gedichte 2*), 492.

[16] Brecht, *Werke 9* (*Gedichte 2*), 503.

[17] Brecht, *Werke 9* (*Gedichte 2*), 556–57.

[18] Brecht, *Werke 9* (*Gedichte 2*), 555.

[19] Brecht, *Werke 8* (*Gedichte 1*), 407.

[20] For a recent discussion of this, see Robert G. Sullivan, *Justice and the Social Context of Early Middle High German Literature* (London: Routledge, 1991).

[21] Brecht, *Werke 9* (*Gedichte 2*), 663–64.

[22] The formulation is Luhmann's: see *Rechtssoziologie* (Opladen: Westdeutscher Verlag, 1983), 42.

[23] Luhmann, *Rechtssoziologie*, 37.

[24] Luhmann, *Ausdifferenzierung des Rechts* (Frankfurt: Suhrkamp, 1981), 97.

[25] On this aspect of Brecht, see Roman Jakobson, "Der grammatische Bau des Gedichts von Bertolt Brecht, 'Wir sind sie,'" in *Hölderlin, Klee, Brecht: Zur Wortkunst dreier Gedichte* (Frankfurt: Suhrkamp, 1976), 107–28.

[26] This would include the reliance on figures of reasoning, especially dialogic ones such as *anthypophora, apophasis,* or *expeditio.*

[27] For a fuller list of rhetorical devices employed by Brecht in exile, see Anna Carrdus, "The Uses of Rhetoric in Brecht's Svendborg poems," in *Brecht's Poetry of Political Exile,* ed. Ronald Speirs (Cambridge: Cambridge UP, 2000), 135–52.

[28] Brecht, *Werke* 8 (*Gedichte* 1), 378–81.

[29] On this, cf. most recently Peter C. Caldwell, *Popular Sovereignty and the Crisis of German Constitutional Law* (Durham, NC: Duke UP, 1997), 164–70.

[30] See also on this question of legal terminology Michael Stolleis, *The Law under the Swastika: Studies on Legal History in Nazi Germany* (Chicago: U of Chicago P, 1998), chapter 4.

[31] Brecht, *Werke* 9 (*Gedichte* 2), 500–501.

[32] Brecht, *Schriften zur Literatur und Kunst* 1 (*Werke* 18), 231.

[33] Steve Giles, *Bertolt Brecht and Critical Theory: Marxism, Modernism and the Threepenny Lawsuit* (New York: Peter Lang, 1998), 47. Giles is especially concerned to point up internal inconsistencies in Brecht's presentation of the case, along with differences from other contemporary reports of the facts.

[34] Brecht, *Dreigroschenprozess, Werke* 18, 184.

[35] Brecht, *Werke* 18, 153.

[36] See Habermas, "Naturrecht und Revolution," *Theorie und Praxis* (Frankfurt: Suhrkamp, 1978), 117.

[37] On this, see again Caldwell, *Popular Sovereignty;* Gierke was himself author of a lengthy study of natural law, published in English translation as *Natural Law and the Theory of Society 1500 to 1800,* trans. Ernest Barker (Boston: Beacon, 1957). For a more liberal variant of this tradition, see Leo Strauss, *Natural Right and History* (Chicago: U of Chicago P, 1953); and for an unabashedly esoteric, if not very consistent, Marxian one, see Ernst Bloch, *Natural Law and Human Dignity,* trans. Dennis Schmidt (Cambridge, MA: MIT Press, 1986).

[38] *Max Weber on Law in Economy and Society,* ed. Max Rheinstein, trans. E. Shils and M. Rheinstein (New York: Clarion [Simon and Schuster], 1967), 293–94.

[39] Brecht, *Werke 8* (*Gedichte* 1), 209–10.

[40] *Hyle* was originally Aristotle's term, but was then used in atomism and alchemism. The theological assumptions tied up with this type of materialism become most evident in later Adorno (*Negative Dialektik*).

[41] Luhmann, *Das Recht der Gesellschaft* (Frankfurt: Suhrkamp 1993), 40.

[42] For trenchant criticisms of this turn, see Luhmann, *Das Recht der Gesellschaft,* 517–18, and *Ausdifferenzierung des Rechts,* 431.

[43] Luhmann, *Das Recht,* 281.

[44] Luhmann, *Das Recht,* 151, Luhmann's emphasis.

[45] Luhmann, *Das Recht,* 484.

[46] Lehmann, *Gesammelte Werke in acht Bänden,* ed. H.-D. Schäfer (Stuttgart: Cotta, 1982), 1:116. See the comments in Uwe-K. Ketelson, "Natur und Geschichte —

Das widerrufende Zeitgedicht der 30er Jahre," in *Naturlyrik und Gesellschaft*, ed. Norbert Mecklenburg (Stuttgart: Klett-Cotta, 1977), 152–62.

[47] Cf. Loerke's last published collection, *Der Wald der Welt* (1936), now in *Die Gedichte*, ed. R. Tgahrt (Frankfurt: Suhrkamp, 1984); Kraus, "Apokalypse," "Die Erde will nicht mehr," in *Untergang der Welt durch schwarze Magie* (Frankfurt: Suhrkamp, 1989). In *Dritte Walpurgisnacht* (Frankfurt: Suhrkamp, 1989), the advent of Fascism is insistently represented as a natural disaster: cf. 15, 20, 27, 199, 216, 242, 273.

[48] Brecht, *Werke* 10 (Gedichte 3), 886. The passage Brecht must have been reading reads as follows: "Sous la fenêtre de ma chambre, un immense platane, qui est bien l' un des plus beaux arbres que j' aie vus. Je reste longtemps dans l'admiration de son tronc énorme, de sa ramification puissante et de cet équilibre où le maintient le poids de ses plus importantes branches. La contemplation d' un arbre séculaire est d' un effet aussi pacifiant que celle des gros pachydermes . . ." (Beneath the window of my bedroom, a huge plane tree, which must be one of the most beautiful trees I have seen. I spend a long time lost in admiration of its enormous trunk, its powerful branches, and that equilibrium with which it supports the weight of its most important branches. The contemplation of an ancient tree has an effect as calming as that of the big pachyderms; Gide, *Journal*, entry of 3 July 1939 [Paris: Pleiade, 1954], 32–33). One wonders what Brecht would have made of the Lucretian materialism of the Resistance fighter and then-Communist party member Francis Ponge's "Carnet du Bois de Pins" (Notebook on a Pine Forest), written in the south of France in August 1940, not long after that country's fall to the Wehrmacht (Ponge, *La Rage de l'expression* [Paris: Gallimard, 1976], 97–172).

[49] On the way this functioned in the aesthetics of German Idealism, cf. Luhmann, *Die Kunst der Gesellschaft*, 312–14.

[50] Luhmann, *Die Kunst der Gesellschaft*, 209.

[51] Luhmann, *Das Recht*, 219.

[52] Brecht, *Werke* 12, 80.

[53] This sets the present reading in severe opposition to Carl Pietzker's (neo-)Freudian readings of Brecht in terms of "mother-loss." There is no nostalgia for the mother in these poems. Compare also the earlier "Von der Willfährigkeit der Natur," *Werke*, 13:347 (*GW Gedichte* 1:194).

[54] Arbeitswissenschaftliches Institut, "Arbeitseinsatz," in *Jahrbuch* 1940/1, 395, quoted by Annemarie Tröger, "The Creation of a Female Assembly-Line Proletariat," in *When Biology Became Destiny: Women in Weimar and Nazi Germany*, ed. R. Bridenthal, A. Grossmann, and M. Kaplan (New York: Monthly Review Press, 1984), 257. For references on the recent debate as to the active or passive role played by women under National Socialism, see *Töchter-Fragen: NS-Frauen-Geschichte*, ed. L. Gravenhorst and C. Tatschmurat (Freiburg: Kore, 1990).

[55] Brecht, *Werke 9* (*Gedichte* 2), 719–20.

[56] Brecht, *Werke 9* (*Gedichte* 2), 815.

[57] Luhmann, *Das Recht*, 507–8.

[58] Gaius, *Institutiones*, 1, 158, cit. in Rudolf Weigand, *Die Naturrechtslehre der Legisten und Dekretisten von Irnerius bis Accursius und von Gratian bis Johannes Teutonicus* (Munich: Hueber, 1967), 78; cf. also the passage from Cyprian on 83 regarding marriage as common to different kinds of law: coniugatio autem ista modo subicitur iuri naturali, alio iuri gentium, alio iuri civili.

[59] Weigand, *Naturrechtslehre*, 291, citing Huguccio.

[60] Benjamin, "Kommentare zu Gedichten von Brecht," *Versuche über Brecht* (Frankfurt: Suhrkamp, 1966), 49–83. "Lyrisches wie einen klassischen Text zu lesen," as Benjamin suggests we do with Brecht, is to fossilize these texts as surely as Lukács's authoritarian notion of "realism" did Balzac and Goethe. ("Classical" to whom, or *for whom*?).

[61] Brecht, "Nachtrag zu: Über reimlose Lyrik mit unregelmässigen Rhythmen," *Werke* 19, 403.

[62] "Unity of a distinction" is a technical term in Luhmann, originating in George Spencer Brown's *Laws of Form* (London: Allen and Unwin, 1969). Luhmann is fond of pointing out that the unity of a distinction is often forgotten for the difference it marks.

[63] The "mutual indifference" of separate systems was criticized by Habermas with specific regard to law in *Faktizität und Geltung* (Frankfurt: Suhrkamp, 1992), 73; compare similar complaints made by Klaus Briegleb in "Gegen die funktionale Literaturwissenschaft," *Unmittelbar zur Epoche des NS-Fascismus: Arbeiten zur politischen Philologie 1978–1988* (Frankfurt: Suhrkamp, 1990), 160–90, and Robert Holub's comments on this in his "Luhmann's Progeny," *New German Critique* 61 (Winter 1994): 148–49.

[64] Luhmann, *Das Recht der Gesellschaft*, 190; for a cognate discussion in the context of art, see Luhmann, *Die Kunst der Gesellschaft*, 314–15.

[65] Luhmann, *Das Recht*, 191.

[66] Cf. Habermas, *Faktizität und Geltung*, 135–50 on the complementary relationship of moral and legal norms, or the book's concluding section on "Recht und Moral," 541–99.

[67] This is the accusation leveled at systems theory by Robert Holub ("Luhmann's Progeny," *New German Critique* 61 [Winter 1994]: 143–59), and it is sometimes borne out by Luhmann's disciples: for one example, see Peter Hühn, "Lyrik und Systemtheorie," in *Kommunikation und Differenz*, ed. Henk de Berg and Matthias Prangel (Opladen: Westdeutscher Verlag, 1993), 114–36; even Peter Fuchs's essay on the differentiation of modern poetry (in Luhmann and Fuchs, *Reden und Schweigen* [Frankfurt: Suhrkamp, 1989], 138–77) is prone to this flaw.

[68] Even more crucial is that we *not*, as many a disciple of Derrida would do, equate differentiation with the banality of mere self-reference or the now-tiresome "free-play of the signifier." Differentiation is emphatically not *l'art pour l'art*, not even in its current academic crossword-puzzle variety, since it is inseparable from structural coupling and hetero-reference as its complement. Recognizing this also provides an answer to the "deconstructive" view of law offered by Critical Legal Studies (on which, see William Galston, "Practical Philosophy and the Bill of Rights: Perspectives on Some Current Issues," in *A Culture of Rights*, ed. Michael Lacey

and Knud Haakonssen [Cambridge: Cambridge UP, 1991], 288–95). As with the current rediscovery of Carl Schmitt on the left, Critical Legal Studies may look at times very much like the Legal Realism of the 1920s and 1930.

[69] The formulation is Harro Müller's: see his book on the historical novels of Second World War exiles, including Brecht, *Geschichte zwischen Kairos und Katastrophe* (Frankfurt: Athenäum, 1988).

[70] Harry Lehmann (*Die flüchtige Wahrheit der Kunst* [Munich: Fink, 2005]) has pointed out that Luhmann had a hard time with the avant-garde, precisely because the latter sought to challenge the differentiation or autonomy of art from politics or other spheres. The present matter of Brecht's emergency lyrics of exile would support Lehmann's point.

[71] Adorno, *Philosophie der neuen Musik, Gesammelte Schriften* 12 (Frankfurt: Suhrkamp, 1997), 126.

[72] Benjamin, *Versuche über Brecht* (Frankfurt: Suhrkamp, 1966), 118.

[73] Brecht, *Werke* 18, 224.

[74] Brecht, *Werke* 9 (*Gedichte* 2), 635–36.

[75] This is the origin of the old debate about Brecht's supposed "Marxist emblematics," particularly with respect to the *Buckower Elegien*. (See Jürgen Link, *Die Struktur des literarischen Symbols* [Munich: Fink, 1975]; Reinhold Grimm, "Marxistische Emblematik," in *Emblem und Emblematikrezeption*, ed. Sibylle Penkert [Darmstadt: Wissenschaftliche Buchgesellschaft, 1978], 502–42, and also the convincing rebuttal of Christian Wagenknecht in the same volume, 543–59.) What commentators took for neo-Baroque was in fact a media effect, one which has not yet been properly investigated. (Paul Peters, "Brecht und die Stimme der Nachrichten," *Weimarer Beiträge* 27 (2000): 3, 352–73 is not informed by any media-theoretical perspective and unfortunately refers Brecht's poetry back to religious concepts of *Offenbarung* — thereby only repeating the Nazi aesthetic of radio inwardness Brecht sought to escape!)

[76] This is what Lacan ironically termed the "alèthosphère" (*Le Séminaire XVII: L'Envers de la psychanalyse* [Paris: Seuil, 1991], 187–88): the authority of science as diffused by modern communications media.

[77] Brecht, *Werke* 9 (*Gedichte* 2), 758.

[78] Brecht, *Werke* (*Gedichte* 2), 819.

[79] Eduard Friedrich Mörike, *Gedichte* (Stuttgart: Reclam, 1977), 61. The result is a microcosm of what Adorno called the bourgeois *Intérieur* (cf. *Kierkegaard: Zur Konstruktion des Ästhetischen, Gesammelte Schriften* 2:61–69).

[80] Luhmann, *Das Recht der Gesellschaft*, 486–87.

[81] Luhmann, *Die Kunst der Gesellschaft*, 83.

[82] Benjamin, *Illuminations*, trans. Harry Zohn (New York: Schocken, 1968), 236–37; *Das Kunstwerk im Zeitalter seiner technischen Reproduzierbarkeit* (Frankfurt: Suhrkamp, 1977), 36.

[83] Freud, *Jenseits des Lustprinzips, Studienausgabe* (Frankfurt: Fischer, 1970), 3:240; the Standard Edition (New York: Norton, 1961), 34, translates this as "quiescent cathexis."

[84] Brecht, "Zu den Epigrammen (Notizen)," *Über Lyrik*, 89–90.

[85] So Peter Whitaker has noted that "the treatment of landscape is not an escapist choice, *but a kind of limitation*. The landscapes of his exile are the *mediating links* between the poet and political conflict; in the thematization of landscape, Brecht recognizes his separation from the centers of the struggle" (*Brecht's Poetry: A Critical Study* [Oxford: Clarendon, 1985], 163, emphasis added).

[86] Brecht, *Werke* 9 (*Gedichte* 2), 634.

[87] See the discussions in "Die Sprache," in *Unterwegs zur Sprache* (Pfullingen: Neske, 1965), and *Zur Sache des Denkens* (Tübingen: Niemeyer, 1976), where the "es ist" is linked to the notion of "event" discussed in chapter 1 here.

[88] Adorno, *Ästhetische Theorie, Gesammelte Schriften* 7, 187. See my comments on this aspect of Trakl in "L'esthétique de l'anasémie," in *Psychanalyse, histoire, rêve et poésie*, ed. Claude Nachin (Paris: Harmattan, 2006), 297–307.

[89] Brecht, *Werke* 9 (*Gedichte* 2): 817.

[90] Brecht, *Werke* 9 (*Gedichte* 2): 814–15.

[91] Brecht, *Werke* 9 (*Gedichte* 2): 817.

[92] Cf. the two wartime California poems, "Vom Sprengen des Gartens" and "Garden in Progress."

[93] Cleanth Brooks, *The Well-Wrought Urn* (New York: Harcourt, 1947), 8.

[94] Brecht, *Werke* 9 (*Gedichte* 2), 723.

[95] Brecht, *Werke* 9 (*Gedichte* 2) 820.

[96] Luhmann, *Die Kunst der Gesellschaft*, 73–74.

[97] Jameson, *Brecht and Method* (London: Verso, 1998), 104, 110.

[98] Luhmann, *Soziale Systeme*, 431; compare also his *Die Gesellschaft der Gesellschaft*, 66 and 446, where this problem of "additional meaning" is explicitly referred to structural coupling for its solution; also *Die Kunst der Gesellschaft*, 86.

[99] On popular misunderstandings of Gödel, see Torkel Franzen, *Gödel's Theorem: An Incomplete Guide to Its Use and Abuse* (Wellesley MA: A. K. Peters, 2005) — a more careful book than Alan Sokal's famous broadside against all poststructural references to science.

[100] Jan Knopf, *Brecht-Handbuch* (Stuttgart: Metzler, 1984), 135.

[101] The present reading has structural similarities with Jameson's idea that "the Brechtian dramatization of contradiction calls for a judgment which is not a choosing between two alternatives but, rather, their supersession in the light of a new and utopian one" (*Brecht and Method*, 121). Jameson's comparison here of Brecht's method to André Jolles's *casus* is certainly relevant to these shorter nature poems, with their "arguing back and forth" (120) and proverbial, lapidary condensation.

[102] Luhmann, *Die Kunst der Gesellschaft*, 288.

[103] Significantly, no example is given of a contingency formula for the art system.

[104] The locus classicus here is Wolfgang Krohn and Günter Küppers, *Emergenz: Die Entstehung von Ordnung, Organisation und Bedeutung* (Frankfurt: Suhrkamp, 1992).

[105] Luhmann, *Die Kunst der Gesellschaft*, 121–22.

[106] Luhmann, *Die Gesellschaft der Gesellschaft*, 134–35.

[107] The moment of metaphor in Luhmann's discussion of self-reference here is in close proximity to the vertiginously unobservable sublime discussed in chapter 1. But we may remember at this point Marius' and Jahraus' critical observations on the inability of deconstruction to break out of its own self-referential circle (see discussion in chapter 3 earlier).

[108] We may recall here the discussion of Kant's constitution (*Verfassung*) between man and nature at the end of chapter 1.

[109] Brecht, *Herr Puntila und sein Knecht Matti, Werke* 4 (*Stücke* 4), 1611.

[110] Wedekind, *Lulu* (Stuttgart: Reclam, 1989), 8.

[111] See also the passage in the *Arbeitsjournal*, ed. Werner Hecht (Frankfurt: Suhrkamp, 1973), 1:390 on the presence of nature in Puntila.

[112] Jameson, *Brecht and Method*, 162, footnote 15.

[113] See the discussion, earlier in this chapter, of Luhmann and medieval law for the idea of an "Umweg über das Tier" and an "Umweg über die Natur."

[114] See note 46 in chapter 1: "That which is originally natural or biological never stops referring to the symbolic level" (Lacan, *Sém. IV*, 96).

[115] To note this need not mean an automatic chiming-in with the chorus of current neo-conservative equivalencies between different forms of "totalitarianism"; yet one must face the problem of Brecht's functionalized art more directly than, for instance, Jameson (whose often-evasive *Brecht and Method* seems to want to reproduce Brechtian "slyness" within an academic context).

[116] Luhmann, *Die Gesellschaft der Gesellschaft*, 238–40 (emphasis mine, LP).

[117] As Alain Badiou has noted in his critique of the current vogue for ethics, "humanity has its root in the identification in thought of singular situations" (*Ethics*, trans. Peter Hallward [London: Verso, 2001], 16). This is the "kairotic" and differential moment we have worked out in Brecht. Badiou wants to define this situation as a Heideggerian "event," framing "a subject which goes beyond the animal (although the animal remains its sole foundation)" (41). Note that the end of his sentence insists that this animal foundation cannot be elided.

[118] Adorno, *Philosophie der neuen Musik, Gesammelte Schriften* 12:192–93.

[119] Luhmann, "Weltkunst," in Luhmann, Bunsen, Baecker, *Unbeobachtbare Welt: Über Kunst und Architektur* (Bielefeld: Haux, 1990), 44; see also Luhmann, *Die Kunst der Gesellschaft*, 136–48 on this.

[120] Luhmann, *Das Recht der Gesellschaft*, 220. Compare also *Die Kunst der Gesellschaft*, 306: "the unity (form) of the distinction self-reference/hetero-reference has the function of sufficing to the system as a representation of the world."

[121] See "Zur Kritik der Gewalt," 179–203 in *Gesammelte Schriften*, 2:1, ed. Tiedemann and Schweppenhäuser (Frankfurt: Suhrkamp, 1977). Derrida's comments on this essay are unhelpful and inaccurate (i.e. his assertion in *Force de loi* [Paris: Galilée, 1994], 77 that Carl Schmitt remained a constitutionalist prior to 1933). Shoshana Felman's *The Juridical Unconscious: Trials and Traumas in the*

Twentieth Century (Cambridge, MA: Harvard UP, 2002) works with an implicitly Derridean opposition between mere legal rationality and an unattainably sublime justice, using the reference to trauma so popular in the 1990s. Felman is right to note that Benjamin's concern with law, like Arendt's later on, was bound up with a "traumatic story of the *loss of Germany*" and an underlying "narrative of a forceful removal across national borders" (239, note 63). The same trauma arguably lies behind Brecht's exile poems. Yet Felman's aporetical claim that "the purpose of the law . . . is to get under control and regain a conscious mastery over the traumatic nightmare," or that "law requires and brings closure and totalization of the evidence and of its meaning" (150–51) does no justice to the real differentiated (i.e. precisely *not* totalizing!) function of law, to which, as this chapter has shown, Brecht was quite attentive. Using Felman's own references, one could just as easily argue that *the law itself* functions, in Brecht, as Benjamin's "expressionlessness" (*das Ausdruckslose*), that is, as a deliberately neutral marker for what cannot be expressed through subjectivity (see Felman, 13 and 163; Benjamin, "Goethes Wahlverwandschaften," *Gesammelte Schriften* 1:1, 181).

[122] On this, see Luhmann, *Die Ausdifferenzierung des Rechts*, 214, footnote 48, with reference to China and Islam.

[123] This may be why later poets engaging Brecht "often . . . take up Brecht's exile poems, especially those of the *Svendborger Gedichte*" (Karen Leeder, "After Brecht: The Reception of Brecht's Poetry in English," in *Empedocles' Shoe: Essays on Brecht's Poetry*, ed. Tom Kuhn and Karen Leeder [London: Methuen, 2002], 231–56, 247).

Appendix: Niklas Luhmann

ALTHOUGH NIKLAS LUHMANN (1927–98) is seen in Germany as one of the most important figures not only in the history of sociology, but also philosophically,[1] he continues to be less well understood in the English speaking world. After a brief period in the 1980s when his work was commented on by David Wellbery and Hans-Ulrich Gumbrecht, interest in Luhmann has been marginalized by the increasing turn, especially in America, toward the Foucault-inspired "happy positivism" of New Historicism or Geertzian cultural anthropology. Luhmann was a latecomer to an university career: after a study of law and ten years' work as an administrator in Hanover, he went to Harvard in 1962 as the student of Talcott Parsons, and was then appointed professor of sociology at the then newly founded University of Bielefeld, where he would remain for the rest of his life. Luhmann's early work remained inspired by Parsons (the only major sociological figure who did not come in for sharp criticism in his writings), although he would later revise Parsons's structural functionalism with borrowings from the autopoietic biology of Humberto Maturana and Francisco Varela. Luhmann's interest in cybernetic models of explanation has its predecessor in Parsons's own work. So does his constant stress on "differentiation" of society, meaning the functional distinction of society into distinct subsystems such as law, economy, art, religion or education. "System" in Luhmann thus means, on one level, these social subsystems, which can no longer be subordinated to any one overarching system of meaning (as in older, stratified social models, where religion or politics could dominate other systems). Each subsystem has its own binary code distinguishing it from others. Thus the economic system works with profitable/unprofitable, the legal system with legal/illegal, and so on. No system can control the workings of another system, although there are "interpenetrations" (Parsons) or "structural couplings" (Luhmann) between them. Thus society must be conceived of in a polycentric fashion: there is no Archimedean point from which to view all of society as a whole, nor can one conceive society in hermeneutical manner, as an organic relation of parts to whole. As is evident, this implies that Luhmann's theory is indeed a theory of modernity.

Luhmann first received wide attention through his controversy with Jürgen Habermas, published in *Theorie der Gesellschaft oder Sozialtechnologie?* (1971). In this volume, Habermas accused Luhmann of an "affirmative" reduction of social theory to scientific models that eliminated subjective agency and reflection in favor of anonymous functioning. Habermas would repeat this criticism in sections devoted to Luhmann in *Theorie des kommunikativen Handelns* (1981) and *Der philosophische Diskurs der Moderne* (1985). Luhmann, in turn, retorted with ironic barbs about the idealism and improbability of Habermas's "ideal communicative consensus." In the meantime, Luhmann's theory had, perhaps somewhat belatedly, reached its final form with *Soziale Systeme* (1984). Here Luhmann integrates the concept of the autopoiesis or "self-production" of society through the production of meaning (*Sinn*). Meaning, for Luhmann, defines the "horizon" of the social world, in a way borrowed from Husserl's phenomenology: everything social is defined by meaning, and there is no escape from the latter. Meaning is not, however, reducible solely to language, which means that language is somewhat devalued relative to its position in poststructuralist thought. (Language, for Luhmann, is not a system, but only a medium.) If, for Habermas — and still for Parsons as well — the basic unit of society is action, for Luhmann it is communication. Yet communication is now conceived of in a way very different from the "communications theory" of the 1960s (e.g. the early Umberto Eco, or Roman Jakobson). In particular, communication is drastically severed from consciousness or perception, which are now seen as "black boxes" ultimately inaccessible to knowledge. This means that communication is conceived of in radically de-subjectivized fashion, an aspect of Luhmann's work which has been linked to poststructuralism. (Although he was always skeptical of psychoanalysis, Luhmann did express qualified admiration for Derrida, as well as for Deleuze.) Moreover, this means a farewell to all older projects of subjective emancipation and autonomy, as they had been conceived of from Kant to Adorno. Luhmann refers, not without irony, to this tradition as "old-European." "Subject" and "subjectivity" are now replaced with "psychic systems" for Luhmann.

After *Soziale Systeme*, Luhmann began to publish the series of nine volumes that would work out the implications of his newly technified theory for all the social subsystems, including *Die Kunst der Gesellschaft* (1995, Engl. trans. *Art as a Social System*, 2000) and *Das Recht der Gesellschaft* (1993, Engl. trans. *Law as a Social System*, 2004). The overarching two-volume summary *Die Gesellschaft der Gesellschaft* (1997) has not yet been translated, and the volumes on religion, politics, and education were only published posthumously. Luhmann also wrote separate books on topics such as the mass media.

Luhmann's ongoing influence remains considerable. In English, Geoffrey Winthrop-Young has compared his work to the media theory of Friedrich Kittler. In Germany, his students Peter Fuchs (b. 1949; *Moderne Kommunikation*, 1993) and Dirk Baecker (b. 1955; *Form und Formen der*

Kommunikation, 2005) have continued to develop his thought on art and social organization. Oliver Jahraus has recently, in a nearly 700-page *magnum opus* (*Literatur als Medium,* 2003), tried to link Luhmann's work back up with the venerable German tradition of hermeneutics. A recent Suhrkamp volume even attempts to connect Luhmann to the very distinct tradition of cultural theory. There have also been commemorative volumes devoted to reminiscences of Luhmann the teacher and person (*Warum haben Sie keinen Fernseher, Herr Luhmann?* 2004). Conferences dedicated to his work also continue to be organized. There has been no decline in his reputation, as so often happens after the death of a major thinker. Luhmann thus remains, a decade after his death, a powerful presence in German intellectual life.

Bibliographical Note

The literature on Luhmann is extensive. A beginning may be made with Henk de Berg, *Luhmann in Literary Studies: A Bibliography* (Siegen: LUMIS, 1995). A shorter version is available as de Berg, "Select Annotated Bibliography to Luhmann's Systems Theory and Its Applications in Literary Studies," *Poetics Today,* 16, 4 (Winter, 1995): 737–41. Among the special issues devoted to his work are: *New German Critique* 61 (Winter 1994); *Cybernetics and Human Knowing* 3, 2 (1995); and *Distinktion* 1 (2000) (ed. Christian Borch).

Notes

[1] A recent German anthology is symptomatically titled *Grosse Theorien von Freud bis Luhmann* (ed. Walter Erhart and Herbert Jaumann [Munich: Beck, 2000]), implying that Luhmann was one of the last great systematic thinkers.

Bibliography

Abrahams, R. D., ed. *African Folktales.* New York: Pantheon, 1983.

Adorno, Theodor W. *Asthetische Theorie. Gesammelte Schriften* 7. Frankfurt: Suhrkamp, 1997.

———. "Engagement." *Noten zur Literatur. Gesammelte Schriften* 11. Frankfurt: Suhrkamp, 2003.

———. "Die Idee der Naturgeschichte." *Gesammelte Schriften* 1. Frankfurt: Suhrkamp, 1997.

———. *Jargon der Eigentlichkeit.* Frankfurt: Suhrkamp, 1964.

———. *Kierkegaard: Zur Konstruktion des Ästhetischen. Gesammelte Schriften* 2. Frankfurt: Suhrkamp, 1979.

———. *Minima Moralia.* Frankfurt: Suhrkamp, 2003.

———. *Negative Dialektik. Gesammelte Schriften* 6. Frankfurt: Suhrkamp, 2003.

———. "Parataxis." *Noten zur Literatur. Gesammelte Schriften* 11. Frankfurt: Suhrkamp, 2003.

———. *Philosophie der neuen Musik. Gesammelte Schriften* 12. Frankfurt: Suhrkamp, 1997.

Adelson, Leslie A. *The Turkish Turn in Contemporary German Literature: Toward a New Critical Grammar of Migration.* New York: Palgrave, 2005.

Andriopoulos, Stefan. "Die Zirkulation von Figuren und Begriffen in kriminologischen, juristischen und literarischen Darstellungen von 'Unfall' und 'Verbrechen.'" *Internationales Archiv für Sozialgeschichte der deutschen Literatur* 21/2 (1996): 113–42.

Anz, Thomas. *Literatur der Existenz.* Stuttgart: Metzler, 1977.

———. *Literatur des Expressionismus.* Stuttgart: Metzler, 2002.

Apter, Emily, and W. Pietz, eds. *Fetishism as Cultural Discourse.* Ithaca, NY: Cornell UP, 1993.

Austin, Linda. "The Lament and the Rhetoric of the Sublime." *19th Century Literature* 53.3 (Dec. 1998): 279–306.

Bachelard, Gaston. *L'air et les songes; essai sur l'imagination du movement.* Paris: José Corti, 1943.

Badiou, Alain. *Ethics: An Essay on the Understanding of Evil*. Translated and introduced by Peter Hallward. London and New York: Verso, 2001.

———. *Le Siècle*. Paris: Éditions du Seuil, 2005.

Baecker, Dirk. "Die Natur der Gesellschaft." Online at http://homepage.mac.com/baecker/naturdergesellschaft.pdf).

———. *Poker im Osten*. Berlin: Merve, 1998.

Balke, Friedrich. "Tristes Tropiques. Systems Theory and the Literary Scene." *Soziale Systeme* 8.1 (2002): 27–37.

Baron, Frank, Ernst S. Dick, and Warren R. Maurer, eds. *Rilke, The Alchemy of Alienation*. Lawrence: Regents Press of Kansas, 1980.

Beck, Ulrich. *Risikogesellschaft: Auf dem Weg in eine andere Moderne*. Frankfurt: Suhrkamp, 1986. Translated by Mark Ritter as *Risk Society*. London: Sage, 1992.

Benjamin, Walter. *Gesammelte Schriften*. Ed. Rolf Tiedemann and Hermann Schweppenhäuser. Frankfurt: Suhrkamp, 1977.

———. *Illuminations*. Trans. Harry Zohn. New York: Schocken, 1968.

———. *Das Kunstwerk im Zeitalter seiner technischen Reproduzierbarkeit*. Frankfurt: Suhrkamp, 1977.

———. *Versuche über Brecht*. Frankfurt: Suhrkamp, 1966.

Benn, Gottfried. *Sämtliche Werke*. 7 vols. Ed. Gerhard Schuster and Ilse Benn. Stuttgart: Klett-Cotta, 1986–2003.

Berman, Nina. *Orientalismus, Kolonialismus und Moderne: zum Bild des Orients in der deutschsprachigen Kultur um 1900*. Stuttgart: M&P, 1997.

Berman, Russell. *Enlightenment or Empire*. Lincoln: U of Nebraska P, 1998.

Bernheimer, Charles. "Fetishism and Decadence: Salome's Severed Heads." In Apter and Pietz, eds., *Fetishism as Cultural Discourse*, 62–83.

Bhabha, Homi K. "The Commitment to Theory." In *Questions of Third Cinema*, ed. Jim Pines and Paul Wellemer, 111–32. London: BFI, 1989.

———. *The Location of Culture*. London: Routledge, 1994.

———. "The Other Question: Difference, Discrimination and the Discourse of Colonialism." In *Literature, Politics and Theory: Papers from the Essex Conference, 1976–1984*, ed. Francis Barker, Peter Hulme, Margaret Iversen, and Diana Loxley, 148–72. London: Methuen, 1986.

———. "Representation and the Colonial Text: A Critical Exploration of Some Forms of Mimetism." In *The Theory of Reading*, ed. Frank Gloversmith, 93–122. Sussex: Harvester, 1984.

Bloch, Ernst. "Herbst, Sumpf, Heide und Sezession." In Bloch, *Literarische Aufsätze*, 439–47. Frankfurt: Suhrkamp, 1984.

———. *Natural Law and Human Dignity*. Trans. Dennis Schmidt. Cambridge, MA: MIT Press, 1986.

Bloom, Harold, ed. *Stéphane Mallarmé*. New York: Chelsea House, 1987.

Blum, Cinzia Sartini. *The Other Modernism: F. T. Marinetti's Futurist Fiction of Power*. Berkeley: U of California P, 1996.

Böhme, Gernot. *Für eine ökologische Naturästhetik*. Frankfurt: Suhrkamp, 1989.

Böhme, Hartmut. *Natur und Subjekt*. Frankfurt am Main: Suhrkamp, 1988.

Bohrer, Karl Heinz. *Nach der Natur*. Munich: Hanser 1988.

Boothby, Richard. *Death and Desire*. New York/London: Routledge, 1991.

Borch-Jakobsen, Mikkel. *The Freudian Subject*. Trans. Catherine Porter. Stanford: Stanford UP, 1988.

Bordwell, David, and Noel Carroll, eds. *Post-Theory*. Madison: U of Wisconsin P, 1996.

Bosse, Heinrich. *Autorschaft ist Werkherrschaft: über die Entstehung des Urheberrechts aus dem Geist der Goethezeit*. Paderborn: Schöningh, 1981.

Boyle, Deirdre, "Post-Traumatic Shock: Bill Viola's Recent Work." *Afterimage* 24 (Sept.-Oct. 1996): 9–11.

Brecht, Bertolt. *Arbeitsjournal*. Vol. 1. Ed. Werner Hecht. Frankfurt: Suhrkamp, 1973.

———. *Werke (Grosse Berliner und Frankfurter Ausgabe)*. Ed. Werner Hecht et al. Berlin: Aufbau; Frankfurt: Suhrkamp, 1988–2000.

Breton, André. *L'Amour fou*. Paris: Gallimard, 1937.

———. *Anthologie de l'humour noir*. Paris: Éditions de Sagittaire, 1940.

Briegleb, Klaus. "Gegen die funktionale Literaturwissenschaft." In *Unmittelbar zur Epoche des NS-Fascismus: Arbeiten zur politischen Philologie 1978–1988*, ed. Briegleb, 160–90. Frankfurt: Suhrkamp, 1989.

Bronfen, Elisabeth. *Over Her Dead Body: Death, Femininity and the Aesthetic*. Manchester, UK: Manchester UP, 1992.

Brook, Peter. "Freud's Masterplot: Questions of Narrative." In *Literature and Psychoanalysis*, ed. Shoshana Felman, 280–300. Baltimore: Johns Hopkins UP, 1982.

Brooks, Cleanth. *The Well-Wrought Urn*. New York: Harcourt, 1947.

Browne, Nick, ed., *Reconfiguring American Film Genres*. Berkeley: U of California P, 1998.

Brulle, Robert J. *Agency, Democracy, and Nature: The U.S. Environmental Movement from a Critical Theory Perspective*. Cambridge: MIT, 2004.

Buchheit, Sabine. *Formen und Funktionen literarischer Kommunikation im Werk Günter Eichs*. St. Ingbert: Röhrig, 2003.

Buber, Martin. *Briefwechsel.* Heidelberg: L. Schneider, 1972.

Budick, Sanford. *The Western Theory of Tradition.* New Haven: Yale UP, 2000.

Butler, Judith. "Imitation and Gender Insubordination." In *Inside/Out: Lesbian Theories, Gay Theories,* ed. Diana Fuss, 13–31. New York: Routledge, 1991.

Cahiers d'Art. Special Max Ernst issue, nos. 6–7, Paris 1937.

Caldwell, Peter C. *Popular Sovereignty and the Crisis of German Constitutional Law.* Durham, NC: Duke UP, 1997.

Carrdus, Anna. "The Uses of Rhetoric in Brecht's Svendborg Poems." In *Brecht's Poetry of Political Exile,* ed. Ronald Speirs, 135–52. Cambridge: Cambridge UP, 2000.

Caudill, David. *Lacan and the Subject of Law.* Atlantic Highlands, NJ: Humanities Press, 1997.

Celan, Paul. *Gesammelte Werke in drei Bänden.* Frankfurt: Suhrkamp, 1983.

Cheek, Pamela. *Sexual Antipodes: Enlightenment Globalization and the Placing of Sex.* Stanford: Stanford UP, 2003.

Clam, Jean. "System's Sole Constituent, the Operation: Clarifying a Central Concept of Luhmannian Theory." *Acta Sociologica* 43, 1 (March 2000): 63–79.

Clifford, James. *The Predicament of Culture.* Cambridge: Harvard UP, 1988.

Copjec, Joan. *Read My Desire: Lacan Against the Historicists.* Cambridge: MIT, 1994.

Cornell, Drucilla. "Enabling Paradoxes: Gender Difference and Systems Theory." *New Literary History* 27.2 (1996): 185–97.

———. *The Philosophy of the Limit.* New York: Routledge, 1992.

Costa, Mario. *Il sublime tecnologico.* Salerno: Edisud, 1990.

Cuomo, Glenn. *Career at the Cost of Compromise: Günter Eich's Life and Work in the Years 1933–1945.* Amsterdam: Rodopi, 1989.

Darwin, Charles. *The Origin of Species.* (1859) Harmondsworth: Penguin, 1985.

Davis, Erik. *TechGnosis: Myth, Magic and Mysticism in the Age of Information.* New York: Three Rivers Press, 1998.

Davis, Whitney. *Drawing the Dream of the Wolves: Homosexuality, Interpretation and Freud's "Wolf-Man."* Bloomington: Indiana UP, 1995.

Dean, Tim. *Beyond Sexuality.* Chicago: U of Chicago P, 2000.

Debrix, François. "Specters of Postmodernism: Derrida's Marx, the New International and the Return of Situationism." *Philosophy and Social Criticism* 25, 1 (1999): 1–21.

de Lauretis, Teresa. *Technologies of Gender*. Bloomington: Indiana UP, 1987.

Deleuze, Gilles. *Nietzsche and Philosophy*. Trans. Hugh Tomlinson. New York: Columbia UP, 1983.

Deleuze, Gilles, and Felix Guattari. *Kafka*. Minneapolis: U of Minnesota P, 1986.

De Man, Paul. *Allegories of Reading*. New Haven: Yale, 1979.

———. "Lyric and Modernity." In *Stéphane Mallarmé*, ed. Harold Bloom, 61–77. New York: Chelsea House, 1987.

———. *The Rhetoric of Romanticism*. New York: Columbia UP, 1984.

Derrida, Jacques. *L'Écriture et la différence*. Paris: Seuil, 1972.

———. *Éperons: Les Styles de Nietzsche*. Paris: Flammarion, 1976.

———. *Force de loi*. Paris: Galilée, 1994.

Diamond, Jared. *Collapse: How Societies Choose to Fail or Succeed*. New York: Viking, 2004.

———. *Guns, Germans and Steel: The Fates of Human Societies*. New York: Norton, 1997.

Devall, Bill, and George Sessions. *Deep Ecology*. Layton: UT: Gibbs Smith, 1985.

Dews, Peter. *Logics of Disintegration*. London: Verso, 1987.

Dilthey, Wilhelm. *Gesammelte Schriften*. Stuttgart: Teubner; Göttingen: Vandenhoeck & Ruprecht, 1961–2006.

Dirlik, Arif. *The Postcolonial Aura*. Boulder, CO: Westview, 1997.

Döblin, Alfred. *Aufsätze zur Literatur*. Olten: Walter Verlag 1963.

———. *Berge Meere und Giganten*. (1924) Olten: Walter-Verlag, 1977.

———. *Berlin Alexanderplatz*. (1929) Olten: Walter Verlag, 1994.

———. *Briefe*. Olten: Walter-Verlag, 1970.

———. *Die Drei Sprünge des Wang-Lun*.(1915) Olten: Walter Verlag, 1960.

———. *Flucht und Sammlung des Judenvolks*. (1935) Hildesheim: Gerstenberg, 1977.

———. *Das Ich über die Natur*. Berlin: S. Fischer, o.J., 1927.

———. *Journey to Poland*. Trans. Joachim Neugroschel, ed. H. Graber. London and New York: Tauris, 1991.

———. *Die Nonnen von Kemnade*. Berlin: S. Fischer, 1923.

Dollenmayer, David. "The Advent of Döblinism: *Die drei Sprünge des Wang-lun* and *Wadzeks Kampf mit der Dampfturbine*." In *A Companion to the Works of Alfred Döblin*, ed. Roland Dollinger, Wolf Koepke, and Heidi Tewarson, 55–74. Rochester, NY: Camden House, 2004.

Dollinger, Roland. "Technology and Nature: From *Berge Meere und Giganten* to a Philosophy of Nature." In *A Companion to the Works of Alfred Döblin*, ed. Dollinger, Koepke, Tewarson, 93–109.

Donahue, Neil. "Fear and Fascination: Rilke's Use of Georg Simmel in *The Notebooks of Malte Laurids Brigge*." *Studies in 20th Century Literature* 16: 2 (Summer 1991): 197–219.

———. *Karl Krolow and the Poetics of Amnesia in Postwar Germany*. Rochester, NY: Camden House, 2002.

Donougho, Martin. "Stages of the Sublime in North America." *Modern Language Notes* 115.5 (2000): 909–40.

Douglas, Mary. *Natural Symbols*. Harmondsworth: Penguin, 1970.

Dotzler, Bernhard. "Benns Woyzeck." *Deutsche Vierteljahresschrift* 78.3 (September 2002): 482–98.

Dusek, Val. *Philosophy of Technology: An Introduction*. Malden, MA: Oxford Blackwell, 2006.

Eagleton, Terry. *After Theory*. New York: Basic Books, 2003.

Eden, Sally. "Environmental Issues: Nature versus the Environment?" *Progress In Human Geography* 25, 1 (2001): 79–85.

Eder, Klaus. *The Social Construction of Nature*. London: Sage, 1996.

Ellrich, Lutz. "Entgeistertes Beobachten. Hegel und Luhmann im Vergleich." In *Die Logik der Systeme,* ed. Gerhard Wagner and Peter Merz-Benz, 73–126. Konstanz: Universitätsverlag, 2000.

Enzensberger, Hans Magnus. *Einzelheiten*. Frankfurt: Suhrkamp, 1962.

Eppelsheimer, Rudolf. *Rilkes larische Landschaft*. Stuttgart: Verlag Freies Geistesleben, 1975.

Evans, Dylan. *An Introductory Dictionary of Lacanian Psychoanalysis*. London: Routledge, 1996.

Fanon, Frantz. *Black Skin, White Masks*. Trans. C. L. Markmann. New York: Grove, 1967.

———. *The Wretched of the Earth*. Trans. C. Farrington. New York: Grove Press, 1991.

Felman, Shoshana. *The Juridical Unconscious: Trials and Traumas in the Twentieth Century*. Cambridge, MA: Harvard UP, 2002.

Fink, Bruce. *The Lacanian Subject*. Princeton, NJ: Princeton UP, 1995.

Foster, Hal. *The Return of the Real*. Cambridge: MIT Press, 1996.

Foucault, Michel. *Les Mots et les choses*. Paris: Gallimard, 1966.

Franzen, Torkel. *Gödel's Theorem: An Incomplete Guide to Its Use and Abuse*. Wellesley, MA: A. K. Peters, 2005.

Freud, Sigmund. *Civilization and Its Discontents*. Trans. James Strachey. New York: Norton, 1989.

———. *Standard Edition*. Trans. James Strachey. New York: Norton, 1961.

———. *Studienausgabe*. 9 vols. Frankfurt: Fischer, 1970.

Frey, Hans-Jost. "The Tree of Doubt." In *Stéphane Mallarmé*, ed. Bloom, 141–49.

Friedrichsmeyer, Sara, Sara Lennox, and Susanne Zantop, eds. *The Imperialist Imagination*. Ann Arbor: U of Michigan P, 1998.

Frost, Robert. *The Poetry of Robert Frost*. Ed. Edward Connery Lathem. New York: Holt, 1979.

Fuchs, Peter, and Niklas Luhmann. *Reden und Schweigen*. Frankfurt: Suhrkamp, 1997.

Fuechtner, Veronika. "Alfred Doeblin and the Berlin Psychoanalytic Institute." Ph.D. Dissertation, University of Chicago, 2002.

Fuss, Diana. *Essentially Speaking: Feminism, Nature and Difference*. London: Routledge, 1990.

Galston, William. "Practical Philosophy and the Bill of Rights: Perspectives on Some Current Issues." In *A Culture of Rights*, ed. Michael Lacey and Knud Haakonssen, 288–95. Cambridge: Cambridge UP, 1991.

Ganguly, Keya. *States of Exception: Everyday Life and Postcolonial Identity*. Minneapolis: U of Minnesota P, 1991.

Gasché, Rodolphe. *The Tain of the Mirror*. Cambridge, MA: Harvard UP, 1986.

Gates, Jr., Henry Louis. "Critical Fanonism." *Critical Inquiry* 17 (1991): 457–70.

Gautier, Théophile. *Émaux et Camées*. Paris: Gallimard, 1981.

Gide, André. *Journal*. Paris: Pleiade, 1954.

Goebel, Rolf. *Constructing China: Kafka's Orientalist Discourse*. Rochester, NY: Camden House, 1997.

Gierke, Otto von. *Natural Law and the Theory of Society 1500 to 1800*. Trans. Ernest Barker. Boston: Beacon, 1957.

Giles, Steve. *Bertolt Brecht and Critical Theory: Marxism, Modernism and the Threepenny Lawsuit*. New York: Peter Lang, 1998.

Goethe, Johann Wolfgang. *Werke*. 14 vols. Ed. E. Trunz. Munich: DTV, 1998. Hamburger Ausgabe.

Goetschel, Willi. "'Land of Truth — Enchanting Name!' Kant's Journey at Home." In *The Imperialist Imagination*, ed. Friedrichsmeyer, Zantop, and Lennox, 321–36.

Graham, A. C., translator. *The Book of Lieh-tzu*. New York: Columbia UP, 1990.

Graham, Elaine L. *Representations of the Post/Human: Monsters, Aliens, and Others in Popular Culture.* New Brunswick, NJ: Rutgers UP, 2002.

Gravenhorst, L., and C. Tatschmurat, eds. *Töchter-Fragen: NS-Frauen-Geschichte.* Freiburg: Kore, 1990.

Graves, Robert. *The Greek Myths.* Harmondsworth: Penguin, 1960.

Grimm, Reinhold. "Marxistische Emblematik." In *Emblem und Emblematikrezeption*, ed. Sibylle Penkert, 502–42. Darmstadt: Wissenschaftliche Buchgesellschaft, 1978.

Guha, Ranajit. "The Prose of Counter-Insurgency." In *Postcolonialism: Critical Concepts*, ed. D. Brydon, 4:1370–1405. London and New York: Routledge, 2000.

Habermas, Jürgen. *Faktizität und Geltung.* Frankfurt: Suhrkamp, 1992.

———. *The Future of Human Nature.* Cambridge: Polity Press, 2003.

———. *Postmetaphysical Thinking: Between Metaphysics and the Critique of Reason.* Oxford: Blackwell, 1992.

———. *Zur Rekonstruktion des historischen Materialismus.* Frankfurt: Suhrkamp, 1976.

———. *Technik und Wissenschaft als Ideologie.* Frankfurt: Suhrkamp, 1968.

———. *Theorie und Praxis.* Frankfurt: Suhrkamp, 1978.

Harth, Dieter. "Die Bühne als Labotorium der Gefühle." *IABLIS* 2003, no page number.

Hegel, Georg Wilhelm Friedrich. *Werke in 20 Bänden.* Ed. K. M. Michel and E. Moldenhauer. Frankfurt: Suhrkamp: 1970.

Heid, Klaus, and Ruediger John, eds. *TRANSFER: Kunst Wirtschaft Wissenschaft.* Baden-Baden: Verlag für kritische Ästhetik, 2003.

Heidegger, Martin. *Identität und Differenz.* Pfüllingen: Neske, 1975; now in the *Gesamtausgabe*, vol. 11. Frankfurt: Klostermann, 1976–.

———. "Die Kehre." In *Bremer und Freiburger Vorträge, Gesamtausgabe* vol. 79, 68–77. Frankfurt: Klostermann, 1994.

———. "Die Sprache." In *Unterwegs zur Sprache.* Pfüllingen: Neske, 1965.

———. *Zur Sache des Denkens.* Tübingen: Niemeyer, 1976.

———. *Der Ursprung des Kunstwerkes.* Stuttgart: Reclam 1982.

———. *Vorträge und Aufsätze.* Pfüllingen: Neske, 1954.

———. "Wozu Dichter?" In *Holzwege.* Frankfurt: Klostermann, 1952.

Heimann, Moritz. *Die Spindel.* Vienna: Bermann-Fischer, 1937.

Heissenbüttel, Helmut. "Der entfirnißte Gottfried Benn." In *Über Gottfried Benn*, ed. Bruno Hillebrand, 2:240–44. Frankfurt: Fischer, 1987.

Heine, Heinrich. *Werke in 4 Bänden*. Ed. W. Preisendanz. Frankfurt: Insel, 1968.

Heizer, Donna. *Jewish-German Identity in the Orientalist Literature of Else Lasker-Schüler, Friedrich Wolf, and Franz Werfel*. Columbia, SC: Camden House, 1996.

Hesse, Hermann. *Gesammelte Erzählungen*. Ed. Volker Michels. Frankfurt: Suhrkamp, 1982.

Hölderlin, Friedrich. *Werke und Briefe*. 3 vols. Ed. F. Beissner and Jochen Schmidt. Frankfurt: Insel, 1969.

Holbeche, Brian. "Benn's 'Palau.'" *Seminar* 22:4 (November 1986): 312–23.

Holub, Robert. "Luhmann's Progeny." *New German Critique* 61 (Winter 1994): 143–59.

Homann, Renate. *Theorie der Lyrik*. Frankfurt: Suhrkamp, 1999.

Hubert, J. D. "Representations of Decapitation: Mallarmé's *Hérodiade* and Flaubert's *Hérodias*." *French Forum* 73 (Sept. 1982): 245–51.

Hühn, Peter. "Lyrik und Systemtheorie." In *Kommunikation und Differenz*, ed. Henk de Berg and Matthias Prangel, 114–36. Opladen: Westdeutscher Verlag, 1993.

Huyssen, Andreas. *After the Great Divide*. Bloomington: Indiana UP, 1986.

———. "Paris/Childhood: The Fragmented Body in Rilke's *The Notebooks of Malte Laurids Brigge*." In David Bathrick and Andreas Huyssen, *Modernity and the Text*, 113–41. New York: Columbia UP, 1989.

Irigaray, Luce. *Ethique de la différence sexuelle*. Paris: Minuit, 1984.

———. *The Marine Lover of Friedrich Nietzsche*. Trans. Gillian Gill. New York: Columbia UP, 1991.

———. *Sexes and Genealogies*. New York: Columbia UP, 1993.

Irwin, Robert. *Dangerous Knowledge: Orientalism and Its Discontents*. Woodstock: Overlook, 2006.

Jakobson, Roman. "Der grammatische Bau des Gedichts von Bertolt Brecht, 'Wir sind sie.'" In *Hölderlin, Klee, Brecht: Zur Wortkunst dreier Gedichte*, 107–28. Frankfurt: Suhrkamp, 1976.

Jameson, Fredric. *Brecht and Method*. London: Verso, 1998.

———. *Ideologies of Theory*. Vol. 1 Minneapolis: U of Minnesota Press, 1988.

———. *The Political Unconscious*. Ithaca, NY: Cornell UP, 1981.

———. *Post-Modernism: Or The Cultural Logic of Late Capitalism*. Durham, NC: Duke UP, 1991.

Jamin, Jean. "L'ethnographie mode d'inemploi." In *Le Mal et la douleur*, ed. Jacques Hainard and Roland Kaehr, 45–70. Neuchâtel: Musée d'Ethnographie, 1986.

Jelinek, Elfriede. *er nicht als er*. Frankfurt; Suhrkamp, 2004.

———. *In den Alpen*. Berlin Verlag, 2002.

Jerushalmi, Yosif Hayim. *Freud's Moses: Judaism Terminable and Interminable*. New Haven, CT: Yale UP, 1991.

Johnson, Barbara. "Les fleurs du mal armé." In *Stéphane Mallarmé*, ed. Harold Bloom, 211–27.

Johnson, Julian. *Webern and the Transformation of Nature*. New York and Cambridge: Cambridge UP, 1999.

Joseph, Betty. *Reading the East India Company, 1720–1840: Colonial Currencies of Gender*. Chicago: U of Chicago P, 2004.

Joseph, Betty. Review of Pamela Cheek, *Sexual Antipodes*. *Comparative Literature Studies* 42.2 (2005): 313–16.

Jonas, Hans. *The Imperative of Responsibility: In Search of an Ethics for the Technological Age*. Chicago: U of Chicago P, 1985.

Kaes, Anton, ed. *Kino-Debatte: Texte zum Verhältnis von Literatur und Film, 1909–1929*. Munich: DTV, 1978.

Kant, Immanuel. *Critique of Judgment*. Trans. J. H. Bernard. New York and London: Hafner, 1968.

———. *Kritik der reinen Vernunft*, I. Ed. Wilhelm Weischedel. In *Werke* III. Frankfurt: Suhrkamp, 1976.

———. *Kritik der Urteilskraft*. Leipzig: Meiner, 1922.

Keller, Evelyn Fox. *Reflections on Gender and Science*. New Haven: Yale UP, 1985.

Kern, Robert. *Orientalism, Modernism, and the American Poem*. Cambridge: Cambridge UP, 1996.

Ketelson, Uwe-K. "Natur und Geschichte — Das widerrufende Zeitgedicht der 30er Jahre." In *Naturlyrik und Gesellschaft*, ed. Norbert Mecklenburg, 152–62. Stuttgart: Klett-Cotta, 1977.

Keyserling, Count Hermann von. *Das Reisetagebuch eines Philosophen*. Vol. 2. Munich: Dunckcr and Humblot, 1919.

Khurana, Thomas. *Die Dispersion des Unbewussten: Drei Studien zu einem nichtsubstantialistischen Konzept des Unbewussten*. Freud — Lacan — Luhmann Giessen: Psychosozial Verlag, 2002.

King, Michael, and Chris Thornhill, eds. *Luhmann on Law and Politics: Critical Appraisals and Applications*. Portland, OR: Hart, 2006.

Kittler, Friedrich. "Benns Gedichte — Schlager von Klasse." In Kittler, *Draculas Vermächtnis*, 105–29. Leipzig: Reclam, 1993.

———. *Discourse Networks 1800/1900*. Stanford: Stanford UP, 1990.

———. "The Mechanical Philosopher." In *Looking After Nietzsche*, ed. Lawrence Rickels, 195–208. Albany: SUNY, 1990.

Kleinbard, David. *The Beginning of Terror*. New York: NYUP, 1995.

Klymiuk, Georg. *Kausalitat und moderne Literatur: Eine Studie zum Werk Alfred Döblins* Frankfurt: Peter Lang, 1984.

Knopf, Jan. *Brecht-Handbuch*. Stuttgart: Metzler, 1984.

Koebner, Thomas. "Der Garten als literarisches Motiv: Ausblick auf die Jahrhundertwende." In *Park und Garten im 18. Jahrhundert*. Munich: Winter, 1978.

Kohlross, Christian. *Theorie des modernen Naturgedichts*. Würzburg: Königshausen und Neumann, 2000.

Kontje, Todd. *German Orientalisms*. Ann Arbor: U of Michigan P, 2004.

Kort, Wolfgang. *Alfred Döblin*. New York: Twayne, 1974.

Korte, Hermann. *Deutschsprachige Lyrik nach 1945*. 2nd ed. Stuttgart: Metzler, 2004.

Kracauer, Siegfried. *Das Ornament der Masse*. Frankfurt: Suhrkamp, 1977.

Kraus, Karl. *Aphorismen (Schriften 8)*. Frankfurt: Suhrkamp, 1986.

———. *Die chinesische Mauer*. (1910) Frankfurt: Suhrkamp, 1987.

———. *Dritte Walpurgisnacht*. (1952) Frankfurt: Suhrkamp, 1989.

———. *Untergang der Welt durch schwarze Magie*. (1922) Frankfurt: Suhrkamp, 1989.

Krauss, Rosalind. *The Optical Unconscious*. Cambridge, MA: MIT Press, 1993.

Kristeva, Julia. *Revolution in Poetic Language*. Trans. M. Waller. New York: Columbia UP, 1984.

———. *La Révolution du langage poétique*. Paris: Seuil, 1974.

Krohn, Wolfgang, and Günter Küppers. *Emergenz: Die Entstehung von Ordnung, Organisation und Bedeutung*. Frankfurt: Suhrkamp, 1992.

Krojanker, Gustav, ed. *Juden in der deutschen Literatur*. Berlin: Welt, 1922.

Lacan, Jacques. *Écrits*. Paris: Seuil, 1966.

———. *Encore*. Trans. Bruce Fink. New York: Norton, 1998.

———. *Séminaire III: Les Psychoses*. Paris: Seuil, 1981.

———. *Séminaire IV: La Relation d'objet*. Paris: Seuil, 1994.

———. *Séminaire VII: L'Ethique de la psychanalyse*. Paris: Seuil, 1986.

———. *Séminaire VIII: Le Transfert*. Paris: Seuil, 1991.

———. *Séminaire XI: Les Quartes concepts fondamentaux de la psychanalyse*. Paris: Seuil, 1973.

———. *Séminaire XVII: L'Envers de la psychanalyse*. Paris: Seuil, 1991.

———. *Séminaire XX: Encore*. Paris: Seuil, 1972.

———. *Seminar II*. Trans. Sylvana Tomaselli. NewYork: Norton, 1988.

———. *Seminar VII*. Trans. Dennis Porter. New York: Norton, 1992.

———. *The Seminar of Jacques Lacan, Book III*. Trans. Russell Grigg. New York: Norton, 1993.

LaCapra, Dominick. *Emile Durkheim*. Ithaca, NY: Cornell UP, 1992.

———. *Representing the Holocaust*. Ithaca, NY: Cornell UP, 1994.

———. *Writing Trauma, Writing History*. Baltimore: Johns Hopkins UP, 2001.

Lattimore, David. "Discovering Cathay." *Parnassus* 1 (1973): 5–26.

Latour, Bruno. *Politics of Nature: How to Bring the Sciences into Democracy*. Trans. Catherine Porter. Cambridge, MA: Harvard UP, 2004.

———. *We Have Never Been Modern*. Trans. Catherine Porter. Cambridge: Harvard UP, 1993.

Leeder, Karen. "After Brecht: The Reception of Brecht's Poetry in English." In *Empedocles' Shoe: Essays on Brecht's Poetry*, ed. Tom Kuhn and Karen Leeder, 231–56. London: Methuen, 2002.

Lehmann, Harry. *Die flüchtige Wahrheit der Kunst*. Munich: Fink, 2005.

Lehmann, Wilhelm. *Gesammelte Werke in acht Bänden*. Vol. 1. Ed. H. D. Schäfer. Stuttgart: Cotta, 1982.

Lepenies, Wolf. *Das Ende der Naturgeschichte*. Munich: Hanser, 1976.

Lethen, Helmut. *Verhaltenslehren der Kälte*. Frankfurt: Suhrkamp, 1994.

Leys, Simon (Pierre Ryckmans). *The Burning Forest: Essays on Chinese Culture and Politics*. New York: Holt, Rinehart and Winston, 1986.

Liliencron, Detlev. *Werke*. Ed. B. von Wiese. Frankfurt: Insel, 1977.

Link, Jürgen. *Die Struktur des literarischen Symbols*. Munich: Fink, 1975.

Loerke, Oskar. *Die Gedichte*. Frankfurt: Suhrkamp, 1984.

Lohner, Edgar. *Passion und Intellekt: Die Lyrik Gottfried Benns*. Neuwied: Luchterhand, 1961.

Loock, Friedrich. *Adoleszenzkrise und Identitätsbildung: zur Krise der Dichtung in Rainer Maria Rilkes Werk*. Frankfurt/New York: P. Lang, 1986.

Lotman, Yuri. "The Origin of Plot in the Light of Typology." Trans. Julian Graffy. *Poetics Today* 1.1–2 (1979): 161–84.

———. *Die Struktur literarischer Texte.* Trans. R. D. Keil. Munich: Fink, 1972.

Lübbren, Nina. *Rural Artists' Colonies in Europe, 1870–1910.* New Brunswick, NJ: Rutgers UP, 2001.

Luhmann, Niklas. *Art as a Social System.* Trans. Eva Knodt. Stanford: Stanford UP, 2000.

———. *Ausdifferenzierung des Rechts.* Frankfurt: Suhrkamp, 1981.

———. *Ecological Communication.* Chicago: U of Chicago P, 1989.

———. *Essays on Self-Reference.* New York: Columbia UP, 1990.

———. *Die Gesellschaft der Gesellschaft.* Frankfurt: Suhrkamp, 1997.

———. *Gesellschaftsstruktur und Semantik.* 4 vols. Frankfurt: Suhrkamp, 1980–1995.

———. "Jenseits von Barbarei." In *Gesellschaftsstruktur und Semantik,* vol. 4, 138–50. Frankfurt: Suhrkamp, 1995.

———. *Die Kunst der Gesellschaft.* Frankfurt: Suhrkamp, 1995.

———. "Das Problem der Epochenbildung und die *Evolutionstheorie.*" In *Epochenschwellen und Epochenstrukturen im Diskurs der Literatur- und Sprachgeschichte,* ed. Hans Ulrich Gumbrecht and Ursula Link-Heer, 11–33. Frankfurt: Suhrkamp, 1985.

———. *Observations on Modernity.* Stanford: Stanford UP, 1998.

———. *Political Theory in the Welfare State.* Berlin: de Gruyter, 1990.

———. *Rechtssoziologie.* Opladen: Westdeutscher Verlag, 1983.

———. *Risk: A Sociological Theory.* New York: Aldine De Gruyter, 1993.

———. *Soziale Systeme.* Frankfurt: Suhrkamp, 1984.

———. *Soziologische Aufklärung 1–6.* Opladen: Westdeutscher Verlag, 1995.

———. "Weltkunst." In Luhmann, Bunsen, and Baecker, *Unbeobachtbare Welt: Über Kunst und Architektur.* Bielefeld: Haux, 1990.

Luo, Zhonghua. *Alfred Döblins "Die drei Sprünge des Wang-lun": Ein chinesischer Roman?* Frankfurt: Peter Lang, 1991.

Lyotard, J-F. "The Sublime and the Avant-Garde." In *The Lyotard Reader,* ed. Andrew Benjamin, 196–211. Oxford: Blackwell, 1989.

Mallarmé, Stéphane. *Oeuvres complètes.* Paris: Gallimard, 1945.

Marinetti, F. T. *Mafarka le futuriste.* (1910) Paris: Christian Bourgois, 1984.

Marius, Benjamin, and Oliver Jahraus. *Systemtheorie und Dekonstruktion: Die Supertheorien Niklas Luhmanns und Jacques Derridas im Vergleich.* Siegen: LUMIS, 1997.

Marx, Leo. *The Machine in the Garden: Technology and the Pastoral Ideal in America.* Oxford: Oxford UP, 1964.

Mason, Peter. *Infelicities: Representations of the Exotic*. Baltimore: Johns Hopkins UP, 1998.

Mattenklott, Gert. "Ostjudentum und Exotismus." In *Die andere Welt: Studien zum Exotismus*, ed. Thomas Koebner and Gerhart Pickerodt, 295–96. Frankfurt: Athenäum, 1987.

Medd, Will. "What is Complexity Science? Toward an Ecology of Ignorance." *Emergence: Journal of Complexity Issues in Organisation and Management* 3, 1 (2001): 45–62.

Menke, Christoph. *Die Souveranität der Kunst*. Frankfurt: Athenäum, 1988.

Merchant, Carolyn. *The Death of Nature: Women, Ecology and the Scientific Revolution*. New York: Harper, 1990.

Miller, Jacques-Alain. "On Perversion." In *Reading Seminars I and II*, ed. Richard Feldstein, Bruce Fink, and Maare Jaanus, 306–20. Albany: SUNY, 1996.

Mörike, Eduard Friedrich. *Gedichte*. Stuttgart: Reclam, 1977.

Mondor, Henri. *Vie de Mallarmé*. Paris: Gallimard, 1941.

Moore, Steven A. *Technology and Place: Sustainable Architecture and the Blueprint Farm*. Austin: U of Texas P, 2001.

Mosse, George. *Germans and Jews*. New York: Fertig, 1970.

Müller, Harro. "Ästhetischer Absolutismus II: Gottfried Benn." In Müller, *Giftpfeile*, 202–20. Bielefeld: Aesthesis, 1994.

———. "Hermeneutik oder Dekonstruktion? Zum Widerstreit zweier Interpretationsweisen in der Moderne." In Müller, *Giftpfeile*, 108–29. Bielefeld: Aisthesis, 1994.

———. *Geschichte zwischen Kairos und Katastrophe*. Frankfurt: Athenäum, 1988.

Münch, Richard. *Die Kultur der Moderne*. 2 vols. Frankfurt: Suhrkamp, 1986.

———. *Die Struktur der Moderne*. Frankfurt: Suhrkamp, 1984.

Muraro, Luisa. *Die symbolische Ordnung der Mutter*. Frankfurt: Campus, 1993.

Neumann, Gerhard. "Einer ward Keiner: Zur Ichfunktion in Loerkes Gedichten." *Marbacher Loerke-Kolloquium 1984*. Mainz: Hase und Koehler, 1986.

Orchard, Karin, and Jörg Zimmermann, eds. *Die Erfindung der Natur: Max Ernst, Paul Klee, Wols und das surreale Universum*. Freiburg im Breisgau: Rombach, 1994.

Parsons, Talcott. "On the Concept of Political Power." In Parsons, *Sociological Theory and Modern Society*, 342–44. Glencoe, IL: The Free Press, 1967.

———. "On the Concept of Value-Commitments." *Sociological Inquiry* 38 (1968): 153–59.

Parry, Benita. "Problems in Current Theories of Colonial Discourse." *Oxford Literary Review 9* (1987): 27–59.

Peters, Paul. "Brecht und die Stimme der Nachrichten." *Weimarer Beiträge* 27 (2000): 3, 352–73.

Pietzker, Carl. *Die Lyrik des jungen Brecht: Vom anarchischen Nihilismus zum Marxismus.* Frankfurt: Suhrkamp, 1974.

Pinker, Steven. *The Blank Slate: The Modern Denial of Human Nature.* New York: Viking, 2002.

Plumpe, Gerhard. "Der Autor als Rechtssubjekt." In *Literaturwissenschaft. Grundkurs 2,* ed. Helmut Brackert and Jörn Stückrath, 179–93. Reinbek: Rowohlt, 1981.

Ponge, Francis. *La Rage de l'expression.* Paris: Gallimard, 1976.

Posner, Richard. *Catastrophe: Risk and Response.* Oxford: Oxford UP, 2004.

———. *Law and Literature.* 2nd ed. Cambridge, MA: Harvard UP, 1998.

Postman, Neil. *Technopoly.* New York: Vintage, 1993.

Powell, Larson. "L'esthétique de l'anasémie." In *Psychanalyse, histoire, rêve et poésie,* ed. Claude Nachin, 297–307. Paris: Harmattan, 2006.

———. "Zufall und Subjekt. Erwägungen zu Cage." In *Mythos Cage,* ed. C. S. Mahnkopf, 203–222. Hofheim: Wolke, 1999.

Prumm, Karl. "Jugend ohne Vater." In *Mit uns zieht die neue Zeit: Der Mythos Jugend,* ed. T. Koebner, R. P. Janz, and F. Trommler. Frankfurt: Suhrkamp, 1985.

Puchner, Martin. *Stage Fright: Modernism, Anti-Theatricality, and Drama.* Baltimore: Johns Hopkins UP, 2002.

Rabinow, Paul. "Assembling Ethics in an Ecology of Ignorance," closing plenary lecture given at the First Conference on Synthetic Biology, MIT, 10–12 June 2004 (online as http://openwetware.org/images/7/7a/SB1.0_Rabinow.pdf).

Reynolds, David. "'Es handelt sich hier um Werdende': The Fiction of the Artist in Rilke's *Worpswede.*" *Seminar* 35:1 (1999): 55–68.

Rheinstein, Max, ed. *Max Weber on Law in Economy and Society.* Trans. E. Shils and M. Rheinstein. New York: Clarion (Simon and Schuster), 1967.

Ridley, Hugh. *Gottfried Benn: Ein Schriftsteller zwischen Erneuerung und Reaktion.* Opladen: Westdeutscher Verlag, 1990.

Rieger, Stefan. *Kybernetische Anthropologie.* Frankfurt: Suhrkamp, 2003.

Rilke, R. M. *Sämtliche Werke.* Frankfurt: Insel, 1955.

———. *Worpswede.* In *Werke in 4 Bänden.* Frankfurt: Insel, 1996. 4: 305–400.

Rittmeester, T. "Heterosexism, Misogyny and Mother-Hatred in Rilke Scholarship: The Case of Sophie Rilke-Entz." In *Women in German Yearbook 6*, ed. J. Claussen and H. Cafferty, 63–81. Lansdale, MD: UP of America, 1991.

———. "Rilke und die namenlose Liebe: Eine vorläufige Bestandaufnahme." *Rilke-Rezeptionen/Rilke Reconsidered*, ed. S. Bauschinger and S. Cocalis, 201–14. Tübingen: Francke, 1995.

Robbe-Grillet, Alain. *Pour un nouveau roman*. Paris: Gallimard, 1963.

Rosenberg, Nathan. *Exploring the Black Box: Technology, Economics, and History* Cambridge: Cambridge UP, 1994.

———. *Inside the Black Box: Technology and Economics*. Cambridge: Cambridge UP, 1983.

Roth, Michael. "Trauma, Repräsentation und historisches Bewusstsein." In *Die dunkle Spur der Vergangenheit*, ed. Jörn Rüsen and Jürgen Straub, 153–73. Frankfurt: Suhrkamp, 1998.

Rothe, Wolfgang. "Benn-Renaissancen." In *Über Gottfried Benn*, ed. Hillebrand, 251–60.

Rumold, Rainer. *Gottfried Benn und der Expressionismus: Provokation des Lesers, Absolute Dichtung*. Königstein: Scriptor, 1982.

Ryan, Judith. "Das Motiv der inneren Landschaft." In *Im Dialog mit der Moderne: zur deutschsprachigen Literatur von der Gründerzeit bis zur Gegenwart: Jacob Steiner zum sechzigsten Geburtstag*, ed. Roland Jost and Hansgeorg Schmidt-Bergmann, 131–41. Frankfurt: Athenäum, 1986.

Sahlberg, Oskar. *Gottfried Benns Phantasiewelt: "wo Lust und Leiche winkt."* Munich: Text und Kritik, 1977.

Santner, Eric. "History Beyond the Pleasure Principle: Some Thoughts on the Representation of Trauma." In *Probing the Limits of Representation: Nazism and the 'Final Solution,'* ed. Saul Friedlaender, 143–54. Cambridge, MA: Harvard UP, 1992.

———. *My Own Private Germany*. Princeton, NJ: Princeton UP, 1996.

Scarry, Elaine. *On Beauty and Being Just*. Princeton, NJ: Princeton UP, 1999.

Schäffner, Wolfgang. *Die Ordnung des Wahns: Zur Poetologie psychiatrischen Wissens bei Alfred Döblin*. Munich: Fink, 1995.

Schama, Simon. *Landscape and Memory*. New York: Alfred Knopf, 1995.

Schank, Stefan. *Rainer Maria Rilke*. Munich: DTV, 1998.

Schelling, F. W. J. *Einleitung zu seinem Entwurf eines Systems der Naturphilosophie* (1799). Stuttgart: Reclam, 1988.

Schenk, Klaus. *Medienpoesie*. Stuttgart: Metzler, 2000.

Scherpe, Klaus. "The City as Narrator: The Modern Text in Döblin's Berlin Alexanderplatz." In *Modernity and the Text*, ed. Andreas Huyssen and David Bathrick, 162–79. New York: Columbia UP, 1989.

Scheuer, Helmut. "Die entzauberte Natur — Vom. Naturgedicht zur Ökolyrik." In *Literatur für Leser* 1 (1989): 48–73.

Schiller, Friedrich. *Sämtliche Werke in 5 Bänden*. Munich: Hanser, 2004.

Schmidgen, Henning. *Das Unbewusste der Maschinen: Konzeptionen des Psychischen bei Guattari, Deleuze und Lacan*. Munich: Fink, 1997.

Schönherr, Ulrich. *Das unendliche Altern der Moderne*. Vienna: Passagen-Verlag, 1994.

Schröder, Jürgen. *Gottfried Benn und die Deutschen*. Tübingen: Stauffenburg, 1986.

Schürmann, Reiner. *Heidegger on Being and Acting: From Principles to Anarchy*. Bloomington: Indiana UP, 1987.

Schütze, Oliver. *Natur und Geschichte im Blick des Wanderers: Zur lyrischen Situation bei Bobrowski und Hölderlin*. Würzburg: Königshausen und Neumann, 1990 = Epistemata, Würzburger Wissenschaftliche Schriften, Reihe Literaturwissenschaft, vol. 47.

Schuster, Ingrid. *China und Japan in der deutschen Literatur, 1900–1925*. Bern: Francke, 1977.

Seel, Martin. *Eine Ästhetik der Natur*. Frankfurt: Suhrkamp, 1991.

Serres, Michel. *Le Parasite*. Paris: Grasset, 1981.

Shepherdson, Charles. "The *Role* of Gender and the *Imperative* of Sex." In *Supposing the Subject*, ed. Joan Copjec, 158–84. London: Verso, 1994.

———. *Vital Signs: Nature, Culture, Psychoanalysis*. London: Routledge, 2000.

Silverman, Hugh, and G. Aylesworth. *The Textual Sublime: Deconstruction and Its Differences*. Albany, NY: SUNY Press, 1990.

Silverman, Hugh. "Lyotard and the Events of the Postmodern Sublime." In *Lyotard: Philosophy, Politics and the Sublime*, 222–29. New York: Routledge, 2002.

Sloterdijk, Peter. *Thinker on Stage*. Trans. J. Daniel. Minneapolis: Minnesota UP, 1989.

Spencer-Brown, George. *Laws of Form*. London: Allen and Unwin, 1969.

Soboth, Christian. "Die Un-Natur der Natur: Zu einigen Gedichten Ernst Meisters." *Text und Kritik* 96 (Oct. 1987): 75–84.

Sollers, Philippe. *L'Intermédiaire*. Paris: Seuil, 1963.

Sophocles. *The Tragedies* I. Trans. David Grene. Chicago: U of Chicago P, 1991.

Spivak, Gayatri. *A Critique of Post-Colonial Reason*. Cambridge, MA: Harvard UP, 1999.

Spence, Jonathan. *Chinese Roundabout*. New York: Norton, 1992.

Stabile, Carol A. *Feminism and the Technological Fix*. Manchester UK and New York: Manchester UP, 1994.

Stäheli, Urs. "Zum Verhaltnis von Sozialstruktur und Semantik." *Soziale Systeme* 4, 2 (1988): 315–40.

Stafford, Barbara Maria. "Leveling the New Old Transcendence: Cognitive Coherence in the Era of Beyondness." *New Literary History* 35 (2004): 321–38.

Stavrakakis, Iannis. "Green Fantasy and the Real of Nature: Elements of a Lacanian Critique of Green Ideological Discourse." *Journal for the Psychoanalysis of Culture & Society* 2, 1 (Spring 1997): 123–32.

Stolleis, Michael. *The Law under the Swastika: Studies on Legal History in Nazi Germany*. Chicago: U of Chicago P, 1998.

Stone, Alison. "Irigaray and Hölderlin on the Relation between Nature and Culture." *Continental Philosophy Review* 36, 4 (December 2003): 415–32.

Strathausen, Carsten. *The Look of Things: Poetry and Vision around 1900*. Chapel Hill, NC: U of North Carolina P, 2003.

Strauss, Leo. *Natural Right and History*. Chicago: U of Chicago P, 1953.

Sullivan, Robert G. *Justice and the Social Context of Early Middle High German Literature*. London: Routledge, 1991.

Surer, Paul. "Explication de texte: 'l'Azur.'" *L'Information littéraire* 19 (1967): 92–96.

Sword, Helen. *Engendering Inspiration: Visionary Strategies in Rilke, Lawrence and H.D.* Ann Arbor: U of Michigan P, 1995.

Theisen, Bianca. "Die Gewalt des Notwendigen: berlegungen zu Nietzsches Dionysios-Dithyrambus 'Klage der Ariadne.'" *Nietzsche Studien* 20 (1991): 186–209.

Thomas, Nicholas. *Colonialism's Culture*. Oxford: Blackwell, 1994.

Theweleit, Klaus. *Männerphantasien* I. Reinbek: Rowohlt, 1980.

Thom, René. *Stabilité structurelle et morphogenèse*. Reading, MA: Benjamin, 1972.

———. *Structural Stability and Morphogenesis*. Trans. David Fowler. New York: Wesley, 1975.

Tobias, Rochelle. *The Discourse of Nature in the Poetry of Paul Celan*. Baltimore: Johns Hopkins UP, 2006.

Tröger, Annemarie. "The Creation of a Female Assembly-Line Proletariat." In *When Biology Became Destiny: Women in Weimar and Nazi Germany*, ed. R. Bridenthal, A. Grossmann, and M. Kaplan. New York: Monthly Review Press, 1984.

Trottein, Serge. "Lyotard: Before and After the Sublime." In *Lyotard: Philosophy, Politics, and the Sublime*, ed. Hugh Silverman, 192–200. New York: Routledge, 2002.

Verschraegen, Gert. "Systems Theory and the Paradox of Human Rights." In *Luhmann on Law and Politics: Critical Appraisals and Applications*, ed. King and Thornhill, 101–26.

von Bormann, Alexander. *"Manche Wörter lockern die Erde, später vielleicht":* Romantische und zeitgenössische Naturerfahrung/Naturdichtung." *Der Deutschunterricht* 38 (1986): 90–100.

von Felbert, Ulrich. *China und Japan als Impuls und Exempel.* Frankfurt: Peter Lang, 1986.

von Regensteiner, Henry. "Die Bedeutung der Romane Alfred Döblins von *Die drei Sprünge des Wang-lun* bis *Berlin Alexanderplatz.*" Thesis, NYU, 1952.

Weber, Samuel. Introduction to Daniel Paul Schreber, *Denkwürdigkeiten eines Nervenkranken.* Frankfurt: Ullstein, 1973.

Wedekind, Frank. *Lulu.* Stuttgart: Reclam, 1989.

Weigand, Rudolf. *Die Naturrechtslehre der Legisten und Dekretisten von Irnerius bis Accursius und von Gratian bis Johannes Teutonicus.* Munich: Hueber, 1967.

Wellbery, David. *The Specular Moment: Goethe's Early Lyric and the Beginnings of Romanticism.* Stanford: Stanford UP, 1996.

———. "Zur Poetik der Figuration beim mittleren Rilke: Die Gazelle." *Zu Rainer Maria Rilke*, ed. Egon Schwarz, 125–32. Stuttgart: Klett, 1983.

Whitaker, Peter. *Brecht's Poetry: A Critical Study.* Oxford: Clarendon, 1985.

White, James Boyd. *Heracles' Bow: Essays on the Rhetoric and Poetics of the Law.* Madison, WI: U of Wisconsin P, 1985.

Whitebook, Joel. *Perversion and Utopia.* Cambridge, MA: MIT Press, 1995.

Whitford, Margaret. *Luce Irigaray: Philosophy in the Feminine.* London: Routledge, 1991.

Young, Robert. *White Mythologies: Writing History and the West.* London and New York: Routledge, 1990.

Zantop, Susanne. *Colonial Fantasies.* Durham, NC: Duke UP, 1997.

Zeeman, E. C. *Catastrophe Theory, Selected Papers.* London/Reading MA: Addison-Wesley, 1977.

Žižek, Slavoj. *The Fright of Real Tears*. London: BFI, 2001.

———. *Organs without Bodies: Deleuze and Consequences*. New York: Routledge, 2004.

———. *The Sublime Object of Ideology*. London: Verso, 1989.

———. *Welcome to the Desert of the Real*. London: Verso, 2002.

———, ed. *Lacan. The Silent Partners*. London: Verso, 2005.

Zupančič, Alenka. *Ethics of the Real*. London: Verso, 2000.

Index

Adorno, Theodor W., 2, 3, 5, 6, 9, 16–18, 24, 26–29, 32, 40–42, 44, 47, 52, 55–68, 83, 86, 87–89, 91–92, 94–96, 123, 132–33, 135, 137, 163, 170, 181–82, 198–99, 203, 217, 219, 220, 223–25, 228; critique of technology of, 2–3, 32; on natural history, 9, 13, 41, 55–56; on nonidentity, 44, 52, 64 n. 113; on sublime, 5, 26, 128, 199
Adorno, Theodor W., works by: *Aesthetic Theory*, 26, 47, 66–67, 83, 85, 89, 91, 123, 128, 203; *Jargon of Authenticity*, 88, 135; *Negative Dialectics*, 27, 52; *Philosophy of New Music*, 198, 217
allegory, allegorical, 4, 6, 7, 41, 47, 52, 64, 65, 69, 71, 74, 87, 102, 105, 118, 122, 125, 141, 142, 149, 158, 166, 174, 193, 201, 209
anthropology, 4, 10, 11, 13, 20, 23, 47, 52, 59, 131, 145, 227

Badiou, Alain, 15, 19, 55, 176, 225
Beck, Ulrich, 4–5, 14, 18, 19, 40, 55, 229
Benjamin, Walter, 8, 9, 17, 18, 41, 50, 52–53, 59, 64, 70, 89, 98, 106, 114, 117, 142, 157, 158, 168, 187–89, 193, 196, 198, 202–3, 217–18, 222–23, 226
Benn, Gottfried, 6–7, 22, 23, 50, 58, 70, 97–133, 155, 156, 161, 174 n. 70, 191, 196
Bhabha, Homi K., 136–38, 152, 154, 156, 158, 169–71, 177

Bohrer, Karl-Heinz, 21–23, 58, 152
Brecht, Bertolt, 1, 7–10, 15 n. 2, 21–22, 25, 50, 60 n. 32, 61 n. 55, 67, 86, 134, 156, 173 n. 48, 175 n. 74, 182–226; and Benjamin, 189, 196, 202–3, 217; relation to Expressionism, 156; and *gestus*, 207; on André Gide, 191–92; contrasted with Kafka, 218; on Karl Kraus, 183; and poetics of exile, 185; on rhymeless lyric, 196; and Rilke, 86; and Trakl, 203
Brecht, Bertolt, works by: "An die Nachgeborenen," 21, 205; *Caucasian Chalk Circle*, 215–17; "Kriegsfibel," 192–93, 203; *Me-ti*, 186; *Threepenny Trial*, 8, 186–88, 198, 199, 213, 217; *Puntila*, 199, 210–15, 225

catastrophe, 1, 7, 19 n. 42, 165, 166, 191, 198
catastrophe theory, 1, 14, 18
Celan, Paul, 11, 17, 21, 42, 47, 57, 63, 127
culturalism, 25, 39
culture, 1, 2, 5, 10, 13, 14, 24, 32, 35, 37, 39, 46, 47, 48, 54, 58, 60, 62, 64, 67, 71, 72, 78, 80, 81, 85, 87, 102, 107, 128, 134, 139, 146, 147, 165, 172, 173, 177, 195, 222
cybernetics, 10, 12–13, 14, 47, 227

Dean, Tim, 58, 61, 136, 139–40, 158, 166, 169–71, 176
deconstruction, 10, 58, 105–6, 225

deep ecology, 16
Deleuze, Gilles, 18, 36, 92, 113, 131, 157, 158, 170, 228
Derrida, Jacques, 3, 5, 8, 10, 13, 15, 17, 23, 25, 51, 58, 59, 64, 105–7, 125, 130, 133, 139, 179, 222, 225, 228; relation to Critical Theory, 3, 5, 17 n. 19; and Judith Butler, 139; on law, 8, 15 n. 5, 25; and Luhmann, 13, 59 n. 29, 64 n. 108, 228
Derrida, Jacques, works by: *Éperons*, 105
differentiation, 9, 17, 25, 36, 39, 40, 42, 46, 49, 53, 55, 57, 127, 157, 158, 168, 179–81, 195, 197–98, 208–9, 222, 223, 227
Döblin, Alfred, 7, 8, 11, 16 n. 17, 50, 60, 134–77; and China, 134, 141–59; and Jewish-German relations, 142–44
Döblin, Alfred, works by: *Berge Meere und Giganten*, 159–65, 167; *Berlin Alexanderplatz*, 157–59; *Die drei Sprünge des Wang-lun*, 141–59, 167

economic system, 45–46, 53, 180, 187, 227
economics, 2, 5, 39, 45–47, 53, 54, 61, 109, 180, 187, 213, 219, 227
Enzensberger, Hans Magnus, 11, 17 n. 29, 18
Ernst, Max, 5, 25, 42–43, 50, 62, 156
essentialism, 3, 16, 21, 23, 24, 39, 139, 169
ethics, 4, 8, 15, 16, 26, 29, 43, 45, 51, 55, 57, 62–65, 146, 153, 176, 178–79, 198, 206, 207, 217, 218, 225
Expressionism, 67, 69, 131 n. 35, 152, 161, 169, 189

Fanon, Frantz, 137, 139, 147, 148, 150, 152, 153, 170 n. 7, 171 n. 22, 173 nn. 51, 54, 55, 174 nn. 67, 68, 175 nn. 76, 77
fantasy, 34, 35, 40, 42–45, 60, 62, 63, 77, 78, 92, 93, 100, 102, 135, 143, 144, 152, 155, 158, 166, 168, 171, 175, 177
feminism, 4, 16, 60
film, 1, 4, 8, 12, 14–15, 18 n. 25, 19 n. 43, 32, 48, 64, 173 n. 45, 188, 198, 201
film theory, 24, 134, 136–38, 169, 177
Foucault, Michel, 10, 11, 22, 27, 41, 92, 137, 179, 227
Freud, Sigmund, 5–7, 13, 20, 26, 29–30, 33–35, 42, 44, 50–53, 55, 60 nn. 33, 34, 44, 62 n, 64 nn. 103, 105, 114, 76–78, 87, 91, 93 nn. 32, 34, 95 n. 70, 98, 104, 124, 125, 128 n. 2, 131 n. 37, 133 n. 65, 135–38, 140, 147, 148, 150, 152, 154, 159, 165, 167–71, 173, 174 nn. 63–65, 72–73, 175 nn. 75, 80, 176 nn. 93, 99, 221 n. 53, 223 n. 83, 229 n. 1; culturalist readings of, 5, 50; Lacan's critique of, 34, 136, 138; on politics of perversion, 87; on "propping" of culture on nature, 34–35, 125; technological mediations of thought of, 42, 124; on trauma, 135, 154, 159, 165–69
Fuss, Diana, 4, 16 n. 13, 171

Gadamer, Hans Georg, 21
Geertz, Clifford, 10, 179, 227
gender, 7, 32, 48, 64, 75, 93, 130, 136, 139–40, 162, 166, 167, 171, 173, 176, 193
Goethe, Johann Wolfgang, 6, 7, 69, 70, 73, 77, 78, 92 n. 12, 93 n. 35, 100–103, 106, 107, 112–14,

117, 120, 121, 127, 128, 129 n. 12, 132 nn. 50–52, 141, 160, 219 n. 10, 222 n. 60, 226 n. 121

Habermas, Juergen, 2–3, 11, 13, 15 n. 5, 16 n. 10, 18 n. 26, 28, 36, 47, 52, 53, 56, 58, 158, 178, 180, 197, 208, 219, 220 n. 36, 222 nn. 63, 66, 227–28; on ethics and morality, 2, 178, 197; and Luhmann, 2–3, 11, 36, 53, 180, 208, 227–28; on modernity, 13, 53
Handke, Peter, 12, 22, 48
Hegel, Georg Wilhelm Friedrich, 2, 16, 55, 70, 86, 87, 91, 92, 95, 99, 107, 108, 123, 130, 132, 138, 164, 176, 198; aesthetics of, 70, 86–87, 123, 164; philosophy of history, 55
Hegel, Georg Wilhelm Friedrich, works by: *Phenomenology of Mind*, 107
Heidegger, Martin, 2, 26, 27, 28, 29, 40, 48, 54, 59, 61, 64, 66, 73, 76, 83, 87, 93, 94, 130, 135, 177, 203, 225
hermeneutics, 9, 10, 12, 21, 26–28, 41, 54, 99, 101, 106–8, 120–22, 124, 145, 157, 171, 196, 207, 214, 227, 229
history, 1–3, 5, 7–11, 13, 14, 19 n. 44, 22, 31, 41, 43, 46–48, 50, 54–56, 60 n. 45, 61 n. 60, 63 n. 94, 66–70, 72, 73, 78, 95, 99, 100, 105, 111, 112, 113, 117, 118, 124, 128, 134, 137, 140–42, 144, 145, 147, 151, 155–63, 165–69, 170 n. 9, 171 nn. 20, 22, 177 nn. 110–12, 114, 178, 189, 198, 201, 204, 205, 211, 220 n. 30, 227; art history, 41, 66–68, 124; literary history, 3, 8, 9, 13, 22, 47, 69, 99, 113, 117–18, 128, 168; and literary studies, 134–40, 168–69, 171 n. 20, 178; of literary theory, 10, 50, 99; nature and, 1–3, 7, 9, 11, 13, 14, 22, 41, 43, 46, 47–58, 55–56, 63 n. 94, 66–67, 70, 124, 128, 145, 147, 159–65, 211; social history, 47, 141–42, 145, 147, 156, 169, 189, 204, 205; within individual subject, 31, 95 n. 70, 112, 144, 158–59, 165, 167
Homann, Renate, 7, 13–14, 25, 36–39, 54, 61
Husserl, Edmund, 6, 12, 18, 54, 67, 228
Huyssen, Andreas, 4, 6, 11, 17, 32–33, 35, 45, 60, 88, 89, 94, 100, 129, 158, 175

imaginary, 1, 8, 22, 23, 24, 25, 31, 32, 33, 34, 36, 43, 46, 49, 50, 58, 60, 68, 69, 74, 76, 77, 79, 87, 90, 93, 101, 105, 106, 117, 134, 136, 137, 138, 140, 147, 148, 151–59, 165–66, 171, 174, 179, 188, 218
Irigaray, Luce, 103, 130 nn. 16, 23, 134, 167, 176 n. 108

Jameson, Fredric, 5, 15, 17 n. 22, 27, 28, 49, 50, 58–61, 64, 128, 207, 213, 216, 224, 225
Jelinek, Elfriede, 5, 26, 48, 49, 64
Jewish-German relations, 7, 142–44, 152, 166, 167, 168, 172 nn. 32, 33
Jugendstil, 5–6, 24, 41, 57 n. 9, 67–68, 80, 83, 87, 90

Kant, Immanuel, 3–5, 9, 23, 25–26, 29, 36–39, 41, 48, 52, 54, 55, 56, 59 n. 22, 61 nn. 56, 57, 69, 72, 73, 75, 79, 92 n. 21, 99, 129 n. 8, 161, 165, 167, 169 n. 4, 180, 216, 225 n. 108, 228; on the imagination, 23; on relation of nature and culture, 5, 26, 48, 52, 54–56, 69, 73, 75; on the sublime, 3–4, 9, 26, 36–39, 72, 99, 161, 165, 216

Kant, Immanuel, works by: *Critique of Judgment*, 4, 25, 36–38, 54–56

Kittler, Friedrich, 9, 10, 18, 28, 49, 58, 63, 69, 88, 92, 94, 98, 99, 100, 106–8, 114, 117, 124–30, 133, 191, 228

Kraus, Karl, 127, 141, 142, 162, 171, 175, 181, 183, 191, 219, 221

Krauss, Rosalind, 5, 49, 50–51, 64

Kristeva, Julia, 5, 33, 40, 88, 96, 131

Lacan, Jacques, 3–5, 9, 10, 12, 13, 17 nn. 19, 21, 18 n. 34, 24, 27, 29–35, 40, 42–44, 51, 53, 59 n. 26, 60 nn. 35–42, 45–47, 61 nn. 48–51, 65, 63 nn. 84–86, 94, 64 nn. 103, 107, 66, 76, 78, 82, 83, 87, 92 n. 18, 93 nn. 30, 34, 39, 40, 94 nn. 40, 54, 95 nn. 60, 67, 69, 70, 96 nn. 73, 79, 80, 105, 121, 125, 130 n. 17, 132 n. 44, 134–36, 138–40, 148, 152, 158, 159, 162, 165, 168, 169 n. 3, 170 nn. 11, 14, 15, 171 n. 22, 173 n. 57, 174 nn. 62, 66, 68, 69, 71, 175 nn. 81, 82, 176 nn. 90, 99; on anxiety, 29–35; and Luhmann, 13; misunderstandings of, 24, 134–38; nature in, 3, 42, 53, 125; on Real, 5, 40, 43, 60 n. 45; on sublime, 4, 29

landscape, 6, 13, 14, 20, 41, 42, 47, 48, 66–96, 101, 112, 124, 132, 166, 199, 202, 203, 213, 224

Latour, Bruno, 5, 26, 62, 64, 65

law, 2, 8, 9, 15 n. 6, 17 n. 21, 25, 29, 30, 36, 39, 55, 56, 60 n. 32, 73–76, 80, 81, 91, 93 n. 29, 94, 99, 101, 102, 136, 146, 152, 165, 167, 173 n. 48, 178–226; natural, 2, 15 n. 6, 55, 102, 173 n. 48, 188–90, 195–97, 207, 209, 214; and positive, 188–90, 207, 214; and rhetoric, 178–79, 187

Lehmann, Harry, 223

Lehmann, Wilhelm, 21, 190–92, 205, 209, 220

Lepenies, Wolf, 11, 17, 92

Luhmann, Niklas, 2–4, 8, 9–11, 13, 14, 16, 18, 21, 61 n. 59, 62 nn. 75, 77, 63 nn. 78–83, 87–88, 91, 64 nn. 100, 103, 108, 114, 65 nn. 115, 116, 120, 123, 124, 129 nn. 13, 14, 130 n. 27, 131 n. 39, 132 n. 62, 177 n. 115, 179, 207, 216–17, 218 nn. 3, 4, 219 nn. 5–9, 12, 22–24, 220 nn. 41–45, 221 nn. 49–51, 57, 222 nn. 62–65, 67, 223 nn. 70, 80–81, 224 n. 102, 225 nn. 105–7, 113, 116, 119–120, 226 n. 122, 227–29; on differentiation of art, 9, 36, 107, 180–81, 197; on historical transitions, 102, 197, 210; on law, 179–80, 187–89, 195–97, 207–9, 214; on nature, 3, 11, 14, 20, 36, 49, 57 n. 9, 59 nn. 29–31, 123–124, 207, 210; on problems of modernity, 13, 40, 44–46, 58 n. 13; on self-reference, 2, 4, 39, 53, 60 n. 32, 107, 137, 181, 197, 208, 215; on structural coupling, 8, 29, 180, 209–10

Lyotard, Jean-François, 4, 25–31, 35–39, 45, 49, 58, 59, 64, 73, 124

Mallarmé, Stéphane, 6, 7, 88, 90, 95, 105, 114, 116–18, 124, 125, 129, 131–33

Marx, Karl, 2, 12, 15, 18, 20, 44, 53, 57, 71, 87, 162, 163, 171, 182, 186–88, 207, 220 nn. 33, 37, 223 n. 75

media, 5, 8, 12, 13, 28, 54, 88, 124, 126–28, 179, 188, 198–99, 202, 228
media theory, 16, 28, 54, 88, 98–99, 106–8, 117, 126–28, 130, 228
metaphor, 1, 12, 31, 36, 42, 48, 56, 63, 69, 71, 74, 75, 77, 80, 81, 86–88, 102, 107–8, 112, 113, 117, 118, 122, 124, 147, 151, 155, 158, 159, 163, 169, 170, 185, 210, 225
metaphysics, 3, 4, 9, 10, 12, 13, 16, 19, 21, 27, 28, 31, 41, 47, 52, 54, 61, 67, 70, 95, 98, 106, 108, 125, 146, 155–58, 168, 192
modernism, 63, 66, 67, 68, 91, 144, 145, 149, 167, 171 n. 25, 175 n. 83, 220 n. 33
Mueller, Harro, 10, 17 n. 20, 129, 223

National Socialism, 21, 221 n. 14
New Subjectivity, 21
Nietzsche, Friedrich, 6–7, 23, 59, 76, 98, 99, 100, 101–8, 113–14, 116–17, 121, 123–25, 127, 128–31, 143, 144, 146

Orient, 123, 172
Orientalism, 7–8, 15, 141–45, 171, 172

paradox, 3, 5, 9, 15, 16, 26, 27, 29, 31, 37–39, 41–46, 49, 51, 55, 64, 72, 91, 98, 100–102, 105, 124, 128–20, 135, 150, 153, 155, 159, 162, 167, 169, 178–80, 182, 185, 188–89, 192, 196, 198–99, 201, 203, 205–10, 212, 214, 215, 217, 218, 219
Parsons, Talcott, 10, 129, 179, 181, 219, 227, 228
political system, 39, 45, 54, 185, 190, 208

politics, 2, 14, 22, 29, 36, 39, 48, 59 n. 22, 62 n. 77, 64 n. 100, 87, 116, 135, 170, 172, 179, 180, 182, 183, 209, 218, 219 n. 6, 223, 227, 228
postcolonial theory, 61, 134–40, 143, 144, 152, 171
postcolonialism, 8, 10, 24, 136, 168, 173
postmodernism, 1, 13, 15 n. 5, 17 n. 22, 22, 23, 59 n. 30

rhetoric, 3, 5, 7, 8, 10, 15, 16 n. 12, 22, 23, 25, 28, 37, 44, 50, 56, 58 n. 18, 59 n. 30, 88, 90, 99, 101, 102, 104, 106–8, 113, 120, 121, 125, 126, 131 n. 34, 132 n. 56, 134–40, 144, 152, 154, 155, 159, 168, 177–80, 183, 185, 187, 193, 196, 198, 199, 208, 215, 218, 220; deconstruction and, 4, 152; hermeneutics and, 10, 108; historiography and, 168–69; law, ethics and, 8, 43–44, 178–80, 198; reduction of theory to, 22–25, 37, 50, 56, 99, 125, 134–40, 178–80, 208; sublime and, 5, 7, 15, 28, 120
Rilke, Rainer Maria, 6, 7, 27, 30, 50, 60, 66–96, 98, 112, 120, 124, 131, 132, 149, 174, 196
Rimbaud, Arthur, 1, 203
Robbe-Grillet, Alain, 11–12, 18, 47, 63
Romanticism, 23, 41, 59, 75, 129
Romantics, 36, 158, 161, 196

Said, Edward, 8, 171–72
Santner, Eric, 167, 177
Schiller, Friedrich, 22, 48, 69, 78, 80, 91
Schmitt, Carl, 9, 180, 186, 188, 214, 216, 223, 225
science, 5, 13, 24, 29, 35, 39, 42, 45, 50, 53, 54, 61, 62, 63, 70,

science (continued):
72, 98, 124, 146, 174, 176, 178, 209, 219, 223
self-reference, 4, 6, 13, 14, 23, 24, 26, 29, 35, 38, 39, 44, 46, 47, 40, 53, 88, 98, 100, 105, 122, 126, 128, 132, 196, 207, 208, 218, 222, 225
semantics, 13, 14, 18, 34, 49, 102, 180, 185, 186, 189, 190
subjectivity, 5, 6, 12, 22, 23, 26, 32, 37, 40, 45, 48, 66, 71, 72, 75, 77, 84, 94, 99, 100–5, 107, 117, 120, 121, 123, 150, 152, 156, 157, 226 n. 121, 228
sublime, the, 1, 3–7, 9, 11, 14, 15, 25–32, 35–39, 45, 49, 52, 55, 58–59, 61, 64, 67, 72, 73, 75, 76, 98–101, 106–8, 111–13, 116–18, 120, 122–25, 127–28, 131, 137, 140, 161, 165, 166, 168, 191, 194, 199, 213–14, 216, 225, 226
Surrealism, 12, 25, 41, 42, 50, 144, 173, 217
symbolic, 5, 23, 29, 30–35, 40, 42, 60, 78, 86, 90, 94 n. 55, 101, 103, 106–7 112–14, 117, 130, 137, 148, 150 151, 152, 157, 158, 164–67, 179, 205, 209, 214, 225 n. 114

technocracy, 3, 20, 21–65, 127, 140, 159, 163, 167
technology, 2, 16, 19, 32, 33, 39, 40, 43–46, 50, 51, 53, 54, 58 n. 18, 59 n. 24, 61 nn. 60–63, 100, 108, 123–26, 130, 161, 167, 176 n. 101, 180, 188, 193, 219 n. 8
theology, 2, 9, 12, 25, 54, 95, 98, 161, 189, 213, 217, 218, 220
trauma, 2, 15, 19, 25, 33, 40, 43–45, 49, 52, 63, 64, 94, 112, 124, 135, 137, 140, 158, 160, 161, 164–69, 177, 203, 225–26

Wellbery, David, 6, 93, 95, 101–4, 106, 107, 109, 112, 114, 121, 129, 131, 132, 227

Žižek, Slavoj, 4, 19, 61, 62, 170